D1223246

Salamanca 1812

Salamanca 1812

Rory Muir

YALE UNIVERSITY PRESS
NEW HAVEN AND LONDON

For information about this and other Yale University Press publications, please contact:
U.S. Office: sales.press@yale.edu   www.yale.edu/yup
Europe Office: sales @yaleup.co.uk   www.yaleup.co.uk

Set in Ehrhardt by Fakenham Photosetting Limited, Norfolk
Printed in Great Britain by St Edmundsbury Press, Suffolk

Library of Congress Cataloging-in-Publication Data

Muir, Rory, 1962–
    Salamanca 1812/by Rory Muir.
      p. cm.
    Includes bibliographical references and index.
    ISBN 0–300–08719–5 (cloth)
      1. Salamanca (Spain), Battle of, 1812. 2. Wellington, Arthur Wellesley, Duke of,
    1769–1852.

DC233.S2 M85 2001
940.2'7—dc21   2001026883

A catalogue record for this book is available from the British Library.

10 9 8 7 6 5 4 3 2 1

Contents

Illustrations

Photographs of the battlefield taken by the author.

Maps and Plans

Maps and plans on pages 8, 49, 53, 63, 89, 99, 125, 127 and 150 drawn by Chris Crothers at the Department of Geographical and Environmental Studies of the University of Adelaide.

Abbreviations

AAG	Assistant Adjutant-General
BL	British Library
DAAG	Deputy Assistant Adjutant-General
DAQMG	Deputy Assistant Quartermaster-General
JSAHR	*Journal of the Society for Army Historical Research*
KGL	King's German Legion
Lamartinière	Official French casualty return for the period 18 July to 8 August 1812 by Général Lamartinière, Chef d'Etat-Major de l'Armée du Portugal in French archives (AHG C7–15: see Appendix III and Bibliography)
Martinien	A. Martinien, *Tableaux par Corps et par Batailles des Officiers Tués et Blessés pendant les Guerres de l'Empire (1805–1815)* (Paris, Editions Militaires Européenes, nd [1980s], first published 1899) and the *Supplément* (Paris, Fournier, 1909)
NAM	National Army Museum, Chelsea
NAS	National Archives of Scotland, Edinburgh
NLS	National Library of Scotland, Edinburgh
Ordnance map	Cartografia Militar de España, Mapa General Serie L, Salamanca 13–19 (478) E. 1:50,000 (1993)
PRO	Public Record Office, Kew
USJ	*United Service Journal* (variations on the title include *Colburn's United Service Journal* and *United Service Magazine*)
Wyld's *Atlas*	*Maps and Plans Showing the Principal Movements, Battles and Sieges in Which the British Army Was Engaged during the War from 1808 to 1814 in the Spanish Peninsula and the South of France* (London, James Wyld, 1841) (Maps surveyed by Sir Thomas Mitchell in the years after the war)

Preface

The battle of Salamanca was Wellington's finest victory. It lacks the fame and the awful grandeur of the bloody slog on the slopes of Mont St Jean, but technically it was far superior. Of all Napoleon's victories, only Austerlitz, Friedland and possibly Rivoli can be compared to its daring conception and skilful execution. After four days of careful, patient manoeuvring in which any mistake could easily have been fatal, Wellington recognized a fleeting opportunity and was able to grasp it. For the first time in the Peninsular War the allied army attacked in the open field, and the French were routed with enormous losses. A French officer described the result as 'the beating of forty thousand men in forty minutes', and although this is an exaggeration – making the action appear less hard-fought than was the case – it captures the enormous shock suffered by French pride and morale. Never again would the French offer Wellington battle in the Peninsula with such confidence, and this was as significant as the liberation of Madrid, the raising of the siege of Cadiz and the French evacuation of Andalusia, all of which resulted from the victory.

Despite its importance, Salamanca has received surprisingly little attention. In almost two hundred years only three slight books, all aimed at a popular or uncritical audience, have appeared describing the campaign and the battle. These works are rightly overshadowed by the famous histories of the war in the Peninsula as a whole, beginning with Napier and including Fortescue's *History of the British Army* and Sarramon's more recent work. The best of these for Salamanca is Sir Charles Oman's *History of the Peninsular War*. Oman's description of the battle is well written, fair and perceptive, illustrated with lively quotations and supported by two invaluable appendices of statistics. It advanced our knowledge far beyond previous accounts and remains the starting point for any new study of the battle. Nonetheless, Oman's account occupies just two chapters out of the twenty-four in a fat volume which covers many other operations, including the sieges of Ciudad Rodrigo and Badajoz and campaigns in Valencia, Andalusia and other parts of Spain. As a result Oman lacks the space to explore fully all the issues raised by the battle. Furthermore, it is almost ninety years since his account was first published, and in that time many new sources have come to light which greatly enrich our understanding of the battle.

The purpose of the present work is to give a detailed account of what happened on 22 July 1812. This apparently simple objective has proved surprisingly difficult to achieve in practice. There is no shortage of sources: scores of officers and men wrote accounts of their experiences either in diaries or letters soon afterwards, or in reminiscences years later, and these personal narratives can be tested against casualty statistics of varying reliability and by visiting the battlefield, which remains today substantially as it was in 1812. But while the sources are plentiful, they do not always fit neatly together; indeed, they are riddled with contradictions, inconsistencies, gaps and uncertainty. Sometimes the only account of an important incident comes from a dubious source; and sometimes two apparently reliable sources flatly contradict each other. The sources are numerous, but not evenly distributed: a great number of British soldiers published their recollections of the battle; far fewer Frenchmen wished to recall their defeat; while Portuguese voices – except for British officers serving in Portuguese units – have proved elusive.

Normally the historian deals privately with these problems, occasionally drawing attention to a particularly thorny issue in the text – perhaps when a novel interpretation is advanced – while alluding briefly to some other difficulties in the notes. This method is inescapable in addressing a large, sweeping subject if the narrative is not to lose its momentum and the reader to miss the thread of the argument. However, it can also mislead the reader by suggesting that our understanding is far more securely based than is the case. Most casual readers of Oman's account of Salamanca probably come away with the impression that there are only a few outstanding difficulties, and that these would be solved easily if fresh evidence came to light.

In fact, almost every aspect of the battle has its complexities, if not its contradictions. I want to explore these problems and examine the various gradations between what we know as surely as we know anything about the past (that a battle was fought a few miles south of Salamanca on 22 July 1812 in which the French were defeated), through what is debatable (the formation of Pakenham's division in its advance, or who gave the order for Pack's attack on the Greater Arapile), to the point where the evidence fails completely. In other words I want to show the reader the historian's building site before the scaffolding has been taken down, the tools put away and the debris swept out of sight. Thus, at one level the subject of the book is the battle of Salamanca; at another, it is a case study of the problems encountered in answering even the comparatively simple historical question of what happened at a particular place on a particular day. Not that I wish to venture into the theoretical or philosophical issues underpinning the writing of history: my objective is much more modest – to show how a simple empirical study is constructed, and how source problems are addressed.

There is a danger that these two goals may conflict. Many readers will only want to know 'what happened' and will have no wish to have problems with the sources paraded before them, feeling that it is the author's task to resolve such questions as best he can. In deference to such readers, and in order to keep the book readable, I have divided the text into a main narrative, which tells the story of the battle as fully as possible, and which includes a discussion of the most important or controversial problems, and a commentary which runs in parallel to the narrative, and which allows for an extended discussion of other problems and the inclusion of supplementary material that would overburden the narrative. Some readers will, no doubt, ignore the commentary completely; others will consult it only for particular points of special interest to them; while a few may, perhaps, find it even more interesting than the narrative.

In writing the history of the battle, I have quoted extensively from the many first-hand accounts which are our principal source for what happened. These are often well written, giving a vivid insight into the author's feelings as well as the actions of his unit. As such, they are an important reminder that the battle was fought by living men, not anonymous, unfeeling cogs in a machine. Many of their experiences were common to soldiers in any battle of the period, not just Salamanca, and thereby give a broader relevance to the work.

I have benefited greatly from two visits to the battlefield, in 1993 and for three days in the summer of 2000. Walking the terrain is an invaluable tool in understanding any battle: some doubtful points immediately become clear, while new, unexpected problems arise. The credibility of some first-hand accounts is confirmed by the accuracy of their description of the ground, while others are cast into doubt. Nonetheless, visiting a battlefield is a supplement to, not a substitute for, hours spent in the library and archives. It is all too easy for the visitor, enjoying the tramp through dry grass under a hot sun, with a head full of images of far-off days, to believe that he or she knows 'what must have happened'. But in the end our knowledge of the battle depends on the testimony of those who were there, for events did not always unfold in the most logical or plausible way.

On the vexed issue of place and personal names I have generally preferred the form made familiar by previous accounts of the battle; for example, the Greater and Lesser Arapiles, rather than the Arapil Grande and the Arapil Chico. Some names are particularly uncertain: Oman spells the French divisional commander General Bonnet with two 'n's, many other sources, including Martinien and Sarramón use only one – Bonet – but 'Bonnet' is the form used in the manuscript of the return of casualties prepared by General Lamartinière, the chief of staff of the French army. Colonel Arentschildt of the King's German Legion is spelt thus by Oman, but without the final 't' by Fortescue and Beamish, while Michael A. Taenzer informs me that he actually signed his name 'von Arentsschildt' (double s and dt). After some reflection I have decided to ignore the double s and follow Oman, for introducing a third form of the name into common use would not eliminate the other spellings and would only increase the confusion. Similarly I have preferred the comfortable if illogical '1st Ligne' for French regiments to the pedantically correct '1e Ligne'.

I am grateful to a number of individuals and institutions for permission to quote unpublished material, and for the good wishes and encouragement which so often accompanied the formal permission. Mr G. Hope allowed me to quote from the Hope of Luffness papers deposited at the National Archives of Scotland, including the full text of a letter from 'H.C.' printed and discussed in Appendix IV. Mrs J. N. Tomes permitted me to quote from the letters of Lieutenant-Colonel Sir Alexander Gordon in her possession. And the National Army Museum, the National Archives of Scotland, the National Library of Scotland and the Public Record Office all gave me permission to quote material which they hold, as well as making it possible for me to see the original papers.

This book was written while I was a long-term Visiting Research Fellow at the Department of History, University of Adelaide (a position I still hold). The facilities, encouragement and resources provided by the department, and by the Barr Smith Library, were immensely useful in bringing the project to fruition. I should particularly mention Professor Trevor Wilson who has explored diverse approaches to military history, matching form to subject with exemplary success. I must also thank the staff of many other libraries and archives for their assistance: the State Library of South Australia and the State Library of Victoria; the British Library, the Public Record Office and the National Army Museum in London; the Scottish Record Office and the National Library of Scotland in Edinburgh; the Brighton Public Library, Sussex; and numerous regimental museums across Britain that replied to my enquiries – in particular, Major Hugo White of the Duke of Cornwall's Light Infantry Museum. Finally, Général Bach and Chef de Bataillon Porchet of the Service Historique de l'Armée de Terre, at Vincennes, for sending me a photocopy of Lamartinière's original casualty return.

When the book was in its final stages I was fortunate enough to spend a month at the University of Southampton as a Fellow of the Hartley Institute. Although the primary focus of my research was on another subject, I was able to devote a couple of productive days to work on Salamanca, including a more detailed examination of the plan of the battle in Wyld's *Atlas*, looking through the unpublished letters of Sir Denis Pack and consulting Oman's own copy of the first edition of Andrew Leith Hay's *A Narrative of the Peninsular War*. I am grateful to the staff of the special collections for making my visit so pleasant, and in particular to Dr Christopher Woolgar for his hospitality, friendship and good advice, not only on this occasion, but over many years.

Mr S. G. P. Ward kindly answered many queries and shared his immense knowledge of Wellington's army in a most enjoyable correspondence. His magnificent gift of books and papers to the University of Southampton has ensured that his collection – including many rare and even unique items – will be both expertly preserved and made readily available to scholars working in the field.

Mr Mark Urban kindly sent me the draft of his fascinating book on Colonel Scovell *The Man who Broke Napoleon's Codes*, as well as copies of several unpublished letters describing the battle from the Le Marchant and other private collections. I have also greatly benefited from his comments on a late draft of chapter six, and from a stimulating and encouraging correspondence with him. Lieutenant-Colonel R. E. R. Robinson generously gave me copies of his notes of the 61st Regiment digest, a manuscript source that I was unable to see for myself. Mark Romans drew on his detailed research into Wellington's intelligence-gathering to answer my queries on that aspect of the campaign. Ian Robertson used his experience in describing terrain and his knowledge of the battlefield to save me from several infelicities in Appendix V. Mrs Alison Thomas translated Wachholtz's journal from the German for me, and John Emerson checked my reading of some doubtful passages in the French sources. Mr Victor Sutcliffe provided me with some important bibliographical information. Señor Pedro Vicente Morales lent me invaluable assistance when I was visiting the battlefield. Mr David Elder read the script, shed light on a number of doubtful points and gave me much encouragement. Dr Paddy Griffith and an anonymous reader for Yale University Press both also read the script and made a number of stimulating suggestions, although they must not be held responsible for any errors or eccentricities that remain. Mrs Chris Crothers of the Department of Geographical and Environmental Studies of the University of Adelaide converted my rough sketches into stylish maps and then accepted innumerable amendments with great good humour.

I have derived great pleasure and benefit from contact with many enthusiasts for the period through the Napoleonic Discussion Forum on the internet (www.napoleon-series.org). Steven Smith of California displayed both his dedication and his bibliographical skills not only in tracking down Oman's vague citation 'Wachholtz' to its source in a century-old German military periodical, but also in obtaining and sending me a photocopy of the article. Bernabe Saiz Martínez de Pisón answered many questions about the Spanish forces at the battle, and generously sent me copies of the maps of the campaign and battle from Arteche's history. Bob Burnham shared his knowledge of British memoirs of the Peninsular War, filling gaps in my collection and answering bibliographical queries. Others have been equally kind. To mention only a few: Tom Holmberg, Bruno Nackaerts, Ron McGuigan, Robert Markley, Michael A. Taenzer, John Cook and George Nafziger have all helped, often repeatedly, both in points of detail and with stimulating ideas.

I must single out for special thanks Howie Muir, another friend made through the internet, whose fascination with the subject, immense enthusiasm and detailed knowledge of the terrain forced me to re-think many casual assumptions and greatly enriched the final work.

My publisher, Dr Robert Baldock of Yale University Press, showed great faith in the proposed work despite its narrow focus, while my editor, Candida Brazil, saw the work through the press with great patience and skill, calmly resolving problems posed by a rather complicated script.

Dr Charles Esdaile is an old and excellent friend whom I have thanked on similar occasions in the past. As always I have enjoyed our correspondence and am grateful for the perceptive comments he made, both in reading the script and elsewhere.

Finally, I must thank my mother, the best of travelling companions, critics and scholarly exemplars rolled into one.

Chapter One
The Campaign

By the end of 1811 the Peninsular War had lasted for three and a half years, and no end was in sight. Napoleon's lightning campaign in late 1808 had driven the Spanish armies from the Ebro in disarray and led to the capture of Madrid, but it had not broken the Spanish will to resist: the war continued and more than 200,000 – at times more than 300,000 – French troops were tied up south of the Pyrenees. Unlike in central Europe, conquered provinces required large permanent garrisons to prevent them bursting into insurrection, while in the more remote regions, which had not yet been overrun, new armies continued to be collected to oppose the French. By removing the Bourbons and placing his brother Joseph on the Spanish throne, Napoleon had made a compromise peace difficult, if not impossible; while the presence of the French armies in Spain, their requisitions, the misdeeds of their soldiers and their punitive atrocities gave constant incitement to resistance. Then there were the British, who provided arms, supplies and money to the patriot forces, especially at the beginning of the war, and whose army had made several interventions in the conflict. In 1808 Sir John Moore had diverted Napoleon from the conquest of Andalusia and dragged his forces into the remote, barren and strategically unimportant north-west corner of Spain. In 1809 Sir Arthur Wellesley had consolidated the British position in Portugal and then attempted to exploit the lopsided distribution of French forces in Spain. His campaign failed only because Soult and Ney had fortuitously evacuated Galicia, and so were able to threaten his lines of communication and force him to retreat, thus making fruitless the allied victory at Talavera. In 1810 a large part of the vast French reinforcements sent to the Peninsula after the defeat of Austria were employed in an attempt to drive the British from Portugal, but Wellington (as Wellesley now was) had made ample preparations to check the long-threatened invasion. Masséna's army received a bloody check at Busaco, where the re-trained Portuguese army showed that it would fight. Turning Wellington's flank, the French resumed their advance, only to grind to a halt before the almost impregnable Lines of Torres Vedras which protected the whole Lisbon Peninsula. Masséna wisely refused to attack such a formidable obstacle and referred the problem to Napoleon, maintaining his position throughout the winter despite severe short-ages of food and the ravages of disease. By the spring he could wait no longer. Napoleon had proved unable to send worthwhile help and Masséna's army was now dangerously weak compared to the allies, who had been fed well and rein-forced over the winter. Masséna retreated back to the frontier: his invasion of Portugal had cost the French army some fifteen thousand men, most of whom had died from sickness and lack of food.

In Spain, however, the French armies appeared to be making progress. Soult had successfully invaded and occupied Andalusia at the beginning of 1810, although he failed to capture Cadiz, which became the capital of the independ-ent Spanish government. A year later, in another winter campaign, he defeated the Spanish Army of Estremadura and captured the great fortress of Badajoz on the Portuguese frontier. Meanwhile, in eastern Spain, Suchet was having simi-lar successes, capturing Tortosa in January 1811, Tarragona in June, then advancing into the rich province of Valencia and capturing its capital, the city of Valencia, in January 1812. The loss of Andalusia and Valencia threatened to cripple the Spanish resistance, for it left only a few poor, isolated provinces under the control of the government of Cadiz, and they had neither the popu-lation nor the wealth to raise regular armies powerful enough to drive back the French.

But equally the French forces in the Peninsula – some 320,000 men at the beginning of 1812 – were now fully stretched, without a significant central reserve or the capacity to meet any sudden disaster. Nor could they look to Napoleon for assistance, for ever since the middle of 1811 he had been turning his attention to the likelihood of a new war in eastern Europe. The steady stream of French reinforcements had dwindled almost to nothing, and selected units, mostly very good troops such as the Imperial Guard and the Polish reg-iments, were withdrawn. So the French could expect to achieve little in Spain in 1812 other than to consolidate their hold over their new conquests, while the loss of Andalusia and Valencia might undermine the Spanish regular forces and the guerrillas might weary of a hopeless struggle. Looking further ahead, if Napoleon's war with Russia was successful – and there was little reason to doubt that it would be – his victory might be followed by heavy reinforcements to Spain, as had happened after the defeat of Austria in 1809; and such forces might be sufficient to overwhelm the allies and subdue the guerrillas, and so eventually bring this difficult and unpopular war to a victorious conclusion.

Wellington's Anglo-Portuguese army was the greatest threat to these hopes, for it was by far the largest and most efficient allied force left in the Peninsula and it had a secure base in Portugal. But in late 1811 French optimists, includ-ing Napoleon, did not regard it as posing too serious a danger. Wellington's efforts at exploiting Masséna's defeat had not been very successful. He had defeated a French attempt to relieve the blockade of the fortress of Almeida in the Battle of Fuentes de Oñoro, but the garrison had escaped through his lines after sabotaging the fortifications. Two sieges of Badajoz had failed, despite Beresford's bloody victory at Albuera, when the French armies of Soult and Marmont (who had replaced Masséna) combined and forced Wellington to withdraw before them. The second half of 1811 was less costly but even less productive as a blockade of Ciudad Rodrigo proved ineffective. Wellington retained the initiative, for the French had no thought of taking the offensive against him or attempting a serious invasion of Portugal, but it seemed that he could be safely contained on the frontier. Napoleon went even further, however, for he concluded that the allied army was incapable of undertaking substantial operations in the midst of winter, and instructed Marmont to detach some of his forces to assist Suchet in Valencia. Marmont saw no danger in obeying these orders and, with a spirit of co-operation rare among the French marshals in Spain, sent even more men than Napoleon had suggested. But Wellington had learnt from his mistakes in 1811 and made meticulous preparations for his next attempt. This time he moved rapidly and with an ample siege train that he had managed to bring forward in secret. Ciudad Rodrigo was besieged on 8 January 1812 and fell eleven days later. Even without the diversion of Marmont's troops it could not have been saved: the attack was too sudden, too rapid and too well prepared to allow the French time to collect their forces and intervene.

Having captured Ciudad Rodrigo, Wellington's next objective would clearly be Badajoz, the more southerly of the great fortresses on the Spanish side of the frontier. Again he made meticulous preparations, although this time he could not hope to surprise the French. The fortress was much stronger than Ciudad Rodrigo, with an excellent garrison which had withstood two sieges in 1811 and so was full of confidence. Wellington expected Marmont and Soult to combine to march to its relief and, while he had some hopes of taking Badajoz before they could intervene, he had made up his mind that, unless the odds were very unfavourable, he would fight their combined forces rather than give up the siege. A victory in such a battle would not only precipitate the fall of Badajoz, it would also open the road to Seville, lift the siege of Cadiz and probably force the French to evacuate all of Andalusia, all before midsummer. But again Napoleon intervened, ordering Marmont not to march to aid Badajoz but instead to invade northern Portugal, which, he believed, would force Wellington to give up the siege in order to protect his bases. Marmont had no faith in the plan, and executed it with little enthusiasm. It was never likely to succeed in its primary object, although it is just possible that with more enterprise it might have gained the consolation prize of re-capturing Ciudad Rodrigo or even Almeida; but in the event it achieved little, despite causing Wellington some uneasiness. Without Marmont's support Soult was too weak to intervene in the siege of Badajoz, and on the night of 6 April British troops stormed the fortress. They met with courageous and ingenious resistance; the attacks on the main breaches failed, and success only came when a diversionary attempt to escalade the castle gained a foothold because most of the garrison was concentrated at the breaches. The cost was very high: 3,713 casualties in the storm alone; 4,670 in the siege as a whole; and the horror of the night was succeeded by days of drunken pillaging, murder and other atrocities before the soldiers could be brought under control again.

In barely three months Wellington had broken the deadlock of 1811, and it was still only April, with the full campaigning season before him. He was tempted to advance into Andalusia and attack Soult directly, but Marmont's incursion into northern Portugal and the vulnerability of Almeida and Ciudad Rodrigo alarmed him. Also, Marmont commanded the most mobile of the French armies in Spain and, if Wellington advanced into Andalusia, Marmont might follow him with most of his forces. But if Wellington moved directly against Marmont, it was most unlikely that Soult would send him any significant aid, both because Soult's resources were already fully committed occupying his vast vice-royalty and because he was generally more inclined to seek than to provide co-operation.

If Marmont received help, it was more likely to be from some of the other French forces in Spain. General Caffarelli commanded the Army of the North, which guarded French lines of communication from Bayonne through Burgos towards Madrid. It was a thankless task which had brought little credit to his predecessors, for their forces always looked substantial on paper but were overextended on the ground, and they were constantly harassed by guerrillas whom they could never subdue. Nonetheless, the Army of the North was under orders to support Marmont if Wellington advanced against him, just as it had supported Masséna at Fuentes de Oñoro, and Marmont when he forced the blockade of Ciudad Rodrigo in 1811. Another possible source of assistance was King Joseph's Army of the Centre, although this was really only strong enough to hold Madrid and the adjacent provinces. Joseph and Marshal Jourdan, his principal military adviser, both saw the need to reinforce Marmont in order to contain Wellington, but were naturally reluctant to withdraw their garrisons from the few areas that recognized royal authority. Theoretically Joseph was, by Napoleon's decree, commander-in-chief of all the French forces in Spain, and he sent the marshals many orders mixed with pleas which generally displayed a fair grasp of the state of the war in the Peninsula as a whole. Sometimes the marshals replied with promises, sometimes with excuses and sometimes they did not reply at all, but Joseph's authority was weak and they seldom, if ever, acted simply in obedience to his orders. The third possible source of reinforcements for Marmont was Marshal Suchet, who now commanded all the French forces in Aragon, Catalonia and Valencia. Wellington feared that Suchet might return the assistance which Marmont had given him at the beginning of the year, especially as he had seen intercepted copies of orders from Joseph which he took more seriously than did Suchet. But Catalonia and Aragon were always very uneasy possessions for the French, and Suchet had more than enough employment for his men without looking to the western half of the Peninsula.

Wellington took some trouble to help distract the French marshals and to give them an excuse not to reinforce Marmont. Through the Spanish government, he asked General Ballesteros, who commanded a small Spanish army in southern Andalusia near Gibraltar, to make a show of activity. Ballesteros did so and, despite suffering a limited defeat at the beginning of June, caused Soult some concern. Wellington also hoped for the co-operation of the Spanish army based in Galicia, which could besiege the French garrison in Astorga and, when it fell (it was not a regular fortress), advance and threaten Marmont's flank. He asked the Spanish forces in the north – notably Porlier in Cantabria and Longa in the mountains above Santander – to make trouble for Caffarelli, which they did with considerable success. They were much assisted by a British naval squadron, complete with two battalions of marines, under Sir Home Popham, which operated on the north coast of Spain throughout the summer, and with its great mobility caused Caffarelli immense problems. Wellington had not asked for this amphibious force, but it complemented his plans perfectly. Equally unlooked-for but welcome was a proposal from Lord William Bentinck, commander of the British forces in Sicily, to mount an expedition to the east coast of Spain. Wellington made optimistic plans for this force, urging that, rather than land in safety in southern Valencia, it should directly attack Tarragona or even Barcelona. He arranged Spanish co-operation, despatched a siege-train from Lisbon and clearly felt that the expedition had a good chance of success; while even if it failed it would achieve his main objective by distracting Suchet.

Wellington's own army was divided, for while he had brought the bulk of it north, he had left a substantial force under his trusted subordinate Lieutenant-General Sir Rowland Hill to guard his southern flank. Hill had some 18,000 men, compared to about 45,000 in the main army, although Hill's force included a higher proportion of Portuguese. His immediate opponent was Drouet's corps of Soult's army, and he had received instructions that, if Drouet were to march north to join Marmont (as King Joseph demanded), he should hasten to join Wellington and so preserve the balance of forces. In a straightforward race between these two corps Drouet might be expected to arrive first, for the French were great marchers and had less far to go, at least as the crow flies. But Wellington had long had his eye on the French bridge at Almaraz, their only crossing of the Tagus for many miles. He gave Hill his orders and, in a beautifully executed operation in the middle of May, Hill seized and destroyed the bridge with only light losses, despite its strong defences. This ensured that any northward movement by Drouet would have to take a lengthy detour as far east as Toledo to cross the Tagus; while at the same time the allied route was shortened by restoring the broken bridge at Alcantara. It is hard to see what more Wellington could have done to ensure Marmont's isolation in the campaign.[1]

Wellington began his advance on 13 June, but it was not until the 16th that the advanced guard first encountered French outposts, only a few miles from

Salamanca. These withdrew before the allied troops, and Wellington entered the ancient university city on the 17 June amidst scenes of great rejoicing. Marmont's army had been widely scattered in cantonments, mainly for logistical reasons, but he had left eight hundred men in three makeshift forts – converted convents – inside Salamanca, and he hoped that these would delay Wellington until he could collect his forces and seek help from the other French armies. Wellington knew of these forts and had even been sent sketches of them, for he had excellent sources of intelligence in Salamanca; but they were stronger than he expected. He had brought forward four iron 18-pounder siege guns and a limited supply of ammunition, but both soon proved to be inadequate. Still, it is not really surprising that embarking on a campaign in open country, with nothing more to worry about than a few fortified convents, he had not encumbered his army with a large, slow-moving siege-train, especially as there were many other pressing demands on his limited transport. But if the initial mistake is understandable, it was soon compounded by others. It was not until 20 June that Wellington sent orders to Almeida to send forward further supplies of ammunition, while the choice of the Sixth Division, which had little or no experience of sieges, to conduct the operation also proved unfortunate. Consequently the attack on the forts made slow, uncertain and costly progress, although its final outcome was never in doubt, unless the garrisons could be saved by outside intervention.

Marmont had not been idle, and he had no intention of sacrificing the garrisons if there was any reasonable chance of saving them. By 19 June he had collected five of his eight infantry divisions, and two more were rapidly approaching. The last division, under General Bonnet, was far away in Asturias; Marmont had summoned it, but could not expect it to arrive until the beginning of July. He had also sent urgent messages to Caffarelli and King Joseph. Caffarelli had already promised, before news of Wellington's advance reached him, that if Marmont was attacked he would send him a substantial force of about eight thousand men, including a brigade of light cavalry and twenty-two guns. Joseph was less encouraging, for Soult was claiming that Wellington was about to attack Andalusia, but if Bonnet and Caffarelli's forces arrived on schedule, Marmont could expect to outnumber Wellington's army within a fortnight. However, the forts were unlikely to hold out this long and, with the bulk of his army near at hand, Marmont decided to advance and see if he could outmanoeuvre Wellington, and either relieve the forts, or at least force the allies to suspend their siege operations.

Wellington was delighted with Marmont's advance and quickly occupied a strong defensive position on the heights of San Cristobal just to the north of the town. Late on the afternoon of 20 June Marmont appeared at the foot of this position and there was some skirmishing, including a spirited fight for control of the village of Morisco. Marmont was certainly rash in approaching the allied position so closely: two of his seven divisions had yet to join, so that he was outnumbered by about three to two, even allowing for the fact that most of the allied Sixth Division remained in Salamanca in front of the forts. Wellington is said to have been tempted to attack, but refrained because he expected Marmont to attack him on the following morning, and that this would lead to a more certain and less costly victory. Before the campaign began he had told Lord Liverpool that he intended 'to bring Marmont to a general action' and expressed his confidence in its outcome; but now he declined an excellent opportunity for doing so.[2] The broken ground at the foot of his position could have hampered such an attack, while in the unlikely event of a defeat the army's retreat, with a town and a river in its rear, would have been extremely difficult. His early confidence had also been sapped by captured papers which indicated that the French forces were generally stronger than he had expected; he was surprised and dismayed that Marmont had flouted Napoleon's order to leave Bonnet's division in the Asturias; and he had begun to doubt the effectiveness of the diversions he had organized.[3] But these reasons, while significant in their way, were hardly sufficient to account for his caution; and there was some surprise and murmuring in the army that he had let an opportunity slip.[4]

Marmont did not attack on the 21st, although his two trailing divisions arrived and he reconnoitred the allied position. He seems to have given little thought to the danger that Wellington might attack him, and Wellington's restraint would only have added to his confidence. That night he called a council of war of his senior commanders and listened as some (including Maucune and Ferey) advocated an attack, while others (Clausel, the senior divisional commander, and Foy) reminded him of the failure of previous such attacks at Vimeiro, Coruña and Busaco. According to Foy's rather hostile account, Marmont was inclined to favour the attack, but would not press forward against such articulate opposition; clearly the summoning of the council of war was itself an indication of uncertainty.[5]

Marmont was probably encouraged to wait by the fact that the siege of the forts was suspended on the 21st, which he naturally attributed to the presence of his army, although in fact it was because the allies had used almost all the ammunition for their siege guns and fresh supplies would not arrive from Almeida for some days. Over the next few days Marmont manoeuvred around Salamanca, transferring part of his army from one side of the Tormes to the other, hoping to force the allies into a mistake. Wellington countered these manoeuvres with relative ease, but was not tempted to take the offensive himself, while his efforts to press forward the siege of the forts with inadequate means led to a costly repulse on the night of the 23rd. The slow progress of the allies encouraged Marmont to hope that Caffarelli's reinforcements might reach him in time to save the forts, but these hopes were dashed on the 26th, when news arrived that Caffarelli was so alarmed by the activity of the guerrillas and Popham's naval squadron that he would not be able to spare any men for some time. With no prospect of reinforcements, Marmont at once embarked on an extremely dangerous attempt to raise the siege. However, before he could fully commit his army, the forts had fallen, thanks to the arrival

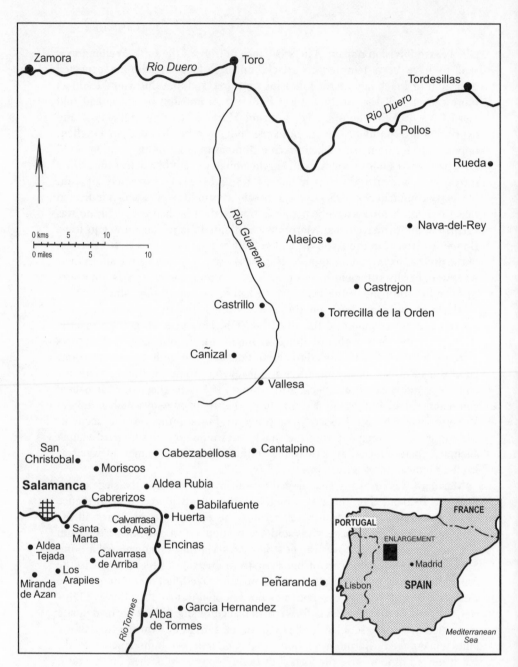

The Salamanca campaign.

of fresh supplies of ammunition. This left the French with no reason to remain so far forward, and over the next few days they made a well-executed withdrawal to the Duero, where they would be closer to Bonnet's division and any reinforcements which could ultimately be extracted from the Army of the North. Wellington followed; he had achieved his initial objectives, but had not brought Marmont to battle, nor had it been a particularly convincing opening to the campaign.

The two armies remained quietly on the Duero for a fortnight. At first Wellington was full of confidence, reconnoitring the fords and talking of attacking the French as soon as the river fell a little. But Bonnet's division joined Marmont on 7 July, bringing the two armies to nearly equal numbers: Wellington had the stronger cavalry, but the French artillery was far superior and occupied strong positions guarding the crossings of the river. Indeed, the more closely Wellington inspected the French positions, the less he liked the prospect of a direct attack, while any attempt to turn Marmont's flank risked exposing his own lines of communication. The best chance was to bring forward the Spanish army, which was besieging Astorga, in the hope that its threat to Marmont's flank and rear would lead to a rearrangement of French forces which might open a way for an attack. But the siege of Astorga dragged on and the Spanish generals appeared unable either to take the town, or to convert the siege into a blockade and advance with the bulk of their force. Meanwhile Wellington was receiving reports that King Joseph was collecting his men with the intention of aiding Marmont, and that he had also ordered Drouet to leave Estremadura and join him. This made Wellington despondent enough to tell Hill, 'I am apprehensive that, after all, the enemy will be too strong for me.' But worse was to come, for on the following day he learnt that Bentinck had decided to send his expedition to the Italian mainland rather than to eastern Spain. Wellington told his brother Henry that this was 'fatal to the campaign', and his staff echoed his despair in letters home which denounced Bentinck's decision in violent terms. In fact, there was never much danger that Suchet would send any aid to Marmont, while Bentinck's decision was soon reversed and his expedition went ahead without appreciable loss of time.[6]

The troops in both armies seem to have found this lull in the campaign pleasant. William Napier, the future historian, who was commanding the 43rd Light Infantry in the Light Division at the time, evokes those midsummer days with some nostalgia:

> The weather was fine, the country rich, the troops received full rations, and wine was so plentiful it was hard to keep the soldiers sober: the caves of Rueda, either natural or cut in the rock below the surface of the earth, were so immense and so well stocked, that the drunkards of two armies failed to make any sensible diminution in the quantity. Many men of both sides perished in that labyrinth,

and on both sides the soldiers, entering the river to bathe, held amicable inter-
course, rallying each other about the battles yet to be fought, and the camps on
the banks of the Duero seemed at times to belong to one army: so difficult is it
to make brave men hate each other.

However, he goes on to say: 'The officers of the allies were anxious to receive
the signal of battle, they were discontented at its being delayed, and many
amongst them murmured that the French had been permitted to retreat from
Christoval. Hence had Wellington been finally forced back to Portugal his
reputation would have been grievously assailed by his own people.'[7] The first
point is confirmed in the journal of Charles Boutflower, a surgeon in the Fourth
Division, who describes large numbers of men from both armies bathing
together in the river while the cavalry brought down their horses to be watered.
But it is seldom possible to please everyone, and Major Rice of the 51st wrote
home to a friend on 6 July: 'We have been wretchedly off for this some time;
scanty fare, bad biscuit, etc. The weather dreadfully hot by day and cold by
night – beyond what I ever experienced. We are lying in cornfields without the
smallest covering. How the men stand this severe work is to me astonishing.'[8]

While Wellington's confidence gradually ebbed and the soldiers bathed in
the Duero, Marmont considered his position. Although Caffarelli continued to
promise some support, if only a brigade of cavalry and a battery of horse
artillery, there was no sign that the troops were on their way. The guerrillas and
Popham were constantly harassing the Army of the North, and by the second
week of July Marmont had despaired of receiving any practical help from
Caffarelli. Nor were his latest despatches from King Joseph any more encouraging. In fact, Joseph and Jourdan were already collecting every man they could
while still leaving a garrison in Madrid – altogether a field force of about fourteen thousand men – with the intention of marching to Marmont's aid. But the
retreat behind the Duero had severed Marmont's direct line of communication
with Madrid and, although Joseph sent duplicates and triplicates of his carefully coded letters, they were all intercepted by the guerrillas, and most found
their way to Wellington's headquarters, where Major Scovell painstakingly
deciphered them. Not for the first time, Wellington knew more of the French
plans than did his immediate opponent.[9]

It was natural, therefore, for Marmont to conclude that he had little to gain
by waiting, and there was the risk that the strategic balance might worsen. The
Galician army might capture Astorga and advance to join Wellington, adding
fifteen thousand men, albeit of inferior quality, to the allied forces. Or
Wellington might summon Hill's eighteen thousand men from Estremadura
and so gain an overwhelming, if temporary, superiority, for even if Drouet set
out immediately he could not arrive until some days after Hill. This was an
alarming prospect, although with hindsight we can see that it was a manoeuvre
more characteristic of Napoleon than of Wellington, who was much less
inclined to stake everything on a single throw of the dice.

On the other hand, Marmont was encouraged by the arrival of Bonnet's strong division, which completed his army and brought it up almost to Wellington's strength. Like most French soldiers, he was firmly convinced that a French army should be capable of defeating any opponent on reasonably equal terms. Busaco and earlier defeats had instilled a degree of respect for British troops defending a strong position, but he could not doubt the immense superiority of French troops manoeuvring and fighting in open country. Twenty years of glorious victories (the defeats in the Revolutionary Wars had been quietly forgotten) and Napoleon's prestige and propaganda had created a spirit which went far beyond pride and became arrogance. This confidence permeated the army and was, in itself, an enormous aid to victory; nor did it often blind French generals to danger or make them foolishly rash – they were too professional for that – but they did operate in a context where their subordinates (and Napoleon) expected enterprise and success. Marmont's failure to rescue the garrisons of the Salamanca forts, his fruitless manoeuvres before San Cristobal and his retreat to the Duero, had produced some discontent in the French army, and the resulting pressure, added to the fear that Wellington might be reinforced, encouraged him to take the initiative.[10]

Although the French controlled the bridges and most of the fords over the Duero, crossing the river in the face of the allied army was still a potentially difficult operation. Wellington had had a fortnight to survey the country and make his plans: he might already have chosen a strong position in his rear in which he could meet the French on his own terms, or he might intend to attack the French army as soon as part of it was across the river and destroy it piecemeal. Marmont devised an ingenious plan to avoid these dangers while exploiting the capacity of his troops to make rapid marches. On 10 July he began repairing the bridge at Toro, at the western end of his line and the point closest to Salamanca. Over the next few days increasing numbers of French troops shifted towards Toro, attracting Wellington's attention and arousing his concern for his communications with Salamanca. On 16 July two French divisions crossed the Duero at Toro and established themselves on the southern bank; Wellington received the news about 7 o'clock that evening and issued orders to move the army to the west where it could form across the Toro to Salamanca road.[11] But that night the whole French army reversed its line of march; the divisions which had crossed at Toro withdrew and blew up the bridge behind them; the bulk of the army crossed the river more than twenty miles to the east at Tordesillas, while the rear divisions, those which had been at Toro and had the longest march, were able to take a short-cut through the fords of Pollos. By nightfall on the 17th the French army was safely across the Duero and well established between Rueda and Nava-del-Rey. Wellington had been completely wrong-footed and was now in some danger, for two of his divisions (the Light and the Fourth) were still around Alaejos and Castrejon, alarmingly close to the French main force and far from support.

COMBATS OF CASTREJON AND THE GUARENA, 18 JULY 1812

On the morning of 18 July Wellington's first objective was to secure the safe withdrawal of these two divisions over some eight miles of open country to the line of the River Guarena, which ran north at right angles to the Duero at Toro, and which would form Wellington's new line. This delicate operation was made easier because the allied cavalry was much stronger than the French, and also because the French troops were weary after their long marches. Wellington brought forward the Fifth Division to Torrecilla de la Orden to cover the southern flank of the retreating troops and to give them some support as they fell back, while their more exposed northern flank would be protected by the heavy cavalry brigades of Bock and Le Marchant.

Wellington reached the divisions about 7 am to find them already skirmishing with the enemy. Sir Stapleton Cotton, the cavalry commander, had taken charge as the senior officer present and had sent out patrols before dawn, which soon discovered that the French were in force. Some skirmishing followed and both sides brought up batteries of artillery and opened fire. Napier remembered:

> Now the cannonade became heavy and the spectacle surprisingly beautiful. The lighter smoke and mist curling up in fantastic pillars formed a huge and glittering dome tinged of many colours by the rising sun; and through the grosser vapour below the restless horsemen were seen or lost as the fume thickened from the rapid play of the guns, while the high bluff head of land beyond Trabancos, covered with French troops, appeared by an optical deception close at hand, dilated to the size of a mountain, and crowned with gigantic soldiers who were continually breaking off and sliding down into the fight.[12]

Wellington and his staff were unexpectedly caught up in this skirmishing when a party of French cavalry suddenly charged two squadrons of the 11th and 12th Light Dragoons who were guarding two guns of Ross's horse artillery – the famous Chestnut Troop. The British cavalry broke – according to Captain Tomkinson, because a staff officer gave them a wrong order – and for a little while all was confusion as generals, staff, horse artillery and cavalry alike had to draw their swords to defend themselves. Fortunately other supports were close at hand, the senior officers and staff found refuge behind some nearby infantry and the French were soon driven off. Captain Kincaid of the 95th Rifles remembered the aftermath:

> I was highly interested, all this time, in observing the distinguished characters which this unlooked-for *turn-up* had assembled around us. Marshal Beresford and the greater part of the staff remained with their swords drawn, and the Duke himself did not look more than half-pleased, while he silently despatched some of them with orders. General Alten, and his huge German orderly dragoon, with

their swords drawn, cursed, the whole time, to a very large amount; but, as it was in German, I had not the full benefit of it.[13]

The allied troops now began their retreat to the Guarena, with the French pressing after them and constantly trying to turn their flank. On several occasions the French were able to bring forward artillery and open fire, inflicting some casualties, while the allied stragglers, whether overcome by the heat or footsore, had to be abandoned. Yet losses were generally low, and the good discipline of the infantry and the protection afforded by the cavalry ensured that the retreat succeeded without giving the French an opening to strike a serious blow. They reached the Guarena in the early afternoon and, although accounts differ, it seems that the Fourth and Fifth Divisions halted for some time on the further bank to drink and rest. Light Division sources, however, say that the French opened fire as soon as they reached the stream, and that they could do no more than snatch a mouthful of water as they waded through, before climbing the further bank and taking cover.[14]

Wellington's army was now collected in quite a good, although not a formidable, position running north–south on the western bank of the Guarena – a small river at that time of the year and readily fordable in most places. His most vulnerable point appeared to be his right flank around Vallesa, where the tributary streams of the Guarena had yet to join and where a successful French advance would again threaten his communications with Salamanca. Marmont recognized this, but he could see that Wellington's troops were already well posted while his own men were badly in need of rest, so he decided to halt for the remainder of the day.

This was not the end of operations on 18 July however, for before Marmont could make his intentions known throughout the army, his northern wing under Clausel had brought on an action. The details of what followed are far from clear, with the sources being unusually patchy and inclined to contradiction. However, it seems that Clausel reached the Guarena with the 2nd and 6th Divisions opposite Wellington's extreme left, and believed that by attacking at once he could turn the allied position and secure a foothold on the western side of the Guarena. Clausel ordered the 6th Division under Brigadier Taupin (French sources all state that he, not Brennier, was in command of the division throughout the campaign) to swing a little further north, ford the river and secure a hill which dominated the position. Protecting their outer, northern flank, rode Carrié's brigade of dragoons. Meanwhile Clausel's own 2nd Division would have time to arrive and could then cross the river and support Taupin, catching any opposition between two fires.[15]

Carrié's dragoons, supported by a battalion of infantry and three light guns, crossed the Guarena in the face of Victor Alten's brigade of light cavalry (1st KGL Hussars and 14th Light Dragoons) which had already played an active role in guarding the flank of the allied retreat. Possibly Alten was caught by surprise with his men dispersed, for he let the French cross unopposed and form on firm ground beyond the sedgy banks of the river before he led his squadrons to attack them. Some accounts say that this attack was initially successful and that the French dragoons were broken and rallied on the supporting infantry; but other sources – including some British ones – make no such claim, and it is fairly clear that Alten's men were falling back in some disorder when the British 3rd Dragoons of Le Marchant's brigade arrived behind them. One of the officers of the 3rd wrote home a few weeks later: 'On the 18th of July, the 3rd were ordered out in a hurry to support the 1st Hussars and 14th [Light Dragoons] who at that Time were completely clubbed and running away, until a charge from the Third turned the Tide.' Other sources support his claim.[16] Alten's men rallied behind the dragoons and the French cavalry were put to flight. Carrié himself was captured: he had been in the thick of the fight, and in the confusion and dust had lost touch with his escort – a company of the 15th Dragoons – and had found himself surrounded by German hussars; he received five wounds before surrendering.[17] Alten's regiments lost 135 casualties between them (including twenty-one killed and thirteen missing), suggesting some rough handling, although these figures include casualties suffered earlier in the day. The 3rd Dragoons lost only ten casualties. There are no reliable figures for French losses, but Martinien names six officers of dragoons as well as Brigadier Carrié as having been killed or wounded on the Guarena, which suggests that they suffered about fifty rank-and-file casualties. Curto's light cavalry suffered similarly, so that the French cavalry as a whole probably lost rather more than a hundred casualties on this day.[18]

While the cavalry combat swayed back and forth, Taupin's division had crossed the river and was climbing the heights beyond. It seems to have been formed in three regimental columns, that is, each regiment advancing on a front of only two companies, one battalion behind the other.[19] A staff officer who accompanied the division, and who wrote some unreliable memoirs many years later, was highly critical of Taupin for crowding his units together and judging the ground poorly, while the French infantry must have been tired from their long marches.[20] Nor was the allied position unoccupied. Wellington had arrived on the scene and ordered General Cole, commander of the allied Fourth Division, to attack the French with two of his brigades. Cole advanced with the British 27th and 40th Regiments of W. Anson's brigade deployed in line, supported on either flank by the Portuguese 11th and 23rd Regiments of Stubbs's brigade formed in close columns. Thus his formation resembled Napoleon's favoured *l'ordre mixte*, though the flanking columns were perhaps more independent.[21] This was a strong force of about 3,200 men (1,200 British, 2,000 Portuguese). If all Taupin's eight battalions were engaged, the French would have had about 4,200 men, but prisoners later said that only six battalions had advanced, giving them about 3,000 men.[22]

A surgeon with the Fourth Division describes what happened: 'the 27th & 40th Regts. ... advanced to the charge in the most undaunted manner ... the French presented a firm front, till our People arrived within about twenty paces of them, when they fired a volley and flew in the utmost confusion.' Lieutenant T. H. Browne, an officer on the staff, confirms this account and adds some interesting details:

> The enemy stood & fired little. They were very firm until within fifty or sixty paces, when our fellows gave them the Bayonet with cheers, routed the column & left of the French about 80 dead & 100 prisoners besides wounded. Our men charged at too great a distance, their ranks were in confusion, & they were so breathless & exhausted when they came up with the French, that they could scarcely use the Bayonet.

As neither of these descriptions makes clear whether the British fired before they charged, it is worth quoting the letter of an officer of the Light Division on the point, even though his account must be second-hand: 'The 4th Division allowed them to come to the top before they fired a shot. They gave them a volley & charged them down the hill, killing them as fast as they could with their bayonets & their officers were obliged to assist with their swords.' Thus, the emphasis in all these accounts is on the charge, whatever the actual number of casualties inflicted in the melee, rather than on British musketry.[23]

British sources stress the role of the two British battalions, but the French officer's account mentioned above attributes the defeat to 'Three or four battalions of Portuguese, [who] having put down their packs, rushed down the hill which they occupied, and hurled themselves on [Taupin's] division, with a rolling fire on our massed troops.'[24] Not all these details may be accurate, but it does seem likely that the Portuguese took an equal share in defeating Taupin.

Many accounts mention that the allied infantry were too weary to pursue effectively, and that although Alten's cavalry joined in the chase they were unable to inflict much damage. It seems likely that the leading regiment of Clausel's own division, the 25th Léger, crossed the Guarena and covered Taupin's retreat.[25] At any rate, this regiment was engaged, losing one officer killed and five wounded, which suggests about a hundred casualties in all, perhaps a few more. Taupin's regiments had lost even more heavily: Martinien lists sixteen officer casualties including four killed and two mortally wounded, suggesting total losses close to five hundred. When the casualties of the cavalry are included it seems probable that Clausel's venture across the Guarena cost the French army about eight hundred casualties, showing that this was no trifling skirmish.[26]

The two British battalions of Anson's brigade suffered 141 casualties, including 21 killed, although these figures would contain at least some losses on the march to the Guarena. Stubbs's losses are less clear, for all the Portuguese losses on the day are aggregated into a single line: 157 in total, including 34 killed and 27 missing; but it is reasonable to assume that the great majority of these were suffered in the fight against Taupin. In all, the allied army lost 542 casualties on 18 July, so that Wellington had not only extricated his army from a difficult position, but actually inflicted more casualties than he suffered – not that such numerical calculations have much significance.[27]

Marmont's elaborate plan of campaign, his deception at Toro and counter-march to Tordesillas thus brought no definite advantage. Napier goes further and strongly criticizes him for not continuing his initial advance from Toro, claiming that the French could have made good their threat to Wellington's communications and so forced Wellington to fight at a disadvantage or igno-miniously to abandon Salamanca.[28] But this is doubtful, and in any case ignores the reasons which lay behind Marmont's manoeuvres: his fears may not have been well founded, but they were not unreasonable. And even if the events of 18 July brought no tangible advantages to the French, Marmont's plan had not misfired. He had brought his whole army safely across the Duero in the face of a superior enemy, and he had seized the initiative, imposing his will on his opponent. Wellington had been out-foxed, and both generals knew it. For the next few days Marmont would dictate the pace and shape of events, while Wellington merely reacted and hoped for a change in fortune. Marmont's natural confidence and Wellington's habitual caution were thus both increased by the opening of the campaign.

Wellington may have expected – even hoped – that Marmont would attack him on 19 July, but the French marshal wisely continued to prefer to man-oeuvre than to take the bull by the horns. He allowed his men to rest all the morning and early afternoon, and this pause permitted many stragglers to join. Then, when Wellington was ready to conclude that the whole day would be spent quietly, Marmont put his army into motion, marching south or south-west, up the Guarena and in the general direction of Salamanca, a little more than twenty miles away. Wellington matched Marmont's movement, attempt-ing nothing venturesome but making no mistake which would give the French the opportunity of striking.

The parallel march continued on the following day and gradually the two armies grew closer as the valley of the Guarena shrank to nothing, leaving the opposing forces less than a mile apart. Many officers commented on the extraordinary and 'beautiful' sight of the two armies marching in close order so near each other. Any mistake – a break in the line, confusion crossing rough ground or one division marching more rapidly than the next – would have opened the way for the other side to attack, but none was made, and after some miles the two armies slightly diverged. Towards evening Wellington called a halt and camped his army around Cabezabellosa and Aldea Rubia, just in front of the position of San Cristobal where he covered all the approaches to Salamanca from the north or north-east. But Marmont pressed on for a few miles, giving his soldiers another gruelling march, halting at last around Babilafuente, with his advanced guard securing the fords of Huerta over the Tormes. This meant that he could continue to turn Wellington's southern flank and might force the allies to choose between attacking the French and aban-doning Salamanca. Charles Cathcart, a well-connected, well-informed staff officer, wrote home that 'Lord Wellington was amazingly angry when He found that the Enemy had reached the River and I believe that if there had been more daylight [he] would have attacked them then, however there was no remedy.'[29]

Early on 21 July Wellington occupied the San Cristobal position again, a month after he had declined the opportunity of attacking Marmont's then much weaker army. This time Marmont ignored the allied position and gradually brought his army across the Tormes at the fords of Huerta and Encinas. He also occupied Alba de Tormes a few miles further upstream where there was a bridge. The castle of Alba de Tormes had been occupied by a Spanish battalion, but this had been withdrawn by Carlos de España, the Spanish commander, who concluded, reasonably enough, that the allied army was in retreat and that if the troops were not withdrawn they would be cut off and sacrificed to no advantage. Unfortunately, he failed to inform Wellington of what he had done – one version of the story even says that, after issuing the orders, España proposed the move to Wellington who rejected it, and that España then lacked the courage to admit that the step had already been taken.[30]

Wellington watched while most of the French army crossed the Tormes in the distance: the armies were now too far apart for him readily to attack the French rear, and in any case Marmont kept his units in hand, with a strong guard of two divisions protecting the passage of the river. By the night of 21 July all but Sarrut's division were on the southern side of the Tormes, and the outposts were holding the village of Calvarrasa de Abajo. Again Wellington conformed to these movements, bringing the bulk of his army across the river at the fords of Cabrerizos and Santa Marta, while leaving the Third Division and D'Urban's cavalry in the San Cristobal position in case Sarrut tried to threaten Salamanca from the north bank.

That night there was a fierce thunderstorm which figures prominently in most memoirs of the campaign. Private John Green of the 68th Foot in the Seventh Division gives a vivid account of what it was like for the soldiers:

[We] encamped about eight o'clock at night. We had not, however, been long at rest, before a most alarming storm came on: the thunder in awful claps echoed through the wood; the flashes of lightning were vivid, and quick in succession; the rain fell in torrents, and, what added to our distress, was, we were exposed to the open air, not having a tent or any thing else to cover us. Several of the cavalry horses broke from their stakes, and caused great confusion in the different regiments of cavalry. The suspense we had been in during the last few days, being in expectation of an engagement every hour, made our situation extremely uncomfortable; indeed at this period the enemy was within two miles of our advanced guard. Notwithstanding the great rains which had fallen during the night, I contrived to keep myself dry, by getting directly under the arm of a large tree, and creeping under the blanket of an old comrade, who is now fixed in business in this country. It was astonishing to see the cheerfulness of the men: I have known them tell tales, sing songs, and crack their jokes, in the midst of danger, and when it was uncertain whether they would live to see another day over. About midnight the storm ceased, the morning was beautiful, the sun rose without a cloud, and everything had a most enchanting appearance. [31]

Other sources agree that the general mood of the allied army that night was less despondent than might have been expected. The retreat from the Duero and the prospect of abandoning Salamanca irritated the army rather than shaking its self-confidence, as Kincaid makes clear with characteristic jauntiness:

There assuredly never was an army so anxious as ours was to be brought into action on this occasion. They were a magnificent body of well-tried soldiers, highly equipped, and in the highest health and spirits, with the most devoted confidence in their leader, and an invincible confidence in themselves. The retreat of the four preceding days had annoyed us beyond measure, for we believed that we were nearly equal to the enemy in point of numbers; and the idea of our retiring before an equal number of any troops in the world was not to be endured with common patience.[32]

Their patience was not to be tried for much longer.

Commentary

The reasons for Wellington's decision not to attack Marmont on 20 and 21 June are discussed further in chapter two (pp. 37–9 below), but some additional evidence can be given here of the dissatisfaction which it caused in the army. Edward Pakenham wrote to Sir George Murray on 24 August:

Marmont you know advanced a day or two after, and committed his people desperately by running slap up against our position, which covered the Town & fords (in a Wild [?] unconnected way) & where he remained for two days playing the Bully. Had it not been for a certain Marshal [i.e. Beresford] (whose nerves latterly have been worse than ever) Marmont would have been lost the first night of his approach, but I believe everything has ended for the best.[33]

And years later a corporal in the First Division recalled:

We expected nothing else but to make an immediate attack upon the whole of the enemy's line. We had a great advantage of the French by our position. ... I thought we might have given them a complete drubbing here; and everyone thought the same, from Graham down to the private soldier. ... Graham was mad to get at them: it was said he went home in two days afterwards, because Wellington would not let him engage.[34]

This gives some plausibility to the statement in a relatively early secondary source that Wellington's decision 'was publicly understood by the army [to be] against the opinion of Graham, Picton, Leith, Cotton and Pakenham; all of whom were urgent for an immediate attack.'[35] Even if this statement is not accepted at face value, it probably reflects the feeling in the army at the time; not that Wellington was ever much influenced by the opinions of his subordinates.

There are many first-hand accounts of the manoeuvring and fighting on 18 July: far more than could be quoted or discussed in the main narrative. Captain Tomkinson of the 16th Light Dragoons gives the most detailed and interesting account of the first part of the day in his diary. He had been sent out on a pre-dawn patrol with six men to discover if the French had really crossed the Duero in force: if not, Cotton had hopes of driving them back to the river. Not surprisingly, he scarcely got beyond the allied outposts before running into strong French forces and was glad to find refuge with the 11th Light Dragoons, who in turn retired on the rest of the brigade. Tomkinson admits that 'We were a good deal pressed, and once obliged to turn round and charge.' The French then brought up some guns and began to bombard the allied cavalry. At first the allied horse artillery were able to respond to this effectively, but more French guns arrived, 'which obliged our guns to retire'. The French then concentrated their fire on the allied cavalry, and with some effect, as Tomkinson admits:

> their fire against my troop ... before I could move off killed Corporal Hardiman and Dragoon Stone (the shot, round shot, hit him on the belly, and sent pieces of his inside all over the troop – a piece on Lieutenant Lloyd's shoulder, the first time he ever was in action – he lived an hour), wounding four others and five horses. It was the sharpest cannonade, for the time, we were, or I, was ever exposed to, and almost impossible to get the men away in complete order.[36]

Frederick Ponsonby, commanding the 12th Light Dragoons in the same brigade, is more prosaic, but admits that there were 'two hours' sharp cannonading and skirmishing. I lost 16 men and 17 horses.' The official return shows that the 12th lost slightly more than this: five men killed, one officer and twelve men wounded and another man missing, or nineteen casualties in all; the 16th Light Dragoons suffered fifteen casualties, and the 11th sixteen.[37]

Kincaid and Tomkinson give the best accounts of the incident in which Wellington and the allied staff were briefly caught up with the French cavalry, but several other sources also mention it. Colonel Campbell, the Headquarters Commandant, wrote home that 'The Enemy's Cavalry showed a great deal of dash, they gave Ld. Wellington and the Hd. Quarters Staff a long Gallop when Reconnoitring this Morning.' George Hennell of the 43rd says that, afterwards, 'All our officers were in a perfect rage', which confirms one aspect of Kincaid's story. T. H. Browne is more explicit: 'two or three of our Squadrons, 11th & 12th did not behave well. They were close to Ld. Wellington & would have lost the two guns attached to them but for the bravery of the Horse Artillery.

Marshal Beresford was nearly taken in endeavouring to rally them.'[38] It is interesting that a staff officer readily puts the blame for the incident on the troops,
while Tomkinson, a regimental officer, blames the interference of some of
Beresford's staff. If Tomkinson was less reliable, one might think he was seeking to divert blame from his own regiment, but his *Diary* is one of the most
highly regarded of all Peninsular sources. It is disappointing that there is no
mention of the episode in the generally excellent – and entertaining – letters of
William Warre, an officer on Beresford's staff.

The retreat to the Guarena is well described by George Simmons of the 95th
Rifles:

> The whole British army were in full retreat, the country all round was one vast
> plain, and the soldiers were moving across it in column of companies at quarter
> distance ready by regiments to form square if the enemy's cavalry should charge;
> the march was taken up literally as coolly as if it had been a field day, taking dis-
> tant points to march upon, and avoiding the villages in order not to lose time
> passing through them. Upon our right as we then faced, and frequently not more
> than five hundred yards distant from us, was a dense mass of Frenchmen moving
> in the same order, horse, foot and artillery.[39]

Major John Burgoyne gives a similar account of the march of the Fourth
Division in his journal, but still it was a retreat under pressure, and Charles
Boutflower admits that 'The enemy pressed us in a manner, and with a spirit,
we were never before accustomed to.'[40]

It is not entirely clear whether or not the Guarena was generally fordable.
British accounts make little of its passage, save as an opportunity to quench
their thirst, and there is no suggestion that units were delayed while others
defiled through narrow fords. On the other hand, Lieutenant-Colonel Castel,
Clausel's ADC, describes searching for a ford for Taupin's infantry and
Carrié's cavalry to cross. Castel's account is generally very interesting but unreliable: for example, he has Marmont take command of the army in the spring of
1812 rather than the middle of 1811, and believes that the battle of Salamanca
was fought on 23 not 22 July, even describing fictitious manoeuvres to fill in the
extra day. Still, if he describes searching for a ford he probably did so, and the
explanation may be that the French were trying to cross the river downstream
of the allied crossings; alternatively, the allies had time to find and mark the
fords before their troops arrived at the river.[41]

Napier strongly criticizes Victor Alten's conduct in the face of Carrié's
advance, blaming him for not charging the French as soon as they reached the
allied bank of the river, and then attacking 'feebly with successive squadrons
instead of regiments'. Historians of the King's German Legion have defended
Alten's conduct and claim that the light cavalry were initially successful against
the dragoons, but fell back to rally when confronted with French infantry.[42]
There is probably some truth in this – Burgoyne describes how the 14th Light

Dragoons had some initial success then got into difficulties – but the letters of William Bragge and the journal of T. H. Browne provide compelling evidence that the light cavalry were thoroughly discomfited when the 3rd Dragoons advanced to support them.[43]

Wellington's dispatch makes it clear that the cavalry were already engaged when he arrived on the scene, and that he then ordered Cole to attack the French infantry. This sequence is supported by Burgoyne, and there is little doubt that Browne is mistaken in reversing the order of events.[44]

The best descriptions of the defeat of Taupin's division are quoted in the main narrative, but a few others may be added here. Charles Cathcart told Graham that the French 'came up in very gallant style and stood the charge of the 40th Regt. until they came within about five yards of them when they were completely Routed and 200 Prisoners taken.' Colin Campbell told Colonel Torrens that 'Genl. Cole immediately advanced upon them and charged them with the Bayonet, put them to the rout and took upwards of 200 Prisoners, but his men were so much exhausted that they could not follow them far.' While Edward Pakenham wrote that on the 18th 'Cole acted with particular conduct and coolness.' The only odd note comes from George Hennell – the Light Division officer quoted in the narrative – who says that the French advanced in close column and then deployed. This suggests that Cole's attack caught the French as they attempted to form line from column, but none of the other allied accounts confirms this, Hennell was probably not a witness and Castel's account, while difficult to follow, tends to contradict it.[45]

The allied casualty figures are based on the original return in the Public Record Office and are given in full in Appendix I. The figures given in Oman (Appendix XII, p. 607) are completely accurate except for those for Anson's brigade of light cavalry, where they are understated by a total of seventeen casualties. The correct total of 542 casualties is given in the brief casualty return in Wellington's *Dispatches* , while Tomkinson gives a detailed return which would be accurate if it were not for two obvious misprints. It is possible that the official figures slightly understate the Portuguese losses, most probably by not counting some lightly wounded officers and men. Almost 22 per cent of listed Portuguese casualties were killed, which is an unusually high figure, and contrasts with only 16 per cent of British casualties being killed. This question is further discussed in Appendix II.[46]

The calculations which lie behind estimates of French losses are explained in Appendix III. Briefly, we have two sources: Martinien's list of French officer casualties, which names individual officers killed or wounded on 18 July and which may be relied upon as accurate, if not absolutely complete; and the official French return of casualties suffered in the campaign as a whole, which significantly understates the true figure, probably by leaving out the lightly wounded who had returned to the ranks by the time that the return was drawn up. By comparing the two, we can make a rough estimate of the losses of each unit on 18 July. For example, if a cavalry regiment had ten officers and one hundred men killed or wounded in the campaign, and Martinien lists three of the officers as being wounded on the 18th and the remaining seven on the 22nd, it is reasonable to suppose than about thirty men were casualties on the 18th. Clearly this is only a rough guide, and there would be occasions when this assumption would be incorrect, but these oddities would tend to cancel each other out.

The combat of 18 July provides an interesting test of the various secondary accounts of the campaign. Napier is remarkably good for so early an account, and gains added interest from including his own impressions as a participant, but he greatly understates the scale of the infantry fighting between Cole and Taupin. Oman is excellent: full, detailed, lively and almost always convincing. Here, as with the battle of the 22nd, he provides by far the most reliable account of each stage of the fighting. Fortescue, however, is disappointing, particularly on the infantry fighting, where he states that only a single French battalion was engaged, despite the clear evidence in Martinien's lists that four French regiments lost quite heavily. Young and Lawford give a popular narrative composed largely of long quotations from Kincaid and Leith Hay; but Jean Sarramon's French account is excellent, mainly following Oman, but adding some fresh details, although it lacks some of the richness which Oman provides.[47]

Chapter Two
Armies and Generals

The two armies camped by the Tormes on the night of 21 July 1812 were almost equal in strength. The allied force was somewhat larger: 51,937 officers and men according to a return of 15 July, adjusted to include some reinforcements which arrived before the battle. But from this total about 1,200 men should be deducted for casualties suffered on the 18th, and men who had fallen out during the long hot marches since the army left the Duero. This gives a nominal strength of about 50,700 men, although the actual fighting strength would have been considerably less, for the return includes some non-combatants such as bandsmen and farriers, while every army contained a certain number of men whose courage failed them and who found their way to the rear whenever serious fighting appeared imminent. It is impossible to quantify this problem even roughly; but good discipline and good morale – and Wellington's army had both – kept it to a minimum.[1]

The French army was a little weaker, with a nominal strength of just under 47,000 men on the morning of the 22nd. Again the last reliable figures date back to 15 July, and so include men who fell out on Marmont's long marches, or who were wounded or killed in the fighting on the Guarena. The return gives the following totals:

French Army, 15 July 1812

Infantry	41,525	or 84 per cent of the army
Cavalry	3,379	or 7 per cent of the army
Artillery	3,437	or 7 per cent of the army
Miscellaneous	1,306	or 3 per cent of the army
	49,647	

About half the 'miscellaneous' were non-combatants, but this is taken into account in estimating the fighting strength of the army. The equivalent figures for Wellington's force are (including the Spanish division):

Allied Army, 15 July 1812

Infantry	45,406	or 87 per cent of the army
Cavalry	4,985	or 10 per cent of the army
Artillery	1,300	or 2.5 per cent of the army
Miscellaneous	246	or 0.5 per cent of the army
	51,937	

Infantry thus dominated both armies to a much greater extent than in Napoleon's battles in central Europe, where cavalry usually formed about 15 per cent of the armies, but conditions in the Peninsula were particularly harsh on horses. Marmont had seventy-eight guns compared to Wellington's sixty-two (including a Spanish battery). However, the French guns were a surprisingly mixed collection: only seven of the famous 12-pounders, twenty-one 8-pounders (equivalent to British 9-pounders), thirty-six old 4-pounders (a mixture of French and Spanish pieces), a single 3-pounder and thirteen howitzers. In other words there was only one battery of 12-pounders, and three of 8-pounders; the rest of Marmont's guns were light pieces normally reserved for horse artillery. Lamartinière's return of losses surprisingly suggests that guns of different calibres were mixed together in the same battery (see below, Chapter 11, p. 211). Wellington's guns were less unexpected: fifteen 9-pounders, thirty 6-pounders, nine 5 1/2-inch howitzers (one per battery), six 24-pounder howitzers, and two 4-pounders with the Spanish cavalry.[2] Three 18-pounder siege guns were sent to the rear.[3] The French batteries generally contained eight guns; the allies' six. By the standards of Napoleon's battles, where there were often three, four or even more guns per thousand troops in the army, both forces at Salamanca were noticeably under-strength in their artillery.

If Marmont's artillery were clearly superior, this was more than offset by the strength of the allied cavalry. This difference was even greater than the simple numbers suggest, for Wellington's cavalry were in fine condition and included five regiments of heavy dragoons, whose primary purpose was to deliver powerful charges in battle: their value was to be clearly demonstrated over the next two days. By contrast the French cavalry were a mixture of dragoons and light cavalry – general-purpose horsemen capable of good service in battle if a favourable opportunity arose, but usually lacking the weight and esprit de corps to create opportunities for themselves.

It was most unusual in the Peninsula for the French not to have a distinct advantage in cavalry, and they were accustomed to their horsemen converting a Spanish defeat into a rout or ensuring success if the day was doubtful. This weakness caused them great anxiety – it is often emphasized in French memoirs. Marmont had done what he could to solve the problem, by appealing to Caffarelli and King Joseph, by raiding a convoy of reinforcements intended for Soult and by commandeering several hundred horses owned by infantry officers over and above the number officially allowed. He paid compensation for these, but even so this move was extremely unpopular. The horses were used to mount hundreds of chasseurs and dragoons who were otherwise standing idle in nearby depots, but their effectiveness must be doubted: not only were horse and rider strangers, the horses themselves were untrained in cavalry movements, or in acting with other horses. Marmont's cavalry was thus far weaker than it appears, and the boldness of his campaign was commensurately greater.

The difference in quality between the infantry of the two armies is much less marked. Marmont's was a homogeneous national force, without any significant foreign element, while the allies were much more mixed: not only were there British, Portuguese and Spanish components, but the 'British' element included the German regiments of the King's German Legion, generally good troops, and two regiments of assorted foreigners, the Brunswick Oels and the Chasseurs Britanniques, who were less reliable. Genuinely British troops thus amounted to marginally less than half the army, while there were more Germans than Spaniards at the battle. On the other hand, if we exclude the relatively small Spanish force (3,360 all ranks), which did not play an important role in the battle, the rest of the army had seen considerable service under Wellington and had built up a tradition of success. British officers differed in their opinion of the Portuguese, who comprised one-third of the army. One stated in his memoirs that they lacked 'that esprit necessary to encounter even the French riflemen', while only the British veterans were able 'to withstand a regular attack from a French column'; but another wrote home shortly after the battle that the 'action was fought chiefly by the Portuguese and they behaved in a manner which could not be excelled'.[4] The truth lies between these two extremes, but rather closer to the latter than the former. In the battle the Portuguese proved to be good troops, and only gave way in circumstances where British troops might also have been broken. In general they were almost, but not quite, as reliable as the British, and took their fair share of the fighting. Indeed, they actually lost proportionally more casualties than the British.

Allied Army, 15 July 1812

British	30,578	all ranks, or 59 per cent of the army
Portuguese	17,999	all ranks, or 35 per cent of the army
Spanish	3,360	all ranks, or 6 per cent of the army
	51,937	all ranks

(Of the 30,578 'British', 5,651 or 18 per cent were in the KGL or other foreign regiments.)

In the summer of 1812 French armies still had immense prestige and confidence in themselves. The soldiers may have hated the war in Spain, but they had a proud tradition to maintain and Napoleon's victories, propaganda and fame gave them good reason to believe that they were the best troops in the world. Nonetheless the glorious days of Austerlitz, Jena and Friedland were now a distant memory, and years of hard campaigning had blunted the sharpness of the troops and eroded their spirit. They were still good soldiers, far better than most of the motley horde Napoleon was leading into Russia; still capable of enthusiastic attack, tenacious resistance and a surprising level of tactical flexibility. On the other side, Wellington's Anglo-Portuguese infantry had established its reputation largely by defending strong positions, and its ability to manoeuvre and attack on a large scale was untested. With hindsight it seems fair to say that the Anglo-Portuguese infantry had a clear advantage over their French counterparts in battle, although not necessarily on campaign or in adversity. However, this difference in quality was not overwhelming, nothing like the enormous gap which was so apparent in the following year; nor was it at all obvious on the eve of the battle.

Marmont's army was organized into eight divisions of infantry and two of cavalry. Each of the infantry divisions was divided into a neat hierarchy of brigades, regiments and battalions: two brigades to each division, usually two regiments to each brigade (though a few had only one), and two or three battalions to each regiment. In all there were 29 regiments and 73 battalions of infantry, each of the battalions having an average strength of 568 officers and men. The strongest divisions were Clausel's (6,562 all ranks on 15 July) and Bonnet's (6,521 all ranks); the weakest were Thomières's (4,543 all ranks) and Taupin's (4,558 all ranks). These totals include the artillery that formed a part of each division, usually amounting to about two hundred men.

The bulk of Marmont's force consisted of the remains of the army which Masséna had led into Portugal in 1810. A few of Masséna's units had been sent home: two weak foreign regiments, the Légion du Midi and the Hanoverian Legion; one good regiment of French infantry (32nd Léger); and seven weak 4th battalions, whose men had been drafted into other regiments and the cadres returned to the depot.[5] However, Masséna's losses had been so great that two complete divisions had to be added to make the French roughly equal to Wellington's force. These were Thomières's division, which arrived from Italy in the second half of 1811 under General Souham, and Bonnet's division, which had been in Biscay and Asturias since 1808. The regiments of Thomières's division were old units with good reputations. They had served in the war of 1809 against Austria, including at Wagram, and had then had time to recruit their strength before being sent to Spain.[6] They should have been among the best units in Marmont's army. Bonnet's regiments had a less distinguished pedigree, for their origins lay in the provisional regiments and supplementary legions which made up Bessières's corps in 1808; but four years of active if desultory service in trying conditions seems to have bonded the men together and made them eager to perform well in this, their first large battle.[7]

Most of Marmont's men were veteran soldiers, but they were not the victors of Austerlitz. Of his twenty-nine regiments of infantry, only two had been present at Napoleon's greatest victory (17th Léger in Taupin's division, and 36th

Ligne in Sarrut's division), although another two had contributed battalions d'élite to Oudinot's grenadiers (2nd and 31st Léger, Sarrut's and Ferey's divisions). Nine further regiments had been part of the Grande Armée of 1805 but not present at Austerlitz (4th, 6th and 25th Léger and 27th, 39th, 50th, 59th, 69th and 76th Ligne: all of Foy's and Clausel's divisions, and 4th Léger in Sarrut's). The regiments comprising the two divisions under Foy and Clausel had been together since the projected invasion of England and the formation of the Grande Armée. They had been part of the 6th Corps, had benefited from Ney's careful training and had shared mixed fortunes in many campaigns since then. Their long and surprisingly stable association must have encouraged a degree of confidence and esprit de corps extending beyond the regiment to these higher formations.

Remarkably, seven of Marmont's regiments appear never to have faced the British in action before the campaign began, while another four, including three which had taken part in the invasion of Portugal, had not been closely engaged with them. In other words, one-third of the army had little experience of being beaten by the British and so should not have been intimidated at facing them; while even the remaining regiments could, with some justice, feel that they were not to blame for the defeats at Busaco and Fuentes de Oñoro. The seven regiments which had not encountered the British were 22nd Ligne in Taupin's division, which went through the invasion of Portugal losing one-third of its strength to deprivation and disease without being seriously engaged; the three regiments of Thomières's division, 1st, 62nd and 101st Ligne; and three of the four in Bonnet's division, 118th, 119th, and 120th Ligne. The four with little prior contact with the British were 25th Léger and 59th Ligne in Clausel's division, the 65th Ligne in Taupin's division (all veterans of Masséna's invasion of Portugal) and the 122nd Ligne in Bonnet's division which had been in reserve at Coruña but had not fired a shot.[8]

French Army at Salamanca

1st Division (Foy)

    6th Léger, 39th, 69th and 76th Ligne (8 btns)   5,147 all ranks

2nd Division (Clausel)

    25th Léger, 27th, 50th, and 59th Ligne (10 btns)   6,562 all ranks

3rd Division (Ferey)

    31st Léger, 26th, 47th and 70th Ligne (9 btns)   5,689 all ranks

4th Division (Sarrut)

    2nd and 4th Léger, 36th Ligne (9 btns)   5,002 all ranks

5th Division (Maucune)

    15th, 66th, 82nd and 86th Ligne (9 btns)   5,244 all ranks

6th Division (Taupin vice Brennier)

    17th Léger, 22nd and 65th Ligne (8 btns)   4,558 all ranks

7th Division (Thomières)

    1st, 62nd and 101st Ligne (8 btns)   4,543 all ranks

8th Division (Bonnet)

    118th, 119th, 120th and 122nd Ligne (12 btns)   6,521 all ranks

Light Cavalry Division (Curto)
    3rd Hussars, 13th, 14th, 22nd, 26th and 28th
    Chasseurs and 1 Escadron de Marche (17 sqdns)   1,879 all ranks
Heavy Cavalry Division (Boyer)
    6th, 11th, 15th and 25th Dragoons (8 sqdns)   1,696 all ranks

Artillery Reserve etc   1,500 all ranks

Miscellaneous   1,306 all ranks

    Total   49,647 all ranks

(A more detailed order of battle is given in Appendix III.)

Wellington's army had slowly grown since his return to the Peninsula in 1809. Its origins lay in a number of less good regiments which Moore had left in Portugal when he advanced into Spain. These had been heavily reinforced in the spring of 1809, giving Wellington the army of twenty thousand British troops which he had led to Talavera. A few units from that army had suffered so much in action or from the rigours of the campaign and disease that they had been withdrawn, but most remained. In the meantime Beresford had been busy reorganizing and re-training the Portuguese army with the assistance of a number of British officers. Early in 1810 Wellington reorganized his forces into five divisions, which had grown to nine by the spring of 1811: numbered one to seven, plus the famous Light Division and a Portuguese division. Of these, the Second and the Portuguese divisions were serving under Hill in Estremadura at the time of Salamanca.

Most of these divisions consisted of two British brigades (each typically of three or occasionally four battalions) and one Portuguese brigade (two line regiments, each of two battalions, plus one battalion of caçadores or light infantry). Thus, a division might have six British and five Portuguese battalions, although on average British battalions were stronger than the Portuguese (572 all ranks compared to 471). However, there was considerable variation on this basic pattern. The First Division had no Portuguese, but three 'British' brigades – a brigade of Guards, a brigade of the line, and a brigade of the King's German Legion – while the Light Division contained only two battalions of caçadores, one attached to each of its two, numerically weak, brigades. Each division had its own force of light infantry, usually consisting of the caçador battalion from the Portuguese brigade, plus two or three companies of specialist light infantry from the 5/60th or Brunswick Oels battalions, which were scattered through the army for this purpose, and the light companies from the line battalions. In addition to these seven Anglo-Portuguese divisions, Wellington had two independent Portuguese brigades at Salamanca under Pack and Bradford (each having two line regiments and a battalion of caçadores) and Carlos de España's weak Spanish division.

There were also six brigades of cavalry: four British and one Portuguese, under the overall command of Stapleton Cotton, and Julián Sánchez's Spanish lancers. There were two brigades of heavy dragoons: Le Marchant's brigade of three regiments, more than a thousand men and the most powerful single force of cavalry in either army, although puny compared to the divisions of cuirassiers and whole corps of cavalry which Murat was accustomed to command; and two regiments of the Heavy Dragoons of the King's German Legion under Bock. There were two brigades of British light cavalry under G. Anson and V. Alten, and a weak brigade of Portuguese dragoons under D'Urban – they were not nearly as dependable as the Portuguese infantry, and although they performed well on 22 July, they were put to flight a few weeks later at Majadahonda.

Finally, there were ten batteries of artillery, eight British (including one King's German Legion), one Portuguese and one Spanish. Three of the British batteries were horse artillery attached to the cavalry, the Light Division and the Seventh Division. Five were foot artillery, attached to each of the other divisions, while the Portuguese battery of 24-pounder howitzers was held in reserve, and the Spanish battery was attached to España's division. Each of the batteries contained six guns (or rather, five guns and a 5 1/2 inch howitzer); three of the foot batteries had 9-pounders (those attached to the First, Third and Fourth Divisions); the remainder, 6-pounders. Sánchez's lancers had two 4-pounders.[9]

Allied Army at Salamanca
Infantry:

First Division (H. Campbell)
two British and one KGL brigades (9 btns)   6,428 all ranks

Third Division (Pakenham vice Picton)
two British brigades (7 btns)   3,678
one Portuguese brigade (5 btns)   2,197 (12 btns)   5,875 all ranks

Fourth Division (Cole)
two British brigades (5 btns)   2,674
one Portuguese brigade (5 btns)   2,544 (10 btns)   5,218 all ranks

Fifth Division (Leith)
two British brigades (8 btns)   4,405
one Portuguese brigade (5 btns)   2,305 (13 btns)   6,710 all ranks

Sixth Division (Clinton)
two British brigades (6 btns)   2,920
one Portuguese brigade (5 btns)   2,631 (11 btns)   5,551 all ranks

Seventh Division (Hope)
two British brigades (6 btns)   3,017
one Portuguese brigade (5 btns)   2,158 (11 btns)   5,175 all ranks

Light Division (Charles Alten)
two Anglo-Portuguese brigades (approx 6 btns)[10]   3,538 all ranks

Pack's independent Portuguese brigade (5 btns)   2,607 all ranks

Bradford's independent Portuguese brigade (5 btns)   1,894 all ranks

Spanish Division (Carlos de España) approx.   2,410 all ranks
Total Infantry   45,406 all ranks

Cavalry:

Le Marchant's brigade		
(3rd and 4th Dragoons, 5th Dragoon Guards)	1,032	all ranks
Bock's brigade		
(1st and 2nd KGL Heavy Dragoons)	771	all ranks
G. Anson's brigade		
(11th, 12th and 16th Light Dragoons)	1,004	all ranks
V. Alten's brigade		
(1st KGL Hussars and 14th Light Dragoons)	746	all ranks
D'Urban's Portuguese Dragoons		
(1st and 11th Portuguese Dragoons)	482	all ranks
Julián Sánchez's Spanish Lancers		
(1st and 2nd Lanceros de Castilla and two 4-pounders)	950	all ranks
Total Cavalry	4,985	all ranks
Artillery	1,300	all ranks
Miscellaneous	246	all ranks
TOTAL	**51,937**	**all ranks**

(A more detailed order of battle is given in Appendix II.)

The Fifth Division was the strongest in the allied army, largely because it was joined by the 1st battalion, 38th Foot on the day before the battle, increasing its strength by eight hundred officers and men. This was the second strong regiment Wellington had received since the campaign began (the other was the 1/5th in the Third Division: 902 all ranks), together with a steady trickle of drafts and convalescents.[11] So there were some inexperienced British troops in Wellington's army, but the great majority had seen a good deal of campaigning in the Peninsula and were acclimatized. The amount of fighting they had experienced varied more widely: the First Division had been heavily engaged at Fuentes de Oñoro in May 1811, while in 1809 – as Sherbrooke's division – it had borne the brunt of the great French attack in the centre at Talavera, and had very nearly been broken. The Third, under Picton's fiery leadership, had seen action at Busaco, El Bodon and, more recently, at the storming of both Ciudad Rodrigo and Badajoz. The Fourth and Fifth were also fighting divisions: both had taken part in the storm of Badajoz; the Fourth had fought gallantly at Albuera, while the Fifth claimed much credit for its role at Busaco – a claim which was much resented by the officers of the Third. The Sixth Division had seen less combat until it undertook the siege of the Salamanca forts; it was probably a little raw, even though some of its regiments had been in the Peninsula for years. The Seventh Division contained a high proportion of foreign units: the two light battalions of the King's German Legion were good troops, but the Brunswick Oels and Chasseurs Britanniques were much less impressive. There were only two British regiments (the 51st and 68th) in

the division, and both of these were very weak (307 and 338 all ranks respectively). The division had been much exposed at Fuentes de Oñoro and had successfully made a difficult retreat. It had also engaged creditably in the
skirmishing at Morisco in front of San Cristobal in June, but it was still the least
cohesive of all the Anglo-Portuguese divisions. Finally, there was the Light
Division, whose numerous memoirists and authors – including most famously
William Napier himself – never tired of extolling its virtues. But it was truly an
elite force, excelling not only in the expected duties of light troops, such as
skirmishing and managing the outposts of the army, but also in close fighting
and manoeuvring in battle, and in taking a leading part in the bloody assaults
on Ciudad Rodrigo and Badajoz.[12]

The Portuguese troops had generally seen less service than the British: they
had defended their positions well at Busaco, and the brigade attached to the
Fourth Division had successfully advanced in line in the face of strong French
cavalry at Albuera – a severe test of their discipline.[13] But in general they, and
to a lesser extent the army as a whole, had yet to prove their ability to manoeuvre and attack in good order in an open field.

The commander of the French army was Auguste Frédéric Louis Viesse de
Marmont, Duke of Ragusa, the youngest of all Napoleon's marshals. He was
born on 20 July 1774, the son of minor nobility, and was always destined for the
army. He was a man of lively intelligence and great organizational abilities; a
fine administrator with a curiosity that extended far beyond purely military
matters. He had been trained in the Artillery School at Châlons, and met his
destiny at the siege of Toulon where he greatly impressed the young General
Bonaparte and became one of his closest aides. Bonaparte's patronage gave him
accelerated promotion and extraordinary opportunities, but also much
heartache. Marmont was not a modest man; well aware of his abilities, perhaps
even exaggerating them, he was ambitious and greatly resented any slight.
When Napoleon created the marshalate in 1804, eighteen generals were given
the honour. They included such distinguished veterans as General Kellermann
(born 1735), who had commanded the army at Valmy, and each of the corps
commanders of the army camped on the Channel coast except one: the thirty-
year-old Marmont. He had never commanded an army in action, but he had
distinguished himself at Lodi and at Marengo, he had accompanied Napoleon
to Egypt and – a rarer honour – accompanied him on his return; he had proved
his loyalty and usefulness in the preparation of the coup d'état of Brumaire; and
had efficiently reorganized the whole French artillery. Considering some of the
other names on the list, he felt he had good reason to be disgruntled, especially
as he alone among the corps commanders was singled out as unworthy of the
honour. But the list was already over-long, and included too many men whose
abilities were not yet widely known and who were closely connected with
Napoleon: Marmont was apparently too young, and too obviously Napoleon's
protégé.

Marmont's corps did not play a central part in the campaign of 1805, and he was not at Austerlitz. In 1806 he was sent to occupy Dalmatia, which had been ceded by Austria. Here he had considerable independence and enjoyed organizing the civil government, building roads and subduing bandits, achievements which were recognized when he was made Duke of Ragusa in 1808; but he was out of sight and Napoleon was winning great victories at Jena and Friedland. Marmont played a useful role in the war of 1809 against Austria, and after Wagram Napoleon made him a marshal at last, only to rob the reward of much of its sweetness by saying that it was granted for friendship, not ability. Marmont then returned to the Adriatic coast for another two years, governing the newly ceded Illyrian Provinces.[14]

In 1811 Napoleon sent Marmont to Spain, where he joined the Army of Portugal two days after its defeat at Fuentes de Oñoro. The task facing him was immense: Masséna's army had not merely been defeated in battle, but starved and demoralized; its senior officers had feuded incessantly, and Masséna's leadership had not been inspiring. Marmont was the perfect new broom: he was young and enthusiastic, and this was his first command of an independent army. He abolished the corps and organized the army into independent divisions, removing one layer of authority between himself and the troops, and sent home several discontented senior generals who resented his being placed over them. He showed a practical concern for feeding his troops and reviving their spirits, and was rewarded with a surprisingly rapid revitalization of the army. As Wellington discovered repeatedly, French soldiers were extraordinarily tough and resilient; they seldom remained beaten for long.

Marmont soon proved his ability in command of the army: his rapid march to aid Soult in June 1811 forced Wellington to lift the siege of Badajoz, while a few months later he not only broke the allied blockade of Ciudad Rodrigo, but caught Wellington in some disarray at El Bodon. Nor was he greatly to blame for the fall of Ciudad Rodrigo and Badajoz in 1812, for his hands were tied by Napoleon's orders, and Wellington's preparations left little room for accident. More recently he had shown great skill and boldness in his advance from the Duero: he had outmanoeuvred Wellington and gained the moral ascendancy. But this proved his undoing: he grew overconfident and, after five days of intense concentration, he relaxed a little too soon.

Assessments of Marmont vary and can be coloured by his betrayal of Napoleon in 1814. Given this, Napier's conclusion is surprisingly generous: 'Marmont was a man to be feared. Quick of apprehension, courageous and scientific, he had experience in war, moved troops with great facility, was strong of body, in the flower of life, eager for glory and although neither a great nor a fortunate commander such a one as might bear the test of fire'.[15] This is judging from events, and if it were not for the publication in 1900 of the diary of General Foy, commander of the 1st Division in the French army, we would have little reason to question Napier's opinion. Marmont speaks well of Foy in his memoirs; there was no quarrel between them. Indeed, Foy had been

Marmont's chief of staff in 1805, which may account for the familiar, even patronizing, tone of his comments, for the diary appears genuinely to have been written at the time and therefore not influenced by the drama of 1814. It is thus the best source we have, although it must be remembered that it is only a single source, representing an individual's view, and even Wellington might appear in an unexpected light if viewed primarily through the eyes of Henry Clinton or Stapleton Cotton. Foy describes Marmont as 'irresolution itself':

> Ardent and enterprising when remote from danger he is frozen and apathetic when in its presence. In discussion he will not face up to difficulties, always seeking to by-pass them. ... He is a good man, worthy and respectable, but he and others have entirely deceived themselves over the nature of his talent. He was not born to command an army. His face expresses too clearly the hesitation of his mind and the anxiety of his soul; the whole army knows his secret. He takes advice too often, too publicly, and from too many people. ... Boinod, the Inspecteur en Chef aux Revues, said to me in 1806, 'General Marmont is like Mont Cenis, in good times his head is clear and sunny; in times of storm it is covered in clouds.'[16]

In a note written later Foy criticizes Marmont's account of the battle, and in particular his failure to give Clausel more credit:

> He does not recall his own lack of ability, his indecision, his agonizing; while his pride and idea of himself makes him regard his friends and generals of division as being in a different class from himself whose petty interests should be sacrificed to his personal vanity. He thinks he has rewarded Clausel sufficiently by referring vaguely in his report to his bravery and constant exposure to enemy fire.[17]

The vehemence of this denunciation suggests that Foy was far from being a cool detached observer, while the criticism of Marmont's pride and willingness to sacrifice his subordinates gives an impression of pique, as if Foy had expected more influence over Marmont than he was able to exert. But his opinion cannot be simply dismissed, even though the evidence of events, and particularly the manoeuvres after the crossing of the Duero, would suggest a more generous verdict.

Evidently one of Marmont's problems was that he lacked moral authority over his subordinates. He was younger than all his generals of division except Foy; his promotion was widely attributed to the Emperor's favour rather than merit; and he had never led an army to victory in battle. This produced a curious mixture of hesitation and uncertainty, combined with a natural confidence, even arrogance. Hence his foolish parade in front of the position at San Cristobal, and the council of war at which he favoured, or at least appeared to favour, a suicidal assault on the British position. Confident generals do not usually call councils of war, and Marmont's real purpose may have been less to seek advice than to implicate the army's generals in a decision not to attack, even if it meant risking the loss of the garrisons of the Salamanca forts – something which would certainly anger Napoleon. In the event the loss of the garrisons and the retreat to the Duero caused discontent within the army, adding to the pressure on Marmont. Eager for a victory or some triumph to establish his authority more securely, he was too wise to attack the allied positions directly, whether on the Duero or the Guarena. Relying instead on manoeuvres, he appeared on the night of 21 July to be on the point of achieving his objective of forcing Wellington to abandon Salamanca and retreat back to the Portuguese frontier; the campaign would be a success, and it might gain additional éclat if he could strike a blow at the allied rearguard.

Marmont's subordinates were not easily impressed, for they were enormously experienced while still being fairly youthful. Of the six generals of division present with the army, the youngest was the 37-year-old Foy, and the oldest was Sarrut, who was forty-seven. All had joined the army at the beginning of the Revolutionary Wars or before, so that they each had nearly twenty years' experience of active service. None had been whisked up the ladder of promotion by a powerful patron as Marmont had, rather they had risen more slowly through a combination of merit, experience and long service; but by 1812 most were barons or counts of the Empire, and had often received other instances of Napoleon's largesse.

General Clausel (not General Bonnet) was the most senior of the divisional commanders.[18] He was two years older than Marmont and in the Revolutionary Wars had served in the Pyrenees, in Italy (at Novi, 1799) and at Santo Domingo under Leclerc. Returning home, he had been shipwrecked and spent some time in the United States. He had been made a general of division as early as 18 December 1802 and had held posts in Holland, Italy and Dalmatia, serving under Marmont in the Austrian campaign of 1809. He had then been transferred to Spain and had commanded a division in Junot's corps in Masséna's invasion of Portugal. Clausel has been much praised, both by contemporaries and by historians; Thiers is among the most lavish:

> General Clausel was young, vigorous both in mind and body, without much experience, it is true, and frequently careless, but imperturbably self-possessed, by turns cool and impetuous, keen-sighted on the battlefield, and although he had never ... commanded in chief, as well fitted to bear the anxieties of such a position as the most experienced officer; esteemed by the soldiers on account of his valour, and loved by them on account of his bonhomie, he was the only one of their officers qualified to retain their obedience, and preserve their discipline by severity, without causing them to revolt.

He ultimately rose to be a marshal of France in 1831.[19]

Bonnet was four years older than Clausel, but eight months junior in rank.

The son of a pastry cook, he had enlisted as a private soldier in 1786. In 1793 he lost his left eye at Hondschoote and was made a provisional general of brigade the following year. He fought at Hohenlinden in 1800 and at many other actions, but gained a reputation for a violent temper and a taste for plunder. He and his division had served in Biscay and Asturias since 1808. It was a frustrating command, but one which gave him considerable independence.

Foy was the youngest of the generals, but he had joined the Army of the North as a lieutenant as early as 1792, when he was seventeen. Since then he had seen much varied service, including spells as chief of staff of a division and – in 1805 – of Marmont's corps, as well as taking part in Sebastiani's diplomatic mission to Constantinople in 1807. He had seen much service against the British in the Peninsula, including Vimeiro, Coruña, Oporto and Busaco. Masséna, faced with the Lines of Torres Vedras, sent him back to France to explain the problem to Napoleon, who was sufficiently impressed by the messenger to make Foy a general of division, even though Foy had voted against both the life consulate and the Empire. In politics Foy was a liberal, and like many liberals he rallied to Napoleon's cause in 1815 and fought at Waterloo. His long involvement in the Peninsula and his excellent diary make him a favourite French general for many British historians.

General Maucune, commander of the 5th Division, was quite a different type. In the course of the Revolutionary Wars he had been shot in the left leg, wounded in the right arm by a bayonet thrust, shot in both thighs and again in the right foot, together with another unspecified wound. His medical record was further extended under the Empire when he was sent to the Peninsula: his right thigh was shattered at Santiago (23 May 1809) and yet again at Busaco, and he was hit twice more at Fuentes de Oñoro, after which his conspicuous bravery was rewarded by promotion to general of division. There is a vivid picture of him in the memoirs of Colonel Girard, the chief of staff of the 5th Division, who describes him as a bully who was determined to intimidate his subordinates and whose foul temper was notorious throughout the army. Girard's memoirs are far from reliable – they are complete with verbatim dialogue in which he always has the last word – but the picture of the general is convincing. Marmont is equally scathing about Maucune in his memoirs, blaming him for endangering his division by advancing too far on the morning of 17 July, 'however it was Maucune's nature never to wait a moment before marching on the enemy.'[20] Plainly Marmont has every reason to emphasize Maucune's impetuosity and disobedience, for they were central to his explanation of the disaster of the 22nd; but still, they accord with other descriptions of Maucune.

The remaining generals are rather less interesting. Ferey had joined the army in 1788 and seen much action including Marengo and Austerlitz, where he commanded a brigade in Vandamme's division of Soult's corps. He had taken an active part in Masséna's invasion of Portugal, and his brigade had suffered much at the hands of the Light Division at Busaco. Oman links him with

Maucune as a fire-eater, always urging action.[21] The last of the generals of division was Sarrut, the oldest at forty-seven. He had distinguished himself in the early days of the Revolutionary Wars, but promotion had come slowly, for he was not made a general of brigade until 1803. He had commanded a brigade in Merle's division of Reynier's corps in the invasion of Portugal.

Two of the French infantry divisions were commanded by brigadiers. Thomières, who commanded the 7th Division in place of Souham, had served throughout the Revolutionary Wars, first on the Spanish front and then in Italy where he took part in Napoleon's first campaigns. He also had some staff experience, including under Lannes in 1806–7, and had been at both Vimeiro and Coruña. Brigadier Taupin, who acted in place of Brennier, was another veteran of the Revolutionary Wars. When Marmont enforced his unpopular order requisitioning officers' supplementary horses, Taupin called his officers together in a village church.

> He ascended the pulpit and thundered against the abuse of horses in the infantry: he would make an end of all baggage carried on mules or asses, but most especially of officers' riding horses. 'Gentlemen,' he cried, 'in 1793 we were allowed a haversack as our only baggage, a stone as our only pillow.' Well – it was a long time since 1793: we were in 1812, and the speaker, this old and gallant soldier, had *six* baggage mules to himself.[22]

The senior ranks of the allied army present a reverse image of the French, with an immensely experienced general at the head, but surprisingly little experience among his immediate subordinates. Wellington was now forty-three years old, and his first independent command of an army was twelve years before. His victories in India have often been discounted both by contemporaries and historians: the context is too unfamiliar and the disproportion of the contending forces seems swollen beyond belief, as if strayed from the pages of Herodotus or Arrian. But Wellington had gained more than a reputation and a modest fortune in India: he had learnt to plan a campaign with unusual thoroughness, to handle an army under difficult conditions and to seize a fleeting opportunity to strike hard at the enemy. Since his return from India he had commanded a division in the Copenhagen Expedition and then been given the command of the small army sent to drive the French out of Portugal. The most striking aspect of this campaign, until it was overshadowed by the controversy surrounding his supersession and the Convention of Cintra, was Wellington's confidence, his refusal to be intimidated by the French and his deft handling of his troops. These qualities were again in evidence on his return to Portugal in April 1809: his aggressive assumption of the offensive against Soult at Oporto and the bold decision to advance into Spain. Talavera was a costly and ultimately barren victory, but it proved that well-handled British troops were equal or superior to good French infantry in battle. The defeat of Austria turned Wellington's attention to the defence of Portugal, despite the widespread opin-

ion in his army that the task was hopeless. The result proved not only his inge-
nuity, thoroughness and breadth of judgment, but also his strength of character. The long months waiting for the French to begin their advance, and then
Masséna's unexpected ability to hold his ground, first at Sobral, then at
Santarem, placed an immense strain on the allied commander. Reward came
with the rapid pursuit of Masséna's tattered army in the first weeks of spring,
but the rest of 1811 proved disappointing as the French thwarted his attempts
to take the frontier fortresses. Their fall, in the early months of 1812, reflected
Wellington's careful planning and a willingness to pay a high price if the objective warranted it. No one predicted that the carnage in the breaches of Badajoz
would be quite as terrible as it was, but after the failed sieges of 1811 no one
expected it to fall easily.

Wellington was a carefully calculating general. He could be very bold, as
he showed at Oporto and, in a different way, in his advance to Talavera; and
he could be very patient, as he showed when facing Masséna. He did not
fight unless he thought he could win, and that he would gain from the victory. He had never yet been defeated in battle, nor had he been manoeuvred
into a position where he had no choice but to fight at a disadvantage, and for
the last three years he had been facing some of the finest generals in the
French army.

The successful defence of Portugal and the capture of Ciudad Rodrigo and
Badajoz had firmly established Wellington's authority in the army, but even his
greatest admirers were puzzled and unhappy at his refusal to attack Marmont
at San Cristobal and the subsequent course of the campaign. A number of
reasons have been suggested to explain Wellington's caution. At the time
Captain Tomkinson wondered if 'orders from England might be to avoid an
action if not prudent'.[23] We now know that this is not true: Wellington's
instructions gave him complete discretion in the conduct of his operations.
However, Wellington may have been influenced by the very uncertain state of
British politics at the time. The Prime Minister, Spencer Perceval, had been
assassinated on 11 May; an attempt to carry on the government under Lord
Liverpool had been defeated; several weeks of intense but fruitless political
negotiations then followed, before Liverpool was confirmed in office on 8 June.
His government was very weak at first and strenuous efforts to bring Canning
into the ministry failed. Wellington had learnt of Perceval's assassination by 9
June, when he told Liverpool: 'You have undertaken a most gigantic task, and
I don't know how you will get through it.'[24] He did not learn of Liverpool's
confirmation in office until 29 June, that is until after the stand-off at San
Cristobal and the fall of the Salamanca forts. In his congratulations to the new
Prime Minister, he admitted that he had expected that the crisis would end
with the Opposition coming to power and it is clear that he thought – quite correctly – that the new government's hold on office was still tenuous.[25] Given
that, until the spring of 1811, the Opposition had vehemently criticized both
the commitment to the Peninsula and Wellington personally, and had then

been converted only to a tepid, half-hearted support for the war, it is reasonable to assume that the thought that they might already be in office made Wellington more cautious at San Cristobal, especially as he had been stung by the taunt that at Talavera he had fought a useless battle in order to gain a peerage. Even when he knew that Liverpool's government had survived a vote of confidence in the Commons, he could have no faith that the ministry's majority would survive the shock of bad news, such as the defeat of the army in Spain. Wellington very seldom allowed political considerations to influence the conduct of his operations, but in June and July 1812 they were a powerful argument on the side of caution.

However, there were other, equally substantial arguments. Wellington had no wish to fight a battle if a victory would bring glory but no tangible reward. He knew, although Marmont did not, that King Joseph was preparing large reinforcements for the French army. These troops would more than make up for the damage suffered in a partial defeat. To be useful, a victory would have to break Marmont's army completely and remove it from the balance of forces in central Spain, giving the allies the unchecked initiative and opening the road to Madrid. Wellington was still happy to fight in a defensive position, where the risk of defeat was minimal and where there was the possibility that a failed French attack would open the way for a devastating counterattack; but he would not risk much without the hope of substantial, lasting gains.[26]

Underlying these calculations was another consideration: Wellington knew that his army could successfully hold and defend a position as it had done at Busaco and Fuentes; he was less certain of its ability to attack over open ground. The critical point at the battle of Talavera occurred in the centre of the allied line. Sherbrooke's division, including the Guards and two brigades of the King's German Legion, had been the object of the main French attack. The allies drove back the first wave of French troops, but were too impetuous and carried their counterattack too far, becoming disordered. As a consequence they were easy prey for the French reserves, and Wellington had only narrowly managed to stem this second attack by scraping together all his uncommitted forces.[27] It was this impetuosity and ill-discipline which gave him cause for anxiety. It had cost the cavalry petty disasters at Campo Mayor (25 March 1811) and, recently, at Maguilla (11 June 1812), when an initial victory had been transformed into a rout; and no one could be sure that it would not equally affect the infantry. After the battle Charles Cathcart wrote home to General Graham:

> Lord W. has now seen that a British Army can attack as well as defend a position and I trust will in future place that confidence in them they so justly deserve. This is the first attack he has made and He was before this Trial afraid that their Impetuosity would be too great and render them unmanageable, the result has however proved the contrary.[28]

An engineer officer attached to the Fourth Division confirms the point, writing after the battle:

> Lord Wellington has at length done what we have so long been wishing him to do, that is, attack the enemy; and it has been attended with the greatest success, as you will see by his Lordship's despatch. He had always expressed himself as afraid of the impetuosity of the British troops in attack, carrying them forward in disorder after the first driving of the enemy, and giving them the only chance they can possibly have of defeating us. The result of this last action near Salamanca has given our army a character of which many thought they were not deserving – that of the highest state of discipline and attention to their officers in the heat of action; which, with their very superior coolness and courage, has enabled them completely to defeat and drive before them a French army of nearly 50,000 men, in nearly as quick time as they could walk over the ground.[29]

Wellington was an extremely self-reliant general, forming his own opinion and little inclined to consult, let alone to depend on, the advice of others. There was no grey eminence whispering in his ear, and he did not tolerate presumption or interference. This self-sufficiency was fortunate, for in July 1812 the senior ranks of the army were remarkably thin. George Murray, the able and efficient Quartermaster-General, had returned home at the beginning of the year, and his place was still being temporarily filled by his deputy, Lieutenant-Colonel De Lancey. The Adjutant-General's office was also vacant: Charles Stewart, Castlereagh's half-brother, had left the army in April 1812, leaving Lieutenant-Colonel Waters to act as head of the department. De Lancey and Waters were experienced officers and quite capable of executing the routine business of their office, but had no wider influence on operations.

The senior officer most in Wellington's confidence was undoubtedly Sir William Beresford, who had reorganized and re-trained the Portuguese army so successfully, but whose mistakes and failure of nerve at Albuera had irretrievably damaged his reputation as a fighting general. Wellington had a high opinion of him, while recognizing his limitations. After Albuera Beresford had suffered a breakdown, but had now largely recovered: Wellington kept him by his side, and throughout the campaign Beresford constantly urged caution and the avoidance of risk. This greatly frustrated Wellington's personal staff, who were overflowing with confidence and eager for action, and there is a story that Ulysses Burgh, one of Wellington's senior ADCs, met Beresford soon after the decision to attack had been made and said, 'Well, we are going to attack at last, and you can't prevent it.'[30] But if Beresford's moral courage was questionable, his physical bravery in action was undoubted: he had been slightly wounded on 18 July, while he would show considerable coolness under fire on the 22nd.

Beresford's status in the army was rather controversial, for while his rank in the British army was relatively low, his position as a marshal of the Portuguese army gave him a claim – which was deeply resented – to seniority over all the British generals except Wellington. This only added to the concern of the British government about who would replace Wellington if he was disabled – a question which was further complicated by Wellington's own lack of seniority in the British army list and by his distaste for having a second-in-command. The problem was temporarily solved when Sir Thomas Graham joined the field army from Gibraltar in August 1811, for he was widely liked and respected, and he acted as commander of the First Division and only incidentally as the most senior British general in the army after Wellington. However, an eye ailment forced him to leave the army at the beginning of July, which left Sir Stapleton Cotton, the commander of the cavalry, as the next most senior officer. Even Wellington, who approved Cotton's dependability compared to that of more adventurous cavalry commanders, admitted that he was 'not exactly the person I should select to command an army'.[31] Opinion in the army was more forthright:

> Sir Thomas Graham has been compelled from ill health to quit the Army, and is gone home to the great regret of everybody: conjecture says he will be succeeded by Sir Edw. Paget, a very deservedly popular Officer. The present second in command is Sir Stapleton Cotton, an officer who has some knowledge of Cavalry Movements, but who is entirely inexperienced in all the detail necessary to make a good Commander in Chief. It would indeed be dreadful, were anything now to happen to Lord W.; to say the least of it, the safety of the army would be endangered.[32]

However, it is only fair to add that another officer, writing of the campaign as a whole just after the battle, said, 'Our Cavalry in particular were very alert, and Sir S. Cotton has profited much by his service in this Country.'[33]

The army suffered not only the loss of Graham, but also Picton, who was still recovering from a wound received at Badajoz, and Craufurd, who had been killed at Ciudad Rodrigo; while Colville, who had temporarily commanded the Fourth Division and was ready for a division of his own, was also absent owing to a Badajoz wound. Of the seven Anglo-Portuguese infantry divisions, only two were under their accustomed commanders: Lowry Cole's Fourth and James Leith's Fifth Division. Cole himself had only recently rejoined the army after six months in England. He was 'a pleasant, sensible, agreeable man', popular with all ranks, although he had a hot temper.[34] He looked after the welfare of his troops, and was supposed to give the best dinners in the army. His initiative at Albuera saved the battle, and the general consensus is that he was a capable, dependable divisional commander, although Alexander Gordon, Wellington's ADC, rejected this view, asserting that Cole was a man of '*very*, *very* moderate talents indeed' and 'quite lost and confused in the field'; but perhaps this isolated comment should not be taken too seriously.[35]

At forty-nine, James Leith was the oldest divisional commander in the army, and his military career dated back as far as 1780. He had commanded a brigade in the Coruña campaign and again at Walcheren, and he had been given the Fifth Division when it was formed in August 1810, leading it at Busaco. He was one of the few generals sent out to the Peninsula at Wellington's explicit request.[36] A recurrence of Walcheren fever forced him home in 1811 and he did not rejoin the army until after the fall of Ciudad Rodrigo. He was fortunate in his staff, for his nephew and ADC Andrew Leith Hay, wrote one of the best first-hand accounts of the battle, which illuminates the role played by the Fifth Division, while William Maynard Gomm describes Leith thus in a letter home: 'I am living with a most excellent man, General Leith, and a higher gentleman or a better soldier I believe is not to be found among us. I am very much indebted to him, and fortunately I find him every day more and more worthy of the respect which I am inclined to pay him on this account.'[37]

The youngest divisional commander was the 34-year-old Edward Pakenham, Wellington's brother-in-law, who had been given command of the Third Division at Picton's request, when that tough old soldier found that his wound had not yet sufficiently recovered for him to take the field. Pakenham had experience both of commanding the Fusilier Brigade in the field and of acting as Adjutant-General and, like most officers, he preferred the active command. George Napier praised him as 'one of the most candid, generous, honourable, active and intelligent general officers in the service', while Edward Costello, a private in the 95th Rifles, says that he was 'beloved by us all' for his consideration of the men. Wellington wrote with uncharacteristic warmth to Colonel Torrens after the battle: 'Pakenham may not be the brightest genius, but my partiality for him does not lead me astray when I tell you that he is one of the best we have.' And, 'he made the manoeuvre which led to our success in the battle of the 22nd, with a celerity and accuracy of which I doubt that many are capable.'[38]

Wellington had no such partiality for Sir Henry Clinton, the commander of the Sixth Division. Indeed, he had successfully prevented both Clinton and his brother William receiving commands in the Peninsula before 1812, when the loss of senior officers left him the choice of either openly admitting his veto or quietly withdrawing it, and he preferred the latter course.[39] When Clinton joined the army in February, Wellington made the best of him; and during the halt at the Duero he corresponded with him in a more confidential tone than with his other subordinates.[40] Later in the campaign he entrusted him with a detached command. Clinton was not popular with his division: his strict discipline and insistence on formality were deeply resented, moving one officer to describe him as 'one of the greatest fools I ever met with ... he makes no allowance for weather, fatigue or any other cause.'[41] But this is not the whole story, for Clinton repeatedly urged the commanders of his regiments to be more sparing in the use of the lash, and was scathing in his official criticism of the 2nd or Queen's Regiment – a most unhappy unit at that time – where floggings were heavy and frequent.[42]

The other senior officers in the army figure less prominently in the course of the battle. Major-General Charles Alten, perhaps the best of the Hanoverian officers, commanded the Light Division and met with the approval of that opinionated, self-regarding force.[43] Major-General John Hope commanded the Seventh Division – this was not the John Hope who had served with Moore in Sweden and Spain, and who would join Wellington in 1813, but a second cousin and exact contemporary. He had served in the Low Countries, 1793–5, the Cape of Good Hope and the West Indies, and on Lord Cathcart's staff on the expeditions to Hanover in 1805 and Copenhagen in 1807. He did not spend long in the Peninsula, although Wellington was – officially at least – sorry to see him go, 'as he is very attentive to his duty'.[44] Finally, Graham's place at the head of the First Division had been taken by Major-General Henry Campbell, a Guardsman, who had already seen much service in the Peninsula, notably at Talavera.[45]

Only one of the brigadiers needs to be noticed here: John Gaspard Le Marchant, the commander of the brigade of British heavy dragoons. Le Marchant had served in Flanders in 1793–4 and devised a new system of sword exercise. A concern for the training of officers led to some years at the head of the precursor of Sandhurst. He arrived in the Peninsula in August 1811 and gained a satisfying small victory at Villa Garcia in April 1812. There seems, however, to have been some tension between him and Cotton, and not all his officers were convinced of his merits. One wrote in October 1811: 'General Le Marchant marched part of the Way hither with our Squadron and regularly treated us with dinners. He is a pleasant Man, highly accomplished and a great Theoretical Warrior, but I greatly fear we shall in him experience how very much Practise exceeds Theory.' Five months later the same officer was still sceptical:

> Genl. Le Marchant has his whole Brigade within reach of him and has therefore begun playing Soldiers in order to prove the efficiency of some miserable awkward Manoeuvres which he has himself been coining. I have no doubt they all occurred to Sir David [Dundas] but were rejected for others infinitely superior. Be that as it may, our Schoolmaster had the three Regts. out yesterday and would I have no doubt treat us with more Field Days should opportunities offer themselves.[46]

Both these letters, to be fair, were written before Villa Garcia, but a private soldier in the 5th Dragoon Guards was more perceptive, even if his spelling was less orthodox:

> Wee have the Genl. that is to command The Brigade of the 5th Dn Guards, 3rd or King's own 3rd Dragoon Guards & Oathers his Name is Le March a French Genrl a Brave warlike Man about 39 years of Age [actually forty-six] a weather Beatten face & can look you Strait without Being Abashed in the least. Old Cathcart cold Not look you Better without Blushing.[47]

This is not the portrait of a desk soldier or a 'Theoretical Warrior'; but then, desk soldiers were not common in either army.

Commentary

It is impossible to calculate the precise strength of either army on the morning of the battle, but an explanation may be given here of the round figures used in the text, and of some of the problems which lie behind them: further information, and the detailed figures, are given in Appendices II and III.

The French army's strength is based on a return of 15 July which gives its total strength as 49,647 officers and men. But from this we may follow Oman in deducting the 768 officers and men of the Equipages Militaires, because they were non-combatants; and go one step further than Oman by also deducting the Gendarmerie (135 all ranks) and the Engineers and Sappers (349 all ranks). These were not actually non-combatants, but they do not appear to have been engaged at all during the campaign: they suffered almost no casualties. We must also make allowance for losses incurred in the week before the battle, both from the fighting on the 18th and from fatigue: Oman puts this at almost 1,200 men, which seems a very reasonable estimate.[48] Finally, French sources agree that one battalion of the 22nd Ligne from Taupin's division was detached on the morning of the battle and took no part in the fighting, and this too should be deducted, for Oman does not count the 12th Portuguese Dragoons, who were similarly detached, in his calculation of the allied total.[49] On the other hand, the battalion of the 27th Ligne (Clausel's division), which garrisoned Alba de Tormes overnight rejoined its division during the day and so must be included. This produces the following results:

French strength on 15 July	49,647
deduct Equipages Militaires, Engineers and Sappers, and Gendarmerie	1,252
	48,395
deduct losses on campaign approx.	1,195
	47,200
deduct one battalion 22nd Ligne approx.	500
	46,700

However, this total is still only a rough approximation and includes a number of men who ensured that they did not come within range of the enemy.

Similar calculations can also be made for the allied army, deducting the waggon train, the Staff Corps (a unit similar to the Sappers) and the Engineers. Oman puts the allied losses during the campaign at about a thousand men, reflecting their lower casualties on 18 July (542 killed, wounded and missing, compared with just over eight hundred French).[50] But as the allies were retreating and the French following in their wake, it seems reasonable to suppose that allied stragglers were more likely to be captured by the French than vice versa and that this would offset the allied advantage on the 18th. It has therefore been assumed that they too lost about 1,200 men during the campaign.

Allied strength on 15 July		51,937
deduct waggon train, Staff Corps, Engineers		246
		51,691
deduct losses in campaign	approx.	1,191
		50,500

On the basis of these figures, Wellington's army was about 3,800 men stronger than Marmont's, although, of course, this figure is only a rough estimate. Such an advantage was useful without being particularly significant: opposing armies are never exactly equal in strength, and the difference at Salamanca was less than in most battles of the period. It was rather more than the strength of the Spanish contingent, but much less than the combination of the Spaniards and Bradford's independent Portuguese brigade, and it is difficult to imagine that the campaign or the battle would have been any different without these units on the allied side. What mattered far more was the quality of the troops and the skill of their generals. Nonetheless, it would be absurd to pretend that Wellington gained no advantage from this numerical superiority, or that he would not have been disadvantaged if it had been reversed.

Many older sources state that the armies at Salamanca were both in the low forty thousands. This seems to derive from Napier's statement that Marmont had 42,000 'sabres and bayonets' and Wellington 'above forty-six thousand'. But these are estimates of rank and file, not the total strength of the army. Oman's comment on such calculations still holds good: 'Why any sane person *should* deduct officers, sergeants, and artillerymen from a fighting total I am unable to conceive, though contemporary British [and French] writers, including Wellington himself, often did so.'[51]

One striking difference which emerges from a comparison of the armies is in their artillery. The French required 3,437 men for 78 guns, or 44 men per gun; while the Anglo-Portuguese needed only 1,300 men for their 54 guns (excluding the Spanish), or 24 men per gun. Looking at the French figures more closely, we see that each infantry division had, on average, 5 officers and 213 men of the artillery attached to it. This would represent an eight-gun battery of foot artillery, including both gunners and drivers (who were organized separately), at an average of just over 27 men per gun. A battery of horse artillery was attached to the cavalry: 3 officers and 193 men, manning and driving six guns (average of 32 men per gun). This accounts for 70 of the 78 French guns, leaving one battery in reserve. However, the 'Artillery Reserve, Park etc.' of Marmont's army on 15 July 1812 amounted to 50 officers and 1,450 men.[52] Of these 1,500 men, two or three hundred might have been needed by the battery of artillery held in reserve – perhaps even a few more if, as seems likely, it was the battery of 12-pounders. But this still leaves about 1,200 men whose function is unclear. Marmont's army was very short of horses; it certainly did not have a pontoon train or a long procession of heavy transport trailing in its rear. Some men would have been needed for the army's reserve ammunition, and for the spare carriages, mobile forges and other impedimenta needed by the artillery, but it seems highly unlikely that their numbers approached 1,200 – or more than one-third of the total artillery in the army. Yet there is no obvious alternative explanation of the anomaly. It is possible that the return of artillery, unlike that of the rest of the army, includes sick, garrisons and other troops not with the field army; but this seems improbable, especially as it is sufficiently detailed to give the strength of the batteries attached to each division.

There are also problems on the other side of the ledger with the allied artillery. The figures for the Anglo-Portuguese artillery, unlike the rest of the army, are not securely based on an original return in the PRO; rather they reproduce statistics given by Oman, and it is not clear what his source was, although he may have seen a return in the Ordnance Papers which is now missing. The weekly state of the army on 15 July in the PRO gives much higher figures for the British and German (excluding Portuguese as well as Spanish) artillery: 121 officers and 2,327 men, or 2,448 all ranks. This is more than double Oman's figure of 58 officers and 1,128 men, 1,186 all ranks.[53] However, this return certainly includes the artillery serving with Hill's corps in Estremadura, and the company of artillery which manned the 18-pounders that had been used against the Salamanca forts and that Wellington sent to the rear before the battle began, which Oman excludes. It *may* also include other British and German companies of artillery in Portugal, although in general the return only includes troops serving at the front, and there is a large number (over 1,000) of artillerymen listed as detached or 'on command' who are not included in the 2,448. So it seems at least possible that Oman's figure is an underestimate, and that the difference in strength between French and allied artillery was less than the figures given in the text would suggest.[54]

The French army included six regiments of light infantry: one each in the divisions of Foy, Clausel, Ferey and Taupin, and two in Sarrut's division. These regiments appear to have behaved no differently from the line regiments in the army, which supports the commonly held view that the distinction between light and line regiments in the French army was almost entirely nominal at this time. In general, the performance of the French skirmishers was disappointing, and it is noteworthy that they made their greatest impact in their attack on the village of Arapiles – conducted by Maucune's division, which consisted entirely of line infantry. However, too many aspects of the French performance in the battle remain obscure for this conclusion to be regarded as definitive.

None of the regiments in Marmont's army had been part of his corps in 1805.

Sarramon gives some interesting figures on the distribution of the horses Marmont gained from his infantry officers and the convoy destined for Soult:

The 3rd Hussars received	68	horses
The 22nd Chasseurs received	71	horses
The 26th Chasseurs received	106	horses
The 13th Chasseurs received	156	horses
The 14th Chasseurs received	134	horses
The 15th Dragoons received	17	horses
The 25th Dragoons received	18	horses
	570	horses

The total number of horses gained was 669, leaving 99 unaccounted for in these figures. However, a comparison of the returns of 1 and 15 July strongly suggests that most of this surplus went to the 15th and 25th Dragoons, which show a total increase of 124 officers and men, 89 more than are acknowledged in Sarramon's figures. The inclusion of such large numbers of untrained horses – amounting to more than a quarter of each brigade of light cavalry and almost one-fifth of the second brigade of dragoons – goes a long way to explain their poor performance in the campaign.[55]

In the return of 15 July, Curto's division of light cavalry includes an 'Escadron de Marche' of 11 officers and 141 men. This does not appear in the previous return, or in Lamartinière's table of casualties. The most probable explanation is that this squadron consisted of reinforcements for the regiments in Curto's division, and that the men were sent to their respective regiments soon after 15 July, their casualties therefore appearing under their regiments.

After the battle Foy made some interesting remarks in his diary on the relative merits of the two armies:

> The English government has by good treatment made a national army from English troops enlisted for silver, German mercenaries without country, and Portuguese wounded in their pride. Our government on the contrary has by its bad treatment transformed our national army into a band of mercenaries. The soldiers have no enthusiasm, no courage, no attachment to their sovereign or their country; they lack physical strength. Their life is generally sad, and their prospects horrible.[56]

If nothing else, these comments show how deeply the defeat shook the pride and self-esteem of the French army, and this in turn helps explain the asperity of Foy's judgment of Marmont.

Chapter Three
Preliminary Manoeuvres and Skirmishing: Morning and Early Afternoon

Well before dawn on Wednesday 22 July 1812, the hundred thousand men and ten thousand horses of the two armies were stirring after their wet and uncomfortable night. The troops stood to arms an hour before break of day as a routine precaution against a surprise attack, necessary when their opponents were so close. But there was no immediate violence and, as the sun rose, promising a fine, hot day, the men were dismissed to clean their weapons and prepare their breakfast, while parties were sent out to gather wood and water. A corporal in the allied Fifth Division, John Douglas of the 3/1st or Royal Scots, remembered:

> we had for a wonder some days' advance of rations, which caused a man to exclaim, 'Well, if I am killed today I will be in with the Commissary for once.' And killed he was. We had not been gone more than half-an-hour when the pickets began to pop at each other and so smartly that I climbed a tree to look into the valley to see how the play went. Scarcely was I mounted when the bugles called us in. The wood and water went to wreck while we double quicked it into line, on with the accoutrements, [and] fell in.[1]

This skirmishing did not signal the beginning of a battle; indeed neither general at this time expected a full-scale engagement. Wellington had made up his mind to fall back on Ciudad Rodrigo if the French continued to turn his flank. On the previous evening he had learnt that Marmont would soon be reinforced by a brigade of cavalry sent by Caffarelli, which had already reached Pollos on the Duero, and this made him decide to break contact and make a clean retreat if no opportunity for turning the tide of the campaign occurred during the course of the day.[2] However, it is evident that, even as he came to this coldly reasoned decision, his spirit was inclined to rebel against such a tame – if prudent – withdrawal before an inferior enemy. The prospect of a further retreat and of abandoning Salamanca, the one tangible prize of the campaign, was very unpopular in the army, which remained confident of its ability to defeat the

French whenever it was permitted to fight. According to one officer, in a letter written a couple of days later, 'the Army began to forget for an instant under whose command they were, and not only repine at their retreat, but to despond of a change of fortune.'[3] But Wellington's determination and authority both held, and orders were given for the army's baggage and heavy equipment to begin its retreat, escorted by a regiment of Portuguese dragoons.

The allied retreat from the Duero had aroused growing apprehension in Salamanca, as it seemed ever more likely that the city would be abandoned to the French. Those citizens who had taken a prominent part in welcoming Wellington cursed their rash enthusiasm and prepared for a hasty flight. Of course, there were others who would welcome the return of the familiar and, in the town, fairly well-behaved French; but they naturally concealed their feelings as best they could. By 21 July some notables had already left, rumours abounded and the town was filled with stragglers and supernumeraries from the allied army: commissaries, camp-followers and even some officers and men who had left their units in search of food, liquor and other comforts. Many of these refused orders and remonstrances to leave the town until at last a staff officer deliberately spread a story that the French cavalry were at the gates. The result was a panic which naturally spread to the civilian population and, though the report was soon contradicted, nerves nonetheless remained frayed and the atmosphere tense, so that the retreat of the allied baggage on the following morning led to some bitterness from their warmest supporters.[4]

The irritation of the allies was matched by growing confidence on the part of the French. Marmont's campaign had already proved remarkably successful: another day's manoeuvring and he would regain Salamanca and force Wellington into a humiliating retreat. Already seven of the eight French infantry divisions had forded the Tormes: Marmont had left Sarrut's division on the northern bank overnight to protect his rear. The French had also discovered that the castle at Alba de Tormes was unoccupied, and the 27th Ligne from Clausel's division had been detached on the previous evening to occupy it and so secure the bridge over the river.

At first light on the 22 July patrols from Foy's division – the leading unit in the French army – pushed forward into the small village of Calvarrasa de Arriba. Marmont and Foy soon followed them, bringing up the main part of the division, while the light troops occupied the formidable position beyond. The heights of Calvarasa de Arriba are a chain of steep bluffs rising perhaps 150 feet from the open valley to their west. The isolated chapel of Nuestra Señora de la Peña is built upon a shelf of flat ground towards their summit, while the Pelagarcia stream (or Rivera de Gaucete) winds northwards around their feet. The Pelagarcia is no more than a creek or small brook lined with reed beds; it is often dry in summer (although the storm of the previous night had left it full on the morning of the battle) and generally poses no obstacle to military movements – unlike the heights which could only be scaled by infantry in loose order.

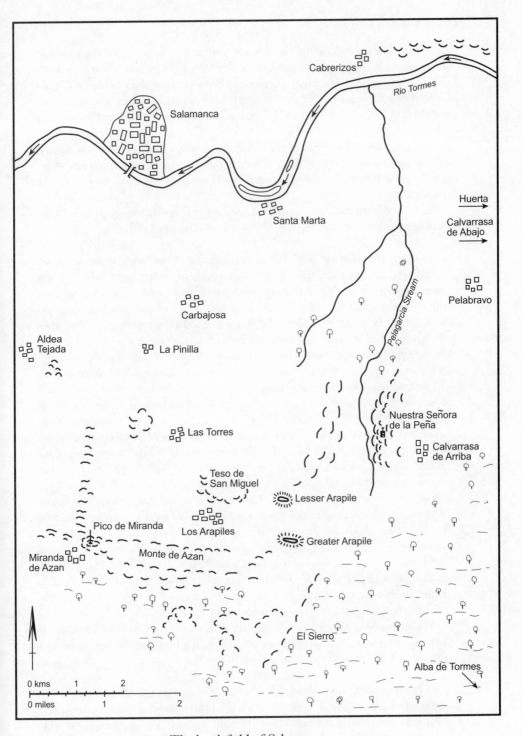

The battlefield of Salamanca.

It was on these heights that the French voltigeurs encountered the outposts of Wellington's army, held by the Brunswick Oels light infantry of the Seventh Division, and a brisk skirmish developed. Both commanders valued the position and so reinforced their front line with fresh units, Wellington sending forward the 4th Caçadores from Pack's independent Portuguese brigade, and the 68th Foot from the Seventh Division. Meanwhile the skirmishing had spread further north along the banks of the Pelagarcia where the riflemen of the King's German Legion came into action, and even onto the plain near the river where the villages of Pelabravo and Calvarrasa de Abajo were held by outposts of the British cavalry.[5]

The best description of the skirmishing near Nuestra Señora de la Peña, where it was sharpest, comes from Private John Green of the 68th:

Early on the morning of the 22nd July, we heard the firing of the advanced guard, and in less than ten minutes our regiment, being light infantry, was ordered forward: having reached the front, we saw the French picquets advancing on ours, and both were sharply engaged. In a moment the left wing was ordered to the front: no sooner did our advanced picquets perceive that they were supported by such a number of light troops, than they advanced on the French picquets, and drove them in confusion to the summit of a high hill; but the enemy receiving strong reinforcements, bore down on my brave comrades, who contested every inch with them. At this period a General came to the front, to see how things were going on: in a fit of passion he enquired, 'Who commands here?' The answer was 'General Hope'. He said, 'Where is he? the whole of the advanced picquets will be taken prisoners.' General Hope came up at the time, but did not appear at all afraid that the men would be taken: he sent one of his aid-de-camps [sic] with directions for a squadron of light dragoons to support the skirmishers immediately: they came forward, and had only just taken their stand, when one of them, a youth of about twenty-one years of age, was killed. The enemy now retired to the top of the hill, and brought six pieces of cannon to play on us. About this time the watering parties of the 7th division came to the valley for a supply of water: the French guns began to play on these unarmed and defenceless men; but not one of them was hurt, although shot and shell fell thickly amongst them. After this the enemy continued firing on us for some hours. In this skirmish Major Miller and several privates were wounded, and one of the latter had to undergo amputation.

We remained in this position until afternoon, but were not allowed to take off our accoutrements. About three o'clock the 95th rifle corps arriving, took our places, and we immediately marched off to join the division.[6]

As Green implies, this skirmishing lasted throughout the morning and well into the afternoon, though generally in a desultory fashion, with neither side pressing the other after the first clash. The allies seem to have maintained control of the chapel, but did not push the French far beyond it, and it remained contested ground for most of the day. Casualties appear to have been light: for example, the 68th lost only four killed and sixteen wounded in the whole day, while the two battalions of King's German Legion light infantry lost only twenty-five casualties between them. Unfortunately, it is impossible to distinguish the losses of the Brunswick Oels or the 4th Caçadores from those suffered later in the day, and these regiments probably bore the brunt of the skirmishing. Equally the French casualties are merged with those suffered by Foy's division on the following day at Garcia Hernandez.[7]

Further north, the skirmishing of the French and allied cavalry was even less bloody, although at one point the appearance of some of Boyer's dragoons caused the allied light horse to fall back hastily, and the position was only restored with the aid of a detachment of Le Marchant's brigade of heavy cavalry.[8] This cavalry affray was more a matter of manoeuvres and threats than of charges or hand-to-hand fighting, but the opposing horsemen did exchange carbine fire, and one French shot hit Major-General Victor Alten, commander of the leading brigade of allied cavalry, in the thigh. Command of the brigade devolved onto Lieutenant-Colonel Arentschildt of the 1st King's German Legion Hussars, and Alten was carried into Salamanca as soon as his wound had stopped bleeding. He left his ADC, Captain Lingsingen, with the brigade, under instructions to send him word if it seemed likely that the army would retreat, as he was determined to avoid capture whatever the risk to his life. In the middle of the afternoon Lingsingen sent him a warning, and Alten – defying both his surgeon and the pain – mounted and set off on the road to Ciudad Rodrigo, returning only when the sound of guns made it clear that the allies were gaining the victory. Remarkably he recovered from his wound, suffering no lasting consequences from his rashness.[9]

While the light infantry were beginning their skirmish, Marmont examined the allied line. Facing him, he could see little more than parts of the Seventh Division and Pack's brigade, which occupied the range of low hills on the opposite side of the valley, rather less than half a mile to the west of Nuestra Señora de la Peña. In the distance he could see that some allied troops (Pakenham's division and D'Urban's Portuguese dragoons) remained in the San Cristobal position on the north bank of the Tormes; while there was movement to the rear near Salamanca – the allied heavy baggage setting out on the road to Ciudad Rodrigo. The rest of the allied army was largely invisible, although it was not far away, breaking camp and shaking itself into formation in the low ground behind Pack and the Seventh Division. In general it occupied a line running roughly north–south, facing east, although some units were further to the rear, and the cavalry by the river were further forward.

Wellington's view was equally restricted – he was with the Seventh Division on the low heights opposite Marmont, and according to Foy the two commanders could see each other clearly. Foy's division and the skirmishers were obvious, and Wellington knew that Sarrut's division had yet to cross the Tormes; but the rest of the French army was concealed by the broken, wooded ground which lay between Foy and the river. According to the account he gives in his memoirs, Marmont's observations led him to believe that the allies were preparing to withdraw to a position at Tejares, three or four miles to their rear, immediately south of Salamanca, 'and as his movements on Tejares would be difficult if our army was brought forward, I decided to concentrate in front of him in order to take advantage of any opportunities.' But Foy goes much further than this, saying that Marmont was greatly tempted to make a frontal attack on the Seventh Division and Pack, fearing that they might otherwise escape him, and only gave up the plan 'after much hesitation, as was customary'. Marmont's account is, of course, self-interested; but if he writes as the accused in the dock, eager to show that the disaster was not his fault, Foy writes more as a witness for the prosecution than as an objective observer: his whole account is pregnant with the impending defeat which he blames squarely on Marmont.[10]

The ground to the south of Salamanca is generally very open and bare, and is well suited to the movement of all arms. It is gently undulating, scarcely deserving the term 'rolling', while the hills, plateaus and ridges that abound in histories of the battle are mostly quite tame, although they still provide a skyline and a reverse slope of considerable significance. Two steep isolated hills, the Greater and Lesser Arapiles, are marked exceptions to this rule, for they stand out boldly on the battlefield, rocky and bare. The Greater Arapile is a short ridge, some three or four hundred yards long, with a flat narrow summit: its ends are very rocky and inaccessible, but the sides, although steep, can be climbed more easily. The Lesser Arapile lies some nine hundred yards north and a little to the west, that is, closer to Salamanca. It is smaller, rounder and slightly lower; more connected with other high ground near it, though it is much higher than these other rises. It was an integral and essential part of Wellington's position, whereas the Greater Arapile could never be more than a detached outpost of the allied line. About a mile to the west of these hills lies the small village of Los Arapiles which was to see some fighting. The land to its north rises in a hill called the Teso de San Miguel which has its highest point a little to the east, so that it fills part of the gap between the village and the Lesser Arapile. South of the village lies a broad tract of higher ground which runs east–west for about two miles and is known as the Monte de Azan – although the name is rather misleading, for it is not a single consistent feature. Directly opposite the village it presents a steep rounded hillside, five or six hundred yards from the houses. Beyond the summit is perhaps a thousand yards of open rolling countryside, before a second, gentler rise, after which the land falls away into open scrubby woodland. Half a mile further west, the first hillside has been elongated into a long, open slope, although the tableland beyond remains much the same – if anything, flatter and more open. Lateral undulations in the ground restrict the view to the east and west. Continuing to the west, the far end of the Monte de Azan, known as the Pico de Miranda, is different again. Here the plateau has contracted to a narrow ridge with steep sides whose flat summit is

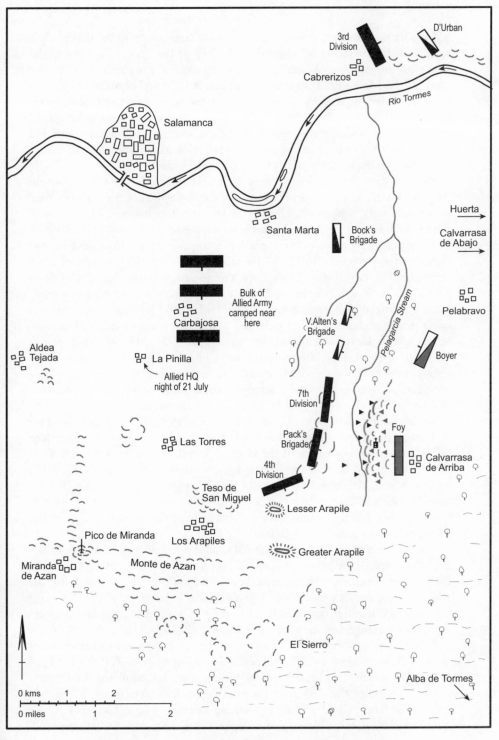

Early morning, 22 July 1812 (all troop positions approximate,
many conjectural).

barely fifty yards across. A low ridge runs off at right angles to the north, while some detached outlying hills continue the line of the Monte de Azan to the west, and the village of Miranda de Azan lies close to the south-west. To the south of the Monte de Azan the land is more broken and partly wooded. The trees are mostly holm-oaks (or ilex), the tattered fringe of an extensive, straggling wood which covered most of the rough country between the battlefield and Alba de Tormes, some eight miles to the south-east. Further south and east, on the edge of the main wood, was a long, low ridge, known as El Sierro, which proved important towards the end of the battle.

Resisting any temptation he may have felt to attack the allied position directly, Marmont gave orders to continue the movement of the previous days to turn the right wing of the allied army by extending his own left. He chose not to make a wide turning movement, which would risk allowing the allies to slip away before he could bring his forces to bear upon them; and instead decided to move across the face of the allied army with only a couple of miles separating the two forces. In practice this meant bringing Sarrut's division across the Tormes, while the other divisions moved south and west in a semi-circle girdling Wellington's position. Foy had a good position from which to cover the early stages of this march, and Marmont brought Ferey's division of infantry and Boyer's dragoons up to support him. He did not expect Wellington to take the offensive suddenly, but manoeuvring so close to the enemy was dangerous and Marmont was taking sensible precautions. The remaining divisions advanced around the edge of the woods in two columns, that nearest the allies being led by Bonnet's 8th Division.

Bonnet's immediate object was to seize the Greater Arapile, which could act as a strong point around which the whole French army could pivot, like a door on its hinge. The possession of the Greater Arapile would protect the flank of the French march as it swung from mainly south to mainly west, while if the allies seized it, Marmont's army would have to swing out in a much wider arc, probably with El Sierro guarding its flank. Not only would the men have to march further, but they would have to move through the forest rather than skirt its edges, and so be further delayed.[11]

The Lesser Arapile formed the natural southern termination of the line of low heights occupied by Wellington's army on the morning of the 22nd. As the highest point in the chain, it dominated these hills, and if the French seized it the whole allied position would become untenable. A detachment of Cole's Fourth Division had therefore occupied it at first light. The Greater Arapile was separate from this range and in the early morning light looked more distant than it really was, so that at first neither Cole nor Wellington, who joined him as it was growing light, recognized its importance. According to Napier, it was not until Colonel Waters noticed French troops stealing towards the hill, that Wellington reacted by sending the 7th Caçadores from Cole's division to secure it, but they arrived too late.[12] Charles Cathcart, writing privately to Sir Thomas Graham only a few days after the battle, gives an unexpurgated account of what happened:

We ought unquestionably to have possessed ourselves of them the very first thing, but through some unaccountable Carelessness, they remained un-occupied. The French saw the importance of these Heights, but did not give us jealousy for them by sending at once a Large Body against them. They sent out some straggling parties in different directions which when they got near the fore-most height ran together and got to the summit before a small party of the Portuguese caçadores which had been sent to prevent them could arrive. They were only in time to save the other height which was immediately occupied in Force by the 4th Division.[13]

Many years later the officer who commanded the caçadores, Major (later Sir) John Lillie, told Napier that when he was sent forward he had no idea that there were French troops in the immediate vicinity and that, when he saw them, he took them for Spaniards. It was not until the two bodies were within a few yards of each other, that the French suddenly opened fire. Although Lillie claims that 'We contested the point so long as anything like an equality of numbers per-mitted us', it seems likely that the caçadores were quickly broken, probably as much by the surprise as by actual losses. This at least is the impression given by another British officer in the Portuguese service, who says that the French 'drove back our people, several of whom were wounded'. Wellington admitted in his official dispatch that by this success the French 'strengthened materially their own position, and had in their power increased means of annoying ours.'[14] French possession of the Greater Arapile cramped Wellington's forces and made even a retreat more difficult, although if the allies had gained the hill they might have found it awkward to hold.

Both sides now consolidated their new possessions. The Lesser Arapile was held by William Anson's brigade of the Fourth Division with the 3/27th on the summit, together with two 9-pounders from Sympher's King's German Legion battery, and the 1/40th in support. The remainder of Cole's division occupied the hill behind the village of Los Arapiles, with Pack's brigade filling the gap between the two heights.[15] The allied line now formed almost a right angle with the Lesser Arapile at the corner. It may have been at this time, or a little later, that Wellington gave orders for Pakenham's division and D'Urban's cavalry to cross the Tormes and to form near Aldea Tejada, some four miles north-west of Los Arapiles. This was far beyond the existing allied line, but in this position they would be well placed to support a retreat or check any wide sweep round the allied flank, while it was clear that the French were committed to operating on the south bank of the Tormes.[16]

Bonnet occupied the Greater Arapile with the 120th Ligne, keeping his other regiments a little to the rear in support, where they were sheltered from allied fire by the hill. Despite the slope the French brought a number of guns up to the summit of the hill: it was too steep for horses to haul them up, so the bar-rels were dismounted and carried to the top by grenadiers, which lightened the gun-carriages sufficiently for them to be dragged up as well.[17] Bringing up ammunition for these guns must have been laborious work, and the steepness of the hill created other problems: a rapid withdrawal was impossible, while there was some 'dead ground' in front, for the gun barrels could not be depressed sufficiently to cover all of the forward slope of the hill, so that attacking troops could gain some shelter there. But the approaches were bare and coverless and could be swept by the guns on the summit, while the position protected them completely from the allied cavalry and vastly reduced the risk of a surprise or flank attack. It also placed the French guns in an excellent position to bombard the allied army, especially the troops occupying the Lesser Arapile, which was well within range.

Marmont soon joined Bonnet on the Greater Arapile. From its summit the world seems open and boundless, but the view is actually less revealing than first impressions suggest. The gentle undulations of ground were sufficient to conceal much, though certainly not all, of Wellington's army, while despite the rain of the night before the thousands of men and horses were already beginning to kick up clouds of dust. Even so, the view and the strength of the position encouraged Marmont to continue his turning movement, although he did so with considerable caution. Foy remained at Calvarrasa de Arriba, where he occupied a strong position guarding the flank and rear of the army, with Ferey's division and Boyer's dragoons in support. In time, Sarrut's division, having crossed the Tormes, would also join him, so that Marmont was well placed if Wellington should suddenly assume the offensive. Bonnet's division holding the Greater Arapile was another bastion of strength, under whose protection Marmont gradually shifted the remaining divisions of his army south-west, heading for the edge of the forest behind the Greater Arapile and for the low ridge of El Sierro. Marmont soon established a powerful battery of twenty guns on this ridge to protect his units as they emerged from the wood and regained their order – for all accounts are agreed that the French movements were rapid but straggling and irregular.

Wellington viewed these manoeuvres with concern, for if the French continued to turn his flank he would soon be forced to retreat, while their possession of the Greater Arapile and the proximity of the two armies would make this a delicate operation full of risks. He had already matched the French movements with some of his own: the First Division had been brought up to support the Fourth and Pack along the line from the Lesser Arapile to the village of Los Arapiles, and most of Victor Alten's brigade of light cavalry, under Arentschildt, had been transferred from the far left to the right of the army, where it deployed on the outer flank of the infantry, beyond the village. But these were merely precautionary moves and would not make a retreat unnecessary, and Wellington was still hoping to avoid the latter.

Late in the morning – some accounts say 11 o'clock, others noon; as usual it is impossible to be precise about the time – he decided to attack the French on the Greater Arapile. Orders were issued and the First Division moved forward, the Guards brigade occupying the village. But then, before the attack could be

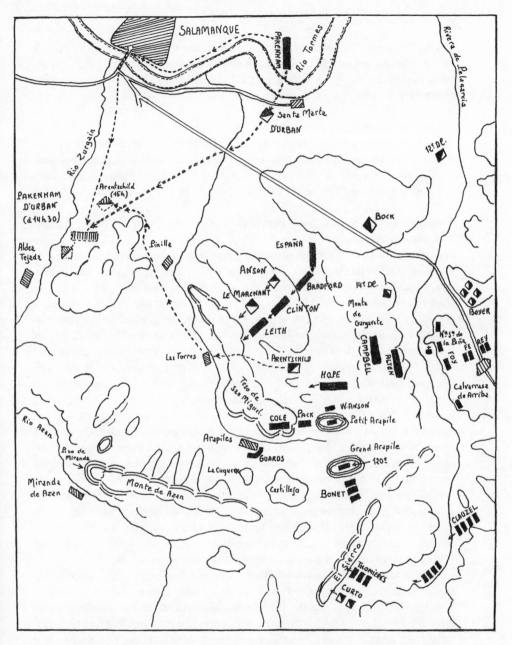

Another view of the battle. Map from Jean Sarramon's *La Battaille des Arapiles*, showing his view of the terrain and the location of the troops between 9 and 11am. (In Sarramon's book the map is rather larger, 230 × 184mm, and with the troops and the river coloured in blue, red and green.)

properly launched, it was cancelled and the troops were withdrawn, leaving only the light companies of the Guards to defend the village.[18] A letter, apparently written by Henry Campbell, commander of the First Division, adds a few interesting details:

> Lord W. at one time determined to attack them, and sent for me, and told me to move forward in two Columns up a Hill in front of our Right, where this Division then was, and attack their left, while the 4th Division was to attack them in front, but I had hardly put the Columns in motion, before I received a Counter Order and moved back to the Ground I had before quitted.[19]

This implies that Wellington's plan was to attack the Greater Arapile in front with the Fourth Division, while the First Division swung round to assault its eastern end and to engage the supporting troops to its rear. What is not clear is whether Wellington intended this as a limited operation to seize the Greater Arapile and so facilitate his retreat if it should be unavoidable, or as the first stage of a full-scale battle. However, the armies were so close that it would have been very difficult to limit the action, while if the initial allied attack had succeeded Wellington would have been well placed to take the French at a great disadvantage. But the French position was extremely strong; the western end of the Greater Arapile is particularly rocky and precipitous, and it was well occupied and well supported. Even with hindsight it is impossible to tell whether the attack would have succeeded or failed.

What is fairly certain is that it was on Beresford's advice that the attack was cancelled. He had been reconnoitring the French position and had observed strong forces to their rear (it was not clear if these were Bonnet's reserves or other French divisions further back) and he urged caution as he had done throughout the campaign. His voice may have been seconded by Stapleton Cotton, for an officer in the Guards who recorded many headquarters rumours reports that 'The two senior officers next to Ld Wellington were decidedly averse to attack.'[20] But more important than Cotton's opinion was the suggestion that the French might be preparing to launch an attack of their own, for Wellington still much preferred to fight on the defensive.

And so the proposed attack was cancelled, and Wellington re-positioned his troops to meet a French assault which never came. But he did not altogether give up the idea of taking the initiative. The sources are too fragmentary to trace the evolution of his plans with confidence, but it seems that he continued to look for an opportunity to strike throughout the afternoon, and that several other plans of attack may have been considered only to be deferred or rejected. Meanwhile, Wellington prepared to retreat if necessary. Early in the day, soon after the French seized the Greater Arapile, he had instructed Colonel De Lancey to draw up plans for a withdrawal, while during the morning or early afternoon orders were issued to the commissariat and other supporting services to begin their march. This caused great discontent among Wellington's staff, who were confident that the army would triumph if only it was allowed to fight, and who deeply resented Beresford's dampening influence on Wellington's initiative.[21]

Among the arrangements Wellington made to resist a French attack was the withdrawal of Sympher's two guns from the Lesser Arapile – they joined the rest of their battery on the hill behind the village of Los Arapiles – and their replacement with two 6-pounders from the battery of horse artillery attached to the Seventh Division. These guns were commanded by Captain Dyneley, and the importance of his task was made clear to him, as he later explained to his brother:

> The order I received had certainly a very awkward signification: 'His Lordship desires you will get your guns up that height and wishes you to defend it as long as you have a man left to your guns. In the event of your being obliged to retire, you will spike your guns and leave them and the General officer commanding has most positive orders that he supports you to the last; in fact,' his Lordship says, 'he must have the hill kept.'
>
> From these orders I made sure of an 'ex' or 'dis'-tinguish. I got my guns up with the assistance of a company of the 40th regiment, unloaded my limbers and sent them and my gunners' horses to the rear, as I thought, if we had to run for it, my men should get away as fast as the infantry. On arrival on the hill I had some satisfaction in finding my friend General Cole in command, knowing there was not any run in him. But the enemy never put us to the test.[22]

Later in the day Dyneley was joined by the remaining four guns in the troop, and they replied to the French battery on the Greater Arapile.

Marmont had observed Wellington's preparations for an attack and had been much encouraged by their cancellation. He thought that Wellington would now retreat and was confirmed in this idea by the sight of troops moving westwards in the allied rear, as Wellington shifted his reserves from his left to his right wing, and perhaps also by the dust raised by Pakenham's division and D'Urban's cavalry as they moved towards Aldea Tejada. But still Marmont did not act precipitately. He did not want a battle which would place the success of the whole campaign at risk; rather he sought to maul the allied rearguard and so gain a triumph which would add éclat to the solid success he had already gained. He would not attack the allies directly until he could be sure that their main body was withdrawing, but in the meantime he would extend his left wing on to the Monte de Azan, thus continuing to turn Wellington's flank and threatening the allies' communications as he had done so successfully in recent days.

Marmont probably issued his orders between 1 and 2 o'clock, an hour or two after Wellington had cancelled his attack. Maucune, with the leading division of the French left wing, would advance on to the Monte de Azan, with Curto's light cavalry acting as a screen in front and on his flank. He would be supported by several batteries of artillery and Thomières's 7th Division, while Clausel's

2nd Division would be in reserve when it arrived, and Taupin's 6th Division would occupy the El Sierro ridge in the rear. It appears that Clausel and Taupin were lagging behind; possibly they had been delayed by the march through the forest, or Clausel may have been waiting to be rejoined by the 27th Ligne, which had been recalled from Alba de Tormes some hours earlier.[23] At the same time Marmont ordered Boyer to leave one of his regiments of dragoons to protect Foy's right flank, and to bring the remaining three regiments of his cavalry division to the centre of the army. Finally, he detached the 122nd Ligne from Bonnet's division to occupy a gentle rise halfway between the Greater Arapile and Monte de Azan.[24]

These movements were not without risk: they would extend Marmont's army in a wide arc perhaps five miles long, with the allied army concentrated inside the arc. The Monte de Azan is open ground, nothing like the strong defensive position of the heights of Calvarrasa de Arriba which Foy occupied; and it was always dangerous to manoeuvre so close to the enemy. The exact degree of risk is impossible to determine, for it depends on the precise location of French divisions – particularly Clausel and Taupin – which we simply do not know. Still, Marmont's whole campaign had been bold, and he had good reason to think that Wellington would not suddenly change character and take the offensive, while, even if he did, the French position was far from hopeless, for Maucune had Thomières, Curto and a powerful force of artillery to provide immediate support, with Clausel and Taupin further back.

Maucune's advance was covered by Curto's light cavalry, who soon began skirmishing with the German Hussars and 14th Light Dragoons of Victor Alten's brigade. The French had the better of this affair, although the fighting was not very serious: a British infantry officer who observed it described it as 'the most beautiful and *stage*-like skirmishing', while a light infantry officer said that watching the spectacle, 'whiled away some hours for us most agreeably'. The historian of the King's German Legion admits that the Hussars generally had the worst of it and suffered some loss, but gives details of one creditable incident: 'Lieutenant Bobers of the regiment, however, made a gallant reprisal, attacking a superior number of the enemy with twenty hussars; rescuing a wounded man from the middle of the enemy's ranks, and bringing in several prisoners.'[25]

In his *Mémoires* Marmont claims that he ordered Maucune to occupy only the near end of the Monte de Azan, but that his hot-headed subordinate pushed forward precipitately and, with his light infantry, attacked the allied troops who were defending the village of Los Arapiles. Whoever was to blame – and Marmont had an obvious motive for attributing the fault to his subordinate, while such behaviour would be in character for Maucune – the result was dangerous. Maucune's division was too far forward, too close to the allied position, and lacked adequate supports. There was a gap of almost a mile between Maucune's right flank and the Greater Arapile, which the 122nd Ligne was quite inadequate to fill, while there was a risk that the fighting in the village might escalate. The problem was not yet insuperable, but it suggests that the French movements were beginning to appear careless and overconfident.

The village of Arapiles was defended by the light companies of the British Guards brigade (First Division) and of the Fusilier brigade (Fourth Division), together with the company of Brunswick Oels light infantry attached to the Fusiliers. Friedrich von Wachholtz of the Brunswickers gives by far the best first-hand account of this fighting in his journal. His company had been deployed in open order in front of the village some hours before: 'We lay on our stomachs on the open field, nibbled on rusks [and] drank fresh water which the inhabitants of Arapiles brought us.' The initial French advance, by a mere company of voltigeurs, was tentative, and Wachholtz's men opened a slow fire to keep their opponents at a distance. But then the French were reinforced and pressed forward, while their artillery inflicted some losses on the allies, including severely wounding Major Dalmer of the 23rd Fusiliers, who was in overall command of the Fourth Division light infantry in the area. The allied skirmishers fell back to the village and were closely followed by the French until the fire of Sympher's guns checked their advance – at this point, seeing their opportunity, the allies charged and drove the voltigeurs back. However, the French were soon reinforced and made a new attack, which carried them into the village before the allied reserves were fed into the fray and drove them out again. This was as far as the French came, although the skirmishing continued for some time. Wachholtz says that his company lost ten men wounded from an initial strength of about fifty-four all ranks. The losses of the light companies of the Fusiliers are merged with those of their parent regiments, but the Coldstream Guards lost thirty-eight casualties, including seven men killed, and the Third Guards suffered twenty-four, with the regimental historians confirming that these casualties came almost entirely from the light companies. Given the small numbers of men engaged, these losses were quite heavy, especially as the allies had the advantage of fighting from under cover.[26]

It is not known why the French abandoned their attack on the village. Perhaps the stiff resistance of the allied light infantry convinced Maucune that there was nothing to be gained by pressing the attack, or he may have obeyed the order to withdraw which Marmont claims to have sent him.[27] Alternatively the sudden appearance of fresh allied troops (Leith's Fifth Division) to the north and west of the village may have persuaded him to retire to a more respectful distance from the allied line. The evidence for Maucune's movements is extremely sparse, but it seems likely that when attacking the village he had brought at least part of the main body of his division to the top of the hillside overlooking Los Arapiles, and that when the attack was given up, he moved further west, occupying the long, gentle forward slope of the plateau, due south of Las Torres.

Wellington had watched the French advance with keen interest and must have hoped that the attack on the village signalled an imminent French onslaught, which would give him the defensive battle which was still his preference. He had responded to Maucune's appearance on the Monte de Azan by continuing the shift of his own forces from left to right. The Fifth Division was ordered to the front line next to the Fourth, extending the line westwards from behind the village. The First Division, except for the light companies which remained in the village, was concentrated behind the Lesser Arapile, with the Sixth Division to its right supporting the Fourth. A little later the Seventh Division would be withdrawn from the left and would form behind the Fifth on the right, leaving only the Light Division, Bock's brigade of heavy dragoons and some light cavalry (12th Light Dragoons and one squadron of 14th Light Dragoons) facing Foy. Bradford's Portuguese brigade, Carlos de España's Spanish division, Le Marchant's brigade of heavy cavalry and George Anson's light cavalry were all in reserve, probably near the village of Las Torres. Finally, Pakenham's division and D'Urban's dragoons had almost completed their march and were approaching the village of Aldea Tejada, where they would rest for more than an hour.

Meanwhile, Maucune had established a powerful battery – British observers put it at about twenty guns – on the Monte de Azan, and this combined with the artillery on the Greater Arapile to open a heavy bombardment of the allied line. The Fourth Division was partly protected by the brow of the hill and suffered relatively little, but the ground to the west of the village, where most of the Fifth Division came into line, provided less shelter, and consequently it seems to have suffered rather more. Nonetheless, Charles Cathcart expressed the common opinion of officers on the staff, and of Wellington himself, when he wrote that the French 'opened a most tremendous Cannonade upon our Line which lasted the greatest part of the day, but not to so much effect as might have been apprehended.'[28]

Soldiers in the ranks could not take such a detached view of the experience, as Corporal Douglas of the Royal Scots, in Leith's Division, makes clear: 'In my opinion there is no situation in which men can be placed so trying as to keep them exposed to a heavy fire and not be allowed the privilege of self-defence.'[29] Two longer accounts by ordinary soldiers, Robert Eadie and John Green, neither of whose units was in the front line, show the psychological strain caused by the bombardment:

> It was about 2 o'clock, p.m. when the enemy extended his line to the left, under the cover of his artillery, the roaring of which was like one continued peal of thunder ... our division, being in reserve, received general orders to cook, which we set about with all dispatch. It being my turn for this duty, I had just commenced kindling a fire, while one of my comrades was preparing the kettle; when my attention was [distracted] ... we were in great danger at the camp kettles, as both shells and shot were coming thickly and rapidly from the enemy amongst us, occasionally exciting a smile at the ludicrous confusion which they caused, by striking a kettle, and upsetting its contents; the men scampering round to avoid being scalded, as they cursed the loss of the precious broth. Two

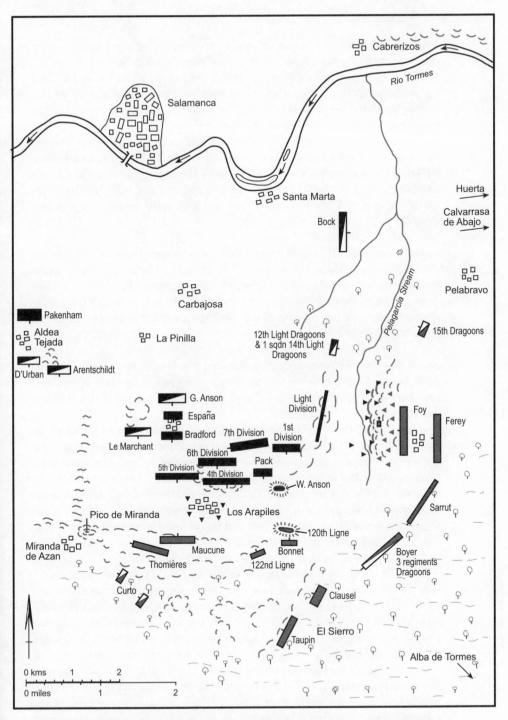

The middle of the afternoon, 22 July 1812, about the time Marmont was wounded and Wellington decided to attack (all troop positions approximate, many conjectural).

of the cooks were killed before we left the ground; but as a precaution against what might equally have been my fate, I took care always to lie down flat on the ground, whenever I could perceive a shell coming in my direction, and which I had time enough to do. The whole of the lines were closely engaged ere we had accomplished the business of cooking, but whenever that was effected, and the measures of beef boiled, the soup was emptied out, and the beef put into our haversacks, and we marched off the hill with the officer to join our division, which we found still lying in close column as a reserve. Just at the moment of our arrival at the regiment, a shell was thrown by the enemy that unpiled a whole company's arms, but luckily enough, no one received any hurt. Shortly afterwards the beef was divided into messes and each man received his welcome share.[30]

This regiment, the 79th, was fortunate and suffered only four casualties in the whole battle, so that most of the shot and shells which disturbed Private Eadie in his cooking had probably overshot their original target. The second account, by John Green of the 68th, shows rather more real danger, although the author exaggerates the number of guns firing, and the casualty figures he gives are higher than those in the official returns:

About this time the cannonading commenced: the French had nearly one hundred pieces of cannon firing on our army ... we had about sixty pieces; and the thunder of these one hundred and sixty guns was terrible, and beggars description.

   Having joined the division [the Seventh], and taken our place on the left of the first brigade; we halted a few minutes, and then advanced to the spot where our artillery were stationed. We now came into an open plain, and were completely exposed to the fire of the enemy's artillery. Along this plain a division of the army was stationed: I think it was the 4th division: the men laid down in order to escape the shot and shells, the army not yet being ready to advance. As our regiment was marching along the rear of this division, I saw a shell fall on one of the men, which killed him on the spot; a part of the shell tore his knapsack to pieces, and I saw it flying in the air after the shell had burst.

   The shot of the foe now began to take effect on us. As we were marching in open column to take our position, one of the supernumerary sergeants, whose name was Dunn, had both his legs shot from under him, and died in a few minutes. Shortly after, a shot came and took away the leg and thigh, with part of the body, of a young officer named Finukin: to have seen him, and heard the screams of his servant, would have almost rendered a heart of stone: he was a good master, an excellent officer, and was lamented by all who knew him. The next thing I have to relate is of the company which was directly in our front, commanded by Captain Gough: a cannon-ball came, and striking the right of the company, made the arms gingle and fly in pieces like broken glass. One of the bayonets was broken off, and sent through a man's neck with as much force as though it had been done by a strong and powerful hand. I saw the man pull it out, and singular to relate, he recovered: three others were also wounded. About this time I had a narrow escape from a cannon-ball, which passed within a few inches of me: although it was nearly spent, yet, had it struck me, I should have been either killed or wounded by it.

After this, we formed column of quarter distance; and several shells fell into our column, and did execution: one shell I shall ever remember: we were in the act of lying down, that it might burst, and do no mischief: the colonel cried out, 'It is a shot!' and we stood up immediately; but while in the act of rising, the shell burst in the midst of the regimental column, and, astonishing to relate, not a man received an injury by it.[31]

As this shows, each casualty in the regiment, and even beyond it, was noticed by the whole unit because there was nothing to distract the men; while in close combat, or even in the excitement of an advance, such losses would have much less impact on the unit's morale. Standing patiently under even distant fire was among the most unpleasant and demanding – but also one of the most common – duties of Napoleonic soldiers in battle.

This bombardment ought to have provided cover for the French to consolidate and secure their position on the Monte de Azan and fill the dangerous gap in their line between Maucune and Bonnet. Instead it saw a further extension of the left which proved disastrous for the army. For reasons which are not clear, Thomières's division, which should have remained in Maucune's rear, moved west along the Monte de Azan, thus becoming the leading division in the army. Neither Clausel nor Taupin was yet in a position to support Maucune or fill the gap to his right. In other words, Maucune and Thomières, who were already dangerously isolated from the rest of the army, ceased to be able to support each other and were strung out over a wide front, lacking depth and solidity.

Marmont recognized the danger and sent urgent orders to Sarrut and Ferey to march from the right wing of the army to the centre, and for Taupin to advance to support the left as soon as his division was in order. He then set out to ride to the left to check Thomières's advance in person and repair the damage, but just as he turned to mount his horse he was badly wounded in the right side and arm by a British shell fired by one of Dyneley's guns on the Lesser Arapile. He was carried to the rear, where the surgeons wanted to amputate the arm: he refused to permit this, and suffered much, but eventually recovered to take the field again in Napoleon's campaigns in Germany and France in 1813 and 1814.[32]

In Marmont's absence the command of the army should have passed to Clausel, the second-in-command, but when messengers reached the 2nd Division, they found that he had just been wounded in the heel by a British shell fragment and had gone to the rear to have it dressed. This left Bonnet as the next most senior officer, but he had scarcely taken command when he was seriously wounded in the thigh. Fortunately Clausel's wound had not disabled him, and he was still able to ride. He arrived at the Greater Arapile soon after Bonnet had been hit and took command, but through this extraordinary chain of events the French army had been left without an effective commander for a crucial hour or more. The British artillery could not match the volume of the French bombardment, but their retaliation had been unexpectedly effective.[33]

Marmont's responsibility for the disaster which followed has been much discussed. His own account, in his dispatches to Napoleon and in his *Mémoires*, is clearly a piece of self-justification designed to shift the blame and clear his reputation. But his arguments are subtle and plausible – infinitely more convincing than the egotistical bombast of most French memoirs of the period – and they may well be largely true, if incomplete: the innocent as well as the guilty have to defend themselves when things go awry. Marmont places most of the blame for the debacle on Maucune's impetuosity and says very little about Thomières. Fortescue makes the suggestion that Thomières and even Maucune may have mistakenly believed that the race of the previous days was to be resumed, and this seems at least possible.[34] But most historians will have none of this and blame Marmont squarely for the defeat. Oman and Sarramon expound this argument most convincingly, and others have followed their lead. According to their account, Marmont was elated by Wellington's aborted attack and was soon convinced that the allies were beginning their retreat. He discounted the danger of an allied attack and worried only that they would succeed in making a clean break and that he would thus be denied the chance to savage their rearguard. Consequently he pushed his left forward prematurely, urging his divisions to advance as soon as they emerged from the wood before they could properly regain their order.[35]

This is a coherent, plausible interpretation of events, and it may well be close to the truth, but it requires us to reject completely Marmont's account, while having little evidence to put in its place. The one piece of testimony which directly supports it appears in the memoirs of Colonel Girard, Clausel's chief of staff. Girard claims that Marmont sent repeated orders to the division urging it to press forward as the allies had begun to retreat. However, Girard is an interested party – he did not want the blame of defeat attached to his division – although less committed than Marmont. Other comparisons are less in his favour: Marmont's memoirs are based on documents written soon after the event; Girard's were composed many years later, and generally lack credibility, being vainglorious and often absurd: he is the hero of every anecdote, and invariably in the right. Girard's account certainly cannot be dismissed out of hand, but it is not compelling evidence in itself.[36] Foy is a far more trustworthy witness, but he was on the other side of the army, near Calvarrasa de Arriba, and could not observe what happened in the centre and left of the army; while the atmosphere in the army after the defeat would not have encouraged dispassionate enquiry. Not that Foy pretends to give a detailed account of events in the centre: he simply and unequivocally blames Marmont for the defeat, and for most historians this has been enough to confirm the presumption of guilt which invariably clings to a defeated general.[37]

Ironically, the one detail which Foy does give counts in Marmont's favour, for he says that the marshal was wounded between 3 and 4 o'clock in the afternoon. This is a little earlier than the contradictory accounts given in other sources would suggest. Marmont himself said 4.15 in his first report, but changed this to about 3 o'clock in his memoirs. Unfortunately, it is impossible to establish the time more precisely, although most accounts place it between 3.30 and 4.15.[38] This tends to support Marmont's account, being soon after Thomières began his disastrous march; but arguments based on the relative time at which events occurred – which would be compelling if the evidence supporting the times was reliable – are worthless when based on such contradictory evidence.

Given this, it seems impossible to declare with confidence whether Marmont's own mistakes were the principal cause of the defeat of his army, or whether this was mainly owing to the errors of his subordinates. In one sense this matters little. Marmont was in command of the army and so must bear the lion's share of the responsibility for defeat – just as he would have gained most of the credit for victory – whatever his personal role. He was also undoubtedly to blame for arranging his army so that the rash Maucune and the junior and relatively inexperienced Thomières were in the lead, although it seems that this was the result of committing Bonnet's division to seizing and holding the Greater Arapile. But the wider case against him is less compelling, more doubtful, than is usually acknowledged.

Whoever was to blame, the overextension of the French left would never have mattered if Wellington had not recognized and used the opportunity it gave him. The story of his sudden vision has been told many times with many variations. Here is his own account as recorded by Charles Greville in 1838:

> He was dining in a farm-yard with his officers, where (he had done dinner) everybody else came and dined as they could. The whole French army was in sight, moving, and the enemy firing upon the farm-yard in which he was dining. 'I got up,' he said, 'and was looking over a wall round the farm-yard, just such a wall as that' (pointing to a low stone wall bounding the covert), 'and I saw the movement of the French left through my glass. "By God," said I, "that will do, and I'll attack them directly." I had moved up the Sixth [sic: Third] Division through Salamanca, which the French were not aware of, and I ordered them to attack, and the whole line to advance. I had got my army so completely in hand that I could do this with ease.'[39]

A few months later Greville collected another version of the story from Fitzroy Somerset, who had been Wellington's military secretary, and perhaps his closest confidant in 1812. This confirms the gist of the Duke's account and adds some pleasing details:

They were going to dine in a farm-yard, but the shot fell so thick there that the mules carrying the dinner were ordered to go to another place. There the Duke dined, walking about the whole time munching, with his field-glass in his hand, and constantly looking through it. On a sudden he exclaimed, 'By G——, they are extending their line; order my horses.' The horses were brought and he was off in an instant, followed only by his old German dragoon, who went with him everywhere. The aides-de-camp followed as quickly as they could. He galloped straight to Pakenham's division and desired him immediately to begin the attack.[40]

It is a delightful anecdote which vividly captures the excitement of the moment, but it is also misleading. It suggests that Wellington made the decision to attack casually, almost impulsively, whereas he had probably been anxiously watching for just such an opportunity ever since he cancelled the earlier attack in the late morning. It implies that it was fortuitous that the army was perfectly placed to exploit the sudden opportunity, whereas Wellington had been gradually shifting his forces to the right all day; he had directed Pakenham's division to Aldea Tejada hours before; and he had carefully used the undulations of the ground to protect his troops both from observation and from the French bombardment. And worst of all, it suggests that the fault in the French deployment was so glaring that every drummer boy in the army must have seen it and understood its significance. But what could Wellington see? He could see Maucune's division deployed on the forward face of the Monte de Azan with a powerful battery in its front. He could see another French division emerging from its rear and pushing westwards along the skyline. And he knew that Bonnet's division was strongly posted around the Greater Arapile. But he did not know that Marmont had been, or was about to be, wounded. He could not see that Clausel's division had only just begun its belated advance to fill the gap between Maucune and the Greater Arapile. Above all, he could not see whether there was another division, or another two divisions in Maucune's rear. *We* know that the French left was unsupported, that Taupin was still at El Sierro and Sarrut behind Foy and Ferey on the right, but it seems most unlikely that Wellington would know this when he decided to attack. He judged that the French left was overextended and vulnerable, and he was correct; but it was not as simple, as easy or as obvious as that charming anecdote makes it appear. Twenty years of intelligent soldiering and careful observation lay behind the decision to cancel the attack in the middle of the day and to launch this new attack four hours later.

Once Wellington decided to attack, his plan was simple, but only because his troops were already in position. Another general might have committed the army to retreat hours earlier, or been so mentally committed himself that he would have seen in Thomières's move only a threat to his lines of communication, not an opportunity to attack. But Wellington had his army completely in hand, ready for whatever course he might need to take: whether to resist a direct French attack, or withdraw in the evening, or suddenly assume the offensive. Pakenham's division, supported by D'Urban's Portuguese dragoons and Arentschildt's two regiments of light cavalry, could advance largely under cover from its sheltered station near Aldea Tejada to the western end of the Monte de Azan, and then push along the plateau driving the French before it. At the same time that Pakenham turned their flank, Thomières and Maucune would be attacked in front by the British cavalry of Le Marchant and Anson, and by the infantry of Leith's division, supported by Bradford's Portuguese brigade, Carlos de España's Spaniards and the Seventh Division. Cole's Fourth Division would advance in the centre, supported by the Sixth Division, while Pack's Portuguese brigade could threaten or, if an opportunity offered, actually make a serious attack on the Greater Arapile. The First Division would remain in reserve behind the Lesser Arapile, while on the left the Light Division and Bock's dragoons would quietly contain Foy and the French right wing. The armies were so close that, if all went well, the French left would be destroyed before its reserves could be brought up and so the army could be defeated piecemeal. It was an excellent plan, but it remained to be seen how it would work in practice and, above all, how the allied army would perform in its unaccustomed role as the aggressor.

Commentary

It is worth drawing attention to the fact that 22 July 1812 was indeed a Wednesday, as a surprising number of the less good secondary sources make it a Sunday, apparently for no better reason than the belief that all Wellington's great victories were preceded by a thunderstorm and fought on the sabbath.[41]

On the evening of the 21st Wellington learnt that General Chauvel with a brigade of cavalry from the Army of the North had arrived at Pollos. Oman puts this force at fewer than 800 cavalry plus a battery of artillery, while Sarramon makes it 900 cavalry and eight guns, which, including the artillerymen, would make a total force of rather more than 1,000 men. This seems much more plausible than Fortescue's 1,700 cavalry with 20 guns, which probably reflects Caffarelli's promise rather than his performance.[42]

There is a vivid picture of the state of Salamanca on the day before the battle in the manuscript narrative by Andrew Leith Hay which differs significantly from his published account:

I went into Salamanca[,] which town appeared in a very different light from what it did when the Army left it to advance. Many people had shut their shops and

fled, and the Countenances of those that remained bespoke terror and conster-
nation – they asked questions which could not be satisfactorily answered as to the
movements of the Army, and any assurances of their safety from the French
were received with distrust. They seemed to think we were going to leave them
to their fate, and a wretched prospect these thoughts laid open to the unfortunate people of Salamanca – but this gloom was but the forerunner of a brilliant
day.[43]

No wonder Charles Boutflower reflected that 'Events may yet turn out well, but
at present I fear we have gained but little popularity by our irruption into the
North of Spain.'[44]

The city of Salamanca stands on high ground on the north bank of the
Tormes, 803 metres above sea level according to the Spanish equivalent of the
Ordnance Survey Map. The ford at Santa Marta a little upstream is 781
metres, which gives a better idea of the level of the river. Alba de Tormes,
some miles further upstream, is 836 metres. On the battlefield itself, the village
of Arapiles is 841 metres; the hill behind it, the Teso de San Miguel, rises to
864 metres, while the Lesser Arapile is 901 metres, and the Greater Arapile 906
metres. Thus, the summit of the Greater Arapile is some 200 feet higher than
the village, which is about a mile distant. The ground further west is generally
rather lower: the village of Las Torres to the rear of the allied position is 820
metres; Aldea Tejada where the Third Division and D'Urban waited is 795
metres; and the hamlet of Miranda de Azan beyond the western end of Monte
de Azan is 824 metres. The highest point of Monte de Azan is 877 metres.[45]

Of the well-known maps of the battlefield, the one which appears the most
detailed and authoritative is that in Fortescue's *History of the British Army*. It
covers the whole area from Salamanca to Alba de Tormes, including Huerta,
where the river turns sharply west, and it shows the rise and fall of the land with
contour lines marking every ten-foot change in elevation. This is a little disconcerting at first, for it makes the country appear more rugged than is the case,
but it promises a degree of precision and accuracy lacking in other maps.
However, a close comparison between it and the modern Spanish ordnance
map reveals significant differences in the distance between points. Both maps
are on a scale of 1:50,000.

	ordnance map	*Fortescue*	
Salamanca bridge to Los Arapiles	140mm (7.0 km)	137mm (6.85 km)	97.9%
Santa Marta to Los Arapiles	126mm (6.3 km)	120mm (6.0 km)	95.2%
Aldea Tejada to Calvarrasa de Arriba	174mm (8.7 km)	157mm (7.85 km)	90.2%
Las Torres to Calvarrasa de Ariba	103mm (5.15 km)	88mm (4.4 km)	85.4%
Las Torres to Los Arapiles	36mm (1.8 km)	29mm (1.45 km)	80.6%
Greater Arapile to Los Arapiles	35mm (1.75 km)	37mm (1.85 km)	105.7%
Greater Arapile to Lesser Arapile	17mm (850 m)	19mm (950 m)	111.8%

There are also a number of other discrepancies, of which the most important is

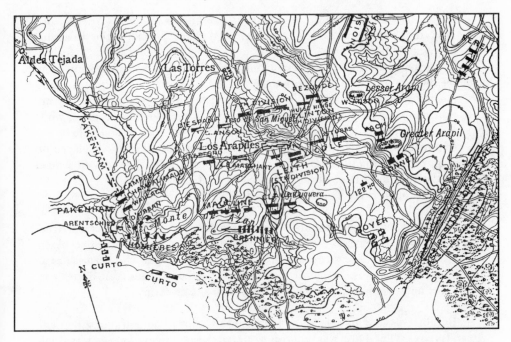

Detail from Fortescue's map of the battle, reduced by approximately twenty per cent.
The whole original is much larger (330 × 350mm) and is coloured brown, green, blue
and red making it much clearer. It is both attractive and impressive, but close
examination casts doubt on its accuracy.

that Fortescue's map shows the Teso de San Miguel lying immediately behind
the village, while the ordnance map (confirmed by personal observation) places
its highest point further east, filling part of the gap between the village and the
Lesser Arapile. Nor do the gradient lines always appear accurate when compared to the terrain on the spot.

Of the other maps of the battlefield, Oman's appears surprisingly accurate,
with no significant difference from the ordnance map in the distances tested
above, while Sarramon's is also generally reliable, although in neither case is the
depiction of the hills entirely convincing. The grandest and most elaborate map
is that specially surveyed by Sir Thomas Mitchell in 1815 and published in
1841 in *Maps and Plans Showing the Principal Movements, Battles and Sieges in
which the British Army Was Engaged during the War from 1808 to 1814 in the
Spanish Peninsula and the South of France* (commonly known, after its publisher, as Wyld's *Atlas*). This large elephant folio is a tour de force of surveying
and engraving and still provides the most accurate depiction of the terrain
of the battlefield; however, it is extremely rare and rightly much prized
by collectors. Two beautiful large maps accompany Marindin's 1906 *The
Salamanca Campaign* (a handsomely produced book whose text is almost
worthless), and there is a fascinating but not entirely accurate map in Arteche's

Guerra de la Independencia – historia Militar de España de 1808 a 1814 (14 vols, 1868–1901, reprinted *c.* 2000), which may have provided the basis for Fortescue's map.

The maps drawn for the present study naturally take their fixed points from the modern ordnance map, with details of the terrain also taken from it where possible, supplemented by Wyld, Oman and personal observation. They are provided as a visual guide and cannot pretend to be absolutely accurate, while the troop locations marked on them are often highly conjectural. There is a common, largely unconscious inclination to accord information displayed on maps greater authority than to that given in the text, but in the end both depend on the same uncertain, partial and often contradictory sources.[46]

In his published *Narrative* Andrew Leith Hay writes:

> The day was fine; the sun shone bright, nor was there any atmospheric obstruction to prevent a clear view of passing events; no haze withheld a distinct observation to the very extremity of the plains upon which the enemy was in movement. Occasional smoke from the firing, and dust, alone created a temporary uncertainty in the view of any movement of either army.[47]

But this was early in the day, and in his manuscript account of the battle Leith Hay says, 'The Dust was so great as to cover the Troops, and appeared one immense moving mass of smoke. The ground was so dry that the instant we began to move it flew up in all directions.'[48] Given the fury of the storm of the previous night, it is surprising to read that the ground was dry, but many other accounts also mention the dust: presumably the hot July sun dried out the ground during the morning and early afternoon. Perhaps also the ground near the Arapiles – village and hills – received less rain than that near the river where most of the allied army camped overnight. Most troops, whether closely engaged or not, could see little of the battle, and only experienced and – usually – mounted officers could hope to form any clear idea of the progress of the day as a whole. One British Guards officer, John Mills, wrote home to his mother:

> I saw our line advance, and occasionally could see through the smoke the contests in the different places, but there was so much noise and such confusion that it was quite impossible to make anything clearly out. I had not the most distant conception but that it was a small body on both sides fighting hard for some ground that both wanted.[49]

In Oman's account of the skirmishing around Nuestra Señora de la Peña, he identifies the Portuguese light infantry involved in the fighting as the 2nd Caçadores from the Seventh Division (and I followed him when discussing the incident in my *Tactics and the Experience of Battle in the Age of Napoleon*). However, Sarramon points out that Wellington in his official dispatch,

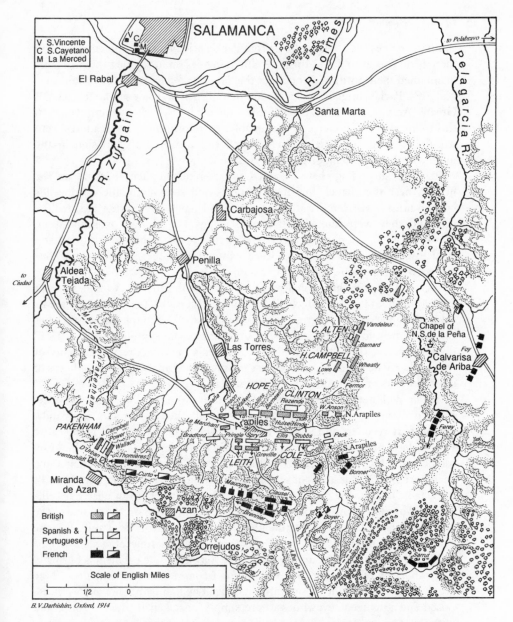

Oman's map of the opening stage of the battle. The original is rather larger (230 × 185mm) and is printed in brown, red and green. Many of the troop locations and some details of the terrain are open to dispute, but it is much more accurate than Fortescue's map.

explicitly names the 4th Caçadores from Pack's brigade as the unit engaged, and there is no reason to doubt this.[50] Wellington goes on to say that the caçadores maintained their position throughout the day. If taken literally, this would suggest that Pack's brigade was without them when it made its attack on the Greater Arapile, but this is directly contradicted by Synge's account, which on this point must be preferred. Presumably, therefore, the 4th Caçadores were withdrawn when the Light Division relieved the Seventh Division in the middle of the afternoon, or possibly even sooner.[51]

It seems surprising that the allied troops retained their foothold on the heights near the chapel, for their supports and reserves in the open valley beyond must have been dreadfully exposed to French observation and artillery fire, and they were almost half a mile in advance of their main position. However, Wellington's statement is explicit and is supported by first-hand British accounts (such as Private Green's quoted in the text), while it is not contradicted by Marmont, Foy or Sarramon.[52]

Victor Alten's rashness in leaving Salamanca despite his wound was not entirely without harmful effects. When James McGrigor, the chief of the medical staff, reported the progress of the wounded to Wellington a few days after the battle, he told him that Alten 'has some unpleasant symptoms but ... I still do not conceive [him] to be in danger'.[53] Alten's rapid recovery is evidence of the good care he received, and is one example among many of the toughness of senior officers on both sides in the Peninsula.

When Wellington discouraged J. W. Croker from writing a history of the Battle of Waterloo, he compared a battle to a ball, then continued: 'Some individuals may recollect all the little events of which the great result is the battle won or lost; but no individual can recollect the order in which, or the exact moment at which, they occurred, which makes all the difference to their value or importance.'[54] Questions of sequence and timing are indeed among the most intractable in studying any Napoleonic battle. Salamanca is not nearly as difficult as Waterloo in this respect and, once the fighting begins, the course of the action is mostly fairly clear, although a few points remain debatable. But the events of the morning and early afternoon, and the time at which actions occurred, remain difficult or impossible to determine. The problem is normally not a shortage of evidence, but a plethora of contradictory statements. There are two explanations for these contradictions. The first is that honest, well-disposed and intelligent eyewitnesses are simply mistaken in their recollection; with the stress and anxiety of battle, time passes unexpectedly quickly or slowly and, with all the other impressions made by the sights and sounds of combat, the time at which events happened does not stick fast in the memory. The second is more prosaic but no less important: there was no radio broadcast of Big Ben striking the hour against which officers could set their watches, and there seems to have been no habit of synchronizing watches or giving orders which depended on the time (except, perhaps, in sieges). In all probability our witnesses could not have agreed on the time within an hour had they met on the battlefield with no other purpose than to discuss this very point. For these reasons all the times which can be given in this or any other Napoleonic battle should be regarded as no more than rough approximations, and histories which divide the day into precise segments, or which pin arguments on fine matters of timing, should be regarded with lively scepticism.

The following collection of times gives some idea of the range and variation, but also of the probable sequence of events on the morning and early afternoon of 22 July:

The skirmishing began at 6 am according to John Mills; 7 am according to John Aitchison.[55]

The French seized the Greater Arapile at around 8 am is Sarramon's plausible estimate, but Lemonnier-Delafosse, in his memoirs, puts it at about 3 pm – one of the easier statements to disregard.[56]

Marmont climbs the Greater Arapile: soon after 8 am in Sarramon's view, but Oman thinks it was not until about 11 am.[57]

The aborted allied attack: Marmont and John Mills both put this at 11 am, and Aitchison rather supports them by saying that it had been cancelled and the troops had resumed their positions by noon. But the normally reliable Tomkinson says that it occurred at about noon and his word convinces Oman – this also receives some slight support from a statement in Ellesmere's *Personal Reminiscences of the Duke of Wellington*.[58]

The French advance onto the Monte de Azan: at 1 pm according to Burgoyne, about 2 pm according to Wellington's dispatch, although Marmont says he only issued the orders about 2.[59]

The French bombardment begins: Leith Hay and Mills agree that this was about 3 pm.[60]

Wellington decides to attack: Sarramon puts this as early as 2.30 pm, Napier makes it soon after 3 pm, Andrew Leith Hay, in an unpublished letter, favours 3.30 pm; but in his manuscript narrative Leith Hay says about 4 pm, while John Mills puts it as late as 5 pm.[61]

Wellington personally gives his orders to Pakenham to attack: at about 2 pm according to Brigade-Major Campbell, at 3 pm according to Pakenham himself (although in another letter he says that this was when his attack began); 3 pm or a little later is also favoured by Sarramon and Moggridge, but Oman makes it around 3.45 and D'Urban puts it after 4.30.[62]

Many more examples could be given, while the most important time of all – when Marmont was wounded – has already been discussed (but see also below, pp. 79–80).

The uncertainty on questions of time, and gaps in other evidence, make it impossible to reconstruct fully the movements of each army on the morning and early afternoon of the 22nd; nonetheless, plausible solutions to some problems can be advanced. The movement of the Third Division across the Tormes has caused some difficulty, with Fortescue making it ford the river at Cabrerizos, while Oman has it cross by the town bridge of Salamanca. Each cites supporting evidence for his view, suggesting that neither is completely wrong. Young and Lawford put forward the obvious compromise, although it is not clear whether there is any basis for their suggestion that another part of the division used the ford at Santa Marta, or for their idea that Pakenham thus divided his division in three on his own initiative. Two sources – Brigade-Major Campbell and Brigadier D'Urban – say that their units crossed the river about noon, which makes it seem likely that they reached Aldea Tejada about 2 o'clock, as both Oman and Young and Lawford suggest.[63]

When Victor Alten's brigade of light cavalry, now under the command of Lieutenant-Colonel Arentschildt, was moved to the right wing of the army, part of the 14th Light Dragoons remained on the left. Beamish states that this detachment amounted to two squadrons, but Wellington's dispatch clearly states that two squadrons under Lieutenant-Colonel Hervey were on the right, implying that only one had been detached. Rather oddly, Arentschildt makes no mention of the detachment in his report to Cotton (although his account implies that a substantial force of the 14th was with him), while Wellington makes none of Arentschildt or the 1st KGL Hussars – possibly Cotton's wound prevented Arentschildt's report reaching Wellington before he wrote his dispatch. There is also great uncertainty concerning aspects of Arentschildt's subsequent skirmishing with Curto's cavalry: where it occurred, when it began, how long it lasted and how it related to other manoeuvres are all quite unclear.[64]

Bonnet's occupation of the Greater Arapile poses slightly different problems. All accounts agree that the hill itself was held by the 120th Ligne, but it is not clear whether all three battalions deployed on the summit, or some of the men remained on the reverse slope. The number of guns dragged to the summit of the hill is also uncertain. Sarramon states that twenty guns were so deployed, but this appears to be based on a misreading of a passage in Marmont's memoirs which actually refers to the establishment of a battery on the ridge of El Sierro well to the rear.[65] Dyneley claims that the French had only four guns on the Greater Arapile and that his own fire silenced them. This may be mere boasting, but the 3/27th, which shared the Lesser Arapile with him and which would have been the most obvious target for French guns opposite, lost only eight casualties all day, and Major Macdonald, Dyneley's commanding officer, later cited this as an occasion on which shrapnel proved its efficacy. Captain Wachholtz, commanding the company of Brunswick Oels light infantry attached to the Fourth Division not far from the Greater Arapile, saw few men on its summit, and states that the French had brought up only a few light cannon, although his view was probably obstructed by the rocky outcrop at the western end of the ridge. Finally, Captain Synge in describing Pack's abortive attack mentions French artillery, but not in a way that suggests he was attacking a large battery. So on the whole it seems likely that the French battery on the Greater Arapile was less powerful than has been commonly thought, even if it was not as insignificant as Dyneley claims.[66]

The letter quoted on page 58, describing Wellington's proposed then cancelled attack on the Greater Arapile, comes from the National Archives of Scotland. It is not an original, but a contemporary copy, presumably made by Colonel Taylor, the recipient, to send to friends in Scotland – it is among the Hope of Luffness Papers. The heading states that it was written by Henry Clinton, commander of the Sixth Division, although the copy has only the initials 'H. C.' in place of a signature, and internal evidence, including the passage quoted in the narrative, strongly points to its having been written by Henry Campbell. The full text is printed as Appendix IV with a discussion of the reasons for attributing it to Campbell.

Even without this letter there is abundant evidence that the First Division was destined to take a prominent part in the proposed attack. John Aitchison wrote in his diary: 'the 1st Division were moved up immediately to the village of Arapiles. ... Ld Wellington immediately issued orders for the 1st Division to attack – we moved therefore into the village of Arapiles, but had hardly entered it when the order was countermanded and we returned and formed in columns of regiments to the ground we had previously occupied.' This is confirmed by John Mills, by Tomkinson and by the letters of an officer of the Scots Guards quoted in Maurice's history of the regiment.[67] These sources make it clear that the whole division was deployed on the right of the Fourth Division behind the village of Arapiles, and that it was only later withdrawn behind the Lesser Arapile; but they provide no hint as to why it was withdrawn and replaced by the Fifth Division, and this remains inexplicable.

There are just as many sources for Beresford's role in having the attack cancelled. Marmont heard the story years later and oddly enough gives the fullest account of the incident, but his version is supported by contemporary British comments. Charles Cathcart told Graham 'Marshal Beresford's advice was too much taken and he was against fight'; while Alexander Gordon, one of Wellington's most trusted aides, wrote home: 'I had all along most strongly recommended Lord W. to attack & particularly on that day, but he was afraid of losing men & Marshal Beresford was much against it.' Lieutenant T. H. Browne later wrote that 'Marshall Beresford's opinion was asked & he was against an attack, considering the strength of the enemy's position, that the river was almost upon our rear, & also upon the principle which had hitherto made Ld. Wellington decline acting on the offensive.' And Tomkinson agrees, although he is the only source to suggest that the Light Division was also destined to play a part in the attack.[68]

The subsequent evolution of Wellington's plans is very much harder to trace: there is a confused but suggestive account in Browne's *Journal* (which was written up years later from contemporary notes), but otherwise only fragmentary references.[69] However, it is fairly clear that Wellington did not commit himself either to fighting or retreating, but kept the choice open. Oman's statement that it was at this point that Wellington told De Lancey to draw up a plan of withdrawal is based on a misreading of Vere: this was done early in the day, although it may have been at this time that orders were issued to the commissariat to retreat.[70]

It is difficult to determine when Dyneley was sent to hold the Lesser Arapile to the last man. It might have been in the early morning when the French had just seized the Greater Arapile, and there was some fear that they might attack its companion. This fits Dyneley's words quite well, but Vere clearly says that the hill was initially held by two guns of Sympher's battery which were later withdrawn and replaced by those from Macdonald's troop (including Dyneley). If this is accepted, then the most likely time for Dyneley to receive his orders was the middle of the day when a French attack again appeared possible. However, Beamish, the obvious source for any point involving the King's German Legion, does not confirm Vere's account; while Young and Lawford say that Wellington gave similar orders to Colonel Maclean of the 3/27th ('You must defend this position so long as you have a man') when his regiment first occupied the hill. Nonetheless, Vere's direct testimony probably carries more weight than the rather tangential evidence which runs contrary to it.[71]

The effect of the French bombardment is discussed further in chapter five. In his official dispatch Wellington described it as 'a very heavy cannonade, which, however, did us but very little damage'. But on the same day he privately told Bathurst, 'I should wish also to be able to equip some more artillery, and of a larger calibre; as it is not agreeable to be cannonaded for hours together, and not to be able to answer even with one gun.'[72] This is an extraordinary statement, almost equal to Wellington's notorious criticism of the British artillery at Waterloo, although it has attracted none of the controversy which surrounds the later letter. Its literal truth is readily disproved by Marmont's wound; but it is not clear whether it has any more general truth. Was the British artillery in the centre and right of the army overwhelmed by the French fire and unable to respond effectively, at least until the allies began their advance? We simply do not know. There were three allied batteries in the area: Macdonald's on the Lesser Arapile, which Dyneley assures us kept firing and had the better of the French guns opposite; Sympher's KGL battery on the hill behind Los Arapiles, which Wachholtz says was important in the defence of the village; and Lawson's battery with the Fifth Division, of which little is known.[73] Of these, Macdonald and Lawson were both equipped with 6-pounders, Sympher with 9-pounders. None of them suffered heavy casualties, for the total losses of all the Anglo-Portuguese artillery in the battle was only four men killed and eleven men wounded. It is also possible that these batteries were supported by Bull's horse artillery attached to the cavalry, Douglas's battery from the Third Division, or the Spanish battery, although there is no evidence that any of these units were engaged at this point. Andrew Leith Hay describes an incident in which Lawson's battery was overwhelmed by French fire and forced to withdraw, but a careful reading of his account makes it clear that this occurred while the Fifth Division was still on the left.[74]

The issue of Marmont's responsibility for the overextension of the French left wing, and hence the defeat of the whole army, has been discussed in the main narrative at some length, but there are a few additional points which ought to be made here. It is sometimes argued, among others by Oman, that if Marmont had really objected to the advance of Maucune and Thomières, he had only to send an ADC with orders and it would quickly have been halted.[75] This would be a compelling argument if Maucune, having climbed onto the Monte de Azan, had advanced along it without halting or interference from Marmont until he reached the far end: but no one suggests that this is what happened. Rather, Maucune advanced against the village, but then halted and perhaps withdrew a little, either of his own volition or in obedience to orders. This was further than Marmont claims that he wished him to advance, but it was not in itself fatal. The true disaster for the French came when Thomières, instead of halting in support of Maucune, continued to advance along the plateau beyond Maucune's position. Marmont saw the error, issued orders to Taupin to bring his division forward as soon as possible, and was in the act of setting out to halt Thomières's advance in person, and to make the best of the situation he found, when he was wounded. There is no need to believe that he recognized the full extent of the danger – that may be being wise after the event – but equally there is no inherent implausibility in his setting off to take command of the left in person: at about the same time Wellington was riding to give Pakenham his orders in person, and it was natural for Marmont to go to the Monte de Azan both to assist Thomières, who was only a brigadier, and to ensure that the headstrong Maucune obeyed orders.

This reconstruction of events is far from certain, but it fits the evidence as well, and is at least as plausible, as the alternative. The other interpretation, best expressed by Oman, but common to most historians of the battle, including Sarramon, is that Marmont became convinced that Wellington had already begun to retreat, and was afraid that the allies would break cleanly away. He therefore pushed Maucune, Thomières and Curto forward as quickly as possible in order to molest and detain the allied rearguard and only realized his mistake, if at all, when it was far too late to correct it. This is quite possible, and Girard's evidence, for what it is worth, tends to support it. But there is no explanation as to why Marmont should have believed that the bulk of the allied army had already begun its retreat, other than vague references to the dust kicked up by Pakenham and D'Urban, and the sight of the allied heavy baggage retreating many hours before. Nor do any of Marmont's other actions suggest that he thought he was only facing a rearguard. The orders given just before he was wounded indicate caution and anxiety, not overconfidence: Taupin was to hurry forward to support the left (we have Castel's word as well as Marmont's for this),[76] while Ferey and Sarrut were to move to the centre. But if Marmont had really believed that he was only facing a rearguard, surely he would have ordered Foy to engage the troops facing him rather than let them escape unhindered?

Marmont's responsibility would be much clearer if we could determine when

he was wounded, but it is impossible to fix the time, or even when it was relative to the allied attack. Some early secondary sources, including Napier, have
him wounded after the battle has begun, when Leith and Cole start their
advance, and Fortescue is inclined to follow them. But Oman and Sarramon,
both of whom are, on the whole, highly critical of Marmont, reject this as being
much too late, and put the wound clearly before Pakenham begins his advance,
and there is little reason to question their judgment on this point.[77]

Almost all authorities have accepted without question Marmont's statement
that he was wounded as he was on the point of setting off to ride to join his left
wing. However, Napier does mention an alternative possibility: that Marmont
was 'at dinner and in the act of holding his plate' when he was struck. This is
evidently based on the testimony of Mercier, an engineer officer attached to
Bonnet's division. If this story could be confirmed, it would seriously damage
Marmont's credibility, but the only other sources which are relevant – Castel
and Parquin – tend rather to contradict it, although they are not conclusive.[78]

One other possibility should at least be mentioned: Marmont may have been
wounded *earlier* than most accounts suggest, while Maucune's men were still
attacking the village. This would explain why he blamed Maucune, not
Thomières, for the defeat, and his apparent belief that the attack on the village
brought on the battle. It is also easy to imagine that the confusion in the command following his wounding was responsible for Thomières's march, or at
least for the failure to halt it. Of course, this is a very convenient theory for
Marmont, as it exonerates him from most of the blame for the defeat, but that
does not make it untrue. On the whole, the balance of evidence is against this
argument, but cannot be completely discounted.

There is a disconcerting oddity in Marmont's *Mémoires*: he implies that
Bonnet was his second-in-command, and makes this explicit in a letter to King
Joseph of 25 July 1812. Oman, and most other historians, naturally follow this,
presuming – reasonably enough – that Marmont could hardly be mistaken on
such a point. It was left to Young and Lawford in 1973 to point out that Clausel
had been promoted to general of division eight months before Bonnet (18
December 1802 and 27 August 1803 respectively). Sarramon has no doubt that
Clausel was in fact second-in-command of the army, and suggests that Bonnet
may have acted in the interim before himself being wounded: it may have taken
some time to locate Clausel if he had gone to the rear to have his wounded heel
dressed. This is as good a reconstruction of events as the evidence will permit,
but it does not really explain Marmont's strange inaccuracy.[79]

If a simple point like this poses such difficulties, it is not surprising that it is
impossible to reconstruct precisely the movements of the French divisions.
Three problems stand out in particular. How far forward was Maucune's main
body when his skirmishers attacked the village, and did he remain in this position or move south or west when the attack was repulsed? Where did Curto's
light cavalry skirmish with those of Arentschildt, and why did they not play a
more prominent role later in the battle? And where was Clausel's division when

Maucune first moved onto the Monte de Azan, and when Thomières advanced beyond Maucune's position? This last is particularly important, for Marmont's orders appear more or less rash depending on whether Clausel should have been in position to support Maucune and Thomières. Unfortunately, there is little or no evidence to answer any of these questions. We do not even really know where or when Clausel was wounded, or whether he was with his division at the time or had ridden ahead. There is some evidence that his troops came into line surprisingly late, after Cole's advance had begun, but even this is not conclusive. Nor is it difficult to ask other insoluble questions. Where exactly was Taupin's division? Where was Sarrut's? Our whole understanding of the battle, and of these early manoeuvres in particular, is much more fragmentary and uncertain than a confident narrative and attractive maps would suggest.

The story of Wellington's sudden decision to attack has been told in many forms. The grain of sand which grew into the familiar anecdote was current in the army at the time. John Mills wrote in his diary of 22 July: 'At five o'clock Lord Wellington having observed that they had detached a considerable body of troops from their left and had occupied the range of hills said, "Now they have driven me to attack them. They will not let me retreat quietly and we will show them we are not to be bullied."' And soon after the news of the victory reached London, *The Times* published a private letter from the army: 'Now arrived the critical moment which decided the fate of the French army. Lord Wellington found the enemy still continuing to open to his left – their impertinence in cannonading us put him out of all patience; and when an officer arrived with information that the enemy were still further off, going to their left, he said – "Then, by God! we will attack them." '[80]

These early versions contain many of the ingredients of the fully rounded tale and help to confirm that at its heart lies a core of truth. Other papers may have published similar stories, or the tale may simply have circulated among veterans by word of mouth. In any case its next appearance in print seems to have been in *Blackwood's Edinburgh Magazine* in May 1828. This was in what purported to be a letter sent home after the battle by one Captain Spencer Moggridge, but which was in fact an article written for the magazine by a regular contributor, Captain Thomas Hamilton, then at work on his *Annals of the Peninsular Campaigns* (1829). Hamilton was a Peninsular veteran who had been wounded at Albuera, but neither he, nor his regiment (the 29th Foot), had been at Salamanca, so that his account is an early but somewhat dubious – because it appeared under false colours – secondary source.

On this height were several officers, one of whom was seated, while his horse was held by an orderly dragoon, and the others standing round him. I had approached within a few yards of them before I observed that the principal object in the group was Lord Wellington. In a moment my attention was arrested. He was at luncheon, and in the act of adding mustard to a slice of meat which had just been deposited on his plate, when the following colloquy took place.

'The enemy are moving, my lord,' said one of the staff officers to his commander, already busily engaged in the office of mastication.

'Very well,' replied his lordship; 'take the glass, Somerset, and tell me what they seem to be about;' at the same time continuing his meal with every appearance of nonchalance. The officer did so for about a minute.

'I think they are extending their left, my lord.'

'The devil they are!' exclaimed Lord Wellington, springing in an instant to his feet; 'give me the glass quickly.'

He took it, and for a short space continued observing the motions of the enemy. 'Come, I think this will do at last!' he exclaimed. 'Ride off instantly, and tell Clinton and Leith to return as quickly as possible to their former ground.'

In a moment all his staff were in motion, Lord Wellington mounted his horse, and I returned to my regiment.[81]

William Grattan reproduces this version of the story almost word for word in his memoirs, which were first published in the *United Service Journal* in 1834, six years after Hamilton's article appeared. Of course, it is possible that Hamilton and Grattan both drew on a common source, or even that Grattan told Hamilton the story (although nothing in the rest of Hamilton's article supports this idea), but the very close verbal similarities between the two tales cast a cloud over Grattan's credibility.

In subsequent years many other versions of the anecdote were recorded. In 1831 J. W. Croker wrote in his diary that Alava told the tale at breakfast in front of Wellington, who listened quietly without the least contradiction. This time the food was 'a bit of bread and the leg of a cold roast fowl' which is unceremoniously tossed away (to Alava's horror) when Wellington himself saw that the French advance had reached a point he had previously determined. Then come the two conversations preserved by Greville and quoted in the main narrative, and several less interesting versions. In the winter of 1851–2 James Thornton, who had been Wellington's cook during the war, was interviewed by Lord Frederick Fitzclarence, then his employer. He recalled that on the day of the battle he had brought provisions to the Duke near the village of Los Arapiles, 'I think about 1 or 2 o'clock in the day.' The food was immediately ordered to the rear (this supports Fitzroy Somerset's account), where Wellington and the staff soon joined them in a farmyard 'and took some refreshment' – neither cold meat nor chicken is specified. Wellington remained less than half an hour, but Thornton makes no mention of staff officers arriving with news, or Wellington leaving at a gallop, let alone the food being thrown away.[82]

There are many other versions, with biographers and historians often introducing variations of their own either inadvertently or to make their narratives flow more smoothly. Some have Wellington on the Lesser Arapile, some behind the village; Napier has him taking a siesta! Others make him remark, 'Mon cher Alava, Marmont est perdu!', or combine incidents from several different versions into a composite, ignoring the inconsistencies which result.

Young and Lawford worry that 'there was no conceivable viewpoint from which Wellington could both eat his lunch and see the French', but the story is too entertaining and too well attested for such quibbles to carry much conviction. Of course, we will never know exactly what happened, let alone the precise words Wellington used. Such anecdotes always lie in the debatable borderland between verifiable fact and the reconstructions of memory; they contain a grain of truth, but soon collapse if an elaborate superstructure of interpretation is built on top of them.[83]

Nonetheless, there is one important question relating to this story which does need to be considered here and, as it also involves a matter of time, the problems are compounded. Some historians, including Fortescue and Young and Lawford, put the 'luncheon' incident quite early in the afternoon, not long after the French first make their appearance on the Monte de Azan. According to this view, Wellington then gave orders for the Fifth Division to move from its position north of the Lesser Arapile to extend Cole's line beyond the village, and that it was not until this was done, almost two hours later, that the orders for the attack were issued. This sequence of events is supported by a literal interpretation of Wellington's dispatch, but creates serious difficulties. It makes a nonsense of Fitzroy Somerset's story, where Wellington sees the French error and immediately rides to Pakenham with orders to attack; while it less directly runs contrary to all the versions of the story which suggest that the resolution to attack was suddenly made and promptly executed. Further, it is hard to see what reason Wellington would have had to attack if all he could see was the leading elements of one French division advance onto the near end of the Monte de Azan. For the story to make sense the French must have overextended their left wing. It may be argued that this happened when Maucune continued his march until he was opposite the village; but the story is much more plausible if it is placed later, when Thomières's division began to advance beyond Maucune's position. This is Oman's view, and it supports his suggestion that Wellington decided to attack at about the same moment that Marmont was wounded.[84]

Chapter Four
Pakenham and Thomières

As soon as Wellington had decided to attack, he set off at a gallop to the far right of his army to instruct D'Urban and Pakenham on their part in the coming battle. By doing this in person he minimized the risk of confusion or misunderstandings – he could point out exactly where he wanted the allied troops to go, and answer any doubts or hesitation. D'Urban noted in his journal that 'Lord Wellington came down from the neighbourhood where he had been examining the Enemy's left, at a rapid gallop accompanied only by Col. Delancey (but followed immediately afterward by Col. Sturgeon) and gave us orders for the attack verbally, – first to me (whom he had first met with) and then to General Pakenham.'[1]

Various anecdotes surround Wellington's meeting with Pakenham. According to Grattan, who always tells a good tale, if not always a reliable one, Wellington's 'words were few, and his orders brief. Tapping Pakenham on the shoulder, he said, "Edward, move on with the third division – take the hills in your front, – and drive everything before you." "I will, my Lord, by G—d!" was the laconic reply of the gallant Sir Edward.' Years later Fitzroy Somerset told Greville that Wellington had 'galloped straight to Pakenham's division and desired him immediately to begin the attack. Pakenham said, "Give me your hand, and it shall be done." The Duke very gravely gave him his hand, Pakenham shook it warmly and then hastened off.' Writing to his brother a few days after the battle, Pakenham himself gives a much more prosaic account of the episode: 'At Three in the afternoon the 3rd Division received instructions to move in double column across the Enemy's Left, which was advantageously placed upon some strong heights, there to form line, carry the heights and sweep everything before it.'[2] This preserves the gist of Wellington's orders: Pakenham would seize the Pico de Miranda, the height at the end of the Monte de Azan, thus turning the French flank, and then advance along the plateau, driving Thomières's division before him. D'Urban's two regiments of Portuguese dragoons,[3] supported by the 1st Hussars of the King's German Legion and the 14th Light Dragoons, under Arentschildt, would support the outer flank of the infantry, protecting them from Curto's cavalry. As Pakenham's men pushed along the Monte de Azan, Leith's Fifth Division and Le Marchant's heavy cavalry would attack the French in front, catching them between two fires.

Pakenham quickly issued his orders. The heavy iron camp kettles in which the soldiers were cooking their meal were overturned and packed onto baggage mules to be sent to the rear, while the men cursed the slow-burning stubble which had been the only fuel they could find for their fires. The infantry regiments uncased their colours, checked the priming of their muskets and fixed bayonets. Colonel Wallace addressed the officers of the 88th, his own regiment and the largest in the leading brigade: 'Gentlemen, the regiment is on this day, as it generally is on such occasions, tolerably strong, and (pointing to batteries which crowned the hill in front) we are likely to have a good deal of noise about our ears. I would recommend you to place yourselves in the centre and front of your companies, which will prevent any mistake.'[4]

Within a few minutes the division was under arms and moved off in several open columns. Captain James Campbell recalls:

> To me, as Brigade-Major of the right brigade, Sir Edward Pakenham, in his quick decided manner, pointed out the direction we were to take, and desired me to tell Colonel Wallace, 88th regiment, the officer in temporary command of the brigade, to move on with as much rapidity as possible, but without blowing the men too much. We soon descended into a kind of valley, or rather hollow, and having brought up our left shoulders a little, we pushed on at a quick pace, but in excellent order, to the right; the side of the hollow towards the enemy concealing our movements from their sight.[5]

Campbell gives one of the few detailed accounts of the advance of Pakenham's division; otherwise we must rely on scraps of information and chance references which are often hard to reconcile – our understanding of what happened in this part of the battle is much less certain than many secondary accounts imply. Matters are not helped by Campbell's reference to Wallace's brigade as 'the right brigade', when other evidence makes it fairly clear that it formed on the left of the division. Campbell's expression may be careless, or he may use it because Wallace's brigade was the senior, leading brigade in the division, which means that it would traditionally, although not on this occasion, have formed on the right of the line, in the place of honour.

From Campbell's account it appears that Wallace's brigade advanced in a long, narrow, open column, with a frontage of a single company, and a considerable gap between each company, so that the whole could wheel into a line facing at right angles at a moment's notice. The second brigade marched parallel to the first to its right (west): if both brigades wheeled to face left, the second would automatically be in a position to support Wallace. The Portuguese brigade either followed the British infantry or formed a third column.

D'Urban's and Arentschildt's cavalry were formed on the outer, or right-hand, flank of the infantry; if the infantry wheeled left, the cavalry could use their superior mobility to continue to protect this flank. The inner flank, to the left of Wallace's advancing men, was covered by a cloud of skirmishers, composed of the light companies of the British regiments, the three companies of the 5/60th attached to the division and the battalion of caçadores from the Portuguese brigade. On this side also were Douglas's battery of 9-pounder foot artillery, and apparently also Bull's troop of 6-pounder horse artillery.

The direction of the allied line of advance is also uncertain. Many maps of the battle show Pakenham advancing from Aldea Tejada in a graceful semi-circle, so that he approaches the Pico de Miranda directly from the west. But this is not supported by the – admittedly thin – first-hand accounts of the advance, while it makes nonsense of the formation described by Campbell. If the infantry approached the hill in this way, the troops in the rear would need to march the full length of the column before they could take their place in the line forming on its head, which would delay the advance and expose them for longer to enemy fire. If this had been the chosen route, it would have been more natural for the regiments of the first brigade to march next to each other in a line of battalion columns, with those of the second brigade following behind – a formation which would make deployment relatively quick and easy. If Pakenham's formation was to make sense he should not march directly towards the Pico de Miranda, but rather march south until he was level with it but further west. A simple left wheel would then bring his whole division into line facing east, ready to climb the hillside and advance along the Monte de Azan. This suggests that Pakenham left Aldea Tejada heading south-east, following a little country by-road which still exists today. After about a mile and a half he could then turn due south towards Miranda de Azan. This route has the great advantage of being screened from French observation for most of its length by the low ridge which extends to the north from just west of the Pico de Miranda.[6]

Further problems are posed by the nature of the ground at the Pico de Miranda. This western end of the Monte de Azan does not rise from a broad plain, but is closely confined by steep hills to the north and west and the village of Miranda de Azan to the south. It is difficult to see how Wallace's brigade, let alone Pakenham's whole division and its supporting cavalry, could deploy in such a limited space. Moreover, the Pico de Miranda itself is so narrow – only fifty yards across its flat summit – that the British line would have extended down its steep slopes and onto the ground beyond, while it would be difficult for the French to bring their full force to oppose them. First-hand accounts of the advance and subsequent fighting provide no solution for these difficulties, which remain intractable. Unsatisfactory though it may be, one can only note them and pass on.

Given this, it is not surprising that it is impossible to reconstruct the French movements convincingly. All we really know is that British accounts say that

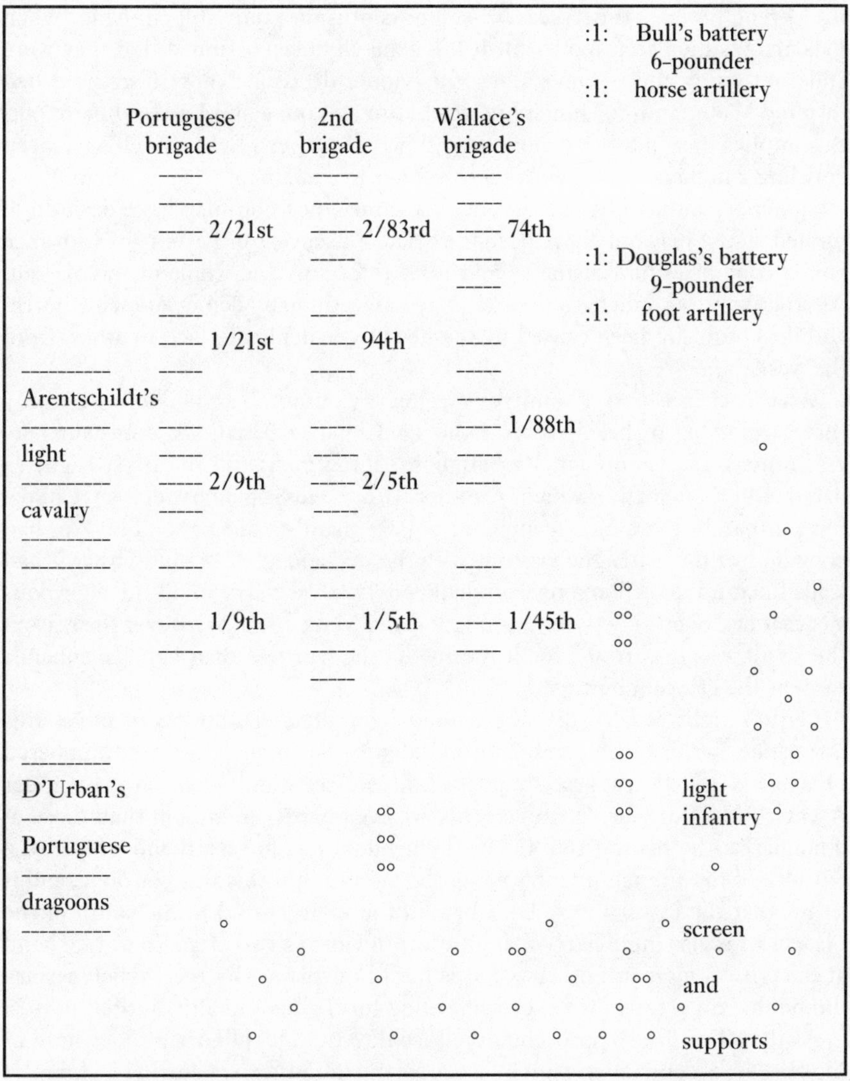

Portuguese   2nd   Wallace's
brigade   brigade   brigade

:1:   Bull's battery
          6-pounder
:1:   horse artillery

----- 2/21st   ----- 2/83rd   ----- 74th

:1: Douglas's battery
        9-pounder
:1:   foot artillery

----- 1/21st   ----- 94th

Arentschildt's

----- 1/88th

light

----- 2/9th   ----- 2/5th

cavalry

----- 1/9th   ----- 1/5th   ----- 1/45th

D'Urban's

Portuguese

dragoons

light infantry

screen

and

supports

Possible formation of Pakenham's division in its advance (heading towards
the bottom of the page). (Not to scale, and there would have been more
lateral space between the columns than is shown here.)

the French were flustered, in some confusion and still moving when Pakenham's men attacked them. It has generally been assumed that they were still continuing the advance along the Monte de Azan whose beginning had inspired Wellington to launch his attack. But as Young and Lawford point out, this implies that they were moving so slowly that they might as well have been crawling on their hands and knees.[7] Two explanations suggest themselves. Thomières's initial advance beyond Maucune's position may have been quite limited, and it may only have been the belated discovery of Pakenham's advance which convinced him of the urgent need to occupy the whole of the plateau. Alternatively, Thomières's division may have originally deployed facing north, and the confusion been caused by the need to re-deploy to face an attack from the west.

What is clear is that Thomières was heavily outnumbered. There were only three regiments in his division – the 1st Ligne (3 battalions, approximately 1,700 men), the 62nd Ligne (2 battalions, 1,100 men) and the 101st Ligne (3 battalions, 1,400 men) – which, together with the divisional battery, gave him a force of barely 4,500 men, compared to Pakenham's 5,800 or so. This was bad enough, but the 1st Ligne was not with the division at this point: either it had trailed behind, or Thomières had deliberately left it to try to fill the enormous gap that had opened between his division and Maucune's. Whatever the reason, the result was disastrous, for it meant that he had less than half Pakenham's force at the critical point.

Curto's light cavalry division should have done something to offset this imbalance, for his seventeen squadrons (about 1,800 men) heavily outnumbered D'Urban's 480 Portuguese dragoons and the six hundred or so men under Arentschildt. But Curto's movements are even harder to fathom than those of Thomières: the natural role for his light horse was to screen and protect the advance of the French infantry along the plateau, but this was not done, and it seems that the cavalry were both behind the infantry and to the south of the plateau. It is also quite likely that only one of Curto's two brigades was on hand at the critical moment: otherwise it is hard to explain why the French cavalry did not have a greater effect, even allowing for the poor quality of their horses.

As the allied force approached the Pico de Miranda, D'Urban rode ahead of his cavalry, accompanied only by a couple of staff officers. Clearing a clump of trees 'a short way up the slope, I came suddenly upon the head of a French column of infantry, having about a company in front, and marching very fast by its left.' D'Urban galloped back to the head of his brigade and led it forward in a charge that took the French completely by surprise. Nonetheless, the French fire was sufficient to check the momentum of the squadron charging frontally and to inflict some casualties, but the squadron on its right was able to wheel inwards onto the defenceless French flank. The battalion then broke and fled uphill, leaving many prisoners in the hands of the Portuguese.[8]

Meanwhile, the allied infantry had formed for their advance up the Pico de Miranda. Wallace's brigade was in the lead, still screened by a thick belt of

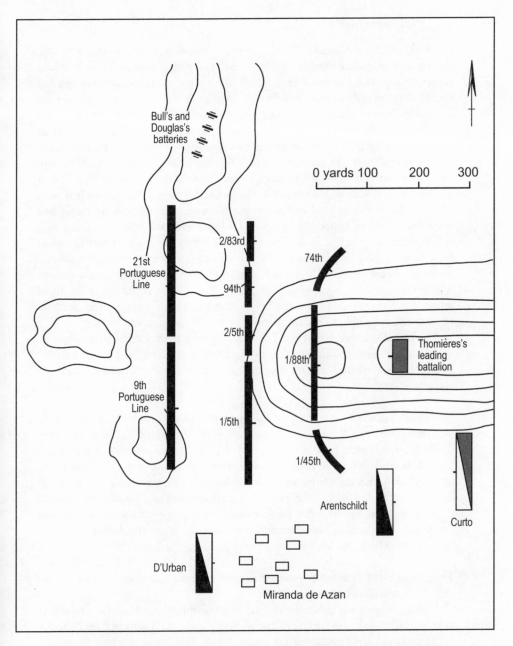

Bull's and
Douglas's
batteries

0 yards 100   200   300

2/83rd

74th

21st
Portuguese
Line

94th

2/5th

1/88th

Thomières's
leading
battalion

9th
Portuguese
Line

1/5th

1/45th

Arentschildt

Curto

D'Urban

Miranda de Azan

Pakenham's attack. The long columns have wheeled into line and Wallace's brigade, leading the advance, has gained the summit of the Pico de Miranda. (Much of this is conjectural, and the troop positions are at best approximate, while the depiction of the terrain has been deliberately simplified.)

skirmishers. The second British brigade followed in support, with the Portuguese brigade probably in their rear. Grattan claims that the line was formed from column without halting, thus disconcerting the French, but another source states that there was a brief pause during which 'General Pakenham rode along the division, addressing, as he passed, a short but inspiriting speech to each battalion.' Final preparations for close combat were made, and in each regiment some of the sergeants were summoned to the centre to help guard the colours.[9]

The French were in some disarray. D'Urban's success had left them with only four battalions in good order to face the onslaught of twelve. Their artillery may have been withdrawn at this point, for the allied advance had been so rapid that it would have had little time to move into position, unlimber and open fire. But the British batteries of Douglas and Bull had now come into action, firing from a rise in the ridge running off to the north. Their fire must have added to the French confusion, for it would catch any troops, infantry or artillery, facing west in the flank and partly enfilade them. Nonetheless, Thomières had little choice but to hope that his infantry could check the allied advance – however desperate the odds – for Pakenham was now too close for the French to be able to retreat in good order.

The allied skirmishers pressed forward against their French counterparts, weight of numbers giving the allies a great advantage. Yet all did not go entirely smoothly, as William Grattan, who had no love of the Portuguese, delights in recording:

> a number of Caçadores commanded by Major Haddock were in advance of us. The moment the French fire opened, these troops, which had been placed to cover our advance, lay down on their faces, not for the purpose of taking aim with more accuracy, but in order to save their own sconces from the French fire. Haddock dismounted from his horse and began belabouring with the flat side of his sabre the dastardly troops he had the misfortune to command, but in vain; all sense of shame had fled after the first discharge of grape and musketry, and poor Haddock might as well have attempted to move the great cathedral of Salamanca as the soldiers of his Majesty the King of Portugal.[10]

Despite Grattan's contempt, such incidents were not uncommon in battle and could affect soldiers of any nationality.

It may have been at this time, or later in the combat, that General Thomières fell, mortally wounded, adding to the confusion and uncertainty in French ranks.

As soon as the British line was formed, Pakenham, hat in hand, personally led its advance. His own account, written just after the battle, is disappointingly vague: 'These instructions your old companions executed in the most admirable style, and, in spite of every resistance, (for the Enemy's Columns remained firm till our line had closed within Ten Yards in the most distant point), were never brought to a check. The crash was magnificent!'[11] Captain Campbell is rather more informative:

The enemy's skirmishers and ours now set to work, yet we did not wait for their indecisive long shots; but advancing still rapidly and steadily, our right soon came into contact with their left, which had opened a very heavy and destructive fire upon us, and which would have lasted long enough had the brigade been halted to return it, but it was instantly charged and overthrown. It was now evident to us all that Sir Edward Pakenham knew how to handle Picton's division.[12]

But for detail and atmosphere – although not for literal accuracy – it is impossible to improve on Grattan:

All were impatient to engage, and the calm but stern advance of Pakenham's right brigade was received with beating of drums and loud cheers from the French, whose light troops . . . [ran] down the face of the hill in a state of great excitement . . . [and] commenced an irregular and hurried fire. . . .

Regardless of the fire of the riflemen, and the showers of grape and canister, Pakenham continued to press onward; his centre suffered, but still advanced; his left and right being less oppressed by the weight of the fire, continued to advance at a more rapid pace, and as his wings inclined forward and outstripped the centre, his right brigade assumed the form of a crescent . . . it so happened that all the British officers were in front of their men – a rare occurrence. The French officers were also in front; but their relative duties were widely different: the latter, encouraging their men into the heat of battle; the former, keeping their devoted soldiers back! . . .

. . . the soldiers, with their firelocks on the rest, followed close upon the heels of their officers, like troops accustomed to conquer. They speedily got footing upon the brow of the hill, but before they had time to take breath, Thomières's entire division, with drums beating and uttering loud shouts, ran forward to meet them, and belching forth a torrent of bullets from five thousand muskets, brought down almost the entire of Wallace's first rank, and more than half of his officers. The brigade staggered back from the force of the shock, but before the smoke had altogether cleared away, Wallace, looking full in the faces of his soldiers, pointed to the French column, and leading the shattered brigade up the hill, without a moment's hesitation, brought them face to face before the French had time to witness the terrible effect of their murderous fire.

Astounded by the unshaken determination of Wallace's soldiers, Thomières's division wavered; nevertheless they opened a heavy discharge of musketry, but it was unlike the former, – it was irregular and ill-directed, the men acted without concert or method, and many fired in the air. At length their fire ceased altogether, and the three regiments, for the first time, *cheered*! The effect was electric; Thomières's troops were seized with a panic. . . .

The French officers did all that was possible, by voice, gesture, and example, to rouse their men to a proper sense of their situation, but in vain. One, the colonel of the leading regiment . . . seizing a firelock, and beckoning to his men to follow, ran forward a few paces and shot Major Murphy dead at the head of the 88th; however, his career soon closed: a bullet, the first that had been fired from our ranks, pierced his head; he flung up his arms, fell forward, and expired.

The brigade, which till this time cheerfully bore up against the heavy fire they had been exposed to without returning a shot, were now impatient, and the 88th greatly excited: for Murphy, dead and bleeding, with one foot hanging in the stirrup-iron, was dragged by his affrighted horse along the front of his regiment; the soldiers became exasperated, and asked to be let forward. Pakenham, seeing that the proper moment had arrived, called out to Wallace 'to let them loose'. The three regiments ran onward, and the mighty phalanx, which but a moment before was so formidable, loosened and fell in pieces before fifteen hundred invincible British soldiers fighting in a line of only two deep.[13]

All this needs to be taken with a pinch of salt: Wallace's brigade was not facing the whole of Thomières's division, and the 'torrent of bullets from five thousand muskets' is no more than a rhetorical flourish. The three battalions of Wallace's brigade amounted to nearly 1,500 rank and file; they formed a single two deep line about five hundred yards long; and it is clear both from Grattan and from other sources that they outflanked the French on both sides, so that parts of the British battalions on each flank curled inwards – Grattan's 'crescent'. This suggests that the French presented a front of at most three hundred yards. A single French battalion formed in column of divisions (that is, with two companies in front) was barely fifty yards wide. It is therefore possible that all four battalions that Thomières had available were crowded together in a single line of battalion columns, with minimal gaps in between each column, although, given the nature of the ground (the southern face of the Monte de Azan is particularly steep at this point), this seems most unlikely. Alternatively, the French could have formed two regimental columns, each having a frontage of only two companies but double the depth of a battalion column; or two battalion columns could have been kept some distance to the rear to act as supports or reserves.

Whatever the details of the French formation, it is clear that they were not in line, and that at best fewer than one-third of Thomières's two thousand infantry could bring their muskets to bear effectively. This is confirmed by the casualties suffered by the British, which were much less severe than Grattan suggests with his 'almost the entire of Wallace's front rank, and more than half of his officers'. In fact, the brigade suffered only 239 casualties from 1,548 officers and men in the entire battle (or 15.4 per cent) and of his seventy officers only two were killed and eleven wounded (18.6 per cent).[14] Significantly, Grattan's own regiment, the 88th, which was in the centre of the line, suffered disproportionately: 135 casualties from 663 officers and men, or 20.4 per cent, a rate almost double that of the other two regiments in the brigade. These heavy losses in the centre help explain why the flanking battalions, facing less opposition, pressed forward more rapidly and the line curved around the French flanks.

It is unlikely that the French expected to halt the British attack through musketry alone: to do so they should have deployed in line. Rather, Grattan's account suggests that they intended their first volley to check and unsettle the British, so gaining a temporary psychological advantage which could then be exploited by charging the shaken line. Against other opponents these tactics might well have succeeded, but, although 'staggered' by the French fire, Wallace's men continued to advance, and this greatly disconcerted the French. Their confidence shaken, the second French volley was 'irregular and ill-directed'; already the allies had gained the psychological ascendancy. The British continued to advance and cheered, displaying a confidence which further shook the French and caused some panic. Finally, as the British soldiers grew impatient, especially at the sight of Major Murphy's body, Pakenham gave the signal, they charged and the French broke before them.

It is worth noting that neither Grattan nor Campbell states that the British line fired at all in their advance, except for the single shot which avenged Major Murphy. Indeed, Campbell is quite explicit in rejecting any attempt to engage in a musketry duel: '[The French] opened a very heavy and destructive fire upon us, and which would have lasted long enough had the brigade been halted to return it, but it was instantly charged and overthrown. It was now evident to us all that Sir Edward Pakenham knew how to handle Picton's division.' This despite the fact that the British were advancing in line and could bring every musket to bear on the enemy.[15]

One last observation on Grattan's account is the emphasis he places on the role of officers: keeping their men under control and seeking to inspire them by personal example. Of course, Grattan was a subaltern himself and so was acutely aware of the pressures on regimental officers in combat, but he paints an interesting picture of the varied roles which relatively junior officers played when their unit was closely engaged – even if he chooses to concentrate on those who displayed particular bravery, rather than those who were anxiously trying to remain inconspicuous. Officers were no more immune to fear than their men, and their prominence could make them decidedly uncomfortable. The colours in the centre of the regiment were an obvious target and junior officers carrying them knew that they must not waver. As the 88th advanced, the King's Colour was borne by Lieutenant John D'Arcy and the Regimental Colour by Lieutenant T. Moriarty. When the French colonel seized a musket and aimed at the centre of the regiment, Moriarty remarked, 'That fellow is aiming at me!' 'I hope so,' D'Arcy replied, 'for I thought he had *me* covered.' But it was Major Murphy riding immediately in front who was hit, and the two young men had to repress their qualms and continue their advance.[16]

At the same time that Wallace's brigade was advancing on the French infantry, Curto's cavalry charged the right flank of the British line. According to one account, the British infantry were 'within about 50 yards of the summit, when a body of German riflemen, belonging to a battalion of the 60th, who had been advancing to the front [as skirmishers], and had already crowned the height, came running back at full speed, exclaiming, "Der Deivel, dere are de French horse coming!" ' This was just sufficient warning for the commander of the 1/45th, the right-hand battalion in Wallace's brigade, to wheel back the three end companies of his line and the advancing cavalry sheered away from their fire. Pakenham, who was riding past, exclaimed, 'Well done, 45th.'[17] But the second British brigade, advancing in Wallace's rear, was less quick to react, and the French cavalry cut in to its end battalion, the 1/5th, and inflicted considerable damage. Private William Brown writes:

> As our brigade was marching up to attack a strongly posted column of infantry, a furious charge was made by a body of cavalry upon our Regiment, and, not having time to form square, we suffered severely. Several times the enemy rode through us, cutting down with their sabres all that opposed them. Our ranks were broken and thrown into the utmost confusion. Repeatedly our men attempted to reform, but all in vain – they were as often cut down and trampled upon by their antagonists. . . . Numerous and severe were the wounds received on this occasion. Several had their arms dashed from their shoulders, and I saw more than one with their heads completely cloven. Among the rest I received a wound, but comparatively slight, although well aimed. Coming in contact with one of the enemy he brandished his sword over me, and standing in his stirrup-irons, prepared to strike; but, pricking his horse with my bayonet, it reared and pranced, when the sword fell, the point striking my forehead. He was, however, immediately brought down, falling with a groan to rise no more.[18]

The 1/5th had only joined the army a few days before, although as it had seen service at Coruña and Walcheren it was not a completely raw unit; but taken by surprise in the flank, it broke. Before the French could exploit their success, however, D'Urban's Portuguese dragoons rode up and drove them off. Pakenham gave the scattered infantry a few minutes to realize that they were safe, stop running and catch their breath, then he rode up to them, 'and very good-naturedly said, "re-form", and in about a moment "advance", adding "there they are my lads, just let them feel the temper of your bayonets." '[19] The troops were rallied with patience and encouragement, not criticism or blame. The battalion lost 126 casualties – although not all of these would have been suffered in this episode. This was considerably more than the combined losses of the other three battalions in the second brigade, but it was a very strong unit (902 all ranks) so that the losses amounted to only 14 per cent of its strength. Even so, this was a higher proportion than any other unit in Pakenham's division except the 88th.

The French cavalry might have secured a more important success if they had been present in greater force, but it seems that only two or three squadrons charged the British infantry. The remainder of the brigade, six or seven squadrons, was already engaged with Arentschildt's horsemen, while Curto's other brigade was evidently too far to the rear to play any part at this point. Arentschildt advanced across a steep gully and then kept the 14th Light Dragoons in reserve while Major Grüben led the 1st KGL Hussars in a charge. The foremost French squadrons were broken, but rallied on their supports, which in turn drove the German Hussars back, only for the Light Dragoons to decide the contest. As usual in cavalry contests, the victor's losses were slight: the Hussars lost only two men killed, five officers and sixteen men wounded, a total of twenty-three casualties from a strength of 399 officers and men, while the 14th Light Dragoons lost only eight casualties from 347 officers and men; in both cases these figures represent their losses over the whole day, and this was not the only episode in which they were engaged. Curto's men lost more heavily, but it is impossible to distinguish which regiments were present at this combat, or when they suffered their casualties. As a whole, his division lost about 250 casualties (including unwounded prisoners), but most of these losses would probably have occurred later in the day. The initial contest, however, was important, both for giving the allies greater confidence in later encounters – and confidence and nerve were vital in cavalry combat – and for protecting Pakenham's flank at the critical moment of his attack.[20]

The Third Division was now securely astride the Monte de Azan advancing triumphantly east, driving the wrecks of the 101st and 62nd Regiments before it. According to Captain Campbell, 'the enemy's infantry were quickly pursued, chiefly by Colonel Wallace, at the head of the 88th, whose impetuosity was found most difficult to restrain. . . . Another charge was intended; the French would not, however, stand, and retired in tolerable order.' This is broadly confirmed by Grattan, who laments that the British cavalry were not yet in a position to exploit the advantage that the infantry had gained, and who admits that although Wallace's men pressed forward eagerly, the French outran them.[21] Thomières's leading regiments had been broken, but they might yet be rallied if they could find supports to shelter behind while they regained their composure and were restored to order. Pakenham's men had won the first round, but now faced the danger that an impetuous advance might leave them breathless, disordered and vulnerable to a French counterattack. The French flank had been turned and an important advantage gained, but the battle was only just beginning.

Commentary

Wellington's dramatic arrival at the head of the Third Division naturally set tongues wagging and eventually produced a crop of well-seasoned anecdotes. Grattan's version is not implausible, but it can hardly have been based on personal observation, for how would a junior lieutenant in the 88th (not the leading regiment in its brigade) have been in a position to overhear Wellington's words to Pakenham? Captain Campbell, as brigade-major of the first brigade, is more likely to have been in attendance, but his account gains credibility by not

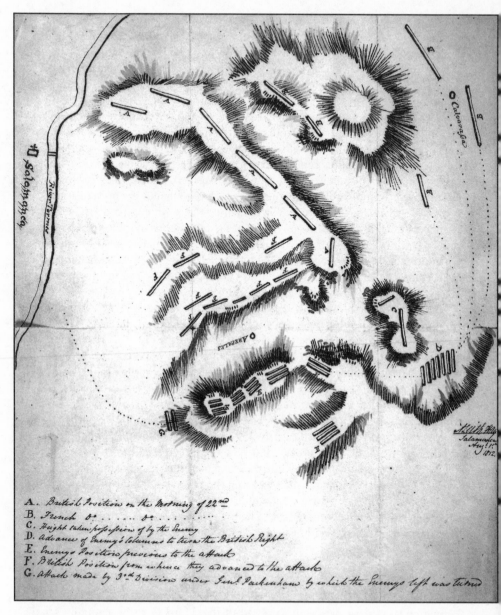

Hand-drawn map of the battle by Andrew Leith Hay. For a more familiar perspective, rotate approximately 45° clockwise.

A is the British position on the morning of the 22 July; B is the French position on the Heights of Calvarrasa de Arriba; C is the Greater Arapile; D is the French advancing behind the Greater Arapile; E is the French troops on Monte de Azan; F is the British position before they began their advance; G is the advance of Pakenham's division which turned the French left flank.

pretending perfect recall of the dialogue: 'Lord Wellington, followed by some of his staff, galloped up to where the 3rd Division was posted; and calling for Sir Edward Pakenham, he gave him certain orders in a few very impressive words, and Sir Edward's reply was quite in character.' Captain Lightfoot of the 45th wrote home from Madrid on 26 September: 'His Lordship's orders to General Pakenham in our hearing were: "Pakenham, you will carry that height where the enemy's left is posted by storm, and when you have gained it, go at them hard and fast with the bayonet." "Yes, my Lord," cried Pakenham, "that I will, by God,"and galloping off, placed himself at our head.'[22] This is a much better source than Grattan or even Campbell, if only because it was written so much closer to the events; but even so, doubts remain. Would Lightfoot really have been able to hear what Wellington said? And would he be able to recall the words exactly more than two months later, when the day of battle had been so full of other momentous events and disturbing impressions?

Other versions of the episode can be traced back to a highly coloured and rather implausible account in *Story of the Peninsular War* (1848) which was an abridged edition of Lord Londonderry's *Narrative of the Peninsular War* (1828) completed, including the account of Salamanca, by George Gleig. Neither Londonderry nor Gleig was at Salamanca, although they both knew Wellington well, and may have heard some version of the story from him:

> Lord Wellington had dined amid the ranks of the third division, and Pakenham, its frank and chivalrous leader, was one of those who shared his simple and soldier-like meal. To him the commander-in-chief gave his orders, somewhat in the following words: – 'Do you see those fellows on the hill, Pakenham? Throw your division into columns of battalions – at them directly – and drive them to the devil.' Instantly the division was formed – and the order executed admirably. As he passed, Pakenham stopped, for a moment, near his brother-in-law, and said, 'Give me a hold of that conquering hand!' and then rode off, watching every movement with a soldier's eye, and directing his columns to their proper places; – while Lord Wellington, turning round, observed to his staff; 'Did you ever see a man who understood so clearly what he had to do?'[23]

Wellington states that Pakenham and D'Urban advanced in four columns; Pakenham writes of his division marching 'in double column'; and D'Urban says that he was directed 'to move in two Columns of Lines upon the Right.' This seems clear enough, but where were the Portuguese infantry? Campbell implies that they followed Wallace's brigade; Grattan has them forming a second line between the two British brigades; while Young and Lawford divide them, with half in the rear of each infantry column. The problem with this is that when the British brigades wheeled to their left, this would have placed the

Portuguese on their left in the front line – which does not agree with any account of the subsequent fighting. Nor do they seem to have been in the second line, or Curto's cavalry would have attacked them in the flank rather than the 1/5th. Their most natural location was as a third line behind the British brigades, and this supposition is supported by their low casualties – which were at barely half the rate suffered by regiments in the second British brigade, even if the unhappy 1/5th is excluded. In this case it would be most natural for them to advance in a third column between the second brigade and the cavalry; none of our sources mentions this, but British writers were sometimes inclined to disregard the Portuguese. However, without further evidence the point cannot be securely settled one way or the other. Strangely, both Oman and Fortescue seem to have been confused by Campbell's habit of calling Wallace's men 'the right brigade' and have his column closest to the cavalry; but it is extremely difficult to see how it could have led the attack on Thomières from there.[24]

Pakenham's formation only makes sense if his division marched across the direction of the French advance and then wheeled into line (in a manoeuvre similar to the naval 'crossing the T'). However, given the difficulty of relating the formation to the actual ground at the Pico de Miranda, it is worth pausing to consider the alternatives. There are two main possibilities: he may have swung his division in a wider arc and approached the Pico de Miranda from the west, but this does nothing to make the troops fit on to the ground more comfortably, while contradicting the evidence of his formation. The second possibility is considerably more interesting, if ultimately unconvincing. According to this theory, Pakenham crossed the north–south ridge and attacked the Monte de Azan from the north. Campbell's evidence of the division's formation must be put aside, and the assumption made that the troops advanced with each brigade in a line of battalion columns which deployed into line before climbing the hill. Thomières's men would still have been flustered by the sudden appearance of such a large force emerging unexpectedly from behind the ridge, and the line of Wallace's brigade would still extend beyond the flanks of the French even if their four available battalions were formed in column along the crest of the hill. The advantage of this theory is that the troops will fit onto the ground quite easily, while the actions of D'Urban, Arentschildt and Curto are not hard to reconcile with it. However, it requires that we discard not only Campbell's detailed account of the formation of the division, but also all the maps and other evidence which refer to Pakenham *turning* the French flank, rather than simply overthrowing the troops that formed the extreme left of the French army. Furthermore, if the thrust of Pakenham's advance was to the south rather than the east, it would require his division to change direction abruptly in the moment of victory, and abandon the pursuit of Thomières in order to press along the plateau to take Maucune in the flank. This presents serious difficulties, although even in conventional interpretations of the battle the role of the Third Division in the later phases is very sketchy.

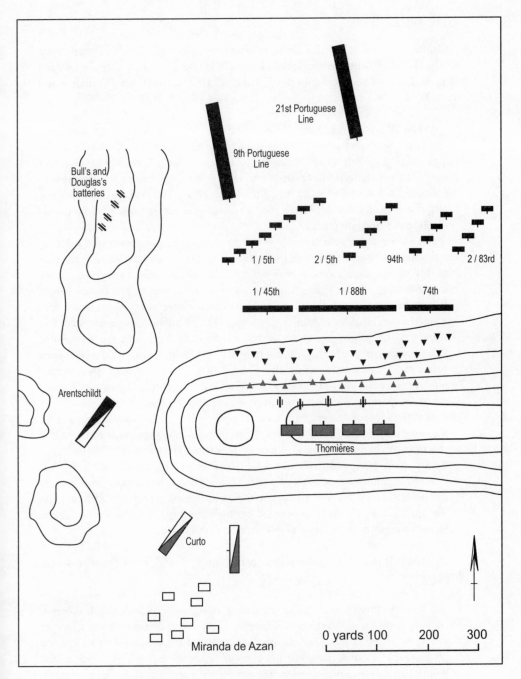

Bull's and Douglas's batteries

21st Portuguese Line

9th Portuguese Line

1 / 5th   2 / 5th   94th   2 / 83rd

1 / 45th   1 / 88th   74th

Arentschildt

Thomières

Curto

Miranda de Azan

0 yards 100   200   300

An alternative interpretation of Pakenham's attack. This is highly speculative;
some of the evidence fits it quite neatly, but the weight of probability is rather
against it.

Grattan's account of the division's advance fits this theory surprisingly neatly. The following comes from his article in the *United Service Journal* for 1834 and, as with other quotations from it, I have substituted Thomières's name for Foy's:

> When all was in readiness, Pakenham departed at the head of ten battalions and two brigades of guns, to force the left of the enemy. Three battalions, the 45th, 74th and 88th, under Colonel Alexander Wallace, of the 88th, composed the first line; the 9th and 21st, Portuguese of the line, under the Portuguese Colonel, De Champlimond, formed the second line; while two battalions of the 5th, the 77th, the 83d and 94th, British, were in reserve. Such was the disposition of the third division . . .
>
> No sooner was Pakenham in motion towards the heights, when the ridge he was about to assail was crowned with twenty pieces of cannon, while in the rear of this battery were seen Thomières's division endeavouring to regain its place in the combat. A flat space, 1,000 yards in breadth, was to be crossed before Pakenham could reach the heights. The French batteries opened a heavy fire, while the two brigades of artillery, commanded by Captain Douglas, posted on a rising ground behind the third division, replied to them with much warmth. Pakenham's men might thus be said to be within two fires; that of their own guns firing over their heads, while the French balls passed through their ranks, ploughing up the ground in every direction; but the veteran troops which composed the third division were not to be shaken even by this.
>
> Wallace's three regiments advanced in open column until within 250 yards of the ridge held by the French infantry. Thomières's column, 5,000 strong, had by this time reached their ground, while in their front, the face of the hill had been hastily garnished with riflemen. All were impatient to engage . . . but Pakenham, who was naturally of a boiling spirit and hasty temper, was on this day perfectly cool. He told Wallace to form line from open column without halting, and thus the different companies, by throwing forward their right shoulders were in line without the slow manoeuvre of a deployment.[25]

Against this must be set the accounts of Campbell and, for what it is worth, Moggridge:

> The division was soon under arms, and moved off rapidly in open column, right in front, the 45th regiment leading. . . . We soon descended into a kind of valley, or rather hollow, and having brought up our left shoulders a little, we pushed on at a quick pace, but in excellent order, to the right; the side of the hollow towards the enemy concealing our movements from their sight.
>
> The whole scene was now highly animating. The left brigade, headed by the 5th regiment, was, I saw, marching parallel to the right, so as to be ready to form a second line. The Portuguese brigade followed the right, and the whole of the

left flank of the columns was covered by a cloud of sharpshooters, composed of light infantry companies, and riflemen of the 5th battalion, 60th regiment.

Having moved a considerable distance in this order, (field officers and adjutants prolonging the line of march,) the head of the column, by bringing up the right shoulder, began gradually to ascend the hill, on the top of which we expected to find the enemy still extending to their left. At length, having fairly outflanked the French left, the whole formed line, and with Sir Edward Pakenham in front, hat in hand, the brigades advanced in beautiful style, covered by our sharpshooters, the right of the first line admirably supported by the left brigade.[26]

And

> The ground through which our route lay was low, and sheltered from observation by the neighbouring heights, and we passed on unobstructed and unobserved by the enemy. In this manner we marched on for a considerable distance, when, emerging into ground higher and more open, we suddenly became exposed to a heavy fire of artillery, which occasioned considerable loss in the ranks.
>
> This, however, did not interrupt our march, and, proceeding onward, I remember we turned somewhat unexpectedly to the right, and entered a narrow valley which ran in a direction nearly at right angles with the course we had hitherto pursued. Having continued our advance in this manner for some time, we halted for a few minutes, and having formed in separate columns of regiments, we were ordered to advance up the heights by which the valley was bounded to the left.[27]

But the most decisive evidence on the point comes from the words chosen by Wellington and Pakenham when describing the advance in letters written within days of the battle. Wellington wrote: 'I ordered Major Gen. the Hon. E. Pakenham to move forward with the 3d division . . . to turn the enemy's left on the heights. . . . The attack upon the enemy's left was made in the manner above described, and completely succeeded. Major Gen. the Hon. E. Pakenham formed the 3d division across the enemy's flank, and overthrew everything opposed to him.' Pakenham wrote: 'At three in the afternoon the 3rd Division received instructions to move in double column across the Enemy's Left, which was advantageously placed upon some strong heights, there to form line, carry the heights and sweep everything before it.'[28] It is difficult to see how these terms could have been used to describe a frontal attack on the north face of the Monte de Azan.

D'Urban's description of the charge of his brigade comes not from his contemporary journal, but from a later narrative which he wrote to support his friend Sir Henry Watson's complaints about Napier's *History*. It is not printed with the published journal, so we must rely on the quotations and paraphrases given by Oman. The most obvious problem with the incident is that it is difficult to understand why the French battalion was so isolated from the rest of Thomières's division and why it was unscreened by Curto's cavalry. A related question is where the encounter occurred. D'Urban implies that it was on the lower slopes of the Monte de Azan, but also says that the French were already beyond the right flank of the advancing British infantry, which rather suggests that the French battalion had advanced beyond the Pico de Miranda onto the low rise to its west. However, this makes Thomières's manoeuvres – already difficult to reconstruct – completely inexplicable. Nor are the details of the actual encounter clear, for Napier, in an appendix, quotes two letters: the first, from Watson, states that the French were in square and that the charge was completely successful; the second, from Colonel Townsend, 14th Light Dragoons, says he was 'almost positive the French were not in square but in line', and that he had no doubt that the charge failed, leaving Watson badly wounded on the field. D'Urban, of course, supports Watson's account, and Oman follows them, although we cannot tell which of the details he gives come from D'Urban and which are his own attempts to reconcile Watson's and Townsend's versions. Oman has the French neither in square nor in line, but in column with the front two companies closed together so as to be six ranks deep; he makes the frontal attack fail while the right-hand squadron breaks in on the defenceless flank.[29]

Thomières's force and deployment are even more obscure, and there are no first-hand French accounts of this part of the battle. The version commonly given is that he advanced beyond Maucune's left flank and 'continued moving in a westerly direction along the summit of the plateau . . . before [he] stopped he had gone nearly three miles.'[30] As D'Urban encountered a French battalion moving hastily westwards, the implication is that the French had only just arrived, breathless and flurried, after a long march. But Thomières did not have nearly as far to go as Pakenham (less than one and a half miles compared to three) and began his march sooner, so it seems likely that he halted for some time on the way. Indeed, he probably never intended to push so far west, and only rushed to seize the Pico de Miranda when he finally discovered Pakenham's advance. Why the French reconnaissance should have been so poor, and Curto's cavalry so ineffective, remains a mystery.

As for Thomières's force, Oman observes that because the division was advancing to the left, the senior regiment would have been in the rear. This is confirmed by the casualty figures, for while the 62nd and 101st Regiments were almost destroyed in the battle (losing 77 and 82 per cent respectively, even on Lamartinière's figures), the 1st Ligne suffered comparatively little (only 13 per cent). Clearly its experience differed greatly from that of the other two regiments, and Sarramon plausibly suggests that it had been left behind as a link (albeit an inadequate one) between Thomières's advance guard and Maucune's division.[31]

None of the primary sources gives details of Thomières's death, and the secondary sources are not particularly helpful. Fortescue declares that he 'fell early on this day'; Young and Lawford that he 'died, vainly trying to rally his men'; while Oman says that he 'died within the English lines after the battle'; and Sarramon refers to the 'mortal wound received by General Thomières at the critical moment of the combat'.[32] Other aspects of the main infantry attack are fully discussed in the main text.

The account of Curto's charge on the British flank requires rather more elaboration. This follows Oman's interpretation that it was the 1/45th in Wallace's brigade which threw back three companies at an angle and drove off the French cavalry, while the 1/5th in the second brigade were caught in the flank and thrown into confusion. This is well supported by the heavy losses of the 1/5th, while the 1/45th lost scarcely more heavily than the 74th, the regiment on the other flank of Wallace's brigade (the 1/45th lost 55 casualties, or 12.4 per cent of its strength; the 74th lost 49 casualties, or 11 per cent). There is also the testimony of Sergeant Donaldson of the 94th in the second brigade: 'The 5th regiment, in attacking a body of infantry posted on a small height, were furiously charged by the enemy's cavalry, and thrown into some confusion . . .' But the other first-hand accounts do not fit this interpretation so neatly: Private Brown, whose graphic account of the resulting melee is quoted in the narrative, served not in the 1/5th, but the 1/45th; while Sergeant Morley of the 1/5th admits that his regiment was broken, but attributes this to the stubborn resistance from French infantry and makes no mention of French cavalry, although he does add that 'at this distance of time, I do not pretend to give a faithful account of the particulars'. This is disconcerting enough and Captain Campbell's account only adds to the uncertainty: 'at this critical moment some of the enemy's cavalry charged in turn, and most gallantly, the right flank of the 45th regiment, but a well directed fire from the 5th, which had been brought up, so as to be close at hand, removed all the apprehensions at that point.' Even Moggridge's account, which appears to support Oman's interpretation completely, is undermined by uncertainty as to whether he is referring to the first or second brigades. All that is really clear is that the 1/45th were not cut up, that their losses do not justify the lurid language of Brown's description and that their attack was not checked. Equally the 1/5th did suffer much more heavily than the other regiments in its brigade; although it is just possible that this was not owing to Curto's attack, but as a consequence of heavy fighting with the French infantry later in the day.[33]

The account of the cavalry melee is based on Arentschildt's official report, as printed in Beamish. It is strange that Wellington in his dispatch refers only to two squadrons of the 14th Light Dragoons accompanying D'Urban and ignores the German Legion Hussars. The suggestion that Curto had only one of his two brigades present is based on the results of the action. Arentschildt believed that he faced 'six to seven squadrons', while Sarramon puts the force which charged the British infantry at two or three squadrons. One of Curto's brigades had eight squadrons, the other ten, averaging one hundred men per squadron. However, there is no evidence for the location or activity of Curto's other brigade.[34]

The difficulties of establishing what happened in Pakenham's attack are greater than with most of the rest of the battle, for the sources are relatively few, and either prove unreliable (Grattan and Moggridge) or lack detail. Even Campbell's account, on which so much of the interpretation given above is based, was written many years after the battle and is not without problems. The lack of a good French eyewitness account is particularly unfortunate, although this is a complaint that will recur frequently. Visiting the battlefield and walking over the terrain can often resolve problems, but here only makes them worse. The most that can honestly be done is to lay out the evidence, explain the problems and point to possible solutions, for any simple, straightforward narrative of this episode must make too many unwarrantable assumptions and leave too many important questions unasked. In other words, we must admit that there is much that we do not know.

Chapter Five
Leith and Maucune

The Fifth Division under Lieutenant-General James Leith was the strongest in Wellington's army, with some 6,700 men in eight British and five Portuguese battalions. It had begun the day as part of the mass of troops which Wellington kept in reserve, hidden in the low ground between Carbajosa and Las Torres; but during the morning it had been brought into the front line, occupying a space immediately north of the Lesser Arapile, which had previously been held by Pack's Portuguese brigade. Here it could see French troops moving south in the skirts of the forest as they followed the advance that Bonnet had already made. Captain Lawson, commander of the division's battery of 6-pounder foot artillery, ventured some long shots into the French columns but was soon compelled to withdraw when the French guns replied in superior force. A little later, Leith thought that the French were massing to attack his position and sent his ADC Andrew Leith Hay with a message to Wellington. Wellington inspected the French positions and sent the leading battalion in Greville's brigade, 3/1st Foot, forward to test the French response. The French guns opened fire, making the British infantry very uncomfortable, but there was no further French reaction, and Wellington, concluding that they did not intend an attack on this side, soon withdrew the 3/1st, much to its relief.[1]

An hour or two later, probably a little after 2 o'clock, orders arrived from Wellington for the Fifth Division to withdraw from this part of the line and march west to take up a new position beyond the right flank of Cole's Fourth Division. This extension of the allied line was in response to Maucune's advance onto the Monte de Azan, and in turn the appearance of Leith's troops may have encouraged Maucune to abandon his attack on the village and move further west to face this new enemy. Leith's division deployed in two lines, each of two ranks, giving it a frontage of about nine hundred yards when allowance is made for the light companies and caçador battalion, who were detached to skirmish in front, and the officers and sergeants who stood behind the main line. Its left was behind the western half of the village of Los Arapiles, and its right extended into open ground where the hill dwindled away, leaving it exposed to the French bombardment.

For more than an hour (from about 3 o'clock to about 4.30, but the times are very uncertain), the division remained stationary under fire, the men lying down behind the crest of the gently swelling ground. Major Gomm, one of Leith's staff, described it as 'the heaviest cannonade I have ever been exposed to', while John Douglas, a corporal in the Royal Scots (3/1st), recalled the way soldiers typically made light of a particularly gruesome incident: 'On the 2nd Brigade forming a man of the 44th was killed and lay for a few minutes, when a shell fell under him and exploding drove him into the air. His knapsack, coat, shirt, body and all flew in every direction. A Dublin lad lying on my right looks up and exclaims with the greatest gravity, "There's an inspection of necessaries." '2

A shiver of excitement must surely have passed along the line when Wellington, accompanied by his staff, rode up at a gallop, spent a few minutes in conversation with General Leith, then rode on towards Cole's division. Wellington had come from the right of the army, where he had set D'Urban and Pakenham in motion; now he gave Leith his orders 'in a clear, concise, and spirited manner'.3 The Fifth Division was to wait until Pakenham's men were engaged, then advance across the shallow valley and attack Maucune's division on the Monte de Azan. Cole would advance on Leith's left; while on his right,

Pringle's brigade (2/4th, 2/30th, 2/44th)	Spry's brigade (11th and 23rd Portuguese line)

Greville's brigade

1/4th	3/1st	1/38th	2/38th	1/9th

G

skirmishers from British light companies, caçador battalion and Brunswick Oels

Formation of Leith's division (advancing south, towards bottom of the page).

linking him to Pakenham, were to be Bradford's brigade of Portuguese infantry, España's division, Le Marchant's heavy dragoons and Anson's light cavalry; and in the rear would be the Seventh Division, ready to support Leith if he needed assistance. By the time Leith was assaulting Maucune's front line, Pakenham – if all went well – would have turned the French flank and would be advancing along the plateau, threatening Maucune's flank and rear. The Fifth Division would be formed in two lines, with Greville's strong brigade in front (3/1st, 1/9th, 1/38th, 2/38th, about 2,600 men) together with the 1/4th Regiment from Pringle's brigade, to equalize the two lines; the second line would be composed of the remainder of Pringle's brigade, and all of Spry's Portuguese brigade. Wellington's instructions concluded 'with commands that the enemy should be overthrown, and driven from the field'.[4]

Having issued his orders, Wellington rode on, leaving the Fifth Division to wait for Pakenham and D'Urban to get into position and begin their attack. Leith rode up and down the line, encouraging his troops and watching how they endured the bombardment. Most were old soldiers, but the 1/38th in Greville's brigade had only joined the army the previous day and, although it had a core of veterans who had served at Coruña and Walcheren, its ranks were swollen with new recruits, for it was a strong unit with eight hundred officers and men. The 2/4th in Pringle's brigade were also newcomers, having joined Leith's division in May from garrison duty in Ceuta. They too had been at Walcheren, although not at Coruña, and so would have had little experience of battle. The rest of the British troops in the division had been in the Peninsula for at least eighteen months and had seen action a number of times, most recently at the storming of Badajoz. Spry's Portuguese had had less fighting. They suffered few if any losses at Busaco, Fuentes or Badajoz, although they had taken part in all of these campaigns and had probably developed some cohesion, as the composition and command of the brigade had been unchanged since March 1811.

As Leith rode along the line, he chatted to the officers and conspicuously disregarded the French cannonade. He also addressed each regiment in turn, letting them know that they would soon have the chance to advance: 'Genl. Leith came up waving his hat and shouting, "Now my lads this is the day for England. They would play at long ball with us from morning until night, but we will soon give them something else!"' An ensign in the 38th records him saying, 'As for you, 38th, I have only to say, behave as you have always done.' And a soldier in the Royal Scots recalls:

> The cannonading at this time was terrible. Addressing the Regiment he says, 'Royals,' on which we all sprang up. 'Lie down men,' said he, though he sat on horseback, exposed to the fire as calm as possible. 'This shall be a glorious day for Old England, if these bragadocian rascals dare but stand their ground, we will display the point of the British bayonet, and where it is properly displayed no power is able to withstand it. All I request of you is to be steady and obey your officers.'[5]

At last Pakenham's attack began and Wellington sent a staff officer, Captain Philip Bainbrigge, to give Leith the word to commence his advance:

> I galloped up to General Sir James Leith, who was riding backwards and forwards along the front of his men, with two or three staff officers; the round shot were ricocheting into and over his line, and as I was about to deliver the order, a shot knocked up the earth close to his horse's nose. He took off his hat to it, and said, 'I will allow *you* to pass, Sir!' The men heard him, and said, 'Hurra for the General.' They were at ordered arms, standing at ease. I delivered my order, and the General replied, 'Thank you, Sir! That is the best news I have heard today,' and turning to his men he said, taking off his hat and waving it in the air in a theatrical manner, and in a tone of voice which was grand in the extreme, said, 'Now boys! we'll at them.'[6]

It was not mere bravado which made Leith welcome the signal to advance, for almost everyone preferred the excitement and risks of close action to the agony of waiting helplessly under fire. Indeed, part of Leith's purpose in addressing his men was to keep them entertained and give them something to think about other than the round shot whistling by their heads and the ordeal that was to come. Humour released some of the accumulating tension, while inspiring words and appeals to regimental pride and patriotism bolstered morale. But what Leith said mattered less than the confidence which he showed and the example which he set: riding along the ranks, fully exposed to the French fire, ignoring the danger or joking about it, while the ordinary soldiers lay under some cover at least.

As it happens, two of these ordinary soldiers in the Fifth Division have left records of their feelings on that day which reveal something of the strain felt by men in the ranks, and the way their religion affected them. First, John Douglas of the Royal Scots:

> I cannot say, as I have heard some say, that they were no more concerned going into action than a common field day, but I am fully persuaded that the man possessed of a belief that there is a God . . . will have a kind of terror over him for which he cannot account, owing to the reflection that the next moment he may be numbered with the dead. For it is an awful thing to fall (particularly unprepared) into the hands of the living God. I am far, very far, from thinking, or wish it to be understood, that it is cowardice. No, but show me the man who knows he has an immortal soul, and advancing under the destructive fire of the enemy, but will in his inmost soul offer up the prayer of the publican. ['God be merciful unto me a sinner.'][7]

The anonymous soldier in the 1/38th also derived rather mixed comfort from scripture:

> Although the scene was dreadfully Awful, I never was in a more composed and

comfortable frame than on that day, for in all that I saw, I saw that I had cause to be truly thankful; not that I had any certainty of Life more than others, but I felt confident that I was under the care and protection of almighty God, and my life was in his hands, and nothing could happen without his divine permission. But I was powerfully struck at the commencement of the action with this passage of Scripture, 'For all they that take the Sword shall Perish with the Sword.' But in my situation I knew I was bound by the law to do my duty as a soldier, besides, I knew that if I did not, my own life was liable to pay for it. And I thought that as providence had placed me in that situation it was my duty to be resigned to his will and prayed that whether it ended in life or in death, it might be for his Glory and my everlasting welfare.[8]

Long before the attack began, Leith's light infantry had been skirmishing with the French voltigeurs in the valley between the main forces. The Fifth Division had a powerful force of light infantry: two companies of Brunswick Oels, the light companies from eight British battalions and the whole caçador battalion, amounting to perhaps a thousand men. They covered the front of the division (about nine hundred yards) and extended beyond it to the right, preventing the French skirmishers approaching or harassing the main allied line. They do not seem to have pressed the combat until the division was ready to advance – as unsupported light infantry, they were vulnerable to enemy cavalry who might be concealed behind the skyline of the Monte de Azan. But when Leith began his advance, he sent Andrew Leith Hay with orders for the allied skirmishers to drive back their French opponents and, if possible, to seize some of their cannon. The French skirmishers gave way – it was not their role to attempt to halt the advance of a whole division – and the guns were safely withdrawn and re-deployed in the intervals between the French battalions. Nonetheless, this gained a welcome respite for the allied troops, for the French infantry was deployed beyond the skyline and the guns in their rear could not fire at an enemy they could not see. In executing these orders, Leith Hay's horse was killed under him, and the young man calmly waited for the main body of allied troops to approach before securing a fresh horse from one of the General's orderly dragoons.[9]

As the Fifth Division advanced, its left wing, including the 9th Regiment and probably part of the 38th, had to pass through the western end of the village of Los Arapiles, but it quickly re-formed and regained its place in the line. The division then continued its advance in excellent order.[10] John Douglas writes: 'Captain Stewart of our company, stepping out of the ranks to the front, lays hold of Captain Glover and cries, "Glover did you ever see such a line?" I am pretty confident that in the Regiments which composed our lines there was not a man 6 inches out of his place.' And Leith Hay adds: 'A blank was no sooner made by the Enemy's fire but it was closed up as if nothing had happened, and as much attention was paid to dressing the Line, as if it had been a common Field day.'[11]

This good order was not achieved without effort. The troops were impatient to press forward and had to be restrained. Before the advance began Leith had sent two of his aides, Captains Belshes and Dowson, to different parts of the line to help curb the pace, while he himself rode in front of the Colours of the 1/38th, in the very centre of the line. Leith's prominent position served several purposes: he was conspicuous, continuing to set his men an unmistakable example of courage; he was a prominent marker, determining the pace and direction of the advance of the whole line; and he was clear of the dust raised by the troops, able to see any sudden threat from the enemy or any irregularity of the ground.

It was vital for the success of the attack that good order be preserved. It was not easy for a line of men nine hundred yards long to maintain its order as it advanced for about a mile under enemy fire. Once the village had been passed, the ground was generally open, but even open ground contains many minor obstacles which can easily cause delay and confusion. One part of the line might press forward, another could fall behind; if the advance was too fast the men would become breathless and flurried, if too slow, the attack would lose momentum. And once disorder began, it would spread very rapidly, sapping the confidence of the troops and preventing them from being able to respond quickly to any sudden threat. It was much easier for infantry to advance in a line of independent columns, which could move more rapidly and worry less about their alignment, than to advance deployed in line. But then, the infantry would either have to fight in column and stake everything on an immediate charge, which would often fail against good troops, or attempt to deploy into line when they approached the enemy, which worked better in theory than in practice.

Leith's division was advancing up the slopes of the Monte de Azan, and the French skirmishers probably still controlled the crest. Beyond lay Maucune's division, which – except for its light troops – was untouched by the day's fighting. And, for all Leith knew, Maucune might be supported by a second French division, or by Curto's cavalry. If the allies became disordered, the French might not wait to be attacked, but instead sweep forward in unknown force and without warning.

Leith's division itself was well supported. Cole was on his left, although Cole's division seems to have advanced rather later than Leith. Bradford's Portuguese brigade should have been on Leith's right, but it had not arrived when the order came to advance, and it trailed behind and was never seriously engaged; its total loss in the whole day was only seventeen casualties, presumably from long-range artillery fire and stray shots; but it would still have been in good position to support Leith if his attack had faltered. Further back, Wellington moved the Seventh Division into the position vacated by the Fifth, so that powerful reserves were available if needed. More immediately relevant, however, was the advance of Le Marchant's brigade beyond Leith's right and Pakenham's division, which was now visibly pushing along the plateau, although the two divisions were still a considerable distance apart.

Unfortunately, we know very little about what was happening in Maucune's division as the allies advanced upon it and the French artillery and skirmishers withdrew back to the main body. It seems to have been formed on a slightly shorter front than Leith's division, for the units at each end of the allied line suffered relatively few casualties, suggesting that they were largely unopposed. Almost certainly the French were not in line. Leith Hay, writing to his father two days after the battle, refers to 'columns & squares of Infantry'; Captain Gomm says 'solid columns'; while John Douglas, whose battalion was towards the right or western end of the line, states that the French were in confusion and attempting to form square. The most probable explanation is that they were originally formed in column and that, just before the allied infantry appeared, the French commander on the left caught sight of Le Marchant's advancing cavalry and ordered his men into square, but that there was no time to complete this change of formation before the British infantry attacked.[12]

The French may have deployed in a single line of nine battalion columns, but it seems much more likely that they were in two lines of columns, with five in the first line and four in the second. The first brigade (15th and 66th Ligne, five battalions) were probably at the western end of the line, with the second brigade (82nd and 86th Ligne, four battalions) on their right. The division may have looked something like this:

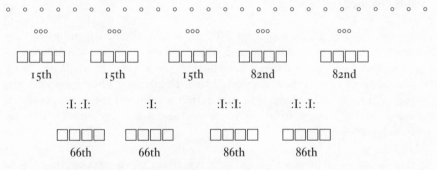

As the British line approached the crest, the allied skirmishers fell back or to the flanks; some were reluctant to go and kept firing at the French despite the risk of being caught between two fires. John Douglas relates a story which, if true, suggests that everything was not quite as calm and orderly as other accounts imply:

At this moment a French officer mounted on a white horse seemed to be very busy endeavouring to keep his men to their work, when a Corporal of the name of Joffrey and I got leave to try if he was ball proof; and running out a few yards in front, kneeled down and fired together, but which of us struck him must still remain a mystery, but down he went. Poor Joffrey, while in the act of rising off his knee, received a ball in the breast which numbered him with the dead also.[13]

Just before the British line marched over the crest, Leith and the mounted officers of his staff had a momentary glimpse of the French infantry waiting for them, perhaps only thirty yards away. Leith Hay, in the centre of the line, writes that the French were

> drawn up in contiguous columns,[14] the front rank kneeling, and prepared to fire when the drum beat for its commencement. All was still and quiet in these columns; – not a musket was discharged until the whole opened. Nearly at the same moment General Leith ordered the line to fire, and charge: the roll of musketry was succeeded by that proud cheer that has become habitual to British soldiers on similar occasions – that to an enemy tremendous sound, which may without doubt be termed the note of victory. At this moment, the last thing I saw through the smoke was the plunge of Colonel Greville's horse, who, shot through the head, reared, and fell back on his rider. In an instant every individual present was enveloped in smoke and obscurity. No struggle for ascendancy now took place; resistance was in vain; the French squares were penetrated, broken, and discomfited; the victorious division pressed forward, not against troops opposed, but a mass of disorganised men, overpowered and flying in all directions.[15]

Captain Gomm, who was also with Leith in the centre, gives a similar, if more highly coloured description:

> the spirit of our people rose in proportion [as they advanced], and when they reached the enemy's solid columns, which opened a fire like a volcano upon them, there was not a moment's hesitation; no check along the whole line, but a general shout of exultation was echoed from all quarters. The enemy wavered, retired from height to height; till at length it was impossible to withstand the ardour of our soldiers, which seemed to increase with every fresh assault, and complete rout ensued.[16]

The accounts of ordinary soldiers are less clear, partly because they wrote less well, but also because their impressions were inevitably more confused as they saw the battle from the jostling ranks amid the smoke and noise of musketry, while Leith Hay and Gomm were mounted and riding a little ahead of the line. The anonymous voice from the ranks of the 1/38th records:

> the French were in a ... square not more than 200 yards from us. As soon as we saw them we gave a shout, opened a tremendous fire and ran into them directly, so that that line was in a few minutes killed and taken prisoner. We then attacked their rear lines and after we had engaged them some time, we were charging them [when] I received a [musket] ball in my right foot.[17]

This still reflects what was happening in the centre of the line; James Hale of the 9th Foot was on the left, where resistance was weaker:

Though their thundering cannon roared tremendously, yet Lord Wellington was determined on victory; therefore we did not fail to let them hear the thunder of our cannon; and as our regiment formed part of the first line, we did not forget to let them hear and feel the effects of our small arms, and according to English custom, as soon as we could make it convenient, we showed them the point of the bayonet, and gave them a grand charge, by which we obliged them to leave three pieces of cannon in our possession in a short time: this part of the enemy's line continued retreating for some considerable distance, and we continued firing advancing, till it was thought necessary for us to halt, which accordingly we did, and remained on our ground for some time, expecting they would advance again; but however, they did not advance on that part of the line any more, so that our division came off rather favourably.[18]

On the right the British infantry were strongly supported by the nearest regiment of Le Marchant's cavalry, which charged the French in the flank, although not – according to John Douglas – before the allied infantry had already had some success:

The enemy, as I before observed, seemed to be rather in confusion. The cavalry on our right was to them a puzzle. The enemy seemed to have formed parts of squares, and parts of lines, and before they could recover from their panic, our murderous fire opened, which swept all before it. Their first line we fairly ran over, and saw our men jumping over huge grenadiers, who lay down exhausted through heat and fatigue, unhurt, in the hope of escaping ...

The first line of the enemy being broken and falling back in confusion, the 2nd lined the side of a deep trench cut by the torrents of water which roll down from the hills near the village of Arapiles, and so deep and broad that it took a good spring to leap over it. Here the 2nd line kept up a heavy fire of musketry, which checked our centre for a few minutes, while our poor fellows fell fast. To remain long in this way was too much to be borne. The cheer was raised for the charge, a general bound was made at the chasm, and over we went like so many beagles, while the enemy gave way in confusion. The cavalry now came in for their share and cut them down in great number[s].[19]

The role of the cavalry will be discussed in the next chapter, but a few points in the descriptions of the infantry combat deserve comment here. Most of the accounts emphasize the same three elements in the British assault: they fired, they cheered and they charged, and these participants give as much weight to the rousing cheer as to the musketry and the bayonet charge. Nowhere did the French stand to meet the charge, and the only hand-to-hand fighting was when the British got in among their fleeing opponents. Douglas claims that the exhausted French grenadiers whom his regiment left in its rear 'did not behave honourably, for as soon as they found us at a little distance they resumed the posture of the enemy and commenced to fire on our rear; but nearly the whole of them paid the price of their treachery with their lives.'[20] This was a common allegation made in many memoirs by soldiers of all nationalities about dozens of different battles. Occasionally it must have been true, although it seems unlikely that overrun troops would often risk their lives in this way. However, in the confusion of battle there were many stray shots flying about, including from friendly units, and it was easy to raise a cry blaming these on enemy soldiers left in the rear. Many innocent men, wounded or taken prisoner, were murdered on this pretext in the heat of battle, and no prisoner could feel safe while still close to the firing line.

The varied experiences of units in Leith's division are reflected in their casualties. Hale's regiment, the 1/9th, was at the eastern end of the line and encountered little opposition. It lost 46 casualties (3 men killed, one officer and 42 men wounded) from 666 present, or 6.9 per cent, less than half the rate of any other unit in Greville's brigade. The first and second battalions, 38th Foot, were in the centre of the line, and lost 17.9 per cent and 16.9 per cent respectively: 143 casualties in the strong first battalion, 51 in the much weaker second battalion. Douglas's regiment, the Royal Scots, was on the right of the brigade and suffered more than any other unit in the division: 160 casualties including 23 killed or 21 per cent. This excess may be owing to the heavy fire they received before they crossed the gully to attack the French second line, or they may have been more exposed to the French bombardment before and during the advance. Equally Wellington's use of them to test French intentions much earlier in the day may also have contributed to their losses. Overall Greville's brigade lost 400 casualties, or 15.8 per cent of its strength. The 1/4th from Pringle's brigade took its place in the front line next to the Royal Scots, but its losses were very light: only 18 casualties, or 3.9 per cent, the lowest in either British brigade. Pringle's other regiments lost: 2/4th, 31 casualties, or 4.6 per cent; 2/30th, 27 casualties or 7.7 per cent; and 2/44th, 29 casualties, or 11.6 per cent, or 87 casualties between them – 105 if the 1/4th is included. Portuguese losses are less certain, but Spry's brigade probably suffered about 150 casualties, or 6.7 per cent of its strength, about the same as Pringle's brigade, even though – unlike the British regiments – it went on to play an important part later in the day. In total, Leith's division lost about 650 casualties, or perhaps a few more, for the losses of the Brunswick Oels companies are not included.[21]

Among these casualties were General Leith and his aides Andrew Leith Hay and William Dowson. The little knot of officers riding so prominently in advance of the centre of the line was too obvious a target to miss and, as well as those who were hit, others such as Colonel Greville, commander of the first brigade, had their horses shot under them. Leith was wounded by a musketball in the arm, which fortunately did not shatter the bone. Leith Hay writes that 'a Musquet Ball entered my left leg about 3 inches below the knee close to the shin bone, and passed out at the Calf, it then went through the Flap of the saddle, the Blanket under it, and entered the Horse's body just under the Flank, of which he died the same afternoon. General Leith and myself remained for the

1. Marshal Auguste Frédéric Louis Viesse de Marmont, Duke of Ragusa (1774-1852).

2. General Clausel (1772–1842), commander of the Second
Division, who succeeded to the command when Marmont
was wounded.

3. General Foy (1775–1825) commander of the First Division
which occupied the heights of Calvarrasa de Arriba.

4. Major William Napier (1785–1860), soldier and historian, who commanded the 1/43rd in the battle and included many personal recollections in his famous *History*.

5. Lieutenant-General Sir Stapleton Cotton (1773–1865), commander of the allied cavalry.

6. Pakenham's attack. The 1/88th charge and break the French infantry, capturing 'Jingling Johnny,' as a trophy.

7. Wellington giving orders during the battle. Drawing by W. Heath, engraved by J. Clarke and M. Dubourg.

8. The Pelagarcia stream in the foreground with the low heights occupied by the allied army on the morning of the battle in the background. Taken from the foot of the heights of Calvarrasa de Arriba. North to the right, south to the left.

9. The view from Nuestra Señora de la Peña across the open valley to the low heights occupied by the allied army on the morning of the battle.

10. The heights of Calvarrasa de Arriba with the reed beds of the Pelagarcia stream in the foreground. Looking north–north–east.

11. The chapel of Nuestra Señora de la Peña on the heights of Calvarrasa de Arriba around which the light infantry of the two armies skirmished on the morning of the battle.

12. The Greater Arapile viewed from the Teso de San Miguel in the centre of the allied line. Looking south-east.

13. The Lesser Arapile seen from the Teso de San Miguel, looking east. This part of the allied line was occupied by Cole's Fourth Division and Pack's Portuguese brigade. Dyneley's guns were on top of the Lesser Arapile.

night at the village of Las Torres and were on the afternoon of the following day removed to Salamanca.' They both recovered, but Dowson was less fortunate: his foot was shattered and he lay out on the field all night; he appears in the returns as 'severely wounded', and he died in Liverpool in 1814, probably from the effects of the wound.[22] However great the inequalities between officers and men in the Napoleonic Wars – and in many respects they were great indeed – they shared equally in the dangers of battle.

These casualty figures show that the French resistance was not completely ineffectual, but the question remains why a complete division of French infantry, which had suffered few previous losses and which was supported by powerful artillery, was broken so easily. Numbers favoured the allies: Leith's division was about 6,700 strong, compared to Maucune's 5,200, but this numerical advantage was never really brought to bear – except for their light troops, Pringle's and Spry's brigades were not seriously engaged; indeed, they probably did not fire a shot, while Greville's brigade did almost all the fighting. It can be argued that the numerical superiority helped give the allies confidence and demoralized the French, but it is hard to give great weight to this argument. Much more important was the advance of the British cavalry, which disconcerted and disrupted Maucune's left even before it charged. There is also the possibility that fugitives from Thomières's division might already have reached Maucune's position, spreading dismay and alarm. But against this, Douglas's account and the casualties suffered by his regiment suggest that the French left fought at least as well as the rest of the division. The importance of the cavalry charge is debatable: it may have done no more than increase the panic of already broken troops, ensuring that they did not rally and that far more of them were captured; or it may have converted the defeat of the French first line into the rout of the whole division, virtually destroying the nearest French regiments and sending the others into precipitate retreat.

Without the cavalry, Maucune's division would probably have resisted more strongly, but it was never likely to succeed in repulsing Leith's attack. There was a qualitative as well as a numerical difference between the two divisions. While Leith's men were mostly veterans and full of confidence, Maucune's regiments had too much experience of the wrong kind. All four of his regiments had suffered greatly in Masséna's invasion of Portugal, losing a quarter or more of their strength mainly through disease and deprivation. The 66th Ligne had also lost heavily in action at the Coa and at Busaco and then again, less severely, at Fuentes. The 82nd had suffered at Busaco and more heavily at Fuentes and the evacuation of Almeida, while years before its third battalion had been cut up at Vimeiro. The 86th had also suffered at Vimeiro, and again at Oporto, although it had not seen much fighting since. These losses would not necessarily have mattered if they had been suffered in the course of a victory, but each of these actions had been a defeat, and the officers and men of these regiments can have felt little enthusiasm for crossing swords with the British again. Only the 15th Ligne had never been broken in battle against the British, although it had been present, if not closely engaged, at many French defeats in the Peninsula, so was unlikely to be much more confident.

But if the psychological advantage lay firmly with the British, the French should have had a tactical advantage. Wellington had frequently proved the great benefits of standing on the defensive and deploying his infantry on the reverse slope, so that they remained in good order while the attacking French arrived breathless and rattled by the fire of skirmishers and artillery, and so vulnerable to an immediate counterattack. Why did Maucune not benefit from the same things, and why was Leith not equally vulnerable? One obvious difference is that the forward slope of the Monte de Azan is open and gentle compared to some of the ridges Wellington chose, most famously at Busaco. Another is that the French attacks relied greatly on impetuosity, advancing rapidly in column, while Leith took great pains to restrain his men and keep them in good order. The advance in line greatly taxed their discipline, but it ensured that there need be no dangerous halt to deploy and that, when they encountered the French, they would bring every musket to bear in their opening volley. Maucune's men, by contrast, were formed in column or square – partly no doubt owing to the threat posed by the British cavalry, but also in readiness to charge the British with maximum effect after the initial exchange of fire. It seems that the British volley overwhelmed them and the British cheer broke their resolution, so that when Leith's line surged forward, the French took to their heels. Ideally, Maucune's second line of columns should have seized this moment to charge forward and attack the British when they were disordered by their success, but they did not do so and were soon broken in their turn by the exultant men of Greville's brigade. Even if they had charged and achieved some temporary success, Pringle and Spry were perfectly placed to check the trouble before it spread.

In the end Leith had too many advantages – his troops were too good, too numerous and too well supported – for the result of the combat to be in much doubt. But the French were far from contemptible opponents, and if the attack had been arranged and executed with any less care the result might have been very different – as the experience of Cole's division was to prove.

Commentary

Oman places the episode involving Lawson's guns and Leith's fears of an impending French attack in the time after Leith had moved next to Cole and was facing Maucune, and links Wellington's observations of the French forces to his decision to attack. This fits into his narrative very neatly, but Leith Hay, who is our only source for both these stories, explicitly states that they occurred before Leith's division moved to the right wing. It is curious that, while Leith Hay specifies that it was Captain Tomkinson's troop of the 16th Light Dragoons which covered Lawson's withdrawal, neither Tomkinson nor Lawson mentioned it in their diaries – although the latter, to be fair, is extremely terse. On the other hand, Leith Hay's account of the incident provides a plausible context for Douglas's strange story that Wellington deliberately sent the Royal Scots forward to draw the enemy fire and test whether the French were really intending to attack Leith's division.[23]

It is rather surprising that Wellington's orders to Leith should have specified how the division was to be formed – normally such matters could be left to the discretion of as capable and experienced a divisional commander as Leith, but Leith Hay is quite definite: 'General Leith was directed to form his division in two lines, the first of which was composed of . . .', and 'all [Wellington] directed was as to time and formation.' And as Leith's trusted ADC, Leith Hay was well placed to know.[24]

Leith Hay says only that 'part of the 4th regiment from General Pringle's brigade . . . [was] brought forward for the purpose of equalising the lines'. The 4th had two battalions in the field, and it seems reasonable to assume that the whole of the relatively weak first battalion (457 officers and men) was brought forward, except the light company which had joined the skirmishers. It is also an assumption that the 1/4th formed on the right of Greville's brigade beyond the Royal Scots, who would take the place of honour in their brigade. Cowper's history of the 4th King's Own supports both statements – though it is not clear whether Cowper had firm evidence or was working from the same assumptions; but he does add some interesting new details, including the fact that the combined light companies of the division were commanded by Major Alured Faunce of the King's Own.[25]

There is some confusion as to whether the 1/38th joined the army on the morning of the battle or on the previous evening, but in his unpublished papers Leith Hay says they 'joined us the day preceding the action', and this is confirmed by the anonymous memoirist in the battalion.[26] Fortescue risks causing confusion on another front when he includes the 2/58th in Pringle's brigade. Technically this is almost correct, but although the orders for its transfer had been issued as early as the beginning of April, they were not implemented until after the retreat from Burgos.[27]

The anonymous recollections of a soldier in the 1/38th are quoted several times during the chapter. These quotations have been edited so as not to distract the reader with their eccentricities; the literal transcriptions are as follows:

> Genl. Leath Came up Waving his Hat and Shouting Now my Lads this Is the day for England they would play at Long Ball with us from Morning untill Night But we Will Soon give them Something else

> altho the Scene was dreadfully Awfull I never was in A more Composed and Comfortable Frame than on that day for in all that I saw I saw that I had cause to be truly thankful Not that I had any certainty of Life more than others but I felt Confident that I was under the care and protection of almighty God and my Life was in his Hands and nothing could happen without his divine Permission.

But I was powerfully Struck at the Commencement of the Action with this passage of Scripture For all they that take the Sword Shall Perish with the Sword But
in my Situation I knew that I was bound by the Law to do my duty as A Soldier
beside I knew that if I did not my hown Life was Liable to pay for it. And I
thought that as providence had placed me in that Situation it was my duty to be
resined to his Will and prayed that wether it ended in Life or in Death it might
be for his Glorey and my everlasting wellfare.

the French were in a ... [here the paper is soiled making one small word illegi-
ble] Square not more than 200 yards from us as soon as we saw them we gave a
shout hopened a tremendous Fire and ran into them directly so that that Line
was in a few Minets killed and taken Prisoners. We then attacked their rear lines
and After we had engaged them some time we where Charging them I received
a Ball in my Right Foot[28]

Leith Hay, writing in his *Memoir* of General Leith, states that the 1/9th had
to pass through the village of Los Arapiles and then 'rejoined the line of their
brigade the moment they debouched from the houses'. This, together with other
praise for the regularity of Leith's advance, seems to override the statement in
Cannon's history of the Ninth that, after passing through the village, the regiment became separated from the rest of the division. Cannon's histories are
unreliable, and James Hale, who was a sergeant in the Ninth, says nothing relevant. More curious is the statement from the anonymous memoirist of the
1/38th that he advanced through a village under heavy fire before closing on the
French. This is strange, for other sources make it clear that the 1/38th was in the
middle of Leith's line, implying that the 2/38th was between it and the 1/9th (as
one would expect: the 1/38th would normally form on the right of the 2/38th).
Does this mean that half of Leith's line overcame the obstacle of the village in the
course of its advance: if so, why do Leith Hay and Gomm not make more of it?[29]

It is much easier to dispose of the claim in Carter's *Historical Records of the
Forty-Fourth*, repeated in Bannatyne's *History of the Thirtieth*, that Pringle's
brigade led the initial advance and was only overtaken by Greville's brigade, if
at all, when it became encumbered with prisoners. All the primary sources suggest that the reverse was the case, and they are supported by the casualties suffered by the two brigades. For the story given in these regimental histories of
the capture of a French eagle, see below, commentary to chapter six.[30]

Maucune's movements are impossible to reconstruct precisely, but it seems
fairly clear that he was on the forward slope of the Monte de Azan when
Wellington made the decision to attack, but had retired behind the slight crest
which marks the edge of the plateau before the British assault reached him.

The description given in the narrative of the formation of Maucune's division is largely speculative, based on French casualties and comments in British
accounts of the fighting quoted in the chapter. The casualties indicate that the
66th and 15th Ligne suffered far more than the 82nd or 86th, and it seems

reasonable to assume that they were at the western end of the line and so more exposed to Le Marchant's cavalry. Most of the British accounts – except Leith Hay, who was wounded in the first clash – imply a succession of opponents, supporting the idea that the French had two lines of columns, not one. Furthermore, if the French had formed a single line of battalion columns they would have been left with relatively small gaps between them – too small for them to deploy if they had wished to do so, although perhaps this is what Leith Hay means when he says that the French were 'drawn up in contiguous columns'.[31] (Nine columns with an average frontage of about 45 yards equals 400 yards, leaving only about 60 yards between each column – eight intervals, not nine – whereas each battalion would need over 120 yards to deploy into three deep lines.) The 66th suffered considerably more than the 15th, which may indicate that it was in the front line; but if the British cavalry charged just as Leith's men were breaking the second line, it is likely that the nearest French battalions in the second line were the ones which suffered the most. Jean Sarramon's ideas on how the French were deployed are discussed below in the commentary to chapter six.

A related question is, how far behind the skyline were the French deployed? In other words, at what range did they open fire on the British infantry? Writing home two days after the battle Leith Hay says that 'we were about 30 yards from them', although he changed this in his published account to 'about 50 yards', while the anonymous memoirist of the 1/38th says that the French were 'not more than 200 yards from us'. Leith Hay was, of course, riding a little in front of the line – but ten, not 170, yards seems an appropriate allowance for this. One can split the difference, or opt for the source written closer to the event or the more conservative estimate (the range was certainly not more than 200 yards), according to taste; but the problem remains ultimately insoluble. The range probably varied in different parts of the line, but this is no explanation, for Leith Hay was with his uncle in front of the centre of the 1/38th.[32]

Most of the questions arising from the descriptions of the climax of the clash between Leith and Maucune are fully discussed in the narrative, while the role of the cavalry must be left to the next chapter. One incidental point remains. Oman's account of this combat consists largely of a lengthy quotation from Leith Hay which makes splendidly dramatic reading. Unfortunately, this is partly because Oman has gently improved the original, mostly by slightly condensing it, correcting the grammar and making it flow more smoothly. No violence is done to the sense of the original, but no indication is given of these changes. Scholarly conventions were less rigid when Oman was writing than they have subsequently become, but even so such practices would have been regarded as surprising and undesirable. Nor is this the only occasion, even in his account of Salamanca, in which Oman's quotations are 'better' than the original.[33] Here are the two versions:

Oman, *A History of the Peninsular War*, vol. 5, pp. 448–9

Leith Hay, *Narrative of the Peninsular War*, vol. 2, pp. 54–9*

'The ground,' writes Leith Hay, 'between the advancing force and that which it was to assail was crowded by the light troops of both sides in extended order, carrying on a very incessant tiraillade. The general desired me to ride forward, to make our light infantry press up the heights to cover his line of march, and to bid them, if practicable, make a rush at the enemy's guns. Our light troops soon drove in those opposed to them: the cannon were removed to the rear: every obstruction to the general advance of our line vanished. In front of the centre of that beautiful line rode General Leith, directing its movements. Occasionally every soldier was visible, the sun shining bright upon their arms, though at intervals all were enveloped in a dense cloud of dust, from whence at times issued the animating cheer of the British infantry.

'The French columns, retired from the crest of the heights, were formed in squares, about fifty yards behind the line at which, when arrived, the British regiments would become visible. Their artillery, although placed more to the rear, still poured its fire upon our advancing troops.

[T]he ground between the advancing force and that to be assailed was also crowded with light troops in extended order, carrying on a very incessant tiraillade. The general desired me to ride forward, make the light infantry press up the heights to clear his line of march, and if practicable make a rush at the enemy's cannon. In the execution of this service, I had to traverse the whole extent of the surface directly in front of the 5th division: the light troops soon drove back those opposed; the cannon[†] were removed to the rear; every obstruction to the regular advance of the line had vanished. In front of the centre of that beautiful line rode General Leith, directing its movements, and regulating its advance. Occasionally every soldier was visible, the sun shining bright upon their arms, while at intervals all were enveloped in a dense cloud of dust, from whence, at times, issued the animating cheer of British infantry.

The confident presence of the enemy was now exchanged for the quiet formation proceeding in his ranks, as preparatives for resisting the evidently approaching shock. His columns, retired from the crest of the height, were formed in squares, about fifty yards removed from the ground, on which, when arrived, the British

---

* This is quoted from Oman's own copy of the first edition, now in the Ward Collection, Hartley Library, University of Southampton (pp. 258–61 of the third edition, that generally used in this book).
† Changed to 'the French cannon' by the third edition.

regiments would become visible. The French artillery, although placed more to the rear, still poured its fire on the advancing troops. In the act of urging forward the light infantry, a ball struck the horse I rode, and passing through his body, laid him dead on the spot. In this dilemma, I waited until the* line approached, and having dismounted an orderly dragoon, proceeded with the general, who continued in the same situation he had occupied when the division commenced its advance; namely, in front of the colours of the 1st battalion of the 38th regiment. That corps, numerous and effective, had joined the army on the previous day, and, being the junior regiment, formed the centre of the first line; its commanding officer, Colonel Greville, having charge of the brigade, in the absence of General Hay.

The second line of the division was about a hundred yards in rear of the first; and between these, during the march towards the enemy, Lord Wellington at one time was observing the progress of the attack.

We were now near the summit of the ridge. The men marched with the same orderly steadiness as at first: no advance in line at a review was ever more correctly executed: the dressing was admirable, and spaces were no sooner formed by casualties than closed up with the most perfect regularity, and without the slightest deviation from the order of march.

General Leith, and the officers of his staff, being on horseback, first perceived the enemy, and had time to

We were now near the summit of the ridge. The men marched with the same orderly steadiness as at the first: no advance in line at a review was ever more correctly executed: the dressing was admirable, and the gaps caused by casualties were filled up with the most perfect regularity. General Leith and the officers of his staff, being on horseback, first perceived the enemy, and had time to observe his formation, before our infantry line became so visible as to induce him to commence

* Changed to 'a line' by the third edition.

firing. He was drawn up in contiguous squares, the front rank kneeling, and prepared to fire when the drum should beat. All was still and quiet in these squares: not a musket was discharged until the whole opened. Nearly at the same instant General Leith ordered our line to fire and charge. At this moment the last thing I saw through the smoke was the plunge of the horse of Colonel Greville, commanding the leading brigade, who, shot through the head, reared and fell back upon his rider. In an instant evey individual present was enveloped in smoke and obscurity. No serious struggle for ascendancy followed, for the French squares were penetrated, broken, and discomfited, and the victorious 5th Division pressed forward no longer against troops formed up, but against a mass of disorganized men flying in all directions ...

When close to the enemy's squares Leith had been severely wounded and reluctantly forced to quit the field; at the same moment I was hit myself, and my horse killed by a musket-ball: thus

observe his formation, previous to the infantry line becoming so visible, as to induce him to commence firing. He was drawn up in contiguous squares,[*] the front rank kneeling, and prepared to fire when the drum beat for its commencement. All was still and quiet in these squares;[†] – not a musket was discharged until the whole opened. Nearly at the same moment General Leith ordered the line to fire, and charge: the roll of musketry was succeeded by that proud cheer that has become habitual to British soldiers on similar occasions – that to an enemy tremendous sound, which may without exaggeration[‡] be termed the note of victory. At this moment, the last thing I saw through the smoke was the plunge of Colonel Greville's horse, who, shot through the head, reared, and fell back on his rider. In an instant every individual present was enveloped in smoke and obscurity. No struggle for ascendancy took place:[§] the French squares were penetrated, broken, and discomfited; the victorious division pressed forward, not against troops opposed, but a mass of disorganised men, flying in all directions.[||]

[Nearly two pages follow describing the rest of the battle; Oman indicates its deletion by ellipsis marks.] When close to the enemy's squares in the commencement of the battle, General Leith was severely wounded, and reluctantly compelled to quit the field;

---

[*] Changed to 'contiguous columns' by the third edition.
[†] Changed to 'columns' by the third edition.
[‡] Changed to 'without doubt' by the third edition.
[§] Changed to 'No struggle for ascendancy now took place; resistance was vain: the French squares ...' by the third edition.
[||] Changed to 'overpowered and flying in all directions' by the third edition.

removed, I cannot detail the further movements of the division.

nearly at the same moment the author of these pages was also wounded, and his horse killed by a musket-ball. Captain Dowson, another of the general's aides-de-camp, had his foot shattered by a shot,* and remained all night without assistance on the field. Colonel Berkeley, Major Gomm, Captain Belshes, and Captain George Hay, acting aide-de-camp in the absence of his father, composed the remaining officers of the divisional staff on this occasion, and, by their activity and gallantry, greatly conduced to the result of the successful service it had the good fortune to perform.

Having been removed from the field, I cannot detail the future movements of the 5th division on the night of the battle.†

---

* Changed to 'a bullet' by the third edition.
† As well as the textual changes noted above, there was some alteration to the punctuation and an increase in the use of capitals between the first and third editions. The changes do not affect the meaning, nor generally bring it closer to Oman's version of the text.

Chapter Six
Le Marchant and the Destruction of the French Left

Wellington did not ride straight from Pakenham to Leith: on the way he stopped near Las Torres, where Le Marchant's formidable brigade of heavy cavalry was waiting. He told Le Marchant

> that the success of the movement to be made by the Third Division would greatly depend on the assistance they received from the cavalry; and that he must therefore be prepared to take advantage of the first favourable opportunity to charge the enemy's infantry. 'You must then charge,' said Lord Wellington, 'at all hazards.' After some brief remarks on the chances of the day, Lord Wellington rode towards the centre, having desired the Dragoons to remain in the same position until the time of action was come.[1]

The heavy brigade was halted in low ground in front of Las Torres, out of sight of the enemy and beyond effective artillery range, although enough long shots came bounding towards it to make the men uneasy, and Le Marchant made them dismount and lie down to be out of harm's way. During the thunderstorm of the previous night many of the brigade's horses had broken their pickets and stampeded through the ranks of sleeping troopers, injuring eighteen men. Most of the horses had been recaptured, but thirty-one from the 5th Dragoon Guards had escaped and galloped towards the French lines. Now one of these prodigals returned, neighing and snorting with satisfaction at having found its accustomed comrades after a night of adventures. Lieutenant Miles recognized it as his charger and rode it for the rest of the day; nor did his luck desert him, for he was unscathed in the fighting.[2]

Such incidents helped fill the time before the brigade could begin its advance; and Le Marchant put this interval to good use, sending Lieutenant William Light of his staff and Lieutenant-Colonel Charles Dalbiac, 4th Dragoons, to reconnoitre the ground over which the brigade would advance and to post videttes to give warning of difficult points.[3] At last, the moment arrived and the heavy brigade moved gently forward in two lines at a walk. It

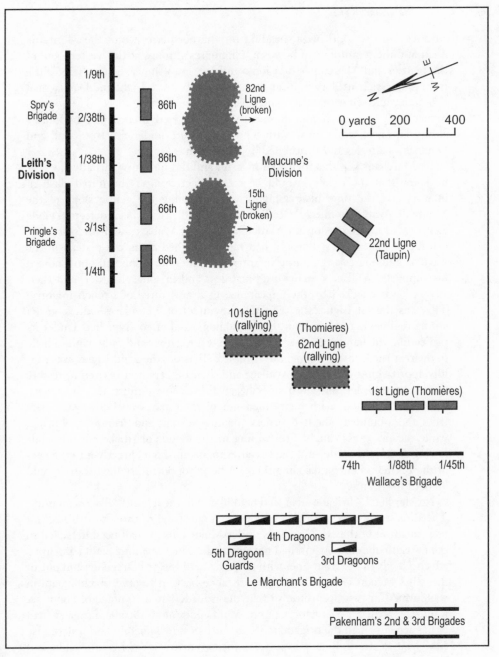

Plan of Le Marchant's charge (all troop positions approximate, many conjectural).

advanced to the south-west, heading for the northern face of the Monte de Azan and the tempting gap between Thomières's troops at the western end of the plateau and Maucune's division a mile or so to the east. It suffered little from the French artillery in its approach, partly because Light and Dalbiac had chosen a route which gave it some cover, but also because there were no guns immediately opposite it, and those with Maucune were preoccupied by Leith's steady advance, while those with Thomières were under fire from Bull and Douglas's batteries and threatened by Pakenham.

Le Marchant kept his men well in hand and did not hurry his advance, for he knew that the cavalry would be most effective after the initial clash of infantry. By the time his regiments were climbing the gentle slope of the Monte de Azan, Thomières's leading brigade had already been defeated, while Leith was rapidly closing on Maucune. Colonel Wallace, with the foremost brigade of Pakenham's division, had rapidly pushed along the plateau in the wake of Thomières's retreating infantry, but in doing so he had outdistanced his supports. Wallace's men were breathless and in some disorder, and their advance was checked by the appearance of a new force of French infantry. This was the 1st Ligne, the remaining regiment of Thomières's division – a strong regiment, 1,700 men in three battalions, and of good quality. Under its protection, the 62nd and 101st began to collect together and rally, while a little to the rear the leading regiment of Taupin's division, the 22nd Ligne, was rapidly approaching. Pakenham, Wallace and their officers hastily tried to restore their men to order, and both sides began firing. There must have been considerable confusion, with many men out of their ranks on both sides, cries from the wounded, shouted orders, drums beating and trumpets blowing, while the dry grass caught fire, adding to the clouds of smoke and dust billowing across the scene, and the late afternoon sun shone directly into the eyes of the French infantry, dazzling them. A better opportunity for cavalry would be hard to imagine.[4]

Le Marchant's brigade advanced behind and to the left of Wallace's infantry. The three regiments of British cavalry each consisted of three squadrons, but one squadron of the 4th Dragoons under Major Onslow had been detached to the far right about noon and had not rejoined.[5] The remaining eight squadrons advanced, six in the front line, with a squadron of the 3rd Dragoons and one of the 5th Dragoon Guards held some distance back in reserve. Each squadron was formed in two-deep line, so that the brigade had a frontage of about six hundred yards. Sir Stapleton Cotton, commander of all the allied cavalry, had either accompanied the brigade in its advance or now joined it, and ordered Le Marchant to attack. Relations between the two men were not comfortable, and when Le Marchant asked what direction the charge should take, Cotton lost his temper and replied sharply, 'To the enemy, Sir.' More furious words were exchanged and the quarrel might not have ended there if both men had survived the battle. As it was, the incident added to Cotton's unpopularity among the heavy cavalry.[6]

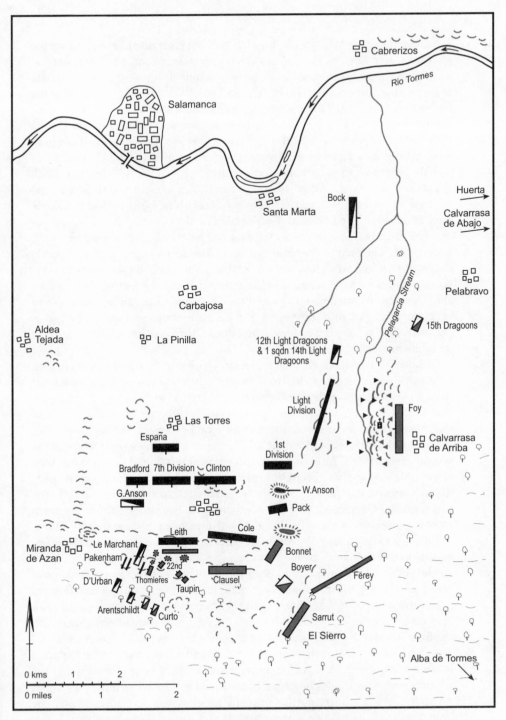

State of the battle when Le Marchant's brigade begins its charge
(all troop positions approximate, many conjectural).

Still seething from this insult, Le Marchant led his brigade forward along the plateau. Unfortunately, the sources are so fragmentary and confused that any account of their charge needs to be heavily qualified, for we cannot be certain of the sequence of events, although the final result is clear. But it seems that the regiments in the centre and right of the brigade approached Wallace's line from behind at a canter. Grattan describes how the British infantry were startled by their sudden appearance, and at first mistook them for the enemy and began to form square. In a moment they were recognized, however, and the order was quickly given to 'Open right and left', creating gaps in the line through which the cavalry passed.[7] Le Marchant's men then quickly re-formed their line, and charged forward at full speed. The French infantry facing them had little time to react: blinded by smoke and dust, dazzled by the sun, they had scarcely recognized the threat and begun to form square before the heavy dragoons were upon them. The men of the 62nd and 101st Regiments had already suffered in Pakenham's initial attack and had not yet properly regained their order or composure. Faced with a determined charge of well-formed heavy cavalry – probably the most frightening spectacle on a Napoleonic battlefield – their nerve broke and they fled in all directions. But the men of the 1st Ligne, who had as yet suffered little, appear to have maintained their cohesion and succeeded in withdrawing relatively unscathed.

Meanwhile, Le Marchant's left regiment – probably the 5th Dragoon Guards, although even this is uncertain – took a slightly different course. It advanced, not through Wallace's brigade, but through the mingled light infantry of the Third and Fifth Divisions which had extended to fill the gap between Leith and Pakenham's main lines. Gathering pace as it swept forward, the regiment came upon the exposed flank of Maucune's division just as Leith's men had broken the second French line. The 66th Ligne suffered the most, but at least one battalion of the 15th seems to have been cut to pieces; meanwhile even the second brigade did not escape completely, for the regimental history of the 82nd Ligne describes how Captain Mottier defended his Eagle against the British horsemen and only got away with difficulty, the staff broken by balls and sabre blows. Maucune's division had already been defeated, but this charge added enormously to its losses and ensured that it could not hope to rally again that day.[8]

Maucune and Thomières had been put to flight, but the charge had yet to spend all its energy. The regiments of the centre and right still pressed forward at full speed. They had become mixed together and were crowded into a solid line, officers riding where they could and the supporting squadrons joined with the front line; but if there was some confusion, they were full of confidence and élan. Soon they spied fresh enemies, for the 22nd Ligne, the leading regiment in Taupin's division, was not far away. The horsemen swept forward and the infantry – whether caught by surprise, disrupted by fugitives from Thomières's division, taken while trying to form square, or simply overwhelmed by the impetuosity of the cavalry – were broken and put to flight with very heavy losses.

With this triumph the scene dissolved into complete confusion. The whole plateau was covered with scattered parties of French, some maintaining good order and bent on escape or further resistance, others fleeing in wild panic. 'The dragoons, excited by the struggle, vied with each other in the pursuit, and galloped recklessly into the crowd of fugitives, sabring those who came within their reach. To restrain them at such a moment was very difficult.'[9] In fact they were completely out of control and vulnerable to a French counterattack, although even the destruction of the entire brigade would not have offset the immense damage they had done to Marmont's army. But there were no French cavalry reserves to exploit the opportunity, and so the British dragoons did not pay the normal price for their reckless impetuosity.

Although Le Marchant's blood was up – he had 'fought like a private soldier, and as many as six men fell by his hand' – he recognized the danger. He sent his ADC (his son) to the rear to look for Cotton, who should have been bringing forward Anson's brigade to support the charge and, if necessary, cover Le Marchant's retreat. It was impossible to rally the brigade, the men were too scattered and too wild, and it seemed best to use their remaining energy and enthusiasm to exploit their success to the utmost. Le Marchant therefore rode forward again and joined Lieutenant Gregory who, with half a squadron of the 4th Dragoons, was preparing to charge a French square. Le Marchant took the lead and galloped forward, closely followed by the dragoons. The French held their fire until the cavalry were almost upon them and Le Marchant was struck by a shot in the groin, which knocked him from his horse. The square dissolved and escaped into the trees, for they were now close to the forest in the rear of the French position, but Le Marchant was dead. His son, returning across the battlefield, his heart filled with joy at his father's triumph, discovered a party of dragoons carrying the corpse. 'Overpowered by this unexpected calamity he threw himself upon his father's body in an agony of grief, which those who witnessed it, accustomed as they were to the miseries of war, felt they never could forget. All were deeply moved, and even many of the common soldiers were observed to shed tears as the corpse was carried along the line.'[10]

The charge was now almost completely over, for the men were mentally and physically exhausted and their horses were blown. Lord Edward Somerset, commander of the 4th Dragoons, is said to have captured a battery of five guns as it attempted to escape, but a scattered charge on the remainder of Taupin's division (17th Léger and 65th Ligne) was repulsed with some loss. Wearily the dragoons made their way back towards their lines, passing the allied infantry who were headed in the other direction, busy collecting prisoners and consolidating the gains that had been made. The whole charge had probably lasted less than an hour – one participant says forty minutes – and had covered about two miles.[11]

The heady excitement, rapid movement and chaos of the charge left most participants with a jumble of confused but vivid images rather than a neat sequence of events in their memory. A letter home from William Bragge of the

3rd Dragoons, written only three days after the battle, conveys something of the raw impression, before frequent tellings and listening to other men's accounts imposed an external order:

> My Dear Father,
>   Knowing the Anxiety you and my Mother will feel upon hearing of a great and sanguinary Battle, in which the Third Dragoons bore no inconsiderable share, I take the earliest possible opportunity of informing you that I escaped perfectly sound, Wind and Limb, together with the Little Bay Mare who carried me through the Day delightfully and I believe to her Speed and Activity I may in a great measure attribute my marvellous escape, as I at one Time had to gallop along the whole Front of a French Brigade retreating in double quick step.
>   ... the Cavalry advanced upon the Backs of the Infantry. Our Brigade literally rode over the Regiments in their Front and dashed through the Wood at a Gallop, the Infantry cheering us in all Directions. We quickly came up with the French Columns and charged their Rear. Hundreds threw down their Arms, their Cavalry ran away, and most of the Artillery jumped upon the Horses and followed the Cavalry. One or two charges mixed up the whole Brigade, it being impossible to see for Dust and Smoak.[12]

Memory of another incident has been preserved because it makes a good anecdote. No doubt the story has been smoothed and rounded in the telling, but it is valuable for showing the unexpected human quirks that lie behind the dry phrases of tactical studies and drill manuals:

> After the third line of infantry had been broken Major Hugonin, who was commanding the left squadron of the regiment [4th Dragoons], had his horse shot under him. He was a sufferer from gout, and wore boot and spur on one foot only, with a large cloth 'shoe' on the other, so without his horse he was helpless. He stood, sword in hand, cursing his ill-fortune until a trooper came up, dismounted and helped the Major back into the saddle. The trooper made his way back on foot while Major Hugonin galloped forward, seeking more Frenchmen.[13]

Lieutenant John Massey (3rd Dragoons) told his brother Dick, 'Our loss in men was trifling all things considered for we charged Infantry which is a thing very rarely done. I can't tell you of any hairbreadth escapes that I had for I don't know of any, but the balls were thick and near enough to be pleasant.' And John Luard, of the 4th Dragoons, came across a French gun limbered up and trying to escape: 'I cut down their leader, turned the horses' heads towards our side, and then galloped on.' Nor was it only the cavalry who were caught up in the excitement. Grattan tells how Captain William Mackie of the 88th disappeared in the confusion and was feared to have fallen. But he returned, 'covered with dust and blood, his horse tottering from fatigue, and nothing left of his sabre –

but the hilt.' He had joined the cavalry as they passed and then taken part in their charge, although if Grattan's account is to be believed, neither his horse nor his sword was really fit for the job.[14]

Captain Parquin, that celebrated raconteur and member of Marmont's escort squadron, gives us a relatively unembroidered glimpse of the fag end of the charge when scattered troops on both sides might engage in personal combats – or seek to avoid them:

> I saw a chasseur of the 20th who was being closely pursued by two English horsemen.
>
> 'Turn and face them!' I cried, going to his help. But he did not stop and one of the Englishmen, whose horse was obviously out of control, cannoned into me and we both went down. Then the second Englishman galloped up and shouted: 'You are my prisoner!'
>
> With his sabre he gestured me to walk ahead of him. The memory of my captivity in Russia flashed through my mind. I noticed that my would-be captor had not drawn his pistol; if he had done so, I would have been forced to obey him. Instead, I parried the blows which he aimed at me with his sabre for I had quickly risen from beneath my horse which made off towards the escort. I endeavoured to strike the legs of his horse so as to unhorse him. When my horse returned without me the other members of the escort became alarmed and two of them came to look for me and to bring me my horse. As soon as they saw me they rode towards us at full speed and the Englishman, when he saw them, retired immediately.[15]

But the most vivid personal account of the charge and its aftermath comes in a letter from Lieutenant Norcliffe Norcliffe of the 4th Dragoons, written three weeks after the battle. This deserves to be quoted at length:

> My Beloved Father,
>
> Thanks to the Almighty, and the very great care of my surgeon, I am quite out of danger from the severe wound I received, but it was perhaps the most hairbreadth escape that ever was heard of, the skull was just injured, and the tenth part of an inch more must have consigned me to an eternal rest. We were pursuing the French Infantry, which were broken and running in all directions. I was cutting them down as well as I could, when in the hurry and confusion I lost my regiment and got with some soldiers of the 5th Dragoon Guards; on looking behind me, I could only see a few of the 5th, and we were in the centre of the enemy's infantry, amongst whom were a few Chasseurs and Dragoons. Nothing now remained but to go on, as we were in as much danger as by going any other way.
>
> I rode up to a French officer, who was, like the rest, taking to his heels, and cut him just behind the neck; I saw the blood flow, and he lost his balance, and fell from his horse. I perceived my sword was giving way in the handle, so I said

to the officer who lay on the ground: *'Donnez-moi votre épée'* – I really believed he was more frightened than hurt; I sheathed my sword and went on with his. I had not gone 10 yards further before my horse was wounded in the ear by a gun shot; he turned sharp round, and at the same instant I was shot in the head. I turned giddy, and fell off. I can recollect a French Dragoon taking away my horse. I was senseless a few seconds, and when I recovered, I saw the French Dragoons stripping me of everything; they began by turning my pockets inside out, to look for money which they stole; my sword and sash, hat, boots, and spurs off my feet, dragging me along the ground in the most barbarous manner, saying: *'Eh ... Anglais, vous n'êtres pas à cheval.'* Another said: *'Eh, je sais* [sic] *bien le garçon, il m'a poursuivi. ...'*; in fact I never saw such usage in my life. *'Allons donc, enlève-toi'* said another; I shook my head as much as to say 'I am unable to rise,' when he held a sabre over me, crying out: *'... je vous mettrai à coup de sabre'.* At last I was left by the cavalry, and the French infantry came all round me, and I expected the same treatment. Judge of my surprise, when I experienced quite the contrary. *'Courage mon ami'.* I asked for water, being very faint from loss of blood, *'Ma foi! je n'ai point de l'eau, pauvre garçon,'* and another *'Etes-vous officier?'* I stammered out: *'Oui, Lieutenant de Quatrième Régiment de Dragoons.'* Presently an officer came up with five [soldiers]; each took a leg and an arm, and the fifth supported my head, which was bleeding profusely, and I will say I never saw men more careful; if ever I groaned, owing to the pain of being carried, they said to each other: *'Gardez-vous, gardez-vous, camarade.'* They carried me into the very centre of the French column, close to a very fine battalion of Grenadiers, with great bear-skin caps. I rested here a little, for I was very weak, and a great number of French officers came round me and were most particularly civil. One, Colonel of Grenadiers, poured some brandy into a cup and wanted me to drink it; I just wet my lips. He then ordered 5 Grenadiers to fall out, and carry me further into the wood. I made a sign that I had rather be carried by the men who brought me there, fearful of falling into fresh hands. Our infantry was at the time advancing again to the attack; the five men who carried me were desired by all the French officers to take particular care that no-one ill-used me, and that if I could not get away, I was to be laid under a tree. The 5 men seeing our infantry advance, laid me down very carefully under an olive tree, and each of them shook hands with me before they left me, and said: *'Je vous souhaite bien, Monsieur,'* and they also desired that I would remember they belonged to the 65th Regiment. Our Infantry I could now see (though it was getting dark) were bayonet to bayonet, and I had at last the pleasure of seeing the enemy running in every direction. I had the presence of mind to take off my jacket and cram it into a bush, and as my boots were off I lay as if I was dead, and when they were running away they all passed my tree and took me for a Frenchman. Several of the musket shots from our men struck the back of the tree where I was, but I lay very close to the root. Drums, muskets and everything they could not easily carry, were thrown away by the enemy. One Frenchman was wounded by a musket ball in the side, and fell close to me. I waited till the French had all passed me, and then ran as fast as my strength would let me towards our Riflemen. I was so delighted at getting back, I actually threw my arms around the necks of our infantry. They led me up to where the 6th Division was, and I fell down quite exhausted at the feet of the Grenadier Company of the 32nd Regiment ... [Norcliffe's wound was dressed by a surgeon, and after a cold night he was carried into Salamanca the following day, and slowly recovered.]

This is the second horse I have lost in action, as also my saddle, bridle, collar, sword, sash, musket, boots and spurs, and pouch. My beloved Father will see I have been obliged to draw largely on the agent owing to these losses. It was a glorious day for our Brigade. They behaved nobly; 4 men killed of the troop I commanded, and several men and horses wounded. It was a fine sight to see the fellows running, and as we held our swords over their heads, fall down on their knees, drop their muskets, and cry: *'Prisonnier, Monsieur.'* You see I am not born to be a prisoner. Love to my Mother.[16]

Norcliffe was rather unlucky to be wounded, for the cavalry's losses were extraordinarily light. Other than Le Marchant himself, only one officer was killed and five wounded, one mortally (this includes two staff officers attached to the brigade). The other ranks lost twenty-two killed, seventy-four wounded and five missing, so that the brigade as a whole lost 108 casualties, or barely one-tenth of its strength.

The damage the charge inflicted on the French left wing bears no relation to these slight losses. Even Lamartinière's return admits that the 62nd and 101st Regiments in Thomières's division were virtually destroyed. The 62nd suffered 868 casualties from 1,123 all ranks, or 77 per cent of its strength; and the 101st lost 1,186 from 1,449, or 82 per cent. The great majority of these were listed as 'killed or captured', and while some casualties would have been inflicted by Wallace's attack and D'Urban's cavalry, the bulk would have come in the mass surrender of demoralized men seeking safety from Le Marchant's attack. The Third Division collected these prisoners by the hundred, some horribly wounded by the cavalry, but many unscathed, and Grattan regarded it as noteworthy that 'Not a man was bayoneted – not one even molested or plundered; and the invincible old third [division] on this day surpassed themselves; for they not only defeated their terrible enemies in a fair stand-up fight, but actually covered their retreat, and protected them at a moment when, without such aid, their total annihilation was certain.'[17]

The remaining regiment in Thomières's division, the 1st Ligne, suffered much less: according to Lamartinière, it lost only 230 casualties from 1,763 all ranks, or 13 per cent. Evidently it was not broken and succeeded in withdrawing in relatively good order, although its movements and part in the battle are difficult to determine.

Maucune's division did not suffer as much as Thomières's, although it too was broken and took no further part in the battle. The 66th Ligne bore the brunt of the British attack, losing 588 casualties from 1,169 all ranks, or fractionally more than 50 per cent. The 15th Ligne lost 607 casualties from 1,667, or 36 per cent. The second brigade was less exposed: the 82nd and 86th Regiments lost 272 and 270 casualties, or 27 and 23 per cent respectively. Many of these losses would have been inflicted by Leith's attack, which had already broken the French before the cavalry intervened, but the cavalry charge magnified the success of the infantry, greatly increasing the panic in French ranks and the number of prisoners taken.

The leading regiment in Taupin's division, the 22nd Ligne, suffered more than any in Maucune's division. Lamartinière lists 1,006 casualties from a nominal strength of 1,547 officers and men, although this includes casualties suffered when the regiment was engaged on the Guarena on 18 July. If the total casualties are divided in the same proportions as the officer casualties recorded by Martinien, the result would be that the regiment lost 193 casualties, or 12.5 per cent, on the 18th, and 813 casualties, or 60 per cent, on the 22nd.[18] This was bad enough, but French sources state that one battalion of the regiment was detached on the morning of the battle, and that the remaining two battalions were left with only 47 men in their ranks at the end of the day.[19] The sacrifice of the 22nd enabled the other two regiments in Taupin's division to withdraw to the safety of the wood in good order. These were the 17th Léger and the 65th Ligne – the latter being the regiment which took such good care of Norcliffe. They probably lost a few men at this point, but did not give way until later in the day when attacked by allied infantry.

A number of cannon were taken, and at least some French cavalry fled from the charge – possibly even the whole of Curto's second brigade, which seems to have made no impact on the battle at any point. The two Eagles taken by the allies were both captured in this part of the battle. Dramatic stories are told of their fall:

> The first Eagle – that of the hapless French 62nd, whose fate has been told – fell to Lieutenant Pearce of the 44th, a regiment in the Fifth Division. He came on the Eagle-bearer while in the act of unscrewing the Eagle from its pole in order to hide it under his long overcoat and get away with it. Pearce sprang on the Frenchman, and tussled with him for the Eagle. The second Porte-Aigle joined in the fight, whereupon three men of the 44th ran to their officer's assistance. A third Frenchman, a private, added himself to the combatants, and was in the act of bayoneting the British lieutenant, when one of the men of the 44th, Private Finlay, shot him through the head and saved the officer's life. Both the Porte-Aigles were killed a moment later – one by Lieutenant Pearce, who snatched the Eagle from its dead bearer's hands. In his excitement over the prize Pearce rewarded the privates who had helped him by emptying his pockets on the spot, and dividing what money he had on him amongst them – twenty dollars. A sergeant's halberd was then procured, on which the Eagle was stuck and carried triumphantly through the remainder of the battle. Lieutenant Pearce

presented it next morning to General Leith, the Commander of the Fifth Division, who directed him to carry it to Wellington. In honour of the exploit the 44th, now the Essex Regiment, bear the badge of the Napoleonic Eagle on the regimental colour, and the officers wear a similar badge on their mess-jackets.

The second Eagle taken was that of the 22nd of the Line. It was captured by a British officer of the 30th, Ensign Pratt, attached for duty to Major Crookshank's 7th Portuguese, a Light Infantry (or Caçadores) battalion, serving with the Third Division. He took it to General Pakenham, whose mounted orderly displayed the Eagle of the 22nd publicly after the battle 'carrying it about wherever the general went for the next two days.'[20]

Unfortunately, there are a number of discrepancies in both these stories. Martinien's list of French officer casualties does not identify either Porte-Aigle of the 62nd as having been wounded, let alone killed, although a Porte-Aigle in the 22nd was wounded. And when one remembers that Leith was lying seriously wounded in Salamanca, while his division was advancing with the rest of the army, one may doubt whether Lieutenant Pearce really presented the captured Eagle to him on the day after the battle. More significantly, Lamartinière's return indicates that the captured Eagles belonged to the 22nd and 101st Ligne, not the 62nd, although this is not accepted by some authorities. Nonetheless, the essence of Pearce's story appears to be true: he did, indeed, capture an Eagle, probably that of the 101st. However, there are more serious difficulties with the claim put forward on behalf of Ensign Pratt. He was an officer in the light company of the 30th, but does not seem to have been attached to the Portuguese. In any case, Crookshank commanded the 12th, not the 7th, Caçadores, although it is correct that his unit was part of the Third Division. Two incidents appear to have been conflated: Pratt himself claimed the capture, not of an Eagle, but of a French standard, that is, a *fanion* or colour carried by each battalion – another *fanion* was claimed by Lieutenant Francis Maguire of the 4th King's Own. The Eagle of the 22nd was secured by Crookshank's caçadores.[21] John Douglas of the Royal Scots writes:

A little before sunset a Portuguese soldier of our Division picked up an eagle and brought it safe into the lines, to the astonishment of all as you would imagine that a sparrow could not escape between the two fires. This eagle was the subject of an account in a book of anecdotes a few years ago, when it was stated to have been captured by an officer of the British. The statement was false. It was taken as I have mentioned. It lay on the ground along with a number of the Regiment to which it belonged, having fallen by our fire, and was free to be picked up by anyone, but it was first discovered among the dead by the Portuguese soldier. But what became of it afterwards I cannot say . . . [22]

It seems likely that this was the Eagle of the 22nd, although Douglas may have been reacting to Pearce's story, not realizing that two Eagles were taken in the same vicinity.

Le Marchant's charge was the finest exploit of British cavalry during the entire Peninsular War. It was perfectly timed and executed, catching the French infantry when they were already shaken, disordered and broken; it converted their defeat into a rout and spread fear and panic throughout the French left wing. This was what cavalry were best at: not dashing against perfectly formed infantry in a desperate attempt to break their will, but taking advantage of a moment of confusion and weakness, so that the infantry dissolved before them with scarcely any resistance. Le Marchant amplified the initial success of Pakenham and Leith, removing any risk that the French left might rally, and reaping a vastly greater harvest of prisoners than the infantry could ever have hoped to gain. Three divisions of infantry, half the army's cavalry and a good part of its artillery were on the French left: after Le Marchant's charge none of it could be brought to face the allies again except the two remaining regiments of Taupin's infantry. Only a calamity in the centre could deprive Wellington of victory.

Commentary

The role of Sir Stapleton Cotton, commander of all the allied cavalry, in the great charge, is far from clear. One might have expected that if Wellington had orders for Le Marchant, he would give them through Cotton, but the memoir of Le Marchant by his son is definite that Wellington gave his instructions in person and directly – indeed, it makes very little mention of Cotton at all. Cotton's life, written by his widow with the assistance of Captain Knollys, is vague on the point, saying only that Cotton 'had been desired by Wellington to take advantage of any opportunity to charge', and it gives few details of the battle. However, this is the only source which describes the quarrel between Cotton and Le Marchant before the charge was launched. The memoir of Le Marchant ignores the incident, while other first-hand accounts refer to it obliquely or in passing. For example, Captain Tomkinson wrote cryptically in his diary: '(Circumstance that occurred with General Le Marchant previous to the attack of the enemy, and his feelings on that occasion.)'[23] But the incident rankled and was made worse by the meagre praise the brigade received for their charge in Wellington's dispatch. Almost fifty years after the battle Lieutenant-Colonel William Legh Clowes, who had served in the 3rd Dragoons at Salamanca, wrote to his brother-in-law Sir George Scovell (who had been on Wellington's staff):

> That due credit was not given to the Brigade was much felt by us all, but the real cause was this: no light Cavalry was engaged in that day, and Lord Combermere [Stapleton Cotton], disliking the Heavys, he thought by naming the success generally of the cavalry under his Command, the public would include the Light among the successful ones.

... His quarrel with poor Le Marchant, and with Elley, determined his hostility to our Brigade and prevented him from doing justice to it.

I have never ceased to feel annoyed at our treatment, which in addition to my being superseded by Lord Charles Manners, drove me out of the service.[24]

Most accounts of the actual charge refer only to Le Marchant, but Napier says: 'Nor were these valiant horsemen yet exhausted. Le Marchant and many other officers had fallen, but Cotton and all his staff were at their head, and with ranks confused and blended in one mass they still galloped on against a fresh column.' This is implicitly rebutted in the memoir of Le Marchant, which goes out of its way to show that Le Marchant was killed at the very end of the charge, even claiming that his was probably the last life lost in it. According to this source, Cotton 'had been too far distant to share in the charge' and only arrived with his large staff when it was over, his attempts to spur the exhausted dragoons into fresh effort meeting with no response. If this suggests a certain understandable hostility, it is at least more plausible than the claim in the life of Cotton that Wellington greeted Sir Stapleton after the charge with uncharacteristic effusiveness: 'By G–d, Cotton, I never saw anything more beautiful in my life! – the day is *yours.*'[25]

The memoir of Le Marchant was written by his son Denis, who became a Liberal MP and Clerk to the House of Commons. This was not the son, Ensign Carey Le Marchant, who had served as his father's ADC in the battle; he had died of wounds in 1814. Lieutenant William Light, another of Le Marchant's ADCs, kept a diary, but unfortunately the entry for the battle is brief and unhelpful. Napier's description of the charge, and particularly Cotton's role in it, is based on the much later testimony of two officers, Colonel Money and General Sir Charles Dalbiac, who both believed that Cotton not only ordered the charge but led it from the outset, or at the very least joined it early on. However, it is rather odd, if Cotton took such a prominent role in the charge, that the accounts written immediately afterwards by Norcliffe Norcliffe and William Bragge, should not mention him. And on other points, where there is independent evidence, it tends to confirm the reliability of the account given in the memoir of Le Marchant.[26]

Cotton's proper place, of course, was not in the forefront of the charge, but at the head of the supports which could exploit success or cover a retreat. The only brigade available for this role was Anson's light cavalry, but there is much doubt as to how they were employed. Napier prints two letters: one from Colonel Money of Anson's brigade, who claims that they took a full share in Le Marchant's charge from the outset; the other from Charles Dalbiac of the 4th Dragoons, who emphatically denies that the heavy dragoons received any support whatsoever, except from the infantry. Other accounts support Dalbiac rather than Money: neither Tomkinson nor Cocks, both in the 16th Light Dragoons, records any great feats of arms in their diaries and letters, while Captain William Smith of the 11th Light Dragoons – Money's own regiment – writes in his journal that 'it was a very easy day for us.' Neither of these regiments suffered a single casualty, while the 12th Light Dragoons, which did lose a few men, had remained on the left flank and was engaged late in the day. A contemporary hand-drawn map in the papers of Major-General Ashworth shows Anson's brigade proceeding, not in the wake of the heavy cavalry, but in a wide circle on the outer flank of Pakenham's division. However, this is probably nothing more than a simple mistake, confusing Anson's with Victor Alten's brigade.[27]

Evidently Anson's brigade was not seriously engaged, and was probably too far to the rear to lend any useful support to Le Marchant, even when the charge was exhausted and the men vulnerable. But Le Marchant's men were not entirely unsupported, for the cavalry of the right wing (Alten's and D'Urban's brigades) took full advantage of the French confusion. Ashworth's map shows a substantial French unit 'charged and routed with very considerable loss by the Portuguese cavalry under General D'Urban' (to quote from the key), and its location implies that this would have been at the end of the charge, about the time Lord Edward Somerset captured the French guns.[28] Arentschildt's report to Cotton gives a more detailed account of the actions of Alten's brigade:

> About this time our heavy cavalry fell upon the French infantry from the other side, and I ordered the hussars to keep on the extremity of the left wing of the enemy's infantry, and cut off whatever they could, *following myself with the fourteenth in close order.* The hussars were then a great way in front, doing great execution among the enemy's infantry, and, according to the nature of the service and ground, (this being in the wood), very much dispersed – when about two squadrons of the French third hussars came up to attack them. But Major Gruben, Krauchenberg and other officers rallied, by great exertion, a body strong enough to oppose the enemy, though they were all mixed; some hussars, some fourteenth, and even some Portuguese. They then fell upon the enemy and drove them back, on which occasion some French officers were cut down; and from that moment the French cavalry never showed their faces again on that side. The pursuit of the infantry was then renewed together with some advanced parties of General Le Marchant's brigade, until they came close to the large hill under the French batteries where you have seen them; four guns have been sent back to the rear by the hussars. ... The number of prisoners is not to be ascertained, for they were driven back in crowds.[29]

It is also possible that Julián Sánchez's Spanish lancers were engaged at this point, although the reference to their role is so brief and cryptic that it might equally apply to the very end of the battle when the whole French army was in flight.[30]

So it seems that at first the heavy dragoons advanced with direct support only from the infantry, and that Arentschildt, D'Urban and perhaps Sánchez joined the charge as it progressed. The brigade itself was formed in two lines. Oman, presumably following regimental sources, states that the 4th Dragoons and the 5th Dragoon Guards were in the first line, with the 3rd Dragoons in support;

but nothing in William Bragge's letter suggests that his regiment was not in the first line from the outset. Ashworth's map has the 4th Dragoons some distance in front of the other two regiments, the whole brigade forming three lines; but again this does not fit well with other sources. The most plausible statement comes from Philip Bainbrigge, an assistant to Colonel De Lancey, the acting Quartermaster-General, who says that the left squadron of each regiment was kept back in the second line.[31]

None of the sources gives a completely reliable statement as to which regiment was on the left, which on the right and which in the centre, but there is some inconclusive evidence that the 5th Dragoon Guards were on the left, that is, closest to Leith's division. The regimental history of the 44th Foot names them as the cavalry which attacked Maucune's flank; John Douglas identifies them correctly, while mistaking the other regiments of heavy cavalry. The charge brought them, as a trophy, the staff of the drum-major of the 66th Ligne, the regiment in Maucune's division which suffered most. But these are slender threads on which to hang an argument, while the unpublished memoirs of an anonymous dragoon in the 5th clearly state that they passed through the ranks of the Third Division – although this is a poor source, and may in any case refer to the light infantry.[32]

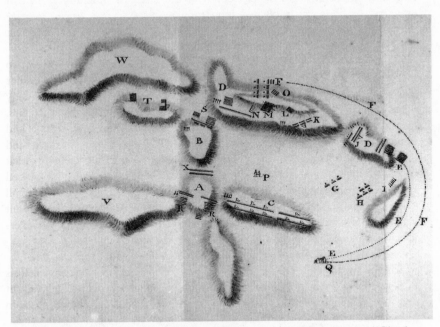

Anonymous hand-drawn map from the papers of Major-General Charles Ashworth. North is at the bottom. A is the Lesser Arapile; B is the Greater Arapile; P the village of Los Arapiles; Q the village of Las Torres; E shows Pakenham's advance; G and H represent Le Marchant's brigade with the 4th Dragoons leading.

Charles Dalbiac told Napier in 1833 that the brigade charged 'with no more than 750 sabres'. This is a surprisingly low figure, given its official strength of just over a thousand officers and men on 15 July. Part of the difference is explained by the absence of Major Onslow's squadron of 4th Dragoons, which had been detached about noon. (Dalbiac is the only source for this but, as he was second-in-command of the regiment on the day, his word must be accepted.) This still leaves a substantial discrepancy, which may be explained in one of two ways. Either Dalbiac's '750 sabres' counts only the rank and file, excluding officers, sergeants and drummers – the phrase 'sabres and bayonets' was quite often used to refer just to the men in the ranks. If this is the case, the total number of men taking part in the charge would have been not far short of nine hundred. Alternatively, the discrepancy may be caused by the large number of supernumeraries – orderlies, farriers, camp-kettlemen and so on – who were part of a brigade of heavy cavalry. A British officer, writing of the Waterloo campaign, estimated that these might amount to at least 120 men in a brigade of this size. We do not know which explanation is correct in this instance, or even if much credence should be placed on Dalbiac's remark, but it does serve as a salutary reminder of the uncertainties concealed even in the apparently simple and transparent figures of a weekly state.[33]

Only one important first-hand account of the charge is not quoted in the main narrative. This was published anonymously in the *United Service Journal* in November 1833, at a time when the ability of cavalry to break formed infantry by an impetuous charge was the subject of much debate.

It was at this critical juncture that the heavy cavalry brigade, 3rd and 4th dragoons, and 5th dragoon guards, received from Sir Stapleton Cotton, their orders to advance; and, moving rapidly forward between the flank attack of the 3rd and the more direct one of the 5th division, which was the right of our infantry line, came first into contact with the 66th (French) regiment, consisting of three battalions, and formed in a sort of column of half-battalions, thus presenting six successive lines, one behind the other. Strange to say, though drawn up in that formidable manner, their fire was so ill-directed, that it is believed scarcely a single dragoon fell from its effects; and no check taking place, the cavalry bore vigorously forward at a gallop, penetrating their columns, nearly the whole of which were killed, wounded, or taken, leaving the broken infantry to be made prisoners by the 3rd division as they cleared the ground before them, to assist in which one squadron of the 4th dragoons was for the moment detached. They presently came upon another column, however, of about 600 men, who brought down some men and horse by their fire, but attempted no stand of any consequence, and, falling into confusion, were left as before to be captured by the advancing infantry.

The nature of the ground, which was an open wood of evergreen oaks, and which grew more obstructed as they advanced, had caused the men of the three regiments of Cavalry to become a good deal mixed in each other's ranks; and the front being at the same time constantly changing as the right was brought forward, the whole had now crowded into a solid line, without any intervals. In this order, but without any confusion, they pressed rapidly forward upon another French brigade, which, taking advantage of the trees, had formed a *colonne serrée*, and stood awaiting their charge. These men reserved their fire with much coolness till the Cavalry came within twenty yards, when they poured it in upon the concentrated mass of men and horses with a deadly and tremendous effect. The gallant General Le Marchant, with Captain White of his staff, were killed; Colonel Elley was wounded; and it is thought that nearly one third of the dragoons came to the ground; but as the remainder retained sufficient command of their horses to dash forward, they succeeded in breaking the French ranks, and dispersing them in utter confusion over the field. At this moment Colonel Lord Edward Somerset, discovering five guns upon the left, separated from the brigade with one squadron, charged, and took them all.

Here terminated the series of attacks we have endeavoured to describe; for by this time, (about forty minutes after the first charge, which took place soon after five o'clock,) it was with difficulty that three squadrons could be collected and formed out of the whole brigade, and any further advance would have been unnecessary as well as imprudent. The spot where Lord Edward captured the guns was about three miles from where the first shot was fired by the Third Division.[34]

Not surprisingly, this article has greatly influenced all subsequent descriptions of the charge, even that in the memoir of General Le Marchant. Yet its very virtues raise questions. How can an account written more than twenty years after the event be so clear, comprehensible and detailed, when letters written within days are generally confused and fragmentary? Could anyone really take such careful note of the formation of the enemy, the range at which they fired and the identity of their units, while galloping straight at them amid the noise, anxiety, excitement and jostling turmoil of a cavalry charge? This is not to suggest that the account is fraudulent; rather, that it contains as much unconscious reconstruction of events as direct, immediate memory. It is still useful and has influenced the narrative at a number of points, but it cannot be accepted without question.

However, the greatest difficulty in understanding Le Marchant's charge lies 'on the other side of the hill', in working out which French units were involved, what they were doing and how they came to suffer so much. Many accounts, of which Oman's is the most important, closely follow the article in the *United Service Journal*, and as a result accept that the charge was primarily directed at Maucune's division. According to this scheme the cavalry first crashed into the unprotected flank of the 66th Ligne (which had two, not three battalions), then broke a battalion of the 15th Ligne (the column of 'about 600 men'), before charging the 22nd Ligne formed in 'colonne serrée' in the fringes of the forest.[35] But several objections can be made to this neat formulation. When it charged, Le Marchant's brigade had a frontage of about six hundred yards, vastly wider than the flank of the 66th, even if the infantry had already been broken. Nor is it easy to see how the 22nd could have been so completely destroyed if it had fought in the skirts of the forest, when the fleeing infantry would have found safe refuge among the trees. Some British cavalry certainly did charge Maucune's flank, but it may not have been the whole brigade, and the *United Service Journal* article may better describe the experiences of the left regiment than the entire force.

Equally, Oman's account fails to explain the enormous losses of the 62nd and 101st Regiments, which are attributed simply to the initial attack by D'Urban and Wallace. Their attack was certainly important, but it is not credible that a frontal attack by a single brigade of British infantry, supported by a few hundred Portuguese dragoons, could kill, wound or capture over two thousand men. It may be that Le Marchant's charge cut off the escape of the fleeing remnants of these regiments, causing many of them to surrender; or that they had already begun to rally upon their supports and were broken a second time by Le Marchant's charge. This second version is adopted in the narrative because it fits more closely with Grattan's account,[36] but the evidence is tenuous and either may be true. However, it is hard to escape the conclusion that the already demoralized men of the 62nd and 101st were among the first victims of the charge.

The remaining regiment in Thomières's division, the 1st Ligne, presents insoluble problems. Where was it? How did it escape so lightly when all around it units were losing half or more of their strength? It suffered 230 casualties, or 13 per cent of its strength, and we can do little more than presume that by good fortune it escaped the main impact of Le Marchant's charge (but how?) and that it then retained enough cohesion to retreat successfully from the field. Other theories might be devised, but there is a lack of evidence on which to base them.

The dreadful fate of the 22nd Ligne, the leading regiment in Taupin's division whose two battalions were reduced to forty-seven men at the end of the day, also requires explanation; but again there is little evidence. If it was still some distance to the rear, advancing to support Maucune and Thomières, it should have had time to recognize the danger and form square. Perhaps it was already in the front line, providing cover behind which the 62nd and 101st might rally? The smoke, the dust, the setting sun and the musketry exchange with Wallace's infantry would explain why it was taken by surprise by the cavalry, and the 1st Ligne may have formed on its left, or southern flank, beyond the line of Le Marchant's cavalry. This is a tempting hypothesis. Grattan identifies his opponent as the 22nd Regiment, but this is less useful than it seems, for he is referring to the initial clash on the Pico de Miranda, not to this second round of fighting; and the number of the regiment is probably fixed in his memory by the capture of its Eagle by the caçadores of the division. And unfortunately, the memoirs of Lieutenant-Colonel Castel, Clausel's ADC, count against this idea (see below).[37]

Jean Sarramon, in his excellent modern study *La Bataille des Arapiles*, suggests a completely different arrangement of the French troops when Le Marchant charged. He believes that Maucune, seeing the threat posed to his flank by the defeat of Thomières and the advance of Pakenham and Le Marchant, had sent his first brigade (15th and 66th Ligne) to guard his flank and rear, leaving only the second brigade (82nd and 86th Ligne) to face Leith. The first brigade joined with the remnants of the 62nd and 101st, and with the main body of the 1st Ligne, to form a new line running north-east to south-west across the plateau. Although formed in some disorder – with some units in line, others in column or square – they succeeded in checking Wallace's advance and repulsed a charge by one of D'Urban's regiments of cavalry. Leith had by now defeated Maucune's second brigade, and was advancing on the flank of the new French line, but at this moment Taupin's division began to arrive and enabled the line to be reconstructed. Pakenham was now in some danger of being defeated, but Le Marchant's cavalry arrived in time to rescue him by charging the 66th, then the 15th, and finally the 22nd Regiments – in other words, when it comes to the actual charge, Sarramon follows Oman's description based on the *United Service Journal* article.[38]

This account is based on familiar, mostly British, sources; and while it is interesting, there are too many problems for it to be ultimately convincing. The whole story of Maucune detaching his first brigade – despite being faced by the steady advance of Leith's strong division – is both implausible and unnecessary. Nor does it shed any light on the role of the 1st Ligne: if this was present with its full three battalions (1,700 men), it would have been quite sufficient to check Wallace's advance either by itself (Wallace's men were breathless and rather disordered, and they had outpaced the rest of Pakenham's division), or with the aid of those parts of the 62nd and 101st which were in reasonable order. Sarramon does not put the 22nd Ligne in the front line, and yet says that the arrival of Taupin's division (of which it was the leading regiment) allowed the line to be rearranged – apparently for the express purpose of making the 66th Regiment expose its flank to the impending charge of the British dragoons. No hypothesis can solve all the difficulties related to the charge, but this raises fresh problems without solving the old ones.

The root of the problem is the absence of reliable first-hand French accounts of this part of the battle. Other than Parquin's anecdote quoted in the narrative and the odd scrap of useful information – such as Captain Mottier's defence of the Eagle of the 82nd – there are only the memoirs of Colonels Girard and Castel. As Maucune's chief of staff, Girard should be most enlightening, but his account is infuriatingly vain and transparently unreliable. For what it is worth, he claims that the French infantry were in the act of repulsing Leith's attack when the British cavalry caused some disorder, and all the heroic efforts of the senior officers were unable to rally their men. As chief of staff his duty was then to save the artillery, and a fanciful account follows of how he did so:

I formed the caissons into square and double-loaded our guns and collected passing infantry and positioned them between the guns. We were not long in this order when the English squadrons arrived at a gallop. But their charge, despite being impetuous and directed against two sides of the square, failed to close on us, although Commandant Blanzot was knocked over by an enemy cavalryman who was himself unhorsed by the servant who fought at his side.[39]

Castel's memoir is much more interesting, but full of difficulties and often confusing. It was written forty years after the event and includes some obvious errors, but also information which appears nowhere else and which seems plausible. Although he was Clausel's aide-de-camp, it was Marmont who sent him with orders for Taupin to move forward to support Maucune, shortly before the French commander was wounded. Castel reached Taupin's division, but was unable to find Taupin himself. Riding forward, he saw that Maucune's division was heavily engaged, so he hurried back and conveyed his orders to the colonel of the 22nd Regiment. Responding to this, the 22nd advanced in two columns, but the other brigade in the division did not follow and soon began to fall back. Here Castel found Taupin, who told him that Curto's cavalry had been driven back 'and that he believed it was prudent to conform to this movement'. Castel remonstrated with him and forced him to halt his retreat by implying that he, Castel, was speaking on the authority of a senior officer. This halt gave some protection to the fleeing troops of Maucune's division, but the first line was already shattered and the 22nd Regiment destroyed. The implication is that if Taupin had acted more positively the 22nd might have been saved, although Castel acknowledges that his retreat preserved the other brigade.[40]

Neither of these memoirs gives any support to Sarramon's suggestion that Maucune re-deployed his division, while, if Castel's account is accepted, the tempting idea outlined earlier, that the 22nd were in the front line and so bore the initial impact of Le Marchant's charge, must also be abandoned.

The official French return states that the artillery in Thomières's division lost four guns: three 8 pounders and one 4-pounder, while Taupin's division also lost an 8-pounder, possibly in this part of the battle. Neither the cavalry nor Maucune's division admitted the loss of any guns. On the whole this return appears credible,[41] even though individual British claims would suggest a higher figure. For example, Lord Edward Somerset is supposed to have taken five guns, and Arentschildt claimed that his brigade captured four. It is impossible to work out exactly what happened, but there was always a tendency for claims of captures to become inflated, while acknowledged losses would be minimized as much as possible.[42]

Another problem relating to the effects of the charge on the French also needs to be mentioned here: how many Eagles were lost, and by which regiments? Lamartinière's return admits the loss of two Eagles, those of the 22nd and 101st, which fits well with the course of the battle and with Wellington's claim to have captured two Eagles. Nonetheless, some authorities disagree: Fortescue suggests that the Eagle of the 66th may also have been captured, while Sarramon follows older British accounts and substitutes the Eagle of the 62nd for that of the 101st. Pierre Charrié, author of the standard reference work on the subject, states that the 22nd and 62nd certainly lost their Eagles in the battle, while the 101st may also have done so. This is sufficient to create a lingering doubt, although the presumption must be that Lamartinière is correct.[43]

By July 1812 only the first battalions of infantry regiments were supposed to carry Eagles – the other battalions carrying only *fanions*. The 22nd, 62nd and 101st Regiments all had their first battalion in the field at Salamanca, but the 66th and 82nd (both in Maucune's division) did not. This rather undermines Fortescue's suggestion that the 66th lost an Eagle, but it also throws doubt on the story of Captain Mottier's gallant defence of his Eagle. Either the regimental history was mistaken and Mottier defended a *fanion*, not an Eagle, or the regiment – like some others – had been slow to return its surplus Eagles to the depot: the decree ordering this was only issued a few months before.[44]

Fortunately, there are fewer problems with British casualty figures. One British officer is listed as killed and three wounded in the regimental tables: Lieutenant William Selby, 3rd Dragoons (killed); Lieutenant Norcliffe Norcliffe, 4th Dragoons (severely wounded); Captain Francis Aicken, 5th Dragoon Guards (severely wounded); and Lieutenant Braithwaite Christie, 5th Dragoon Guards (severely wounded). To these need be added General Le Marchant (killed), Captain William White, DAQMG to the brigade (mortally wounded, dying on the following day) and Lieutenant-Colonel John Elley AAG to the brigade, who was slightly wounded.[45] It is noteworthy that the 5th Dragoon Guards suffered much more heavily than either of the other regiments in the brigade: 56 casualties compared to 20 in the 3rd Dragoons and 29 in the 4th Dragoons, all the regiments being of approximately equal strength. However, much of the excess may be owing to the stampede of horses on the previous night, in which 18 men were said to have been injured, rather than their service in the battle, for Tomkinson says that the horses lost owing to the storm were recorded as lost in the battle.[46]

Chapter Seven
Collapse and Recovery in the Centre

While the French left was being so comprehensively routed, the battle in the centre was hard-fought, with fluctuating fortunes. Here, Wellington's front line consisted of Cole's Fourth Division and Pack's Independent Portuguese brigade, supported by the Sixth Division with the First Division further back in reserve. Cole's division was one of the weakest in the allied army: some 5,200 officers and men on 15 July, while the week's campaigning and the fighting on the 18th, in which it played a prominent part, had probably reduced it to just under five thousand men. Half of these were Portuguese in Stubbs's brigade; the remainder formed two weak British brigades under William Anson and Henry Ellis. Both British brigades had seen much service: Anson's brigade (3/27th and 1/40th) had lost very heavily in the storm of Badajoz (421 casualties between two regiments); while Ellis's Fusilier brigade (1/7th, 1/23rd and 1/48th) had not only suffered at Badajoz (504 casualties), but had also been cut to pieces the previous year at Albuera. Stubbs's Portuguese had also been at Albuera: the two line regiments (11th and 23rd) had suffered little – only thirty-two casualties – but the 7th Caçadores had lost 171 casualties or 30 per cent of their strength. However, the Portuguese had not been engaged much since, for they had not taken part in the storming of either Ciudad Rodrigo or Badajoz.[1]

Cole himself had been wounded at Albuera, then fell ill towards the end of 1811 and spent six months recuperating in England. He returned to the Peninsula at the beginning of June, but was not in good spirits: 'I am once more embarked in the business, and if I keep my health and present resolution shall not quit till it is over. . . . The fact is, I nearly despair of being able to gratify the first wish of my heart, viz. to be able to settle and live comfortably near you all . . . I have lost almost every friend and every good officer with at least a third of the Division at the siege of Badajos.'[2]

Early on the day of battle, William Anson's brigade had been committed to the defence of the Lesser Arapile, while soon afterwards the Fusilier brigade occupied the Teso de San Miguel. The wide gap between the two British brigades was filled by Stubbs's Portuguese and Pack's Independent Portuguese brigade, meaning that in this part of the line the normal proportion of two British soldiers to one Portuguese was reversed. Nor were these brigades numerically strong enough to allow Cole to form his men in two lines, as Leith did to his right. Indeed, one of the few criticisms which can legitimately be made of Wellington's handling of the battle is that he did not replace Pack's brigade with either the First or Sixth Division in the front line, and consolidate Cole's division either behind the village or near the Lesser Arapile.

No one recorded Wellington's orders to Cole, but they must have been similar to those he gave Leith, except that Cole's troops advanced in a single line (two ranks deep), the three battalions of Fusiliers on the right, the four Portuguese battalions on the left. They had a frontage of about a thousand yards and were preceded by the usual strong screen of light infantry: the light companies from the three British battalions, the company of Brunswick Oels attached to their brigade, and the 7th Caçadores – perhaps seven hundred men in all. Their advance probably began a little after Leith's, and seems to have been further delayed when the Fusiliers passed through the village. According to Charles Vere, who was Assistant Quartermaster General to the division, the infantry 'went through the village of Aripeles [sic] by files from the right of companies, covered by the Light Troops; and when through, the companies formed up upon their Sergeants regularly sent out; and then the line advanced in great order and regularity.'[3]

A British officer who had recently joined the 23rd Portuguese, Captain Barralier (or Barailler), records that, when the advance was about to begin, his entire regiment went down on their knees, offered a short prayer and then rose with great firmness and resolution. And Captain Wachholtz of the Brunswick Oels company wrote in his journal with disarming honesty: 'Cole came to me, "You will go in front with the Portuguese caçadores; move on!" "Very well," I said, but thought, "It's not 'very well'"'; however it's no use being afraid.'[4]

The division advanced with rapid steps, flags flying and bayonets fixed, past the village, up the hillside and across the open plateau beyond. The French responded with heavy artillery fire, but it seems that when Cole's advance began, there may have been no French infantry on the opposite heights to support the guns, although Clausel's division was approaching rapidly and soon took its place in the line. Evidently it formed some distance to the south-east of Maucune's division, while a gap had also opened in the allied line between Leith and Cole, so that each division fought independently.

As he advanced, Cole was much more concerned with his left flank than his right. On his left, Pack's brigade faced the Greater Arapile, but Cole could see further bodies of French infantry massed behind the height, while a single French regiment (the 122nd Ligne of Bonnet's division) occupied a gentle rise halfway between the Greater Arapile and the plateau. This regiment posed the most immediate threat to the allied flank, and Cole sent the 7th Caçadores – probably supported by part, or even all, of Stubbs's main line – to drive it back.

Faced with this advance, the French regiment fell back, apparently without much fighting. The 122nd was a strong regiment, 1,600 men in three battalions, but it may have felt isolated and lacking in support. The 7th Caçadores were left to watch it and the rest of Bonnet's division, while Cole's infantry continued its advance.[5]

Having crossed the plateau, the allied line climbed the hillside which bounded it to the south. Just beyond the crest it was met by Clausel's 2nd brigade, the 50th and 59th Ligne, five battalions, almost three thousand officers and men, so that the French were only slightly outnumbered. One British account claims that the French were deployed, 'in line, ready formed to open their fire on our four [sic] battalions as soon as they should crown the hill'; although a French authority states that they were in a line of columns with artillery in the intervals.[6] What followed is not entirely clear – the sources on this stage of the combat are very meagre – but it seems that there was probably a sustained exchange of musketry before the French fell back in some confusion, but far from broken. The British and Portuguese did not pursue and were themselves rather disordered and shaken. It was probably in this fighting that Cole fell: 'A musquet ball struck him a little below the left shoulder, broke the rib and passed out through the breast-bone – the lungs are very slightly touched.'[7] Another painful convalescence lay ahead, but he was able to resume his command in the middle of October.

The French did not retreat far. Clausel's other brigade (25th Léger and 27th Ligne, also five battalions and slightly over three thousand men) was only a couple of hundred yards to the rear and seized the perfect moment to counterattack. Taken at a disadvantage, the allied line hesitated, stood firm for a moment, then broke and fled. Fortunately, we have two good descriptions from close observers of what happened, which are all the more interesting as few memoirists or diarists linger over episodes in which they were worsted. The first comes from a letter written five days after the battle by an unknown British officer:

> The Fuzileers on the left [sic] of the 4th Division had gain'd the most commanding point of the position where they immediately found themselves exposed to a heavy fire from the ground mark'd as the 2d Position & a French Regt. of 4 Battalions (about 12000 [sic] men) below at a very short distance & regularly formed. The Fuzileers in this situation unsupported at the moment commenced firing without forming after its first attack. The French regiment form'd close column with the Grenadiers in front and closed the Battalions. (I was very close on the right flank of the Fuzileers, & witnessed the whole proceeding). They then advanced up the hill in the most beautiful order without firing a shot except a few individuals in the rear of the column. When about 30 paces distant our men began to waver, being still firing & not properly formed. The Ensigns advanced two paces in front & planted the colours on the edge of the hill & Officers stept out to encourage the men to meet them. They stopt with

an apparent determination to stand firm, the enemy continued to advance at a steady pace & when quite close the Fuzileers gave way: – The French followed down the hill on our side.[8]

The second description comes from John Burgoyne, the engineer officer, who was with the Fusiliers in their attack. He wrote to his sister on 25 July:

Our troops had but just gained [the height], and had not had time to form again in order, but even then they did not give it up, although ours was a much smaller regiment, until the enemy's column was close to them. The French regiment came up the hill with a brisk and regular step, and their drums beating the *pas de charge*; our men fired wildly and at random among them; the French never returned a shot, but continued their steady advance. The English fired again, but still without return; they stood their ground however with great courage. But men in such confusion had no chance against the perfect order of the enemy, and when the French were close upon them, they wavered and gave way. The officers all advanced in a line in front, waving their swords, and cheering their men to come on, but the confusion became a panic, and there was a regular *sauve qui peut* down the hill.[9]

These accounts make clear that the Fusiliers were broken by Clausel's counterattack, but this was not the only blow which Cole's regiments suffered at this moment. Bonnet's division sallied forth from behind the Greater Arapile and fell on Cole's exposed flank, easily overpowering the 7th Caçadores, despite gallant resistance. Some British witnesses attribute the defeat of Cole's attack to this sudden new threat, and Bonnet's advance would probably have made Cole's position untenable, even if Clausel had not gained the upper hand.

A column of French Grenadiers with hairy caps from the right of their line came on at a run with drums beating, and charged the left of the Portuguese, taking them obliquely in the flank. Nothing could be better done on the part of the French. The Portuguese gave way like a wave of the sea, first on their left, then by degrees all the way to the right. It then became a question of whether the Fusiliers would stand it, but, finding their friends on the left gone, a tremendous fire directed upon them in front, and the victorious French column coming on with shouts on their left flank, taking them also in flank, and perceiving that their own fire did not bear upon these fellows close to them, they, in like manner, gave way.[10]

At about this time Pack was also repulsed in his ambitious attack on the Greater Arapile (see chapter eight). These two defeats tore a great hole in the centre of the allied line, and appeared to offer the French a chance of gaining an advantage which might offset the defeat of their left. It is not clear whether Clausel consciously determined to grasp this moment and gamble on a slender

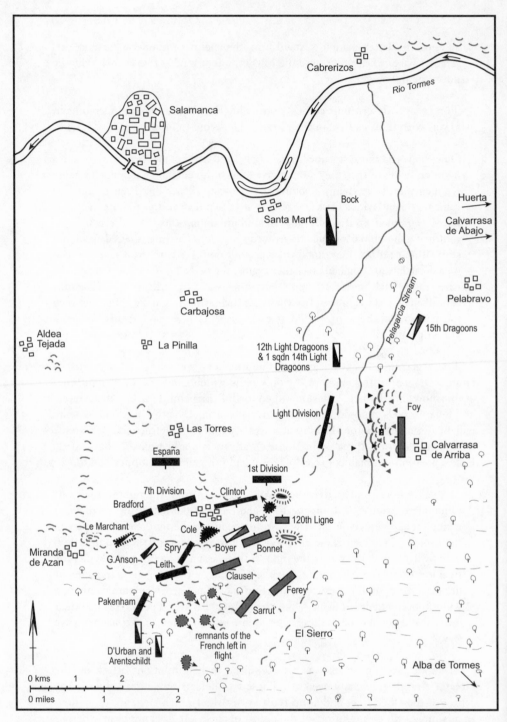

The French counter-attack (all troop positions approximate, many conjectural).

hope of victory, rather than use the opportunity to withdraw, salvaging all that could be saved of Marmont's army, but admitting defeat. It is just as likely that the French units acted independently, with little co-ordination, carried forward by their own momentum and striking wherever they saw an opportunity. Indeed, Clausel's own division – showing admirable discipline – only made a limited advance and soon halted its pursuit, probably because its commander realized that the defeat of Maucune exposed his left flank.

The sense of danger on the allied side at this moment is well conveyed in the recollections of a staff officer, Philip Bainbrigge, who, with his chief, Colonel De Lancey, the acting Quartermaster-General, was riding in the rear of the Fourth Division when it broke:

> they ... gave way like a wave of the sea; I can compare it to nothing else. My heart was in my mouth, and they all came down into the hollow in the rear, where they halted.
>
> Colonel Delancey said to me 'For God's sake bring up the 6th Division as fast as possible,' then dashed in amongst the Portuguese, seized the colour of one of the regiments and endeavoured to rally them. I galloped off to the rear; as to restoring order and reforming the regiment it required some time and the work of regimental officers.[11]

But in fact the danger was less real than it appeared. The Sixth Division was well placed to fill the gap in the allied line, and beyond it, behind the Lesser Arapile, the First Division lay untouched in reserve. The French counterattack would not be defeated without hard fighting, but the odds were always heavily against its success.

Wellington ordered the Sixth Division forward even before he saw Cole's attack falter. Clinton's regiments advanced in two lines of columns – that is, each battalion in column and enough space between them for the whole to deploy into line – the British brigades in front, Rezende's strong Portuguese brigade (almost half the division) some distance behind them. No mention is made in the sources of sending the light infantry forward as skirmishers, and they may well have remained in the ranks. Hinde's brigade (2nd Foot, 1/32nd and 1/36th) was on the right; Hulse's (1/11th, 2/53rd and 1/61st) on the more exposed left flank, with the 2/53rd on the extreme left. They were generally good troops and had had plenty of campaign experience in recent years, but, by a quirk of fate, only the 1/61st had been seriously engaged in battle (at Talavera). More recently, the division had been responsible for the costly attacks on the Salamanca forts.

Meanwhile, on the French side, Clausel's division had not advanced very far, and the 120th Regiment in Bonnet's division remained on the Greater Arapile. The thrust of the French counterattack came from Bonnet's other three regiments, the 118th, 119th and 122nd Ligne, all strong, three-battalion units, amounting to 4,500 men when the battle began. They were supported by three regiments of Boyer's cavalry, 6th, 11th and 25th Dragoons, perhaps 1,100 horsemen, more than in Le Marchant's brigade, but much inferior in quality.

Boyer's men took the lead at first and did some damage to the broken men of Cole's division; but the bulk of the Portuguese and Fusiliers rallied and formed hasty squares, or gained the protection of the advancing Sixth Division before they had suffered much. The dragoons had more success further east, where they attacked the 2/53rd, the regiment at the eastern end of Clinton's line. It is not clear, precisely, what happened, but it seems that this battalion had been slightly detached from the rest of the division, and two first-hand accounts show beyond doubt that it got into serious difficulties. 'Our regiment was formed on the left of the line,' wrote its adjutant, Lieutenant John Carss, on 25 July,

> and a little from the division, to support a pass in order to prevent the enemy from flanking us. We had fired about 10 rounds ... when about two or three hundred of the enemy's cavalry supported by infantry made a charge and totally surrounded us. They called out 'Surrender'. We answered 'No'. Our brave fellows kept up such a blaze on them that in about five minutes we drove them off after killing and wounding nearly one half; in this charge we had about five officers wounded and about 40 rank and file killed and wounded. We formed line and advanced.[12]

The commander of the battalion, Lieutenant-Colonel George Bingham, wrote on 24 July:

> our left was uncovered just as the French gained a temporary advantage on our right. In this situation, unsupported, we were attacked by the enemy's Heavy Dragoons; we retired in good order, in line, and twice stopped their advance by halting and firing. At last a circular rocky hill, about two hundred yards in the rear, offered an advantage; I determined to profit by it; the Dragoons being too near, and the ranks too much thinned to attempt a square, we made a dash for the hill. The Dragoons came thundering on the rear, and reached the hill just as our people faced about. The fire checked them and it was soon obvious that they would make no impression. At this moment I saw a part of the Regiment which had not reached the rock, running down the hill in great confusion, without however being pursued by the Dragoons. Giving the charge of the hill to Mansell, I dashed through the Dragoons, who made way for me, and succeeded in rallying the men round the Regimental Colour that I had with me. The several attacks of the Dragoons on the mass failed, although at one time they seized the end of the King's Colour, and there was a struggle who should have it; when a sergeant of grenadiers wrested it from the Dragoon who held it, or rather tore the silk from the pole, which I rather think remained with the enemy; at the same time our people gained ground on the right, and the Dragoons retired in confusion.[13]

The 2/53rd was not a strong battalion: on 15 July it had twenty-five officers and 316 men, and in the battle as a whole it lost twenty-six men killed, and eleven officers and 105 men wounded, or 142 casualties in all – more than 40 per cent of its strength. No doubt the great bulk of these losses occurred in this incident, for although the 2/53rd rallied, it does not seem to have taken any further part in the battle.

This was the limit of Boyer's success. If the dragoons charged any of Clinton's other regiments, they made little impression, nor do they reappear later in the battle. The three regiments lost quite heavily: about two hundred casualties or almost one-sixth of their strength; but they had made little impact on the course of the battle. Stubbs's Portuguese brigade, already broken and fleeing – the perfect target for cavalry – probably suffered five to six hundred casualties (about 20 to 25 per cent) – and many, perhaps most, of these losses were inflicted by Clausel's and Bonnet's infantry. The Fusiliers suffered proportionally more (28 per cent, or 380 casualties), but as they were further from the cavalry, and went on to play a more active part later in the battle, it seems unlikely that the French dragoons were responsible for more than a fraction of their casualties. Only a single weak battalion, the 2/53rd, was knocked out of action for the remainder of the day. The contrast between the results achieved by Le Marchant and Boyer is striking, yet both charged when the infantry facing them were already disordered and broken. The good discipline of the allied infantry and the advance of the Sixth Division no doubt helped limit Boyer's success, and he might have done better if he had charged rather later, after Clinton's line had been weakened and disrupted by fighting Bonnet's infantry, but the crucial difference lay in the quality of the two brigades of cavalry. One was well mounted, full of confidence and eager for action; the other was intimidated by the knowledge that for once the allied cavalry were clearly superior.

Bonnet's infantry advanced in the wake of Boyer's dragoons. They had already broken Stubbs's 7th Caçadores, and they next encountered the 1/40th from William Anson's brigade of Cole's division. Anson had kept the 3/27th on the Lesser Arapile as a garrison, but had detached the 1/40th – possibly on Wellington's orders[14] – to help fill the gap between Pack's attack on the Greater Arapile and Cole's advance. With Pack and Cole both defeated, the 1/40th was left exposed. Unfortunately, the sources for what followed are again inadequate, for neither Sergeant Lawrence nor Charles Boutflower, who are usually so helpful for the affairs of the 40th, shed light on this incident. Instead we must rely on a letter written to Napier many years later by Major J. Scott Lillie, who was with the 7th Caçadores in the battle.

I happened to be at the time with some companies of the Caçadores and the 40th Regiment . . . This was one of the few occasions on which I saw the bayonet used; the 40th under the late Colonel Archdall, having come into close contact with Bonnet's French brigade in consequence of this movement, which was directed by General William Anson in person; he was moving on with the 40th, leaving the [Greater Arapiles] on his left and in his rear, on which a corps moved from behind the hill in rear of the 40th for the purpose of attacking it, the regiment being at the time engaged in front. I happened to be between the 40th and the enemy, and rode after the former to tell Colonel Archdall of his situation, on which he wheeled round and charged the enemy's column with the bayonet and this terminated the contest at that point.[15]

This is hard to follow, for Lillie seems to be saying that the 40th singlehandedly drove back Bonnet's advance, which is manifestly absurd. Charles Vere, on the other hand, says that the regiment was 'overpowered' and forced back to its original position near the Lesser Arapile, but gives no details.[16] It is even possible that some mixture of the two is correct: that the 40th repulsed a threat to its flank as described by Lillie and so secured its retreat; or that it advanced a second time on the left flank of Clinton's division and that Lillie's description belongs to this phase of the combat. All that we can really state with confidence is that it was heavily engaged, for it lost twelve men killed, five officers and 115 men wounded: 132 casualties in all from an initial strength which would have been considerably below the 582 officers and men present on 15 July, owing to its losses on the Guarena on the 18th.

French accounts of this part of the battle often tell the story of the heroic Sous-Lieutenant Guillemot of the 118th Ligne, who is supposed to have sprung into the enemy ranks, seized a flag, cutting off the arm of the man who held it, and made his escape despite a severe bayonet wound.[17] It is hard to know what to make of this tale. The only British colour arguably lost was that of the 2/53rd, whose fate has already been described, and it is possible that Guillemot ended with the credit for its capture. Oman suggests that the 7th Caçadores may have lost a colour; however, it appears that the caçador battalions, like many other light troops, did not carry standards in the field.[18] This leaves the possibility that the flag belonged to a line regiment in Stubbs's brigade or, less plausibly, in Rezende's brigade. However, the failure of Marmont and the other French writers who make so much of Guillemot's exploit to so much as mention the dragoon's capture of the pole and some of the silk of the 2/53rd's King's Colour leaves the impression that only one allied flag was taken, and that the credit for the incident was misdirected. On the other side, J. Scott Lillie claims to have personally captured a French flag. This was presumably the *fanion* of one of Bonnet's battalions and, as the allies captured half a dozen of these in all, there is no real reason to doubt Lillie's claim.[19]

Meanwhile, the 11th and 61st Regiments of Hulse's brigade, forming the left of Clinton's division, took a prominent part in repulsing the French counter-attack. An unpublished contemporary account of the services of the 61st states that the division was ordered forward at the double even before the Fourth Division had been broken. As they were forming line from column, a confused mass of fleeing men mixed with some pursuing French descended upon them.

The leading companies of the regiment which had deployed opened fire and checked the French advance, although not without hitting some of Cole's men as well. This gained time for the brigade to complete its deployment and for the broken allied units to pass behind it. The French, their confidence high, now made an impetuous assault on the two British regiments, but 'being met with 3 cheers, a volley and an instant charge' were driven back in disorder. Hulse pursued them, but halted his line before his men could get completely out of hand. This enabled the French to rally (or perhaps they had fallen back on supports), and their skirmishers and artillery opened a heavy fire on the brigade. When the British battalions had caught their breath and regained their order, they renewed their attack and were again successful.[20]

Many of these details are confirmed, with a few variations, in an account written many years later by 'Major Nott' (in fact, probably Major Frederick Newman) of the 1/11th:

> our brigade advanced in contiguous columns ascending a rising ground, you may recollect that, just before we reached the top, the 4th Division came over in a state of disorder, the enemy close upon them, the French officers in advance, and actually making use of their swords against our retreating men: our brigade was immediately halted and began to deploy. By the time three companies had formed, the portion of the 4th Division opposite to the 11th passed round the right flank; these companies at once opened their fire and swept away nearly the whole of those officers; this checked them, and after some firing they turned about and fled ... The brigade now advanced in line, and when we rose the hill a body of French cavalry was coming up at a hand canter, either to cover their retreating infantry, or to put a finishing hand to the 4th Division; we at once halted and gave them a volley which sent these cavaliers to the rightabout in much quicker time than they came, leaving several horses and men on the ground. The brigade then again advanced in line and entered the plain in front of the enemy's position, and within range of their batteries, which commenced a fire upon us. We advanced but a short distance before we were halted by Headquarter Staff, and in this situation remained considerably more than an hour.[21]

Other sources provide some further corroboration. For example, John Aitchison of the Guards wrote: 'At one point the first line was attacked after gaining the summit of a hill and driven back, but the second line moved up into its support and the 61st Regiment made one of the most brilliant charges ever recorded.' And Edward Brackenbury, an officer in Spry's brigade of the Fifth Division, wrote home describing the wounds suffered by his brother, Lieutenant William Brackenbury of the 61st,

> which he received *when having grasped the Colours of the 61st Regt. within 25 yards of the French Column.* He received the first ball through the Left foot, which

passed through the bone, but as it has neither touched the ankle Joint, nor the Joints of his toes, his foot is safe, nor will he (I hope) be lame in consequence of it, although the cure may be tedious: the second ball he Received in the left side of his Face which broke the Jawbone; it is now setting; the wound is suppurating. He converses freely and takes nourishment without much pain.[22]

William Brackenbury survived, but retired from the army in 1816 (aged twenty-six) owing to the lasting effects of his wounds. He was awarded a pension of £70 per annum in 1815, which was increased to £140 in 1824.[23]

However, this was clearly not the whole story. Bonnet's three regiments had over 1,200 casualties between them, even according to Lamartinière – the true figure is probably rather higher, perhaps 1,500 or a few more. In other words, they lost between one-quarter and one-third of their strength, and the great majority of these casualties must have been suffered at this time. Most accounts suggest that they lost heavily when they pressed their attack close to the British batteries on the Lesser Arapile and the Teso de San Miguel. But even so, Bonnet's nine battalions can hardly have been defeated simply by the 1/40th and the two remaining regiments of Hulse's brigade (leaving out the 2/53rd). Unfortunately, there are no first-hand accounts from either Hinde's or Rezende's brigades which appear to relate to fighting at this time. However, it seems probable that at least the Portuguese, and perhaps both brigades, were engaged, albeit less heavily than Hulse's gallant regiments.

Whatever the details, the French counterattack in the centre collapsed and Bonnet's infantry followed Boyer's dragoons in headlong retreat. Clinton's division followed in their wake, still in good order, despite the heavy losses which they surely must have suffered. Their advance exposed the right flank of Clausel's division, which already had more than enough troubles to deal with. Clausel seems to have limited his pursuit of the Fourth Division, presumably because he felt that his own left flank was threatened by the defeat of Maucune and Leith's advance. The danger was real, for Beresford, who was riding in the rear of Leith's division, reacted quickly to Cole's defeat, taking personal command of Spry's brigade and wheeling it round at a right-angle so that it faced almost due east. Thomas Henry Browne describes what happened:

> The Portuguese Brigade of the 5th Division from being on the left took these Battalions of the enemy completely in flank; but there was so much hallooing that instead of charging they began firing which was as dangerous to the British as to the French. Marshal Beresford & his staff put a stop to this firing, and he was making a disposition to charge the enemy in flank, which these Regiments, the 3rd and 15th Portuguese[,] were not very willing to try – a few companies made a sort of shabby charge which these French troops would scarcely have regarded but that the 4th Division again attacked & the 5th took them in rear. They then moved off & the greater part were killed or taken prisoners.[24]

Yet Edward Brackenbury, who was serving in the 15th Portuguese Line, told his parents: 'I fought with my Portuguese Regt. who behaved well and bayonetted a Column of French, you will scarcely believe how I could have Escaped when I assure you I was cutting away in a Solid Column with my Common regulation Sword: but Providence protected me as it did at Badajos.'[25] However a letter written by William Warre, Beresford's ADC, tends to support Browne's account, although his main concern is with his chief:

> It was near sunset, and in endeavouring to make a Portuguese Brigade charge the enemy, (who were driving the 4th Division back with 5 Battalions) in flank, that our excellent Marshal was wounded, while exerting himself, as he always does with the greatest zeal and gallantry, and by his noble example, to cover the 4th Division by this flank charge. But they soon rallied and regained the ground they had lost by the sudden attack of the enemy, and the heights were retaken just as the Marshal was hit.[26]

Spry's brigade lost only about 150 casualties, or 6.7 per cent, in the whole battle, only a marginally higher proportion than Pringle's brigade (the other unit in Leith's second line); so despite Brackenbury, it does not appear to have been engaged heavily against Clausel. Nonetheless, it probably helped to gain time for Cole's infantry to rally, and many accounts suggest that the Fourth Division returned to the fray and eventually drove Clausel's men from the plateau. This seems superficially implausible, but Clausel's division *was* driven back, and if it was not done by Spry, nor by the Fusiliers, it is hard to see who did do it, for we must assume that the Sixth Division was fully occupied with Bonnet. Clausel's losses were not slight: even Lamartinière admits 1,700 casualties, although about a hundred of these would have occurred on the 18th.

The memoirs of a French officer in the 59th Ligne, in Clausel's second brigade, suggest an alternative explanation which is worth considering, even though there is no support for it in other sources, and many of its details are obviously wrong. The author was Captain Alphonse d'Hautpoul:

> General Clausel led us in a charge on the troops of General Hill who was facing us. The English opposed us resolutely when we began firing at half musket range; they fired battalion volleys on us with the same precision as if on manoeuvre. Their flag was in the centre of their line; we could hear the orders of their officers. The divisions of Ferey and Clausel were not halted by this first fire although more than 800 men had been killed or wounded. We charged the enemy with the bayonet; his line was broken; the regiments of Scots Guards who were facing us could not rally. We pursued them vigorously over ground covered with their dead.
>
> In the centre, we believed that the battle was won, but Wellington, seeing Marmont's mistake in overextending his line, had sent all his reserves and cavalry to his right flank and made an all-out charge with eight thousand cavalry on

our left wing. The cavalry of General Curto could not stand the shock and were broken. Thomières's division on the extreme left was charged in the flank without having time to form squares, and could resist no longer. Whole regiments were put to the sword and General Thomières was killed. The divisions of Taupin and Maucune were charged in turn and broken. General Clausel, who was pursuing General Hill, seeing that his left was outflanked by numerous cavalry, halted his line and tried to form it in squares, but he lacked time, and his regiments, taken by surprise, were broken. General Hill, reinforced by a corps of Portuguese, resumed the offensive and a frightful melee ensued. At this moment I received from a Scottish sergeant – whom I'd just dealt a sabre blow – a musketball in the hip and at the same time a bayonet which pierced my right arm. I fell covered in blood.

A few moments after I received my two wounds the English cavalry rode over our line, taking it in the rear. Monsieur de Loverdo, my colonel, who had succeeded Colonel Caste, saved the regiment's Eagle by carrying it at a gallop into the squares of Ferey's division, behind which the debris of Clausel's division tried to rally. Stretched on the ground I lay at the mercy of the enemy. During the charge, two squadrons passed over but the horses instinctively leapt over me. I saw their feet almost crush me: my position was critical, but I was powerless to do anything and had to resign myself.[27]

It is hard to know what to make of this: d'Hautpoul's many mistakes about the allies – General Hill, the 'eight thousand' cavalry, fighting the 'Scots Guards' – are all disconcerting, but do not really discredit his account. It is one thing to mistake a regiment of Fusiliers for a regiment of Scots Guards, and not to know the name of the enemy general who commanded them; but being ridden over by enemy cavalry was direct personal experience, unlikely to be imagined even in a wound-induced fever. If the story was self-serving, designed to show how heroic d'Hautpoul had been in action, it would be easy to dismiss it; but it is relatively free of bombast, while Colonel de Loverdo's saving of the Eagle by abandoning his regiment was far from the tales of glory often associated with such incidents. And yet it is hard to believe that Le Marchant's charge really penetrated this far, breaking Clausel's division in addition to those of Thomières and Maucune and half of Taupin's. If it did, why does no British account claim it? D'Hautpoul's uncorroborated testimony is insufficient basis on which to re-write the history of the battle; but equally his account is too credible to be dismissed out of hand. The question, like so many others, must remain open.

Commentary

The experiences of the Fusiliers at Albuera (16 May 1811) are well known, but it is worth giving some details of their losses. The three regiments began the day with five battalions in the field (not all brigaded together), amounting to 2,964 officers and men, and suffered 1,668 casualties, or 56 per cent of their strength. As a result, the surviving men of the 2/7th and 2/48th were drafted into their first battalions and the cadres sent home. The 1/7th, and probably the other regiments, also received substantial drafts of fresh recruits from Britain (ten officers and 370 men sailed to join the 1/7th in July 1811); while many of the men wounded at Albuera would have rejoined their units in subsequent months. Nonetheless, the brigade had only 1,413 officers and men on 15 July 1812, less than half its strength on the morning of Albuera. Such losses were, of course, extraordinary, but the constant attrition caused by sickness led to a high turnover of men even in units which did not see much fighting.[28]

The sources for Cole's initial advance at Salamanca are thin, but pose few major problems. Several accounts say that the division suffered much from flanking fire from French batteries on the Greater Arapile, but the western end of the hill is extremely rocky and precipitous, and it is not easy to see how any guns could have been positioned there to fire on the allied flank. In any case the French troops on the hill were more likely to be preoccupied with Pack's brigade. However, there may have been a battery deployed behind the hill, facing north-west, whose fire would have taken the Fourth Division in the flank.

Vere says that Cole was wounded 'soon after the line passed through the village of Arapiles'; but this seems too early in the advance, for Colonel Wade states that it occurred when Cole 'was leading his division on to storm the heights', and also that the wound was caused by a 'musquet ball'. Clausel's division does not seem to have been in position early enough to send out skirmishers to harass the allied advance, so unless the musketball came from a canister fired by the French artillery, Cole probably suffered his wound in the fighting on the plateau.[29]

It is not certain whether the initial clash between Cole and Clausel occurred on the hillside a few hundred yards to the south of the village of Arapiles (that is, on the north face of the Monte de Azan), or at the crest on the further side of the plateau, perhaps a thousand yards to the south. However, the latter seems more probable: descending the steep slope of the Teso de San Miguel and passing through the village would inevitably cause some confusion, which would be risky if the main body of the enemy was so close. Moreover, there are hints that Clausel's advance had been delayed and that Cole came into action well after the initial clash between Leith and Maucune. Not everything fits this hypothesis perfectly: Clausel's limited pursuit of Cole, the ineffectiveness of Boyer's dragoons and the rapid intervention of the Sixth Division would fit the more northerly ridge better; but weighed against all this, Cole's left flank would not have been much exposed by such a limited advance, while it would have been highly vulnerable had he crossed the breadth of the plateau. The intervention of Spry's brigade also points to the fighting occurring further south, as does the retreat of Bonnet's 122nd Ligne, which would otherwise be inexplicable.

By a curious chance, there is no good description of the first round of fighting, in which Clausel's leading brigade was broken, but there are no fewer than five accounts of the second round, in which Clausel's reserve brigade broke Cole's disordered line. Three of these descriptions are quoted in the main narrative; the other two present a problem, for they suggest that Cole's flank was threatened by French cavalry, and that this was the reason it broke. However, this is not supported by the other, earlier sources, and may be owing to no more than some confusion regarding the sequence of events. Whatever the explanation, these two additional descriptions are quite interesting. Thomas Henry Browne writes that the Fourth Division,

> after driving the enemy from a hill, which he had warmly contested, were in their turn charged by five Battalions of Infantry drawn up six deep, & probably would have withstood even this tremendous fresh formation, had not some Squadrons of French dragoons charged the Portuguese in flank, & broke them, which also for a moment, disordered the Fusileers [sic], & the five French Battalions succeeded in retaking the hill.[30]

Lieutenant Cameron of the 7th Fusiliers recalls:

> We were at this moment ordered by Colonel Beatty to retire and form square, a most hazardous movement when the enemy's Infantry were advancing, and within thirty yards of us. The order was only partially heard and obeyed on the right, while on the left we kept up a hot fire on the enemy, who were advancing up-hill, and within a few yards of us. The Companies on our right having retired in succession we found ourselves alone, but the ground the enemy were ascending was so steep that we got off without loss and joined the rest. Luckily while we were forming square to receive the cavalry, the 6th Division came up and received the charge intended for us.[31]

What happened next is also open to debate. Burgoyne claims that the Fusiliers rallied at the foot of the hill and immediately returned to the fray:

> No sooner had they arrived at the bottom, than they came to their senses, and were furious with themselves for having allowed the enemy to gain the advantage. In about five minutes, they were formed in perfect order at a short distance below, and they then reascended the hill most gallantly, and drove the French down the other side as quickly as they themselves had been driven before.[32]

This seems unlikely, as even the best troops would take some time to rally and regain their order, while Burgoyne's version of events leaves no time for Beresford to intervene on Clausel's flank with Spry's brigade. Wachholtz provides a more plausible account of this phase of the combat. When Clausel's division delivered its counterattack, he found himself with the 7th Fusiliers and was surprised when the allied line crumbled and broke. 'Before I could decide if I should remain or go with them,' as he quaintly puts it, 'I found myself instinctively already at the fastest gallop which I have ever made in my life. I covered an enormous distance at each stride ... Finally, when we reached the valley, the shouting of the officers began to have an effect, particularly as everyone was out of breath.' But then the disordered infantry caught sight of the French cavalry, supported by Bonnet's infantry. Hastily they formed square, British and Portuguese mingling together. Fortunately, the squares were not put to the test, for the Sixth Division advanced to support Cole's men before the cavalry could charge. Wachholtz records that Clinton's men said as they passed, 'Be ashamed, Fusiliers!', while the two accounts from Hulse's brigade both make clear that the Fourth Division did not rally until the Sixth had driven off their pursuers.[33]

It would be interesting to know why Beresford was riding in the rear of the Fifth Division when he took command of Spry's brigade and led it against Clausel. Similarly, what were De Lancey and Bainbrigge doing behind the Fourth Division when it collapsed in front of them like a wave of the sea? Where was Wellington: at the head of the Sixth Division, or on the Lesser Arapile or some other convenient observation post? We simply do not know. The sources give us glimpses of these figures at memorable moments, but not enough information to construct a continuous narrative of their movements, let alone analyse their activities. And naturally the sources are even less helpful for the French generals.

The account by 'Major Nott' is printed in H. A. Bruce's *Life* of William Napier; however, as R. E. R. Robinson points out in his history of the 11th, no such officer appears in the *Army List*. The full text of the letter makes clear that the author took command of the regiment when Lieutenant-Colonel Cuyler was wounded, which strongly suggests that it was written by Major Frederick Newman, the second-in-command. Presumably the signature was unclear, and Bruce – or his printers – hazarded a guess.[34]

Most elements of the French counterattack are uncertain to a greater or lesser extent, and any account of this episode must include some guess-work. Oman memorably describes how the defeat of Cole and Pack gave Clausel the choice between risking all in the hope of victory, or admitting defeat and withdrawing what could still be saved of Marmont's army. 'Being an ambitious and resolute man', Clausel preferred the former, and it is evident that Oman sympathized with his choice, even though he later admits that it proved unwise – indeed, it is noticeable that almost all British accounts are distinctly well disposed towards Clausel. Other historians, even Jean Sarramon, have followed Oman's lead, with only Young and Lawford questioning whether Clausel would have seen his decision in these stark terms. But unless Oman is drawing on some unmentioned source, we do not even know that Clausel made *any* decision, for Boyer's dragoons and Bonnet's infantry may have been acting independently in seizing the tempting opportunity presented by Cole's exposed flank and Pack's defeat. Oman's description superbly captures the state of the battle as a whole at an important moment and fixes the reader's attention – which is why it has so often been repeated – but it appears to be based on no more than supposition.

Similar criticisms can be made of most descriptions in secondary accounts of the fighting between Clinton's and Bonnet's infantry. As we have seen in the narrative, the first-hand accounts of this episode are meagre and confusing. According to Oman, however, Clinton's men 'fell upon, overlapped at both ends, and thoroughly discomfited in close musketry duel the nine battalions of Bonnet's division'. Fortescue follows Oman in substance, but adds his own rhetorical touches: 'now the Sixth Division came striding over the plain to recover the ground that had been first won and then lost by Cole ... the red-coats engaged the nine battalions of Bonnet in a bitter contest of musketry. As usual the British fire prevailed; and presently Bonnet's troops ran back dis-comfited to the hill in their rear.'[35] Evidently, this is too tame and vague for Young and Lawford, who have their own ideas of what happened:

> As the British division drew near a ferocious combat developed. The French returned volley for volley; but their position was fast becoming untenable ... When the range had dwindled to little more than ten yards, the French wavered; their leading line began to disintegrate; the 6th Division went in with the bayo-net and the French ranks broke up. As they went back through a vortex of fire, the 6th Division pressing mercilessly on their heels, all order was lost.[36]

None of these accounts cites a source for its claims, but in the end they rest on just two facts: Clinton's division was responsible for Bonnet's defeat, and Bonnet's three regiments lost heavily. The rest is pure speculation. Some of this is highly plausible – there probably was some close musketry, for both sides seem to have lost heavily – but note the way the rhetoric escalates from Oman's 'close musketry duel', to Fortescue's 'bitter contest of musketry', to Young and Lawford's 'returned volley for volley ... the range had dwindled to little more than ten yards'.

Perhaps we should not be too critical, for the authors are simply trying to maintain the flow of their narrative by papering over a gap in the evidence – something every historian has to do quite often. It would not have been appro-priate for Oman or Fortescue to interrupt their works, which embrace a much larger subject than this single battle, with a lengthy digression every time the sources were less than perfectly full and explicit. Equally, Young and Lawford were writing for a popular audience. But even if this 'making bricks without straw' is understandable, it still has unfortunate consequences, especially if it is done carelessly. Young and Lawford write of the troops returning volley for volley at little more than ten yards, not because any source says it about this encounter, but because they believe that this was what often happened. But in fact very few first-hand accounts ever write of combat in these terms; rather, the idea gets copied from one secondary source to another, developing credibility simply through repetition. This in turn leads to further absurdities, such as overly bold calculations that X number of infantry fired Y number of shots, in this number of minutes at such-and-such a range, and inflicted that number of casualties, which means ... absolutely nothing, for every step in such calculations is built on sand, because the sources are not that precise or reliable, even if, for once, two accounts agree on what happened.

In fact, the accounts which we do have of the experiences of Hulse's brigade mention the normal British tactics of cheer, fire and charge, rather than a sustained exchange of musketry, while suggesting that the brigade's heavy losses were largely owing to periods of inactivity under heavy skirmisher and artillery fire.[37] However, this may not be true of the rest of the division, and many questions remain unanswered about this part of the battle. The 61st Regiment source quoted in the narrative states quite clearly that the regiment – which apart from the 2/53rd was at the eastern end of the divisional line – passed through the village of Arapiles in its advance.[38] This is extremely odd: it has always been believed that Clinton's division formed a second line behind Cole, occupying the space between the Lesser Arapile and the village, so that only the most westerly regiment should have passed among the houses. If the Sixth Division formed so far west, it was as much behind the Fifth as the Fourth Division, suggesting that the Seventh Division was even further west, while there would be many other implications for the deployment of the allied army. It also suggests that the fighting between Bonnet and Clinton may have been on a front running almost due north-west, with the French advance directed more towards the village than to the gap in the allied line. French claims to have advanced to the edge of the village at this time give this idea some credibility, although it is also possible that they are a muddled reference to Maucune's earlier attack.[39] In the end, the evidence is simply too fragmentary and uncertain to reconstruct precisely what happened.

Understanding the role of Clinton's other brigades in the fighting is also hampered by inadequate sources. Most accounts state that the two British brigades formed the front line of the division, with Rezende's brigade making the second; but it is possible that the Portuguese moved into the middle of the line and helped in the defeat of Bonnet, while Hinde's brigade may have been employed to watch Clausel and protect the flank and rear of the division. This is almost entirely speculation, but there is some slight support for it in Philip Bainbrigge's brief account: 'I galloped to the 6th Division and met them coming up in columns, they, that is two brigades, the left British (General Hulse's) and the Portuguese soon passed the 4th Division, deployed into line, and opened a tremendous fire on the enemy, who, having contented themselves with checking the 4th Division, began to retreat.'[40]

If the brunt of the fighting against Bonnet was borne by Hulse and Rezende, it would explain why the sources in Hinde's brigade – notably Captain Harry Ross-Lewin of the 32nd – do not make more of this part of the battle. It is notoriously dangerous to argue on the basis of what sources do *not* say, but

Ross-Lewin's account does not suggest that his regiment was heavily engaged at this point:

> By this time the loss sustained by the enemy was considerable. One of their colonels lay immediately in front of the colours of my regiment; he was badly wounded, and begged hard to be removed from the field; and our commanding officer humanely directed the drummers to take care of him. I saw him afterwards perfectly recovered at Salamanca.
>
> Close to the wounded colonel one of his own men was seated with his leg broken; he had a large calabash of wine slung by his side, and as soon as some of our men caught a glimpse of it they determined to make free with its contents; but he understood what they said, and instantly raising the calabash to his head, endeavoured to empty it with all possible expedition. Two soldiers ran forward to stop him, but he sturdily resisted their efforts; and when they at length succeeded in wresting the calabash from him, they found to their disappointment that he had transferred all that made it valuable to his own interior.[41]

Of Bonnet's regiments, the 118th and 119th both had colonels wounded, while the 122nd had a chef de bataillon who might easily have been taken for a 'colonel'.

Meanwhile Lieutenant Smith of the 11th makes a familiar claim:

> The advance of the brigade was so rapid, that very many of a body of riflemen, more numerous than the British, covering the retreat of the main body of the defeated enemy, had not time to get out of our way, threw themselves on the ground as dead, and were run over. It was known that many of them fired at the back of the advancing line. One, it is certain, drove his bayonet through the back of a grenadier of the Eleventh, and before he could withdraw it, he was cut down by Brigade-Major Cotton who was following the regiment on foot, his horse having been killed, and in that position both lay dead.[42]

Whatever the truth of these individual tales, they are a useful reminder that a battlefield is much less neat and orderly than a simple narrative would suggest.

Chapter Eight
Pack's Attack on the Greater Arapile

Cole's initial defeat was not the only setback suffered by the allies in the centre: Pack's independent Portuguese brigade had made a bold attack on the Greater Arapile and had been repulsed with heavy losses. Fortunately, we have an excellent account of this operation in a lively personal narrative by Captain Charles Synge, Pack's aide-de-camp, which also sheds much light on the experience of the battle.

Pack's brigade consisted of the 1st and 16th Portuguese line regiments (two battalions each) and the 4th Caçador battalion: 2,607 officers and men on 15 July. It was the second strongest Portuguese brigade in the army, after Rezende's brigade in the Sixth Division. However, it also had much the lowest proportion of officers: only one officer to every twenty-nine men, compared to one to twenty or better in most of the other brigades. The composition and command of the brigade had been unchanged since August 1810, and two years' active service had presumably given its commander a sense of its abilities, and the troops some esprit de corps. Pack himself had seen much service and, according to Colville, 'has the character of a more than ordinarily zealous and alert officer'. Some complained about his 'fidgety and irascible temper', but Charles Synge writes of him with real affection.[1] His brigade had performed well at Busaco, repulsing the attack of Maucune's brigade of Marchand's division, and had been in the vanguard of the allied army in the pursuit of Masséna in the spring of 1811. It was entrusted with the blockade of Almeida, but had been relieved of this duty before Brennier made his escape. It played a creditable part in the storming of Ciudad Rodrigo, when its diversionary attack captured the outwork in front of the Santiago gate. In the months since then it had seen little action, so it is reasonable to regard it as a seasoned unit, experienced but far from jaded, and full of confidence.

On the morning of the battle, the 4th Caçadores had taken part in the skirmishing around Nuestra Señora de la Peña. There is no evidence of the casualties they suffered, but it seems unlikely that they were heavy, and the men had plenty of time to regain their composure before advancing into action again.

The rest of the brigade had suffered only from the effects of the French artillery bombardment. It occupied a position in the allied line between the Lesser Arapile and Stubbs's brigade of the Fourth Division. As the Lesser Arapile is somewhat to the west, as well as to the north, of the Greater Arapile, and as Pack's troops were to its west, it was not directly opposite the French battery on the larger hill, which probably concentrated most of its fire on Anson's infantry and Dyneley's guns on the allied height. Pack's brigade was opposite the gap between the Greater Arapile and the beginning of the plateau – the position occupied by the 122nd Regiment of Bonnet's division.

There is some doubt over the nature of the orders Pack received. In his official dispatch, Wellington implies that he gave the order for Pack to attack the French position: 'I ordered ... and Brig. Gen. Pack should support the left of the 4th division, by attacking that of the Dos Arapiles which the enemy held.' Pack's own later account agrees with this: 'My "cacadores" stood well at Bussaco and Ciudad Rodrigo, much to my wonderment, but my mind misgave me somewhat when I received the order to attack the hill at Hermanito [the Greater Arapile], the strongest part of the enemy's position; it is the duty of a soldier to obey and not to question, hence we advanced up the hill.' And: 'No one admires Lord Wellington more than myself, but I fear he expected over-much from my "Hidalgos", whose courage is of a vastly changeable nature.' This is quite clear and unequivocal, but it is directly contradicted by Charles Synge's account. Synge was writing years later and his memory may have led him astray, but he liked and admired Pack, and would certainly not have consciously distorted the record to Pack's discredit, while as Pack's aide-de-camp he would surely have known the gist of the orders even if he did not hear them from Wellington. Yet he says: 'The orders Sir Denis Pack had received were discretionary. He was to watch and mark the Arapiles, and not to let any of the enemy come down from it to molest the flank or rear of our left Division (Cole's). He was to exercise his own judgment, and if he saw a favourable opportunity, he was authorized to try and carry the Hill of the Arapiles.'[2]

There is also some doubt over when Pack's attack was launched. Wellington and a well-informed Fourth Division source say that Bonnet only attacked Cole's flank after Pack's attack had been repulsed, while Synge states that Pack's assault only began when he saw that the Fourth Division was in difficulties and received an appeal for help from Cole.[3] This is not a problem which can be resolved definitively, although it seems rather unlikely that Pack would attempt such a difficult and dangerous operation as an assault on the Greater Arapile when he could see that the nearest allied troops were struggling. It is easier to imagine that the attack was launched in a spirit of confidence, when Cole's advance was progressing well, and that, on this point at least, Synge is mistaken. The decision to attack, while always ambitious, is certainly easier to justify if Cole's advance was succeeding. If the Fourth Division was already faltering, it was an extremely risky and uncertain way of attempting to help it, when it would have been much simpler and more effective to have advanced to cover its retreat.

These problems may cast a slight shadow over Synge's credibility, but he is the only witness who gives us the details of Pack's attack, while the outline of his account is amply confirmed by all the other relevant sources. According to Synge, Pack deployed his troops as if he was going to attack a fortress. They were led by a storming party of one hundred men of the 4th Caçadores under Major Fearon who, before the assault was launched, 'were ordered to gain as much ground up the Hill as the enemy would let them, and then lie down'. The remaining caçadores were to advance on either side in open order, taking advantage of any cover they could find; presumably, their role was to provide covering fire for the attack, although Synge does not actually say so. The storming party was supported by the four grenadier companies (one from each battalion) under the command of Lieutenant-Colonel Neil Campbell. Rather oddly, these were deployed in line. The remainder of the brigade followed in two columns: the two battalions of the 1st Regiment under Lieutenant-Colonel Noel Hill on the right; the two battalions of the 16th under Colonel Pizarro on the left.

Because the only hope of success lay in a determined charge which might carry the hill in a rush, Pack ordered that all the troops should advance with

Formation of Pack's brigade attacking the Greater Arapile.

unloaded muskets, for 'once such troops as we had began firing they would never get to the top'. If the momentum of the attack was lost the assault would fail, and nothing could be gained by having the men stand on the open hillside blazing away against the French, who would remain secure on the summit. All but the boldest and best-disciplined infantry rapidly lost their forward impetus once they began firing, so that it was often the task of the officers and NCOs in an attack to keep their men moving forward and prevent them from opening fire. Nonetheless, it was rare to make an attack in the open field with unloaded muskets, although it might be done in storming fortifications. The reasons are obvious: with unloaded muskets the infantry were vulnerable to any sudden change of fortune, the unexpected appearance of cavalry on their flank or deter-mined resistance from their immediate opponents. More importantly, it is likely that they *felt* vulnerable and defenceless. All might go well so long as the attack prospered; but if it was checked, the men would struggle to load their muskets under pressure and were likely to panic. Still, attacking the Greater Arapile at all was highly risky, and Pack evidently felt that it was worth increas-ing the danger of defeat if it minimized the chance of the attack stalling halfway up the hill.

The French held the Greater Arapile with three battalions of the 120th Ligne – some 1,800 officers and men – and a battery of probably no more than eight guns, which they had hauled to the summit. The flat table-top of the hill facing north made it easy for the guns and infantry to deploy, and the sweeping views in all directions ensured that they could not be taken by surprise.

Charles Synge describes the attack so graphically that it would be a shame not to quote him at length. The order to advance has just been given:

> In a moment all the commanding officers were under weigh [sic]. As the General and I were riding to Major Fearon's storming party, he remarked that both on the right and left of the point of direction which the storming party were taking there appeared better openings to get to the top, and he added, 'I wish I had divided Fearon's party into two and sent half towards each of the openings, but it is too late now.' I said, 'Not if you choose to let me gallop at once and give him the order, and allow me to take command of one.' He hesitated for a second, but on my repeating the offer and urging the necessity of my being off or it would be too late, he consented. I was soon up with Major Fearon. He took fifty to the left, and I the same number (not that we stopped to count) to the right. Immediately after this change my direction led through a patch of standing rye, where several of my little party fell, at first I supposed killed, for the enemy opened their guns as soon as they saw what we were about; but one man near my horse fell in such a manner that it struck me it was sham, and as he lay on his face I gave him rather a sharp prod with my sword – there was no time for any other appeal to his 'honour' – on which he turned up perfectly unhurt! What became of him afterwards I know not; I had other matters to think of ... While I was appealing to feelings of all sorts and had just got through the last of the rye, Pack

overtook me, and said in a whisper, 'Synge! I think those fellows won't carry it for you.' I said 'Oh! yes, they will, we are over the worst of it.' I meant the ground. The roar of the enemy's guns was tremendous as we approached the top, and somewhat unusual in its sound, for they tried to depress the muzzles of their guns as much as possible, and though they could not do so much harm, so steep was it, it sounded as if all but touched the top of our heads. I have never heard the like before. Those following in support fared worse.

The last part of the ascent was so steep that it was almost impossible for a horse to climb it; even the men did so with difficulty – but I had a horse that would do what scarcely any horse would attempt. It was not until I was close upon the summit that I knew what we had to contend with, for I found the ground, which had at a little distance the appearance of a gentle slope, formed a natural wall of I suppose between three and four feet high, at the top of which it spread out into a level table-land, on which the enemy were drawn up in line about ten yards from me. We looked at each other for a moment. I saw immediately that what we had undertaken was impracticable, as the men could not mount the scarped ground without first laying their arms upon the top, and even then in such small numbers that it would be absurd – but I also saw that we were so easily covered by 'the wall', and the enemy so exposed from head to foot, that if we fired they could not remain an instant. At this critical moment the head of Sir Noel Hill's column, which had followed me in support, was close up, and Hill himself called to me to ask what to do and what was before us (he could not see). I said, 'Be quick, and let your leading company close up to this bank and fire away while the others deploy as fast as they can and fire as they get up – the enemy are exposed and we are protected by this parapet.' To my horror Hill replied, 'You forget we are not loaded!' 'Well,' said I, 'we have no other chance. Load away as fast as you can.' He gave the word of command, and the men were in the act – I was addressing some few words of encouragement as well as the breathless state of anxiety I was in permitted (my poor old Ronald with great difficulty keeping his position on the steep), and two or three of the storming party were trying to scramble up the scarp, when the whole line opposed to us fired, knocked me over and literally cut to pieces the few that had climbed the 'wall'. My thigh was broken, and in falling, having no hold of the saddle, I could not in any manner save myself. Ronald made a couple of springs down the hill while I was falling, and this, together with the mangled bodies of those who fell back off the scarp on to the head of Hill's column, which in the confusion of loading was unable to see what was happening above, caused a sensation of panic which was complete.

The French line followed up their volley by charging up the the edge of the scarp, down which they leapt when they saw our confusion.

Sir Niel [sic] Campbell's Grenadiers, the left column and all, went! – the disaster was complete. I had fallen to the ground on the near side of my horse, it being the left thigh that was broken, and was in great agony owing to a sort of instinctive effort to use the broken limb in which the marrow also seemed to be breaking. A gallant little fellow, an ensign, who was adjutant of Hill's Regiment, ran up to me and put his arms under mine to try to raise me, and if his strength had equalled his courage and goodwill he would have carried me off, but he was of the smallest stature. I told him that my thigh was broken, and that it was of no use. The bayonets of the charging army were all but touching him before I could persuade him to save himself, and I actually pushed him away. A lot of the French ran over where I was, and amongst them an officer, cheering them on. As he passed over me, seeing me twirling about in frightful agony owing to the position in which I had fallen, he called out at the appalling spectacle my state exhibited. 'Oh! mon Dieu!' and then asked, 'Est-ce-que vous êtes Anglais?' I said, 'Yes,' and he pointed to a man by his side as he ran by and told him to save me. The man, who I suppose was a non-commissioned officer, did stop for a second or two, which perhaps saved my life. Some of the enemy then began to plunder those who had fallen, wounded, dying or dead, and several began at me. I was in Hussar uniform, and wore all my riches about me, with some smart things about my neck, which there was a scramble for. Most foreign soldiers, at least such as I have known, conceal their money in the waistband of the dress or inside the leg of the boot. To see if I had any such store some began cutting my clothes off, as you might have seen a sheep in the act of being shorn, and one began to pull off my boots. This was horrid, for my overalls were fastened down by curb-chain piping, and the attempt to get the boot off the broken limb was intolerable. I was soon left to go out of the world nearly as naked as I had first entered it.

Just then my attention was called from my own state to a fine young fellow of the 1st Grenadiers, who was defending himself with his musket against four or five men who surrounded him, and who were all trying to bayonet him. I called to them to spare him as he was now their prisoner. Someone, who I believe was in authority, thought I wanted something for myself, and seemed disposed to ascertain what I stood in need of, but when he learnt I was appealing for the young Portuguese sergeant, he turned away. 'Oh! as for these canaille!' was all I heard, and how it ended I do not know, for I myself became an object of the same sort of extinguishers. Suddenly they were called off to re-form on their original position on the top of the Arapiles, and I and the bodies of my comrades were left to our fate.[4]

Relations between the British and French soldiers in the Peninsula were remarkably friendly, with much mutual admiration, fraternization between the outposts and other gallant gestures. But this spirit extended only partially to the Portuguese soldiers under Wellington's command, and scarcely at all to the Spanish forces. At bottom, the goodwill rested on a sense of reciprocity as each army gradually learnt to trust the other: they were professional soldiers fighting in a cause which did not arouse their deepest passions, and could take a detached, admiring view of their opponents. The Spanish and Portuguese had a much greater personal stake in the war – many had private horrors to avenge

– while they were not always as well disciplined. But these are generalizations: soldiers of any nationality were likely to be ill-treated and even murdered when first taken prisoner, just as soldiers of all armies left the ranks during and after a battle to plunder the fallen.

Synge's account sheds light on other issues. He gives an example of the often hazardous role which an aide-de-camp might play in battle – imagine his prominence as he rode, clad in his brilliant hussar uniform, up the hill at the head of a small party of dark-uniformed infantry, a tempting and obvious target. His description of the Portuguese soldier who pretended to be hit in order to fall out and avoid the last stage of the advance highlights a common problem which is not always given sufficient weight. Many unwounded men found their way out of the ranks on various pretexts whenever a unit was heavily engaged. Some would pretend that their musket was broken, or that they were out of ammunition; others would assist a wounded man to the rear. Some did it purely from fear, others with an eye to plunder. The problem was universal, although good units suffered less than poor ones, and winning armies less than those which were being defeated; but it is impossible to quantify it.

Synge comments on the fact that the French artillery could not sufficiently depress the muzzles of their cannon to fire effectively on the storming party, and that the supporting units suffered more. It was probably only because of this protection that the attack made as much progress as it did. It is also worth noting the intimidating sound of the guns, even when the storming party escaped their fire, posing another test of the morale and resolution of the advancing infantry.

Several aspects of Synge's account are confirmed by Captain Dyneley, who watched the Portuguese attack from the Lesser Arapile.

> Our infantry, two Portuguese regiments, then stormed the hill which the French let them get to the top of before they opened much musketry. Then they did pepper them most dreadfully and beat them down again, and notwithstanding the fire we had upon them, they advanced within range of our canister which, however, it was impossible for them to stand, and they fell by hundreds. The enemy had a party without arms in their rear for the purpose of stripping and plundering our wounded, which I saw them do; for they had the poor fellows naked before they had been down two minutes.[5]

However, in his next letter Dyneley admits that 'the Portuguese, are just as bad, for in riding over the field a short time after, I found the poor wretches of Frenchmen lying in every direction without a stitch of clothing on.'[6]

Pack's attack proved a costly failure. His brigade probably lost about 470 casualties, or 18 per cent of its strength, and far from helping Cole, it added to the breach in the allied centre. Still, the consequences do not seem to have been serious. The French pursued Pack's fugitives, but did not venture on a serious attack on the Lesser Arapile – Dyneley rather exaggerates the importance of the part played by his guns in checking their advance. The 120th Ligne appears to have suffered much less than the other regiments in Bonnet's division – probably about 225 casualties, including lightly wounded men who soon returned to the ranks.[7] Few of these would have been owing to Pack's infantry; more, perhaps most, to Dyneley's guns; but the regiment may also have lost casualties at other points during the battle. Indeed, it is even possible that one of its battalions took part in the attack on Cole's flank, or the fight with Clinton.

Napier comments on Pack's attack that the Portuguese 'were scoffed at for the failure, but unjustly, no troops could have withstood that crash upon such steep ground, and the propriety of attacking the hill at all seems questionable.'[8] This conclusion is particularly valuable because Napier learnt in the Pyrenees in 1813 what excellent troops could accomplish. Nonetheless, it is worth asking what it was which made the task so formidable. Pack's brigade had a significant, although not overwhelming, numerical advantage (2,600 men compared to 1,800 infantry plus gunners). Against this there was the French battery; but it is the 'steep ground' which Napier emphasizes, not the French artillery. Climbing a steep slope slows the advance, depriving it of momentum and making the men breathless and disordered. Equally important is the psychological effect of the enemy being above, coming down upon the troops while the latter 'look up' to them as a child has to look up to an adult. Mentally as well as physically the advantage lies with those on the higher ground.

Clearly the task was beyond Pack's brigade, and the decision to launch the attack, whether made by Wellington or by Pack, proved a mistake. It would have been better if the hill had been masked frontally, while a stronger force should have been sent to protect Cole's left flank, which would inevitably become exposed as he advanced. Still, there were ample reserves ready to contain the allied setback in the centre, while it would be unrealistic to expect that a battle fought on such even terms would not see some mixture of fortunes.

Commentary

Charles Synge's account, on which so much of this chapter depends, was written years after the events he describes. However, it was based on a notebook which he kept at the time, although, given the severity of his wound he probably did not write it up until some time after the battle. Some of the incidents he reports from other parts of the battle, such as Pakenham's attack, are probably inaccurate, and must be based on hearsay rather than his own observation. But his account of his own experiences rings true. The ascent of the Greater Arapile is just as he describes it, and the natural 'walls' of rock near its summit are still there today. His writing is free of the obvious vanity and self-importance which often distort first-hand accounts, and there is no reason to suspect that he exaggerates the events he describes, or his own part in them. The tale has been smoothed and rounded by frequent repetition, and the dialogue can hardly be verbatim, but almost all of the story can be accepted at face value.

The one point where Synge's account appears doubtful is on the responsibility for the decision to attack, and its timing. This has already been discussed in the main narrative, but it is worth giving the evidence more fully here. Synge's version is detailed, circumstantial and at first sight convincing. Having said that Pack was ordered to protect Cole's left flank and rear, he continues: 'We saw, that, having ascended the heights he [Cole] was being roughly handled and after some time, though fighting desperately, he was losing ground.' And:

> In a short time Sir Denis received a message from Cole to send him some assistance.
>
> There appeared to Sir Denis Pack, and also to myself, to be so fierce a struggle just at this moment between Sir Lowry Cole's Division and the enemy, that it must be over, one way or the other, in a few minutes – long before we could get to his support, which at the shortest time would have been half an hour. He explained to the Aide-de-Camp who brought the message what the Duke's orders were, and that, if we moved to try to get to Sir Lowry, the fellows on the Arapiles would be down on our flank and rear before we got half way. In this dilemma he decided on rushing on the instant to try to carry our own hill, very properly arguing that if we succeeded we should soon be with Cole, and if we failed our attack must have the effect of preventing those on the Arapiles from detaching any men to add to Sir Lowry's difficulties.[9]

But against this there is Wellington's explicit statement, made only two days after the battle that the Fourth Division 'was obliged to give way ... after the failure of Brig. Gen. Pack's attack upon the Arapiles'. And Charles Vere is just as definite:

> At this moment, it became evident that the danger to which the left of the line of the two Brigades of the 4th division was exposed, in their forward movement, had not been lightly estimated. General Pack had attempted to gain the height opposite to him (the highest of the Aripeles [sic]) and failed – and the left battalion of the Portuguese Brigade of the 4th division, had been arrested in its forward movement in the plain, by a movement of the enemy from behind the Aripeles upon it.[10]

This sequence of events has been accepted without question by Napier, Oman, Fortescue and all other historians of the battle, but of these only Oman gives evidence of having read Synge's account. They may well be right: Wellington's contemporary statement must carry great weight, and it seems intrinsically more likely that Pack would launch such an ambitious attack if Cole's advance appeared to be prospering. On the other hand, Synge was on the spot and appears otherwise reliable. Given this it is impossible to decide the question with any confidence unless fresh evidence comes to light.

Synge's account implies that Pack's brigade advanced directly up the north face of the Greater Arapile, but as we have seen they began their advance well to the west, beyond the Lesser Arapile. Presumably they actually advanced obliquely in a south-easterly direction. This would have made their approach march longer, but it would also have meant that they were not advancing quite so directly into the mouths of the French cannon. It is even possible that they clambered up the north-west corner of the hill, which is much more rugged than the middle of the north side, although Synge's reference to the rye he advanced through, the natural wall near the summit and the fact that he could remain mounted almost rule this out.

Pack's choice of formation is interesting, and even rather surprising. The four grenadier companies under Lieutenant-Colonel Campbell which provided immediate support for the storming party were deployed in line. They probably amounted to about 400 men, giving a frontage of 130 yards or so (in two ranks), so it would not be difficult to maintain alignment if the ground was reasonably even. But there seems little advantage in advancing in line when the ground was so steep and rough, the men's muskets were unloaded and success depended upon the impetus of the attack. (Possibly the formation was chosen to reduce the damage inflicted by the French artillery.) Conversely, the remainder of the brigade formed in two columns, each containing two battalions minus their grenadier companies, or about eight hundred men. Synge does not say whether these columns were formed on a one- or two-company front: the former was probably more common in the allied army, but it would have produced a column with 50 men in each rank, 16 ranks deep. This would have been as heavy and vulnerable to artillery as anything used by the French in the campaign. Even if these columns had a two-company frontage, they would still have been 8 ranks deep. It is not a formation one expects to see Wellington's infantry employing in open battle, and perhaps it is putting too great a burden of interpretation on Synge's words to assume that it was actually adopted. After all, his main concern was with the troops leading the advance, not with the formation of the reserves.

When Synge states that all the Portuguese infantry advanced with unloaded muskets, he presumably intends to exclude those members of the 4th Caçadores who were not part of the storming party, as their role was to provide some covering fire for the advance. He also refers to the 'French line' charging forward. This may or may not be intended to indicate that the French were deployed in line, but it was the obvious formation for them to adopt when defending a position such as the Greater Arapile. Finally, there is no doubt that Pack's brigade was thoroughly broken, although it probably rallied as soon as the French ceased their pursuit. Dyneley records an interesting incident which must have occurred during this panic: 'At the battle of Salamanca I caught one [Portuguese] officer, with his sword drawn, running away. I stopped him short and made all the men at the guns hiss and abuse him, then gave him over to the 40th regiment, who hooted him from right to left; but the fellow did not care, he saved his head which was his object.'[11] Such informal sanctions were far more common than formal accusations of cowardice in the face of the enemy, at least in the allied army. Even the best troops might break and run if caught by surprise or placed under intolerable strain, and this was understood, although they were expected to rally at the first opportunity.

Pack's own account of the fighting is brief: 'we advanced up the hill and were within thirty paces of the top when the hidden French reserves leaped on us from the rocks on our front and flank. I did what in me lay, but the Lisbon Volunteers disappeared sooner than smoke.'[12] Lieutenant Ingilby, of Gardiner's company of Royal Artillery, attached to the First Division, says: 'The Portuguese advanced to within musket shot of the crest of the hill, but were suddenly driven back and overwhelmed by the fire of the French, who had screened their force on the slope of the opposite side of the hill.' Ingilby then adds a fresh detail, not recorded in any other account: 'I was advanced to sustain the defeated Portuguese with two pieces, a gun and a howitzer.' Presumably Ingilby, if he arrived in time, added his fire to Dyneley's and so helped encourage the French to withdraw back to the Greater Arapile. Ingilby's movement may have been supported by Wheatley's brigade of the First Division – there are obscure hints of this in the sources but nothing definite, while the trifling losses suffered by the brigade show that it was not seriously engaged.[13] J. Scott Lillie of the 7th Caçadores, who had been driven from the Greater Arapile early in the day, criticizes the attack: 'it was in my humble opinion an injudicious one, having been made at the point where I could not ascend on horseback in the morning.' And he goes on to imply a much later time for the attack than any other account – when Bonnet's counterattack was already being defeated. But Lillie's account was written many years later, while on the day he was naturally preoccupied with the misfortunes of his own regiment, so his evidence may be safely disregarded.[14] Finally, it is worth pausing to smile at Marmont's account of the episode in his memoirs. No one can blame the defeated marshal for seeking to make the most of whatever successes French arms achieved in the battle, but in claiming that Pack's brigade lost eight hundred dead he risks becoming the object of ridicule. The true figure, for the whole battle, was 102 killed.[15]

Chapter Nine
Ferey and the French Last Stand

The defeat of the divisions of Clausel and Bonnet left no doubt that the French had lost the battle. More than half of Marmont's army had been broken; thousands of French troops had been captured and the remainder were streaming to the rear in great disorder, even panic. But there was still a large number of men – almost half the infantry in the army – who had yet to be seriously engaged, and who remained in good order. With skill and luck these units might be salvaged from the wreck, but first they were needed to check the allied pursuit of the rest of the army; otherwise the panic would spread and further enormous losses would be inflicted. The long afternoon was drawing into evening; if a couple of hours could be gained, night would cover the flight of the broken divisions.

Three and a half French infantry divisions remained intact. Foy, on the far right, had only been engaged in the morning's skirmishing. He could do little to cover the retreat of the rest of the army at this stage and was in some danger of being separated from it, although, even if this had happened, he could still have crossed the Tormes at the fords of Huerta and Encinas. Ferey's division was in the centre; it had advanced in support of Clausel and Bonnet but had not been involved in their ruin; now it would cover their retreat and attempt to halt, or at least delay, the allied advance. Further south and west lay half of Taupin's division – five battalions of 17th Léger and 65th Ligne – which was all that remained of the left wing; and Sarrut's division which had been sent by Clausel to try to stem the allied advance and cover the flight of the left.

There is little reliable evidence for the activities of Taupin's brigade and Sarrut's division in this phase of the battle. Most historians – French as well as British – suggest that Taupin's regiments were either so demoralized that they dissolved almost of their own accord, or that they were constantly driven back by the steady advance of the allied Third and Fifth Divisions. But Norcliffe Norcliffe is quite clear that the French infantry who treated him so well were from the 65th Ligne (see above, p. 132) and that the British infantry who drove them back included the 32nd Foot from Hinde's brigade of the Sixth Division. If this is correct, Taupin's regiments had either fallen back in good order, carrying Norcliffe with them, and joined the French rearguard on the ridge of El Sierro; or, less plausibly, Hinde's brigade engaged them separately before it attacked the final French position. Taupin's losses are more than usually difficult to establish, as the casualties suffered at Salamanca are combined with those incurred four days earlier at the Guarena. Lamartinière gives totals of 262 casualties (23 per cent) for the 17th Léger and 359 (23 per cent) for the 65th Ligne. While these losses suggest similar experiences, the distribution of officer casualties differs sharply: according to Martinien, the 17th Léger lost 8 officers (including two killed and one mortally wounded) on the 18th, and only 3 on the 22nd; while the 65th lost 3 on the 18th (two of them killed), and eleven on the 22nd (one killed, two mortally wounded). These figures would seem to indicate that the 17th Léger was only lightly engaged at Salamanca, having lost quite heavily on the Guarena, while the 65th Ligne suffered four-fifths of its losses (271 men) in the battle. So perhaps the 17th escaped or dissolved and joined in the flight of the rest of the French left, while the 65th retreated in good order back to El Sierro.[1]

According to one French account, Sarrut's division advanced onto the Monte de Azan with its first brigade (2nd Léger and 36th Ligne, six battalions) deployed in line, and its remaining regiment (4th Léger, three battalions) in columns on its left to guard against the British cavalry. The mere appearance of this new force checked the allied advance. Many of the allied troops were still far to the rear, collecting prisoners and attending to the wounded. Pakenham's infantry in particular were tired by their long march in the heat of the day, and the initial excitement of combat may now have passed. The allied reserves which might have taken over at this point – the Seventh Division, Bradford's Portuguese and the Spanish Division – had not been brought forward. And the allied commanders were probably most anxious not to let their troops get out of hand and so jeopardize the success which had already been achieved. Whatever the reason, Sarrut was able to gain time without being seriously engaged, and Pakenham's men took three hours to advance the three miles from the Pico de Miranda to El Sierro.[2]

Sarrut's losses in the battle were very light. Martinien records only eight officer casualties in the whole division (or 4 per cent of the 198 officers present on 15 July), and none of these was killed. Lamartinière's figures are actually higher than this would imply: 384 casualties, or 8 per cent of the division. But of these, 158 were 'killed or captured'; and while some would have been wounded men who could not escape, others were probably men who lost touch with their unit in the retreat and were subsequently taken prisoner.

Meanwhile, in the centre, the defeat of Clausel and Bonnet had made the French position on the Greater Arapile untenable. The light companies of the King's German Legion brigade in the First Division turned its eastern flank; Clinton's advance had already passed it to the west; and Cole's division, now rallied and restored to order, was advancing on it frontally. There was no resistance: Colonel Bouthmy of the 120th withdrew his regiment in good order, although it is said to have suffered heavily from British fire before it could make a clean break.[3]

Ferey's division had also fallen back in the face of the allied advance and now occupied the ridge of El Sierro. This was a long, low ridge, smooth and easy of ascent, but giving no cover to troops advancing from the north-west; behind it were the low trees and rough scrub of the 'forest' which stretched towards Alba de Tormes. Clausel ordered Ferey to hold the position until night fell, so that the rest of the army could escape. Ferey's division consisted of nine strong battalions, almost 5,700 men on 15 July if the divisional artillery is included. He deployed in a single line (three ranks deep) along the forward face of the ridge, with a battalion at each end of the line formed in square to protect its flanks. Behind and above the infantry, presumably firing through gaps in their ranks rather than over their heads, were fifteen guns. This well-posted rearguard attracted support from fragments of other divisions. As we have seen, it is likely that the 65th Ligne from Taupin's division joined it, as the 119th Ligne from Bonnet's division may also have done. On the other hand, Sarrut's division appears to have withdrawn beyond it and was not engaged in its support, although it may have helped to protect its outer, or southern, flank.[4]

The sight of this new opposition brought Clinton's advance to a halt. His division had already fought hard to break Bonnet's attack and needed time to reorganize and gather support before plunging into fresh combat. Unfortunately, it halted within range of the French guns, and the men of the Sixth Division are said to have suffered severely in the interval before they resumed their advance. Gradually additional units arrived, ready to support or take part in the impending attack. The Fusilier brigade of the Fourth Division, now fully restored to order, formed on the left of Clinton's line. Wellington directed the remaining brigades of the Fourth Division – Stubbs's Portuguese and W. Anson's two British regiments – to turn Ferey's right (or north-eastern) flank. They would be assisted by Gardiner's battery of artillery from the First Division, whose fire took Ferey's line in the flank in the later part of the combat, and more distantly by the advance of the First and Light Divisions. The Third and Fifth Divisions were ordered to support Clinton's attack, but they might have been better employed turning Ferey's southern flank. According to Napier – who in this case was writing as a historian, not a witness, for his regiment was several miles away – Pakenham urged Clinton to delay his attack until the Third Division could turn the French left, but an unnamed staff officer suddenly ordered Clinton's troops to advance.[5] Thomas Hamilton, writing as Spencer Moggridge, gives an elaborate version of this story, but it must be remembered that, despite the use of the first person, he was not at the battle.

> At length, an aide-de-camp of Lord Wellington, – who, during this interval, had been engaged in reconnoitring the new position of the French, – came riding

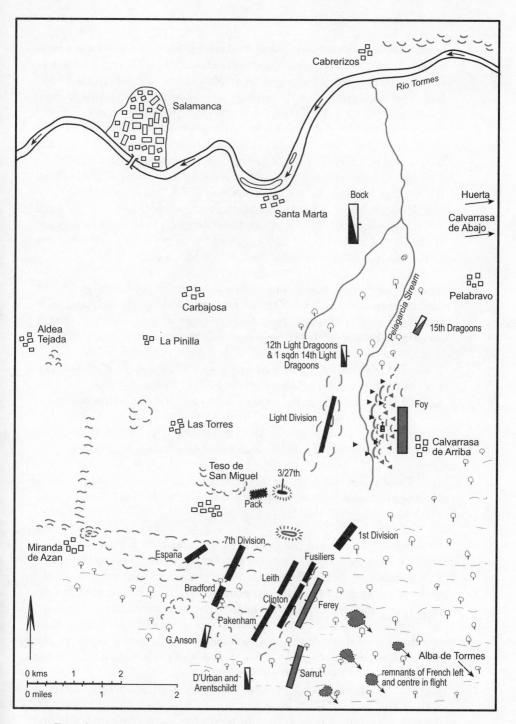

Ferey's rear-guard (all troop positions approximate, many conjectural).

up at full speed, with orders to General Pakenham. These were, for I heard them delivered, – that the 6th division, commanded by General Clinton, were to lead the attack on the front of the heights occupied by the enemy, and that the 3d division were to support them. 'I shall do so with pleasure,' rejoined General Pakenham; 'but tell Lord Wellington that my decided opinion is in favour of a flank movement. To storm that height,' he continued, his voice becoming more elevated and his eye more sparkling as he spoke, 'is nothing less than an inhuman sacrifice of life. Everything can be gained by operating on the flank.'

'General,' replied the aide-de-camp, 'it is not for me to judge of such matters. It is my duty merely to deliver the orders with which I am intrusted.'

'I know, I know,' rejoined Pakenham; 'but, nevertheless, tell my Lord Wellington what I say. Tell him my opinion is decidedly in favour of taking them in flank – to do otherwise, is taking the bull by the horns.' The aide-de-camp bowed and rode off, and so ended this extraordinary colloquy.[6]

There is no confirmation of this remarkable story in the letters written by Pakenham immediately after the battle. However, an unpublished letter from Colonel De Lancey, the acting Quartermaster-General, to his old chief, George Murray, reveals considerable unhappiness with the attack:

> The 6th Division afterwards were brought into Action, but I think unnecessarily at about two or three Miles from the Field of Action.
> The Enemy retired from the Field of Action towards Alba de Tormes and to cover his Retreat occupied a strong Height on the Road. Part of our Force was already between the Height and Alba de Tormes. The Height however was attacked and carried by the 6th Division but at the expense of 1,000 men.
>
> ... Hulse is very highly spoken of in the Attack of the 6th Division. I understand he executed it extremely well and had nothing to say to the planning of the attack.[7]

Unfortunately, we do not know nearly enough about the position of the various units at the time to be able to judge whether this criticism is justified or not. If all had gone well, an attempt to turn Ferey's southern flank might have dislodged him as quickly, and much more cheaply, than a frontal assault. But the attempt might not have succeeded: it might have encountered Sarrut's division, which – according to one French source[8] – was in a perfect position to block such a move; or it might have taken too long to organize and execute, so that Ferey would have achieved his objective and been able to withdraw under cover of night before his line of retreat was seriously threatened.

Rather than turn the French flank, the allied troops advanced up El Sierro in a costly frontal assault. There are a number of first-hand accounts of the subsequent fighting, but unfortunately most were written years after the battle, and they contain numerous contradictions and inconsistencies. We do not even know whether the whole of the Sixth Division was in the front line, or whether Rezende's brigade was – initially at least – in a second line in support; nor whether the combat involved one round of fighting or two. Nonetheless, both its severity and its ultimate result are clear.

Major Newman, of the 1/11th in Hulse's brigade, describes the wait under fire in front of El Sierro, and the subsequent fighting where it was hottest:

> During this time their artillery played incessantly on us with shot and shell, by which I lost about forty men; and the loss increased so fast by their getting the range, that I told Hulse something should be done, either in retiring or by the line lying down. The latter he agreed to, and we had hardly a casualty after ...
>
> The next advance of the 6th Division was to the attack of the French position. As soon as the French saw this, a cloud of their skirmishers came down to the foot of the hills forming their position, and as we neared them opened their fire, supported with terrible effect by their artillery with grape; however, the brigade kept moving on, and in spite of every obstacle carried the position. Not a shot was fired by the 11th until we reached the top, when we gave them a farewell discharge. By this time the loss of the 61st and 11th was most severe: the Portuguese brigade in attacking their portion of the position found the ground steeper and more difficult of access, which enabled the enemy to retain that part, and eventually the French came down and attacked them in turn. I saw this and proposed to Hulse to wheel up the 11th to their right and attack them in flank, but for the present he declined, thinking we were too much reduced. After a while poor Bradford, the assistant adjutant-general, came up, and instantly went to the rear and brought up our support a brigade of the 4th Division which had been reformed; the 61st and 11th then changed their front to the right, and attacked this hill and carried it. This was the last of the engagement, and at this period the 61st and 11th had about five officers and eighty men each left.[9]

Captain Harry Ross-Lewin of the 32nd Foot in Hinde's brigade tells a similar tale, if with more striving for literary effect:

> It was half-past seven when the sixth division, under General Clinton, was ordered to advance a second time and attack the enemy's line in front, supported by the third and fifth divisions. The ground over which we had to pass was a remarkably clear slope, like the glacis of a fortification – most favourable for the defensive fire of the enemy, and disadvantageous to the assailants, but the division advanced towards the position with perfect steadiness and confidence. A craggy ridge, on which the French infantry was drawn up, rose so abruptly that they could fire four or five deep; but we had approached within two hundred yards of them before the fire of musketry began, which was by far the heaviest that I have ever witnessed, and was accompanied by constant discharges of grape. An uninterrupted blaze was then maintained, so that the crest of the hill seemed to be one long streak of flame. Our men came down to the charging position, and

commenced firing from that level, at the same time keeping their touch to the right, so that the gaps opened by the enemy's fire were instantly filled up. At the very first volley that we received, about eighty men of the right wing of my regiment fell to the rear in one group; the commanding officer immediately rode up to know the cause, and found that they were all wounded.

Previously to the advance of the sixth division, the light companies of the right brigade were formed on the right of the line, and, as we moved on, one of the enemy's howitzers was captured by the light company of the 32nd regiment. It had been discharged once, but before the gunners could load it again, it was taken by a rush.[10]

These accounts can be broadly confirmed by that of John Douglas, of the Royal Scots (3/1st) who was advancing in their rear:

> While this was occurring on the right, the 6th Division on our left was ordered to charge a hill crowned with cannon. The day was extremely warm. Our poor fellows, having to bear up against the united fire of cannon and musketry, had their ranks equally thinned ere they commenced to ascend the hill. So determined were the enemy to maintain this post that one brigade of our division was cut off. Fortunately, our work was settled on the right as the enemy were falling back in confusion. We brought up our right shoulder and flanked the hill, on which they gave way here also, abandoning their guns in disorder. 'Twas now near sunset, which appeared as red as sunset through the dense clouds of smoke, while the cheers of the British advancing to the charge, and the peals of musketry which seemed to increase, was a scene so awfully grand that no pen could describe it. The 2nd Queens, the 11th and 61st were the Regiments which composed the Brigade I have mentioned ... I never saw the British casualties so thick, while we passed on in pursuit, striving to avoid treading on the wounded, who were calling for a little water for God's sake, which was entirely out of our power to give; or in the more feeling accents of comrades they pleaded, 'Don't trample on us.'[11]

The casualty figures leave no doubt of the severity of the fighting in the centre. The 1/11th, Newman's battalion, suffered 341 casualties from 516 all ranks, or two-thirds of its strength; and the 1/61st in the same brigade suffered just as severely. Newman was probably exaggerating little, if at all, when he said that each regiment was reduced to a handful of officers and eighty rank and file by the end of the fighting, for many unwounded men would have left the ranks in the course of the day and failed to find their way back. (Each unit was left with a nominal total of about 180 unwounded rank and file.) Hinde's brigade suffered much less: 344 casualties from 1,456 officers and men, or one-quarter of its strength. The 1/32nd, Ross-Lewin's unit, lost 137 of these casualties, so that his story of 80 men wounded at one blow is possible, if unlikely. The remaining brigade in the division, Rezende's Portuguese, suffered almost as heavily as Hinde's: probably rather more than 600 casualties from its strength of 2,631 all ranks. All these casualties, of course, were suffered in the battle as a whole; many, perhaps most, in the earlier fighting with Bonnet.

The Fusilier brigade from the Fourth Division formed on the left of Clinton's line and took part in the assault on the French position, although the distribution of casualties within the brigade rather suggests that the outer half of it may have extended beyond Ferey's main line and consequently encountered little effective opposition. Charles Vere, the Assistant Quartermaster-General of the Fourth Division, describes the part played by the Fusiliers:

> The Brigade of the 6th division, under General Hulse, was ordered by Lord Wellington to attack the right of the enemy in his new position, and the Fusilier Brigade of the 4th Division, commanded by Lieutenant-Colonel Wilson of the 48th Regiment, was moved forward to the attack, on the left of General Hulse's Brigade.
>
> The attack was spirited, and well executed. The Fusilier Brigade moved up the heights under a heavy fire, without returning a shot; and drove the enemy in its front, from his ground. The Brigade then brought up its left, for the purpose of assisting General Hulse, by a flank and raking movement. But the formation was no sooner effected, than the enemy gave way before the General, and the defeat was completed. As the day had closed, the troops halted and picquets were pushed into the wood.[12]

Much of this is confirmed by Wachholtz, whose Brunswickers were on the outer or northern flank of the Fusiliers as they wheeled around Ferey's flank. Evidently there was some confusion caused by the growing dark and the fact that the troops were among the trees. Some Portuguese infantry attempted to take Wachholtz prisoner, and tempers flared before the difficulty was over-come. Wachholtz also notes the effectiveness of the British artillery enfilading the French line, and saw some men from the 23rd Regiment capture a French gun. (This was either the 23rd Fusiliers, or the 23rd Portuguese Line from Stubbs's brigade of the Fourth Division: Wachholtz does not specify which, although the former seems rather more likely.)[13]

Finally, we are fortunate in having a detailed French account of the later stages of the fighting, written by Captain Jean-Baptiste Lemonnier-Delafosse of the 31st Léger. According to Lemonnier-Delafosse, there were two distinct phases in the combat. In the first, Ferey's division checked the advance of the British, but was ultimately forced to withdraw to the skirts of the forest in its rear. In the second, it repelled an attack by Clinton's Portuguese, but finally succumbed to a renewed British assault acting with increased pressure on its flanks. The quotation begins at the end of the first phase:

> The cruel fire cost us many lives. Then, slowly, having gained almost an

hour's respite for the army, we retired, still protected by the squares, to the edge of the wood which stretched away to Alba de Tormes. Here Ferey halted his half-destroyed division, and formed in line it still presented a respectable front to the enemy. Here he made his stand despite the enfilading fire of the English batteries; here he found the death most desired by a soldier, that caused by a cannon-ball.

The 3rd Division thus formed on the edge of the wood, deprived of its artillery, saw the enemy advance on it in two lines, the first composed of the Portuguese, the second of the English. Left alone to fight, its position was critical, but it awaited the shock. The two lines marched on the division; their order was so regular that we could see the officers in the Portuguese lines maintain company intervals by striking their men with their swords or canes.

We opened fire on the enemy as soon as they came within range, and the fire of our front two ranks was so effective that it halted their advance, and although they tried to return our fire, they melted away completely – but they were Portuguese. The second line, composed of English soldiers, now advanced upon us; we should have tried to receive it like the first, without yielding an inch, despite the fire of the enemy's batteries, but a sudden blow on our left was too much. The 70th Ligne was turned and broken by cavalry and their flight carried away the 26th and 77th [sic – 47th] regiments. My own 31st Léger, although only two battalions strong, held firm and halted the enemy who continued to fire until we finally retired a few hundred yards into the wood.[14]

Lemonnier-Delafosse then goes on to give more details of the experiences of his own unit, from which it is clear that it suffered much from the enfilading fire of the British artillery:

In my company ten [men] were carried away by the fire of the battery which cut us to pieces. My company was number 4 in the first battalion; all the others, especially the carabineers, had large holm oaks to the right which gave them cover from the flanking fire, so all the cannon shot hit my company, whilst the voltigeurs did not lose a man. A gap opened on my left. In the midst of this carnage a farcical event made us laugh, a soldier was hit twice by one bullet, his pack was full of flour which powdered all our faces.[15]

After this, it is rather disconcerting to find that Ferey's losses were among the lowest in the French army: of the infantry divisions, only those of Foy and Sarrut, neither of which was seriously engaged, suffered less. According to Lamartinière's return, Ferey's division suffered 1,001 casualties, or 17.4 per cent of its strength. These are not trifling casualties, and Lamartinière's return generally understates the true figure, although in this case Martinien's record of officer casualties tends to support the return. (According to Martinien, the officers of the four regiments in the division lost 19.6 per cent, 13.6 per cent, 25.4 per cent and 10.2 per cent, or 17.5 per cent overall.) Other French regiments who joined Ferey would also have suffered in the action, but the evidence is too uncertain to attempt to estimate their losses.

Several factors contributed to keeping Ferey's losses lower than might have been expected. The fact that most of the allied troops had already been heavily engaged probably reduced the effectiveness of their musketry significantly, and may also have reduced their impetuosity, preventing them from charging through the French fire and so resolving the combat rapidly. The powerful French artillery must also have greatly helped Ferey's cause, while the British guns only played a part late in the action, when a battery from the First Division was able to enfilade the French line. The fading light and the steepness of the slope probably reduced the accuracy of the fire on both sides, although here the advantage lay with the allies, for it was more difficult to fire effectively downhill than up, while the setting sun would have shone longer on the French on top of the westerly facing ridge than on the allies at its foot. More important is Ross-Lewin's statement that in the initial advance the French opened fire at two hundred yards, while Lemonnier-Delafosse implies that in the second round, against both the Portuguese and then against the British, the French opened fire 'as soon as they came within range'. But Napoleonic muskets were very inaccurate even at two hundred yards, and at that range a musketry duel could be sustained for some time before significant casualties would accumulate; especially as the effectiveness of each round would diminish as the men became dazed by the noise, blinded by the smoke, and began making mistakes in the complicated procedure of loading their muskets. It is significant that Ferey's fresh troops lacked the discipline to hold their fire until the British were at closer range and, equally, that fire at such a long range was sufficient to check the impetus of the British advance. Finally, there was no effective pursuit of Ferey's division after the fighting had finished: it fell back in considerable disorder, but the wood and night covered its retreat, while the Sixth Division was too badly battered to advance any further.

Lemonnier-Delafosse's account raises some other questions. This is the only source which suggests that the combat fell into two distinct phases, or that Rezende's brigade attacked separately from the rest of the allies and was repulsed. This does not mean that his account is not correct: Ross-Lewin was wounded and had to leave the front before the combat was over, and Major Newman may well have conflated two episodes into one. Lemonnier-Delafosse's story is intrinsically plausible and appears convincing, but it should be noted that some details are demonstrably wrong – Ferey was mortally wounded, but not killed outright – while the account of other parts of the day is unconvincing. If his was the only first-hand description of the fighting, one would accept it with gratitude but, as we are faced with a number of conflicting accounts, doubts arise that cannot be dismissed. Even if fresh evidence were to be discovered, it seems unlikely that we would ever know precisely what happened in this combat.

Nonetheless, it is quite clear that Ferey achieved his principal objective. His task had been to cover the retreat of the French army, even if this required the sacrifice of his division. In the event his men suffered heavily – although not as heavily as might have been expected – and fell back in disorder, joining the flight of the rest of the army. But vital time had been gained: darkness had fallen and the main thrust of the allied advance had been halted. Ferey appears to have handled his division with considerable skill, while his regiments fought with resolution, neither disrupted nor demoralized by the flight of the rest of the army. Wellington's men in a similar position might have achieved even more, decisively repulsing Clinton's assault, but defensive linear tactics were not the French forte, and the performance of Ferey's division was certainly among the most creditable of all Marmont's troops on the day. In the end, the fighting could have only one outcome, for Ferey had no choice but to withdraw: his flanks were vulnerable and, once night had been gained and protection afforded against allied pursuit, it would serve no purpose to remain. Indeed, his division had to be across the Tormes by morning or it would certainly be cut off and destroyed.

The handling of the attack aroused some discontent in the allied army, although not enough to cloud the joy of victory. Two issues are involved: the decision to attack frontally rather than operate on Ferey's flanks, which has already been discussed, and the actual execution of the attack. Colonel De Lancey, while criticizing the first, speaks highly of Hulse's conduct in regard to the second, and Major Newman emphatically agrees, 'Hulse's conduct during the whole of the battle was beyond praise.' It is not clear why both officers refer to Hulse rather than Clinton: there are no reports of the latter being wounded, nor any other reason for doubting that he remained in command of his division throughout the day. However, Colonel Bingham, of the 2/53rd, said in a letter written soon after the battle that Clinton's 'conduct on the day of the action, was such as does not add to his popularity'. This is suggestive, but without further evidence – and there is none – it would be dangerous to leap to any conclusions.[16]

Lieutenant T. H. Browne of the staff also presents a more critical view of the attack, although he names no names: 'the Troops of that Division [the Sixth] were not quite satisfied with the mode of attack by which they were brought up in front & then halted to fire at an enemy who had better ground.' And Andrew Leith Hay elaborates with some comments which may disconcert those who still believe that British success in the Peninsula rested on the firepower of their infantry: 'The 6th [Division] suffered very much having been halted when advanced about half way – which is a system that never will answer, the only way is to get at them at once with the Bayonet, that they can never stand, but as to firing they will do that as long as you like, and fire much better than we do.' That this was a common view at the time is shown by an anonymous second-hand account of the battle, published in the *Royal Military Panorama* for December 1812: 'The Sixth Division ... deployed at the bottom of a hill, of easy ascent, and then began to fire regular vollies. In consequence, they suffered very severely, for the French, it is well known, will exchange shots with you as much as you please.' Even Charles Boutflower, who, as a surgeon, knew how few wounds were ever actually inflicted by bayonets, agreed, remarking of the battle in general: 'The whole business was performed by the Bayonet, & the most sceptical must now be surely convinced how superior in the use of it is the British Soldier to every other in the world.'[17]

Whether the Sixth Division was in fact deliberately halted to return the French fire – as Leith Hay implies – must be doubted. Any such order would have been most unwise and most uncharacteristic of British tactics in the Peninsula, which always emphasized the search for a quick decision through a bayonet charge, rather than a prolonged, mutually destructive exchange of musketry. It seems far more likely that the allied advance, made by troops who had already been blunted by hard fighting, simply faltered when faced with an extremely strong position held by fresh, determined troops, sensibly deployed. The wonder is not that the British brigades did not press home their initial attack, but rather that they sustained it so well and eventually forced Ferey to withdraw. Clinton's division and the Fusiliers suffered more than twice as heavily as any other comparable unit in the allied army, except Stubbs's Portuguese brigade from the Fourth Division. But they had borne the brunt of the battle in the centre where the French fought with great courage and resolution – and some skill – and they had triumphed. The cost was high, but probably not excessive.

Commentary

By far the best secondary account of this late stage of the battle is in Jean Sarramon's *La Bataille des Arapiles*, which adds considerable new information to Oman's narrative. In particular Sarramon sheds light on the hitherto mysterious movements of Sarrut's division, basing his account on unpublished papers and an obscure biographical notice of one of Sarrut's brigadiers, General Fririon.[18] Nonetheless, much still remains unclear about the role played by this division, and even more about Taupin's remaining brigade and the related movements of the allied Third and Fifth Divisions. All we can really say with confidence is that the advance of the allied right wing was slower than might have been expected, and that the casualty statistics do not suggest any serious fighting at this point. Sarramon states that when Sarrut's division withdrew from the plateau it took up a position to the left and in the rear of Ferey's division; but if so, it is rather strange that its casualties remained so light and that it did not give Ferey more effective assistance.

Ferey's division was not one of the more distinguished in Marmont's army: only the 31st Léger had played a noticeable role in the campaigns of 1805–7 (at Friedland), while all four regiments had seen long and mostly unhappy service in the Peninsula. Three regiments (31st Léger, 47th and 70th Ligne) had been heavily engaged at Coruña and had gone on to take part in Soult's invasion of Portugal. In the following year all four had again invaded Portugal in Reynier's corps of Masséna's army, and all except the 47th lost heavily at Busaco. The campaign as a whole cost the division between 30 and 50 per cent of its strength, mostly due to illness and famine. The unfortunate 70th Ligne had particular reason to dread the prospect of another encounter with British infantry, for it had been engaged, generally with heavy losses, at Roliça, Coruña, Oporto, Busaco and Sabugal. Admittedly the division had not been in the thick of the fighting at Fuentes, but nonetheless its performance is all the more creditable given its previous experiences.

A minor oddity concerns the strength of the 70th Ligne. Both Oman and Fortescue state that this regiment had two battalions with the army, amounting to 1,163 officers and men, on 15 July. However, it is not clear whether both historians checked the original returns in the Archives de Guerre independently, or whether the return was among the transcripts 'of French dispatches for 1812' which Fortescue lent Oman.[19] The question arises because the return of 1 July printed by Sarramon, which is based directly on the original manuscript, states that the 70th Ligne had three battalions in the field. There is no disagreement over the numerical strength of the regiment, which Sarramon puts at 1,175 officers and men present on 1 July; it is only the number of battalions which is in dispute. If Sarramon is correct, the battalions would have been unusually weak, averaging fewer than four hundred men each, while the 582 men per battalion implied by Fortescue and Oman is very close to the average for Marmont's army. It thus seems probable that Sarramon is mistaken, and one might believe that this is no more than a misprint if his text as well as his appendix did not refer to Ferey's ten (rather than nine) battalions.

Several sources comment on the allied decision to attack Ferey's position frontally, although none adds much to the question of whether Pakenham really protested against it and advocated a turning movement. Wellington says simply: 'I ordered the 1st and Light divisions, and Col. Stubbs' Portuguese brigade of the 4th division, which was reformed, and Major Gen. W. Anson's brigade, likewise of the 4th division, to turn the [enemy's] right, while the 6th division, supported by the 3rd and 5th attacked in front. It was dark before this point was carried by the 6th division.'[20] This makes it fairly clear that the Third and Fifth Divisions advanced in the rear of the Sixth, and that no attempt was made to turn Ferey's outer flank. Captain Campbell, the brigade-major of the first brigade of the Third Division, evidently regretted this decision:

> We, however, committed one mistake, in following up the enemy, for we had
> inclined too much to our left, and had thereby thrown away the advantage we
> would have had in still acting, even after dark, upon the French left and rear.
> Had the 3rd Division been kept more to the right, instead of coming at dusk
> almost in the rear of troops engaged with the enemy upon our left; and had it,

supported by our cavalry, continued to act even in the dark, I cannot imagine how the enemy could have been able to recross the Tormes.[21]

But if Sarramon is right and Sarrut's division had formed in Ferey's left rear, an attempt to turn the French flank may have proved costly and time-consuming. Yet again the information is too vague and uncertain to allow us to judge with confidence.

There is considerable difference of opinion over how long the Sixth Division waited in front of El Sierro before launching its attack. An anonymous source in the 61st Regiment says that it remained under heavy skirmisher fire 'for near three quarters of an hour'. Napier vaguely says it was kept waiting 'a long time', while Thomas Hamilton, who was not present but who draws on evidence which has not otherwise survived, says that the Third Division lay idle for 'about an hour and a half ... gazing on the new and formidable position in which the enemy had sought temporary refuge', and implies that the French artillery fire was quite heavy. Ross-Lewin, on the other hand, states that 'Lord Wellington was not long in preparing for the attack; but the hour, unfortunately for him, was very late.'[22]

The 61st Regiment source gives a rather different impression of the assault than most other witnesses, although some of his details tally neatly with Major Newman's narrative:

> The Major-General finding that the brigade was losing many men from the fire of the enemy called the C.O.s of the Regiments to him to intimate his intention of attacking the hill in front ... [and told] them to make the same known to their respective corps. The communication was received by the two corps with an instantaneous shout of 'Yes, we will!' and three cheers. This was followed by an immediate advance unchecked by the destructive fire from the French artillery and numerous sharpshooters. The movement was performed by the Regiments with sloped arms, by order, until the hill was crossed.
>
> On the arrival of the brigade at the summit of the hill, the enemy again formed their troops into column and faced a proportion of their files outward to receive the attack of the 11th and 61st who threatened their flank. The two Regiments formed to the right, on the right file of the 11th and then opened their fire upon the column ... and soon compelled it to retire.[23]

Napier gives a dramatic and picturesque description of the appearance of the fighting from a distance:

> in the darkness of the night the fire showed from afar how the battle went. On the side of the British a sheet of flame was seen, sometimes advancing with an even front, sometimes pricking forth in spear heads, now falling back in waving lines and anon darting upwards in one vast pyramid, the apex of which often approached yet never gained the actual summit of the mountain, – the French

musketry in opposition, rapid as lightning, sparkled along the brow of the height with unvarying fulness, and with what destructive effects the dark gaps and changing shapes of the adverse fire showed too plainly.[24]

A letter from 2nd Lieutenant Frederic Monro of Greene's battery of 6-pounders (no. 10 Company, 8th Battalion, RA), which was attached to Clinton's division, suggests that the fighting was less fierce and protracted than later accounts claim, but the weight of evidence is overwhelmingly against it: 'The 6th division advanced up the principal hill, and an incessant fire of musketry commenced; it was now getting darkish and the fire was grand beyond expression (take the word *'incessant'* in its full extent). The enemy staid till our men arrived at the top of the hill – then threw down their arms and ran. Mem. – *Frenchmen fine goers.'* [25]

On the other hand, Ross-Lewin's claim that the light company of his regiment captured a French howitzer is supported by a contemporary letter from his brother, which states that they took two guns, and the brigade as a whole, five.[26] To these must be added the gun which Wachholtz saw captured, so that the allies claimed the capture of at least six guns. Lamartinière's return acknowledges the loss of an 8-pounder and three 4-pounders from Ferey's division; Sarrut's division lost a 6-inch howitzer; and it may have been at this point that Clausel's division lost a 4-pounder or Bonnet's division an 8-pounder. So for once the claimed captures and the admitted losses can be reconciled, although if the allied sources were fuller, the number of claims for captured guns might rise.

Lemonnier-Delafosse's credibility suffers from his claim that Ferey was killed outright by a cannonball. Martinien does not accept this, recording that Ferey was severely wounded but did not die until 24 July, and this is confirmed by several British sources which describe his grave miles from the battlefield. Similarly his statement that Ferey's division was finally broken when allied cavalry charged it in the flank is unsupported by any other source and is intrinsically most unlikely – it is hard to imagine which allied cavalry unit might have made this charge. But the most damaging part of Lemonnier-Delafosse's tale is the far-fetched claims he goes on to make in passages not quoted earlier. Put briefly, these include the statement that his regiment spent the night only a few hundred yards behind its first position, as it would not retreat without formal authorization from a general; and that Lemonnier-Delafosse spent several hours – despite a sprained ankle – wandering through the chaos of a routed army, trying to persuade any senior officer he met to return to the battlefield to give the requisite command. This strange mixture of bureaucratic *punctilio* and *Boy's Own* derring-do fails to convince.[27]

The losses of the Fusilier brigade are referred to in the main narrative, but not discussed. They were a little heavier than those of Hinde's brigade: 380 casualties, or 28 per cent. As the brigade had certainly lost heavily in its fighting with Clausel's division, this supports the idea that it was less seriously engaged against Ferey. One of its three regiments, the 1/7th, lost far more than the other two: 195 casualties, or 40 per cent of its strength; the 1/23rd lost 106 casualties, or 24 per cent; and the 1/48th lost only 79 casualties, or 18.5 per cent. This rather suggests that the Fusiliers may have extended beyond Ferey's main line, and that only the 1/7th (on the right of the brigade) received the full weight of French fire. There is some support for this in Wachholtz's account. His light infantry were on the extreme left of the Fusilier brigade, and he notes that they encountered virtually no opposition.[28]

One technical point needs explanation: the reason that it was more difficult to fire accurately downhill than up was that the initial trajectory of a ball leaving a perfectly level musket was slightly up; troops might correct for this at short range and aim for the enemy's knees, but could not be brought to add a further correction for falling ground, effectively aiming in front of their opponents. The effect was well known at the time, with one Peninsular veteran writing that firing uphill 'is far more destructive than firing down, as the balls in the latter case fly over.'[29] Wellington's tactic of deploying his infantry on the reverse slopes of hills allowed his opponents the psychological advantage of gaining the crest, but his men had the compensating advantage of firing up at them.

The French casualty figures given in the narrative are based on Lamartinière's return, and in this case Martinien's record of officer casualties matches them quite closely. Inevitably there is still a difficulty. Lemonnier-Delafosse clearly states that his regiment (31st Léger) lost 360 casualties, of whom 80 were dead, while Lamartinière shows only 276, with 68 killed or captured. It is not uncommon for old soldiers confidently to give casualty figures in their memoirs that do not match those in contemporary documents, while, as has already been mentioned, Lamartinière's return is incomplete. It seems probable that total casualties suffered by the 31st were between the two figures given (perhaps around 330); Lamartinière's figure for the number of men killed or captured can be accepted as fairly accurate. The proportion of killed to wounded in the figures given by Lemonnier-Delafosse would be most unusual.

Finally, in Andrew Leith Hay's manuscript narrative account of the battle, which was written after the war and which varies both from his contemporary letters and from his published works, he adds some further comments on the reasons why the Sixth Division suffered so much:

> The Charge of the Bayonet as usual carried everything, and it was owing to the 6th Division halting and firing at the Enemy that our loss was so great. Those Divisions who rushed upon the Enemy without hesitation not only did not lose nearly so many men, but did the business much better, and nowhere did the French Columns stand for an instant when fairly attacked with the Bayonet.[30]

Chapter Ten
Foy and the French Retreat

The battle was almost over, and yet many thousands of allied soldiers, and even some thousands of French, had not fired a shot, or made a charge or confronted an enemy face to face. The Spanish contingent – Carlos de España's division and Julián Sánchez's lancers – lost only two men killed and four wounded in the whole day. This produced a rather sour reproach from a Scottish sergeant in one of Pakenham's regiments:

> During the battle, the Spanish army, under Don Carlos d'Espagne, had remained at a respectable distance on a height in our rear without having been engaged; they seemed to be perfectly contented with seeing us fighting for their country, without having a hand in it themselves, and when we were successful, they threw up their caps in the air, and cheered as heartily as if they had earned the victory; they had only one or two men wounded of their whole army, while ours lost nearly half of its number in killed and wounded.[1]

Sergeant Donaldson's figures are, of course, wildly inaccurate: his own regiment, the 94th, had less than one-tenth of its strength killed, wounded or missing, and this was fairly typical of the allied army as a whole. His hostility to the Spanish troops may have been felt by many in the Anglo-Portuguese part of the army, but it was not universal. The anonymous author of an annotated contemporary plan of the battle found among the papers of Major-General Charles Ashworth is much more generous, writing 'The village of Las Torres occupied by the Spaniards under Don Carlos d'Espagne, until moved out before the attack commenced. This Corps were very steady under a heavy cannonade and advanced in high order.'[2]

The Spanish division suffered fewer casualties than any other allied force of comparable size, but a number of other allied units were barely engaged. Bradford's independent Portuguese brigade, which was to have advanced on Leith's right flank but instead lagged behind, never caught up with the front line or seriously came into action. It probably lost about twenty casualties, from an initial strength of two thousand. As with España's men, these would have been the result of long-range artillery fire, stray shots and accidents.

The Seventh Division suffered rather more: about 150 casualties from 5,175 officers and men, or 2.8 per cent of its strength, but these figures include all the losses of the Brunswick Oels Regiment, three of whose companies were attached to brigades in the Fourth and Fifth Divisions. The Seventh Division had also taken the lead in the morning skirmishing around Nuestra Señora de la Peña, and this is probably where most of its casualties occurred. Later in the day it was transferred to the right wing of the army and suffered a little from the French bombardment on its march; it ultimately advanced in the wake of the Fifth Division.

These three units, the Seventh and Spanish Divisions and Bradford's Portuguese, amounted to over ten thousand men, but played no significant part in the battle. They formed the second line or reserve for Wellington's right wing and would have been called upon if Pakenham or Leith had got into difficulties, just as the Sixth Division had filled the hole created by Cole's defeat. Ideally they might have advanced sooner and taken over the pursuit of the French left from the weary men of the Third and Fifth Divisions, and perhaps even acted more effectively against Ferey's flank. But few battles go entirely smoothly, and none without missed opportunities.

There was an even larger force on the allied left flank, and it too saw little action, at least until late in the day. Here was the First Division (except for the light companies of the Guards which had been detached to the village of Arapiles) and the elite Light Division, as well as Bock's brigade of the Heavy Dragoons of the King's German Legion, and the 12th Light Dragoons from George Anson's brigade, apparently supported by at least one squadron of the 14th Light Dragoons from Victor Alten's brigade. In addition to the batteries of Ross and Gardiner, attached to the Light and First Divisions, this wing also contained a battery of 24-pounder iron howitzers under the immediate command of Captain Arriaga, although Lieutenant-Colonel Dickson spent the battle with them. Altogether there were more than eleven thousand men on the allied left, and for most of the day they did little more than watch the French troops opposite them, with occasional desultory skirmishing and exchanges of artillery.

This passive watching and waiting was not easy, even for veterans. There was the strain of knowing that at any moment they might be sent forward into close combat and, simultaneously, a paradoxical feeling of being left out of the great event. Edward Costello expresses this lightly:

Although every moment expecting to be sent into the thick of it, we kept undisturbed possession of our ground, from whence we could see the column of the enemy on the heights engaged in attempting to repel the advance of our troops. When the 'glad sounds of victory' reached us, a general feeling of pleasure pervaded our ranks, mixed perhaps with some regret that we had not taken a more active share in the battle. But all we could do we did, which was to pepper the French well in their hurried retreat from the field.[3]

In the middle of the day, the French right wing was even stronger than the allied left it faced. Foy's division in the front line, with Ferey in support and Boyer's dragoons on the outer flank, amounted to some 12,500 men, not counting Sarrut's division further to the rear. But just before he was wounded, Marmont had summoned Sarrut and Ferey and three of Boyer's four regiments to the centre, leaving only Foy and the 15th Dragoons – some 5,500 men – to guard the right. Wellington might have tried to exploit this relative weakness by sending his left forward to attack, but Foy's division was strongly posted in a formidable position, and the First Division, which was all that gave the allied left its numerical superiority, was carefully placed behind the Lesser Arapile so that it could support the left or centre with equal ease. Until the battle in the centre had been decided – with the breaking of Bonnet and Clausel – it would have been unwise to commit the First Division permanently to the left, unless it were absolutely necessary.

Foy remained inactive until the battle was clearly lost. There was nothing he could do to turn the tide. If he had tried to move his division to the centre, this would have freed the much larger allied force facing him either to turn the French right, or to join the fighting in the centre. If he had tried to attack, even as a diversion, he would have courted destruction for no possible gain. Simply by remaining in position and by keeping his division intact, he contained the allied left wing and protected the right flank of the French army – this was not enough, but it was all that his force could achieve. And when the time came to withdraw, he did so skilfully, while continuing to protect the army's flank. His own account is clear and convincing:

At this point I received orders to quit Calvarrasa de Arriba with my division and join the rest of the army. I arrived at the edge of the wood half an hour before sunset. The battle continued to be extremely bloody; one could hear nothing above the continuous musketry and cannon fire. The French took flight. I decided not to enter the wood but to take a position very near by, behind a ravine, in order to cover the retreat of the army. There was time; the victorious enemy was advancing towards Alba de Tormes between Calvarrasa and the wood, with two strong bodies of infantry, six cannon and 1,500 cavalry. I sent my skirmishers to delay their advance and they engaged them with artillery and musketry. Night saved my division and those I was protecting; without it I would probably have been broken and the enemy would have arrived at Alba de Tormes before the remains of our seven broken divisions. For an hour after sunset the English cavalry continued its charges on my regiments formed alternately in line and *en masse*. I had the good fortune to have my division in hand at all times and maintain its good order, although many of the broken units coming onto our left threatened to carry disorder into our ranks. The enemy's pursuit stopped near Utero de Maria Asensio, and all our forces found their way to Alba de Tormes where the army was gathered about 10 at night.[4]

One of Foy's officers gives us a glimpse of the anxiety of this difficult withdrawal, when the object was to delay the allied advance without involving the division in serious fighting:

The general wishing to share in the dangers of the army and protect it from a great disaster offered battle on the bank of a steep ravine and disputed its passage. Baron Desgravier[s], commanding our brigade, (who was killed in this position) crossed the ravine with two companies of our regiment in order to stop, or at least retard the enemy's advance, but they did not show any fear or hesitation. Time was precious, and I resolved, by myself, without consulting or orders from anyone, to advance on their head. On my heavy, ponderous horse I climbed the steep bank and arrived at the top at point-blank range from the English. Having thus gained time until night fell, the regiment fell back and I retraced my path, not without danger of being thrown from my horse whose rapid leaps down the slope were dangerous. I saw with regret that a sergeant-major, many voltigeurs and their captain had fallen in action.[5]

Foy's division retreated east then south-east, from its position in front of Calvarrasa de Arriba towards Alba de Tormes, where the leading fugitives of the French army were already crossing the river. But Wellington believed that the Spanish garrison still held the castle at Alba, and consequently that the French would have to retreat by the fords at Huerta and Encinas, some six to eight miles further north. In daylight, or in more open country, this illusion might soon have been dispelled, but night was falling and the country between the French position and the river was broken and heavily wooded, so that it was almost impossible to see troops moving even a little way off. Apparently Wellington did not entirely ignore the possibility that at least part of the French army might try to escape via Alba (there were fords above and below the town, as well as the bridge which the castle dominated), for there is some evidence that he directed the Sixth and Third Divisions to advance on it, but they were too tired to make any progress that night.[6] However, his main effort was directed to the north-east: Wellington must have hoped that if he could seize these fords rapidly he might prevent much of Marmont's army from escaping, or at least force it to abandon its heavy equipment and scramble across the river at inferior, less well-known fords, increasing its disorder and demoralization. There was another reason for heading north-east: once they crossed the Tormes, the French would almost certainly direct their retreat on Peñaranda, almost twenty miles to the east, and the fords offered the more direct route in this direction, while passing through Alba would add several miles to the army's march. Even if the allies failed to catch the French on the river, the fords thus offered the best chance of intercepting their march on the following day.

Wellington personally led his left wing in their advance, to the east initially, then north-east, although the order to move forward was brought by one of his aides – the Prince of Orange, according to one account.[7] As usual when the Light Division was present, there is a good narrative of what followed:

> At seven, one of the Duke's aides-de-camp rode up and ordered our division to move on the left to attack. We moved towards the Table Mountain, right brigade in front, in open column; having passed it, we then closed to column of quarter distance. The enemy's skirmishers soon advanced and opened a brisk fire. The shades of evening now approached, and the flashes of cannon and small arms in the centre and on the heights were still vivid, while the enemy were making their last struggle for victory. . . .
>
> The enemy's light infantry increased, and retired very deliberately; the ascent was gentle. The first brigade deployed, supported by the second; the First Division was marching in reserve.
>
> Our skirmishers were obliged to give ground to the obstinacy of the enemy. The line of the 43rd was one of the finest specimens of discipline I ever saw, as steady as rocks, with Col. William Napier twenty yards in front of the corps, alone; he was the point of direction. Our skirmishers ceased firing, and the line marched over them, dead and alive. I expected to see our chief unhorsed, and carried away in a blanket.
>
> Appearances indicated a severe fight, for we were near the enemy's reserves. The Duke of Wellington was within fifty yards of the front, when the enemy's lines commenced firing. I thought he was exposing himself unnecessarily, the more so, as I heard he had put every division into action that day. The Duke ordered us to halt within two hundred yards of the enemy. They gave us two volleys with cheers, while our cavalry galloped forward to threaten their right flank. At this time I heard that a musket-ball had perforated the Duke's cloak, folded in front of his saddle. As we were about to charge, the enemy disappeared. This advance was beautifully executed.
>
> Night coming on, the firing died away. . . . Our line continued to advance until *midnight*. A French cavalry picquet fired on us at ten; the *ruse de guerre* would not do. We bivouacked round a village.[8]

William Napier himself confirms the story of Wellington's being hit by a spent musketball: 'After dusk . . . the Duke rode up *alone* behind my regiment, and I joined him; he was giving me some orders when a ball passed through his left holster, and struck his thigh; he put his hand to the place, and his countenance changed for an instant, but only for an instant; and to my eager inquiry if he was hurt, he replied, sharply, "No!" and went on with his orders.'[9] Another Light Division source, although much briefer, confirms the first account and adds a further glimpse of Wellington:

> We were ordered to march about 7 o'clock & came up with the enemy about

sunset. We never load until we come close up. When we came under the hill the enemy were upon, Ld. Wellington passed us & said, 'Come fix your bayonets, my brave fellows.' We did, and sent out skirmishers & advanced in a line that delighted Lord Wellington. I hear he talked of nothing else next morning at breakfast.[10]

It seems fairly clear that, although the Light Division advanced confidently and in good order, it was unable to press Foy hard. The French rearguard waited at the ravine until almost the last moment as the British prepared a full-scale assault, but before it could be launched, the French infantry slipped away into the trees. In the whole battle the Light Division suffered only about fifty casualties, which indicates pretty plainly that most of the French fire was at long range. Foy's losses are impossible to determine, for both Martinien and Lamartinière's official returns combine them with casualties suffered on the following day at Garcia Hernandez. However, they would certainly have been heavier than those of the Light Division – for they had taken part in the morning's skirmishing – but still relatively light: perhaps about two hundred killed, wounded and missing.

The Light Division's left flank was covered by the allied cavalry. Bock's German dragoons made no impression – they suffered no casualties and are not mentioned in any account of this part of the battle unless we include them in Foy's rather hyperbolic '1,500 [enemy] cavalry'. But Frederick Ponsonby, who was commanding the 12th Light Dragoons, told his mother, Lady Bessborough, that his regiment had been in action:

it was getting very dark when Lord W. advanced the light division and first against their Right. I covered them with a squadron of the 12th and one of the 5th: we charged twice, and in the last went thro' two battalions of Infantry. I was unfortunate enough to lose Dickens in this charge; he was leading a Squadron, and received a ball in his left breast. Just as we came up to the enemy's columns the officer who commanded the other Squadron was also shot in the breast, but not killed.[11]

It is difficult to know what to make of this. No other source suggests that any of Foy's battalions was broken by cavalry or otherwise seriously damaged in the retreat, although this does not mean that it is impossible. Equally it is unclear what Ponsonby means by a squadron of the '5th' taking part in the charge: Le Marchant's brigade had assisted in the skirmishing on the left early in the day, but it would be very surprising indeed to discover that a squadron of the 5th Dragoon Guards had remained there all day. It is more likely that Ponsonby's words have been mistranscribed and that the reference is to the squadron of the 14th Light Dragoons which is known to have remained on the left when Arentschildt led the remainder of the brigade to the right flank. The identity of the anonymous wounded officer, which might solve the problem, remains impenetrable, and none of the officers of the 14th is listed as wounded. Dickens presents no such difficulty: he was Captain Frederick Dickens of the 12th Light Dragoons and, incidentally, nephew of the Archbishop of Canterbury.[12] The regiment also lost two men killed and two wounded: five casualties from 340 all ranks, which does not suggest that it met with any very serious opposition.

The role of the First Division in the final allied advance has been much misunderstood. For example, Sarramon states that 'Campbell's division advanced to the east of the two Arapiles but soon halted in an intermediary position for no good reason', while Fortescue damns Campbell for not obeying his orders and declares that, had Graham still been in command of the division, 'the victory would have been far more decisive.'[13] However, a hitherto unpublished letter, almost certainly written by Campbell himself, makes it clear that the First Division provided support to the Light Division throughout its advance:

> [The French] Right then formed on a Hill and made a last effort, where they were attacked, just as the Moon was rising, by the Light Division in two Lines supported by the 1st [Division]. They kept up a smart fire as we ascended the Hill, but on some Guns opening from a Hill on our Left they turned and ran for it, and must have made very good play for we followed them in the same order, the Light Division in two Lines, and the first [Division] in two Columns, one on each of its Flanks to support it, till near 1 o'clock in the Morning, going all the time at a rate of near 4 miles an hour, without overtaking more than a very few stragglers and wounded, but as a great deal of our way was thro' a very thick wood, we must have passed a great many that were picked up by others in our Rear. It is the first time I suppose, that ever Troops marched in Line for four hours across Country in the night, and they were in a very good Line when they halted, and our Columns also were in order to have wheeled into Line directly. We halted about one near the Village of Calvarrasa de Abajo.[14]

Except for a little exaggeration – the total distance covered by the division was only about six miles, so they were not moving at four miles an hour for four hours – this account carries conviction. Other sources also confirm it, such as a letter from Colonel Jackson to Sir Thomas Graham, the previous commander of the division:

> Lord Wellington with wonderful celerity collected together the German Brigade of the 1st Division (no part of the 1st Division but the Light Companies having been engaged) & the Light Division supported by the Guards and Gen. Wheatley's [brigades], and pushed Foy's Division upon Calvarrasa de Abajo and towards Huerta where it crossed the River. Our Troops halting at 12 at night at Calvarrasa de Abajo.[15]

It is interesting that even a couple of days after the battle, when Jackson wrote this letter, he still believed that Foy's division had crossed the river at Huerta rather than Alba de Tormes – proving that Foy had not only made a clean break with his pursuers, but had left them, literally, in the dark as to his line of retreat. A Guards officer in the First Division, John Mills, admits as much in a letter home: 'Our division was first in the pursuit. We were for some time at their heels, but they desisted from firing, and the wood was so thick we could not see them, so we lost them.'[16]

The human side of this night march is expressed in the *Recollections* of Robert Eadie, a private in the 79th Regiment:

> I declare that never before, or since, have I felt so perfectly tired. – We had so many large fields, covered with white stones, to pass, that our feet were much hurt; a great many prisoners, however, fell into our hands, but I confess, I thought the best thing to be taken alive, would be a sheep from the many flocks we passed on our way. Wearied as I was, I succeeded in catching a pretty fat one, which I got upon my back, and carried along in the march for nearly four miles till we halted. The captain of the company repeatedly called me to let go my prize, but his mind was changed when the savory smell of mutton curled up from the cooking fire. – I could then almost have refused him a mess, for which he anxiously asked, but he partook along with some of my comrades.[17]

Relations between officers and men in the army on active service were far from the simple world of the parade ground, drill books and official regulations.

The main body of Wellington's weary advanced guard camped for the night a few miles short of the Tormes, but Cotton pressed on to the river and established some cavalry picquets at the ford of Huerta. This done, he rode back to the army with a small party; they were not recognized in the dark, and when Cotton failed to respond to the challenge of the Portuguese picquet, the sentries fired and both Cotton and his orderly were wounded. Despite being badly hurt, Cotton managed to ride on to Calvarrasa de Abajo, where 'he was carried from his horse into a miserable pillaged hovel, and placed in a pig trough, the most comfortable place that could be found.' The bullet had shattered one of the bones in his left arm and the surgeon of the 14th Light Dragoons, who inspected the wound, urged an immediate amputation. But Cotton determined to wait for Dr McGrigor's opinion and was rewarded, after an extremely painful night, with the news that the arm might be saved. And so it was, although it remained partially disabled for the rest of his life and he had to give up playing the violin which he loved.[18]

Meanwhile, the great majority of the French army, including Foy's division and all the units which retained any order, retreated by Alba de Tormes. We know almost nothing about how this retreat was managed: who gave the order to head for Alba, or how the troops – who had not passed through it in their advance – found their way there in the dark. There were paths, even roads, through the woods which headed in the right direction, and staff officers may have been placed at junctions to point out the direction. Marmont himself was

carried to Alba when he was wounded and this may have acted as an example;
or the baggage, reserve ammunition and similar supporting services may have
been directed there earlier in the day, before the fighting began, as a routine
precaution: we simply do not know. Indeed, no aspect of Napoleonic battles is
as poorly understood as the immediate consequences of defeat, simply because
soldiers naturally did not like writing about it. Fortunately, there is one first-
hand description of the chaos in the French rear. It is by Lemonnier-Delafosse
– not the most reliable source, and his account may be exaggerated, but it gives
a vivid impression of the panic and confusion which could grip a defeated army:

> What a spectacle I found on the road through the middle of the forest. What did
> I see? A formless mass of men, flowing like a torrent! Infantry, cavalry, artillery,
> waggons, carriages, baggage, the artillery park, mixed with cattle pell-mell; the
> soldiers crying, swearing, altogether without order, each seeking his own safety.
> A true rout, it was an inexplicable panic to me, who had just left the field of battle
> . . .
>   No enemy pursuit could explain such terror. But alas! I know well that if the
> French have boldness and extreme impetuosity in attack, if they fail they are
> shameless and irresponsible in flight. All my experience teaches me that it is only
> the fear of being captured that gives our soldiers wings.
>   . . . Officers, soldiers, all were swept away and I had to keep to the sides to
> avoid the same fate.[19]

This suggests that the entire French army dissolved in panic into a formless
mass of fleeing men, but Lemonnier-Delafosse also claims that his own regiment spent the night only a few hundred yards from its final position on the
battlefield. While this is implausible, Sarramon argues that Foy's division,
Fririon's brigade of Sarrut's division and Lemonnier-Delafosse's 31st Léger all
retreated in fairly good order, providing a shield for the broken troops who had
preceded them.[20] This seems quite likely, although the sources appear insufficient to confirm it clearly, and in such a situation fear and panic might spread
even among soldiers who had suffered little. If the British cavalry had been
directed to pursue them vigorously towards Alba de Tormes, it is possible that
they might have increased the French panic and collected thousands more prisoners; but it is also possible that they might have been repulsed by the French
rearguard or lost their way in the difficult country. With his customary caution
Cotton had ordered the allied cavalry to retire when darkness fell, and
Ponsonby's light dragoons were the only allied horse which took part in the
final stage of the battle.[21] While this may have been a missed opportunity, there
were few allied cavalry left in any position to act: Le Marchant's, Alten's and
D'Urban's brigades must all have been exhausted by this time, while Bock's
was too far away on the extreme left. This left only the 11th and 16th light dragoons of George Anson's brigade, neither of which lost a man all day. They
might perhaps have done more, but it would need exceptional boldness to lead

the pursuit of an entire army at night, through broken wooded country, with only 650 British light dragoons.

In any case, Wellington and, presumably, Cotton assumed that the French were making for the fords and that the pursuit could best be conducted by the left wing of the army. Two days later Wellington wrote privately to Lord Bathurst:

> If we had had another hour or two of daylight, not a man would have passed the Tormes; and as it was, they would all have been taken, if Don Carlos de España had left the garrison in Alba de Tormes as I wished and desired; or, having taken it away, as I believe before he was aware of my wishes, he had informed me that it was not there. If he had, I should have marched in the night upon Alba, where I should have caught them all, instead of upon the fords of the Tormes.[22]

Unfortunately, this statement has too often been taken at face value, with no allowance made for Wellington's weariness or his understandable exasperation with España's compounded offence of not only withdrawing the garrison, but also failing to inform Wellington that he had done so. If Wellington had known that the bridge at Alba was unguarded, he would have directed his pursuit towards it, but even so he would not have 'caught them all'. The nearest allied troops to Alba were the exhausted men of the Sixth and Third Divisions who were in no state to mount a vigorous pursuit. Fresh troops might have been brought up: the Seventh Division and España's own division, or the allied left might have advanced south-east rather than north-east, but they could not have reached Alba before the bulk of the French army had crossed the river. Such a pursuit would have been useful: it would have increased the disorganization and demoralization of the French, and might have yielded several thousand additional prisoners – stragglers who crossed the bridge after the main part of the army – but probably no more than this. Equally, if España had not withdrawn his garrison, the result would have been rather worse for the French, but not dramatically different. Their retreat to the fords would have been longer and more exposed, running against, rather than with, the lie of the land. More men would have been lost to exhaustion and straggling, and Foy's division might have been forced into serious combat in order to cover this line of retreat. But their escape would probably not have been intercepted, for as we have seen the First and Light Divisions spent the night bivouacked near Calvarrasa de Abajo, several miles short of the fords, and while their men slept, the fleeing Frenchmen would have made their escape. España's mistake was, as Wellington himself put it, 'a little misfortune', which only slightly reduced the exceptionally thick icing on the cake of victory. Such 'misfortunes' are common in war, and the well-directed, sustained pursuit, idealized in theory, was extremely rare in practice.

Night had long since fallen, and most of the allied soldiers were settling down to get some sleep if thirst and the excitement of the day would let them. The French, urged on by fear, made their way to Alba and so across the river, which gave them a reassuring sense of security. The wounded called out for help or struggled towards the camp fires, while the dying slipped in and out of consciousness, and the dead grew cold. The battle was over.

Commentary

It is rather frustrating that the sources for Foy's retreat and the advance of the allied Light and First Divisions are so much more complete and coherent than those for many more interesting aspects of the battle. Foy's account, as well as being inherently convincing, is corroborated by those of Duplan and Marcel, while there are good sources for the advance of both the Light and First Divisions. Unfortunately, this rich seam of material does not extend to other events which were occurring at the same time. For example, the suggestion that Wellington ordered the Sixth and Third Divisions to advance on Alba de Tormes that night appears only in a single source: the normally reliable diary of Captain Tomkinson. It seems strange that the Sixth Division, which had seen so much fighting, should be ordered to lead the advance, but we know too little about the incident, or even the relative position of the other divisions, to be able to judge the question fairly. Tomkinson, however, clearly believed that Cotton's withdrawal of the cavalry was a mistake.[23]

Fortescue's criticism of Henry Campbell may not be wholly unfounded, for there is a hint of discontent at missed opportunities in at least one well-informed letter written soon after the battle from an officer in the First Division. Napier goes much further and says that when Wellington 'had restored the fight in the centre he directed the first division to push between Foy and the rest of the French army, which would have rendered it impossible for the latter to rally or escape; but this order was not executed.'[24] However, the only confirmation of this story comes in the recollections of an anonymous corporal in the 42nd Highlanders, who clearly could have had no direct knowledge of Wellington's orders to Campbell and whose account simply reflects the gossip in the division at the time:

> It was said, that the general who commanded our division, that was Major-Gen. Campbell, received orders from Wellington to bring the division into action at the time the battle was raging with such fury. We were to have dashed forward, they said, and formed in some large fields of wheat, in front of those heights, the enemy having a very strong line at the farther side of them.
>
> The light companies of our brigade were sent out to skirmish on our new position; but it was long ere we were marched from the high ground. I think General Campbell took his own time to form the division on this new position, knowing that there would be a great deal of bloodshed, had he obeyed the orders sent him by Wellington. This is what was said at the time in the division; and I report what I saw and what I heard from those who looked farther than I did perhaps.

The truth is, General Campbell saw the victory was our's without this move-ment and sacrifice; it was then complete in his eyes; but it would have been a per-fect annihilation of the enemy if our division had been pressed forward at the moment Wellington commanded us to move. We should then have had the brunt of the battle in its close, and the French would have been overthrown inevitably. At last, our brigade marched, and formed line in the wheatfields, but did not advance, as the enemy's line had fallen back.

By this time the French army was all in confusion, making the best of its way from the field of battle; and now it was almost sun-set. But our division having received orders to pursue the retreating foe, we were marched off the wheat-fields; yet it was not marching, it was rather running.... We continued in this manner till a little before daylight next morning, when we were halted, expect-ing, as the day dawned on us, to behold a great many of the enemy surrounded by our division; but, to our great surprise, we were a long way out of our course. General Campbell had a guide, but I could never learn whether he or the guide was in fault. The general in a few days more quitted the division, and went home to England, they said.[25]

Whether or not this story has any foundation – and it may simply reflect the discontent of the troops at not having taken a more active part in the victory – it is clear that it refers to an episode before the pursuit began, not to any lack of enthusiasm for the chase.

The description of the Light Division's advance shows clearly that Wellington's infantry did not always act in line. The division had spent most of the day in open column, and it retained this formation at the beginning of its advance, then changed into close columns – 'column of quarter distance' – only deploying into line when it approached the French position. Whether it then remained in line for the rest of the evening or reverted to columns is open to dispute. William Napier, writing on 25 July, is clear: 'Although we had not as much as we wished of the battle, yet I am much pleased with the conduct of the regiment, which marched in line near three miles under a disagreeable fire from the French, with a degree of correctness that I never could persuade them to do on a field day.'[26] However, George Hennell's more detailed description, writ-ten on 10 August, gives a different idea:

By this time it was quite dark [and] our skirmishers (3rd Caçadores) opened upon them upon the brow of a hill and the French immediately returned it which passed mostly over our heads. We had express orders not to fire until ordered. Our regiment was well prepared to give them an excellent charge but they had received another lesson that afternoon that they will not forget in a twelvemonth. Had they stayed still till we came up twenty yards further they might have given us a most destructive volley but they rapidly fired a volley or two that passed mostly over our heads and they ran away. Both the sergeants of my company were slightly wounded.

We advanced in line 1/2 a mile over corn and ploughed land. Then [we] formed sections of a company, keeping our distance & marched 2 or 3 miles over bushes and ploughed lands. On passing a wood our skirmishers, who were always about 300 yards in advance, opened a fire. We were in a good line in 5 minutes (it was only a few cavalry in a wood) & advanced dressing by the Colours over horrid roads with numerous pebbles another league. We halted and slept.[27]

Several sources, including Napier and Sarramon, state that when Foy checked the allied advance at the ravine, the French left flank was threatened by the advance of the Fourth Division. There is nothing intrinsically improbable about this, but it is difficult to discover the origins of the idea, for neither Foy nor Vere – the obvious Fourth Division source – mentions it. The suggestion may have arisen from the Fourth Division's role in turning Ferey's right, although in fact the two episodes were quite separate: perhaps two miles apart, and probably not simultaneous. Still, Napier was himself a witness and had many sources that have never appeared in print, so his account cannot be lightly dismissed. Here is the relevant paragraph, which delicately combines intense pride in his own division with respect and admiration for Foy's ability:

Foy, throwing out a cloud of skirmishers, retired slowly by wings, turning and firing heavily from every rise of ground upon the light division, which marched steadily forward without returning a shot save by its skirmishers, and for two miles this march continued under musketry, which was occasionally thickened by a cannonade, yet very few men were lost, the French aim being baffled by the twilight and by the even order and rapid gliding of the lines. The French general Desgraviers was however killed, and the flanking brigades from the fourth division having now penetrated between Maucune [sic – Ferey] and Foy, it seemed difficult for the latter to extricate his troops from the action, nevertheless he did it with great dexterity. For having increased his skirmishers on the last defensible ridge, along the foot of which run[s] a marshy stream, he redoubled his fire of musketry and made a menacing demonstration with his horsemen just as the darkness fell, whereupon the British guns immediately opened, a squadron of dragoons galloped forwards from the left, the infantry crossing the marshy stream with an impetuous pace gained the summit of the hill and a rough shock seemed at hand; but the main body of the French had gone into the thick forest on their own left during the firing, and the skirmishers fled swiftly after, covered by the smoke and darkness.[28]

Napier barely mentions the part played by the British cavalry in the pursuit of Foy's division; Foy, on the other hand, is surely exaggerating when he writes, 'For an hour after sunset the English cavalry continued its charges on my regiments', just as he stretches the truth when he says that he was opposed by 1,500 horsemen.[29] Bock's brigade are said to have bivouacked near Pelabravo, to the south-west of Calvarrasa de Abajo, which does not suggest that they had advanced far or seen Foy's troops since the French began their retreat. Ponsonby's light dragoons had, of course, been in action, and a letter from his proud mother gives some third-hand, and probably unreliable, details:

> Lady Bathurst was told by Lord Clinton [Wellington's aide who brought home the dispatch announcing the victory] that Lord W. order'd F[rederick Ponsonby] to command the three squadrons he mentions – 12th, and 5th and 1st – and to accompany him and take his orders directly from himself. Ld. Clinton added: Never were orders more clearly given or more correctly executed, and that two charges particularly Lord Wellington quite exclaim'd at, and said, '*That is gallantly done* – nothing can be better.' Is not this a delightful thing to hear – to know that F. had the advantage of being directed by the greatest general that ever liv'd, and the glory of being approv'd by him?[30]

This need not be taken too seriously, and only adds to the confusion of what cavalry were under Ponsonby's command; but it is a significant moment when a great Whig hostess such as Lady Bessborough calls Wellington 'the greatest general that ever liv'd'.

However, not everyone was as satisfied with the pursuit. Many officers followed Wellington's lead in blaming Carlos de España for the evacuation of the castle at Alba de Tormes. For example, Alexander Gordon told his brother Lord Aberdeen: 'If we had had two hours more daylight & Don Carlos had not withdrawn the Garrison from Alba de Tormes, I really believe we should have destroyed their whole Army.'[31] But Thomas Henry Browne, writing years later, took a more sceptical, independent view:

> The night & the woods thro' which the road to Alba de Tormes lays, made it difficult to follow up our victory, & the best way to avoid the uncertainty of night operations even against a defeated enemy, appeared, it was understood, to Ld. Wellington to move by his left upon Huerta, at the angle of the Tormes, by which he had a shorter road than the enemy, to fall upon him the next morning – the justice of this movement may be seen on the map, & that our line was shorter than that of the French to Peñaranda. The light Division which led, had no guide, & after marching till near midnight found itself at Calvarasca d'Abaxa [Calvarrasa de Abajo] where it was halted for the night. Some Officers were of opinion, that if the whole army had marched upon Huerta, the enemy must have been brought to action the next day, or if he had been followed up, by pressing with all our force upon the Alba de Tormes road, that he could not have crossed the river without great difficulty & loss. Ld. Wellington's arrangement of intercepting the French Army by moving upon Huerta seemed an Excellent combination, but it failed, for want of guides.[32]

Edward Cocks also complains of a lack of guides: 'But for the darkness I believe the battle of Salamanca would have completely dispersed the enemy's army but night and darkness impeded our pursuit. Not a peasant could be met with for a guide, the enemy fled through the woods where we blundered till midnight.'[33] No doubt the absence of guides was a problem, although hardly a decisive one. Advancing at night through broken country with the possibility of stumbling into an enemy rearguard at any moment was sufficiently unnerving with or without a guide.

Several commentators on the battle have criticized Wellington for persisting in his march on the fords when, they claim, the lack of stragglers and of human and material flotsam, must have made it obvious that he was not following the route of a defeated army.[34] There is some merit in this argument, but it is less compelling that it initially appears. First, the Light Division *did* encounter scattered parties of French troops in its advance: for example, Napier describes how 'a squadron of French dragoons . . . bursting from the woods in front of the advancing troops soon after dark fired their pistols and then passed at full gallop towards the ford of Huerta, thus indicating great confusion in the defeated army, and confirming the notion that its final retreat would be in that direction.'[35] Second, Wellington's line of advance was not identical to the presumed line of French retreat, but rather converged upon it, so that he would not expect to find the debris of a whole army upon it. And finally, what alternative did he have, even if he realized that the French were not heading for the fords? It was simply impractical suddenly to re-direct the advance of the Light and First Divisions from north-east to south-east in the middle of the night when advancing over unknown country: such a move might cause untold confusion and lead to fighting between allied units who failed to recognize each other in the dark. In any case, if the infantry was too weary to reach the fords, they certainly would not have had the energy to reach Alba. With hindsight Wellington might have organized the pursuit differently, but the whole question is more complicated than it first appears.

Finally, we may quote the description of the French retreat given by Colonel Girard, Maucune's chief of staff. Part of this is obviously wrong, and part plainly self-interested; but whether there is a residue of fresh material when these elements are discounted, or whether the whole is worthless, is open to question. Girard is not a particularly credible witness, and if there were better sources for this aspect of the battle it would be easy to ignore his account, but where there is so little evidence, one is reluctant to throw any aside.

> Wellington moved against this position in strength but could not force us to abandon it. He renewed his attack with even greater force but still failed to gain any advantage. We fought until the barrels of our muskets were touching the chests of the men in the first rank. When we advanced to cross bayonets with the enemy he retreated, abandoning the ground which was covered with thousands of dead and wounded.
>
> We ourselves were almost completely *hors de combat* and in a most critical situation for our only line of retreat was across the Tormes a little below Alba. The

enemy might easily have seized the bridge. Fortunately he spent the night collecting his forces and preparing to pursue on the following day. General Clausel
took advantage of this to get his troops across the river, and in order to ensure
that this was achieved without confusion, he placed General Maucune at the
head of the bridge until the army was assembled on the further bank.

In order to protect the passage, General Maucune and I – the only senior officers remaining! – had with great effort collected a thousand or 1,200 men and
Blanzat's battery, now reduced to ten guns. Our advanced posts were so close to
the enemy that we heard their voices. Wellington might, in the course of the
night, have got some of his cavalry across the Tormes and attacked us simultaneously at both ends of the bridge. But fortunately he did nothing. It was dawn
before his advance guard prepared to attack us. Our army was safely across the
river, but it had not had enough time to reform and be ready for battle.

General Maucune told me to cross the river and help rally the bulk of our
troops. I asked to leave this until we had halted the enemy's advance by our vol-
leys and artillery fire, and so forced him to deploy. We would still have time to
disengage and retreat across the bridge, while our cannonade would alert the
general that the enemy had begun their advance. Maucune accepted all my suggestions, and it turned out as I predicted.[36]

Chapter Eleven
The Victory

The battle of Salamanca was the greatest French defeat for over a decade. Other reverses had cost more men, for example, the capitulation of Bailen, or the failure of Masséna's invasion of Portugal; or had involved Napoleon more closely, such as the repulse suffered at Aspern-Essling. But not since the dark days of 1799 had a French army of almost fifty thousand men been broken in open battle and fled into the night. Equally, it was the greatest British victory, not just of the Peninsular War, or even of the whole Revolutionary and Napoleonic Wars to date, but for more than a century, and officers on both sides drew the inevitable comparisons with Marlborough. 'Certainly the greatest [victory] that has been gained by any British army since the days of Marlborough'; 'this Victory is certainly the most splendid he [Wellington] has gained and is more decisive than any we have had since Blenheim'; 'this most glorious victory, which revives the recollection of, and equals the glory of, the Victories of Marlborough'; and, finally, Foy's well-known tribute:

> the battle of Salamanca is the most masterly, the most considerable, allowing for the number of troops, and the most important in its results, battle that the English have gained in modern times. It raises Wellington almost to the heights of the Duke of Marlborough. Previously one recognized his prudence, his choice of positions, his ability in using them; at Salamanca he showed himself a great and able manoeuvrer; he kept his dispositions hidden almost all day; he watched our movements in order to determine his own; he fought in oblique order; it was like one of Frederick the Great's battles.[1]

There are no precise figures for the French casualties, but Marmont's army appears to have lost about 12,500 men killed, wounded or taken prisoner in the battle, or one-quarter of its strength. (The figure of fourteen thousand casualties which is often given includes the fighting on the Guarena and at Garcia Hernandez on 23 July.) Not surprisingly, the heaviest losses were on the left, where, even following Lamartinière's figures, Thomières's division lost over 50 per cent of its strength, Maucune's division almost 35 per cent and Taupin's division almost 30 per cent.[2] Four regiments in the French army lost more than half their strength in the battle:

66th Ligne in Maucune's division suffered 50.3 per cent casualties
22nd Ligne in Taupin's division suffered 60.0 per cent casualties
62nd Ligne in Thomières's division suffered 77.3 per cent casualties
101st Ligne in Thomières's division suffered 81.8 per cent casualties

All four regiments were on the French left, and it is likely that their exceptionally heavy losses were caused, at least in part, by Le Marchant's charge. But the heavy fighting in the centre also exacted its toll: Clausel's division suffered 26 per cent casualties, Bonnet's 23 per cent and Ferey's 17 per cent. The French cavalry failed to make any significant impact in the battle, but still lost over 400 casualties (13 per cent of Boyer's dragoons, 14 per cent of Curto's light cavalry).[3] The only divisions in the French army which lost less than one-tenth of their strength were Sarrut's (8 per cent) and Foy's (perhaps 4 per cent, but this is just a guess); although the artillery also seems to have escaped remarkably lightly, suffering fewer than 150 casualties, only 4 per cent.

The figures for the allied army are much more reliable, although still not without problems. Overall, Wellington's army lost 5,220 casualties in the battle: 694 killed, 4,270 wounded and 256 missing.[4] The British suffered nearly 61 per cent of these casualties (3,176 officers and men), the Portuguese 39 per cent (2,038 officers and men), while the Spanish division lost only 6 casualties, or 0.1 per cent of the army's losses. These casualties amount to almost exactly 10 per cent of the army's strength, with the Portuguese suffering slightly more, proportionally, than the British.

British suffered 3,176 casualties from 30,578 all ranks, or 10.4 per cent
Portuguese suffered 2,038 casualties from 17,999 all ranks, or 11.3 per cent
Spanish suffered 6 casualties from 3,360 all ranks, or 0.2 cent

By far the heaviest allied losses were in the Sixth Division, where the three battalions of Hulse's brigade suffered 849 casualties from an initial strength of 1,464 officers and men, or 58 per cent (the 1/11th and 1/61st both lost two-thirds of their strength; the 2/53rd lost 'only' 42 per cent). The other brigades in the division suffered much less, but still heavily: Hinde's brigade 24 per cent; Rezende's brigade 23 per cent. The Fourth Division also suffered considerably: 21 per cent casualties overall, with the 1/7th Fusiliers losing 40 per cent. All Cole's regiments suffered, with the sole exception of the 3/27th, which remained in garrison on the Lesser Arapile and lost only one officer and seven men wounded from an initial strength of around six hundred all ranks. Pack's brigade lost 18 per cent of its strength, mostly as a result of its unsuccessful assault on the Greater Arapile; this was a little more than the leading brigades of the Third and Fifth Divisions (Wallace's brigade lost 15.4 per cent, Greville's 15.9 per cent). The losses of the cavalry were extraordinarily light: fewer than two hundred in all. More than half of these were in Le Marchant's brigade, which lost 105 casualties, or 10.2 per cent, a remarkably small cost given the brigade's impact on the battle. Most of the remainder were in D'Urban's Portuguese and Victor Alten's German hussars. The artillery suffered only fifteen casualties, spread among the 1,300 officers and men present, which once again proves it to have been a surprisingly safe occupation. But it was not only the artillery which suffered little: many allied regiments suffered negligible or no casualties, including such a renowned unit as the 1/52nd, which lost only two men wounded from 799 officers and men present. Almost half of the army was scarcely engaged: the First, Seventh, Light and Spanish Divisions, Bradford's Portuguese brigade and Bock's heavy dragoons all lost less than 3 per cent casualties; while even in divisions which were closely engaged, there were units such as the 3/27th which may never have fired a shot. However, this does not mean that these troops were wasted or unnecessary, let alone that the battle could have been won without them. Most were deployed in the second line where they could be brought into action if the need arose; and it was just the absence of such well-placed reserves which made the French left wing so vulnerable.

The battle took an extremely heavy toll of senior officers. Marmont and Bonnet were seriously wounded, Ferey mortally wounded, Thomières killed and Clausel slightly wounded. In other words, the commander of the French army and the commanders of four of its eight infantry divisions were hit by allied fire. Brigadier Desgraviers from Foy's division and Brigadier Menne from Ferey's were also wounded, Desgraviers mortally, while five staff officers and no fewer than eight aides-de-camp were also casualties. If Clausel's wound had been a little more serious, the command of the whole army would have devolved onto Ferey almost before the battle had begun; while if Ferey had still been wounded late in the battle, the task of organizing the retreat would have been left to Foy. Marmont's wound had already left the army leaderless at a critical point in the day, but at least in Clausel he had a capable and confident successor. Ferey had neither the temperament nor the ability to command the army, while Foy – who may have had both – was too far away to do so effectively. Bad as the French luck was, it might very easily have been much worse.

Allied generals suffered almost as much: Beresford, Cotton, Leith and Cole were all wounded, as were the commanders of two Portuguese brigades, the Conde de Rezende (Sixth Division) and the one-legged Richard Collins (Seventh Division), while Le Marchant was killed. As Cotton's wound was inflicted after the fighting was over, either he or Beresford would have taken command of the army if Wellington had been incapacitated. But if Wellington had been killed or wounded the following day at Garcia Hernandez, the command would have fallen to Henry Clinton, who before the battle was the sixth most senior officer. No doubt Hill would soon have arrived from Estremadura

14. Pakenham's advance. The unsealed road leading south-east from Aldea Tejada. The low north-south ridge which concealed Pakenham's division is clearly visible.

15. The Pico de Miranda from the edge of the village of Miranda de Azan. Pakenham's infantry scrambled up this steep hill with fifty pounds of equipment on their backs, under enemy fire and trying to remain in close formation.

16. Maucune's view. Looking north from the summit of Monte de Azan to Las Torres in the middle distance. The village of Los Arapiles is just to the right of the picture. It was up this slope that Leith's division advanced.

17. Leith's view. The wide, open, gentle but not perfectly smooth forward face of Monte de Azan, (rather flattened by the camera). Leith's division advanced up the slope in good order, Maucune's skirmishers and artillery falling back before them.

18. Looking south from the summit of Monte de Azan across the open plateau to a further rise before the land falls steeply away to the south. General Leith and Andrew Leith Hay were probably wounded close to the spot where the photograph was taken, while a little later in the battle Le Marchant's cavalry swept across the plateau from right to left.

19. Looking south at the forward face of Monte de Azan from the edge of the village of Los Arapiles. The slope is much steeper here, where Cole's division advanced, than further west in Leith's path.

20. The Greater Arapile viewed from the foot of the Lesser Arapile. Pack's brigade had to cross eight hundred yards of open ground, bare of cover, before it could begin its assault.

21. The view south across the Monte de Azan from the top of the first hillside: one thousand yards of open ground and then a second hillside before the land falls steeply away to the south. Clausel defeated Cole's initial attack at the top of one of these hillsides.

22. The task facing Pack: the north face of the Greater Arapile with the natural rock wall clearly visible just below the obelisk.

23. A closer view of the slope and the rock wall. It was near this spot that Charles Synge lay, severely wounded, stripped and under fire of the British guns on the Lesser Arapile, for hours until the French abandoned the position and help arrived.

24. The long low open ridge of El Sierro where Ferey's rearguard covered the retreat of the French army.

25. Looking south-east from El Sierro across the broken wooded country through which the French retreated. Alba de Tormes and the safety of the river were still five miles away.

26. Looking across the bridge to the Castle of Alba de Tormes. Even if Carlos de España had left a garrison in the castle, could it really have blocked the passage of a whole French army made desperate by defeat?

27. The bridge at Alba de Tormes.

28. Stripping the dead after the battle. Many wounded were also killed by looters after the fighting was over. The practice was universal and soldiers of all nationalities, not just camp-followers, took part. From an etching by Francisco Goya.

29. An endless column of French prisoners marching into Salamanca on the day after the battle. The allies took between six and seven thousand prisoners, including those captured at Garcia Hernandez.

and taken the command into his own safe hands, but the possibility of such carnage in the senior ranks must have been a shock to those in London who had always been anxious to provide Wellington with a competent deputy as a safeguard against misfortune.

The allied army took between five and six thousand prisoners in the battle, many of whom were wounded, but there were also many unwounded prisoners: men who surrendered in the face of Le Marchant's charge.[5] Lamartinière's return acknowledges the loss of twelve guns: six 8-pounders, five 4-pounders and a 6-inch howitzer. According to the return:

Clausel's division lost one 4-pounder;
Ferey's division lost one 8-pounder and three 4-pounders;
Sarrut's division lost one 6-inch howitzer;
Taupin's division lost one 8-pounder;
Thomières's division lost three 8-pounders and one 4-pounder;
Bonnet's division lost one 8-pounder.[6]

This suggests that the French batteries were not all formed of guns of a single type, but in some cases at least contained a mixture of 8- and 4-pounders, despite the obvious problems this would cause.

British accounts usually claim the capture of twenty guns, following Wellington's statement in his dispatch that 'The official returns only account for eleven pieces of cannon, but it is believed that 20 have fallen into our hands.' However, the details of the official return (in the PRO) coincide closely with Lamartinière's statement, listing six 8-pounders, four 4-pounders and one 6-inch howitzer. It thus seems probable that Wellington had been misinformed – possibly with several units claiming the capture of the same gun – and that only a dozen artillery pieces changed hands.[7]

Other trophies included two French Eagles, six French battalion flags or *fanions*, and many other prizes, such as the famous 'Jingling Johnny' captured by the 88th and a highly decorated drum-major's staff taken by the 40th. These objects had considerable symbolic importance, as Sergeant Lawrence of the 40th makes clear:

I found that our regiment had taken at the famous battle of Salamanca a splendid drum-major's staff from the enemy, which was stated to be worth at least £50, and it must have come in very useful, for ours was terribly worn and knocked about, being very old, having been itself taken from the French in Holland, during the commandership of the Duke of York.[8]

On the other hand, the French have some claim to have taken the King's Colour of the 2/53rd, and possibly one other allied flag.[9]

Salamanca was predominately an infantry battle, reflecting the composition of the two armies. The powerful French artillery was strangely ineffective. Its initial bombardment was noisy but seems to have done little or nothing to daunt the allied troops. Its flanking fire is said to have troubled Cole's division in its first advance, and the guns on the Greater Arapile helped to repulse Pack's attack, while Ferey's rearguard must have gained much support from the powerful battery deployed on the summit of El Sierro; but this was a meagre return from a force of nearly eighty guns employing 3,500 men. The allied artillery had a far greater impact with the single shot which disabled Marmont, and must also be credited with the death of Bonnet, the wounding of Clausel and all the resulting confusion in the French command. Other than this, its part was fairly marginal: Bull and Douglas gave useful, but hardly decisive, support to Pakenham's initial attack; the batteries in the centre are supposed to have played an important part in checking the French counterattack; and late in the day Gardiner's battery from the First Division enfiladed Ferey's position on El Sierro. But with the exception of the extraordinary losses among the French generals, Salamanca was not a good advertisement for the value of artillery. It was the wrong type of battle, with too much rapid movement and quick, decisive combat, whereas artillery was at its best in a protracted, grinding combat of attrition.

Cavalry also played a limited part in the battle. Le Marchant's charge, perfectly timed and executed, yielded far greater results than anyone could have hoped or expected, and proved just how effective a relatively small force of confident, well-led heavy cavalry could be against a disorganized and demoralized opponent. D'Urban and Arentschildt on the allied right were useful, both in protecting Pakenham's flank and exploiting the advantage he gained, but did not have a dramatic impact on the course of events. George Anson's brigade was scarcely engaged, although his two regiments in the centre ought to have been employed in supporting Le Marchant's brigade more closely. And Bock's heavy dragoons saw no fighting at all, although they more than made up for this on the following day at Garcia Hernandez. On the other side, the French cavalry were uniformly disappointing. Curto had almost two thousand horsemen under his command, but had less influence on the battle than Arentschildt with only one-third of that number. Boyer's dragoons were presented with an opportunity almost as promising as that facing Le Marchant, but failed to take much advantage of it. Excuses such as the introduction of untrained horses are insufficient to explain such a lamentable failure, and it appears that the French cavalry were both poorly commanded and overawed, all too aware of their unusual inferiority.

The French infantry, by contrast, generally fought well whenever they were given a reasonable chance of doing so. It is true that the left wing collapsed without much resistance, but the troops there were taken at a great disadvantage, and their defeat was primarily owing to the mistakes of their generals. In the centre, where the terms of the contest were more even, the French infantry did much better. Clausel and Bonnet repulsed the initial attack of Cole and Pack, and there was much hard fighting before Clinton's fresh division defeated their counterattack. Ferey's rearguard may have been somewhat less heroic than Lemonnier-Delafosse suggests, but it checked the allied advance and gained crucial time for the army to retreat. The French may not have displayed the tactical flexibility, verve and high morale of Napoleon's army at its very best, but they employed line, column and square as appropriate, manoeuvred rapidly and generally showed considerable spirit both in attack and defence, although their skirmishers were rather disappointing.

Nonetheless, there is no doubt that the Anglo-Portuguese infantry of Wellington's army proved their superiority in the battle. They displayed great confidence and élan in attack, eagerly pressing forward to the charge and so bringing each combat to a rapid decision. Yet when necessary they had the endurance and discipline to sustain a protracted musketry duel and to emerge victorious from it. When they were defeated and broken, they rallied quickly and, in the case of Cole's division, returned rapidly to the fray. With one or two possible exceptions – Wallace's brigade from Pakenham's division springs to mind – their impetuosity was kept within safe bounds, and they did not recklessly pursue their advantage too far and so become vulnerable to a counter-attack. Wellington's doubts about his infantry thus proved to be unfounded: they were as effective in attack as when standing on the defensive, being robust, combative, confident and yet well disciplined.

The battle was won and lost on the French left. Thomières, Maucune and Taupin between them lost more than five thousand casualties (including prisoners) compared to the 1,346 suffered by their immediate opponents, Pakenham, Leith and Le Marchant. Yet the allied forces in the immediate area were no stronger than the French; indeed, if Curto is included on the French side, and the brigades of D'Urban and Arentschildt on that of the allies, the French outnumbered their opponents 16,224 to 14,845.[10] (However, the allied right had powerful reserves available to support it if its advance was checked: the Spanish division, Bradford's brigade and the entire Seventh Division.) The real problem for the French was not lack of men on the left, but the fact that they were poorly deployed. Taupin's division was too far to the rear to provide effective support for Thomières and Maucune. Thomières's advance along the Monte de Azan left him exposed at its far end facing Pakenham's entire division with a force barely half its strength. Inevitably the leading French brigade was broken, and Curto's cavalry, which had failed to protect it, also failed to exploit the potential opportunity provided by Wallace's enthusiastic pursuit.

The defeat of Thomières put the whole French left at a disadvantage. An attempt was made to halt the allied advance and rally the broken troops under the protection of the 1st Ligne, Thomières's remaining regiment, with the leading regiment of Taupin's division, the 22nd Ligne, providing support. It is doubtful if this could have succeeded against the triumphant advance of the Third Division, but before it could really be put to the test Le Marchant's cavalry decided the combat. The shaken and disordered French infantry were in no state to resist the British heavy dragoons, whose charge transformed the defeat of the French left into a wholesale disaster and explains most of the disproportion of losses in this part of the field, less through the men they killed or wounded than by the hundreds or even thousands whom they terrified into surrender.

Le Marchant's charge also ended any hope that Maucune's division might successfully resist Leith's attack. This was in any case unlikely, for although the French had the advantage of standing on the defensive and a strong force of artillery, their infantry were considerably outnumbered (5,244 French facing 6,710 allies). It also seems that the French preparations were disrupted by the sight of Thomières's defeat and the advance of the British cavalry, which led at least some of Maucune's infantry to form in square – which further reduced their chances of repulsing the allied infantry. In these circumstances, Le Marchant's cavalry charging in upon their flank was almost superfluous, although it greatly increased the losses of the two nearest French regiments.

Le Marchant's charge finally exhausted its impetus, and the few units which remained in good order on the French left – notably Taupin's second brigade – took advantage of the lull which followed to make their escape. The allies had undoubtedly fought better than the French in each of the encounters in this part of the battle, but they had also had superior numbers at each critical point and had acted with a speed and decision which gave them tactical advantages which more than offset the slight benefits the French received from the terrain.

The contest was much more fiercely fought in the centre. Here, too, the French (Clausel, Bonnet and Boyer's three regiments of dragoons) had a slight numerical advantage over their immediate opponents (Cole, Pack and Clinton: 14,436 French against 13,376 allies).[11] If Ferey's division is included the imbalance becomes more marked, even if Spry's brigade is added to the allied total (the figures are 20,125 French and 15,681 allies). But again, these figures do not include allied reserves which were available but never needed: in this case, the First Division (6,428 men), which more than makes up the difference. The actual numerical advantage of the French in the centre was less important than the fact that the allied attack there was less well conceived and executed than that on the flank. Cole's division was spread too thinly and Pack's attack on the Greater Arapile was almost certainly a mistake, while the French in the centre were not caught in such disarray. This led to the failure of the initial attacks by Cole and Pack, but the French proved unable to exploit their advantage, for Wellington's attacks were well supported. The Sixth Division was perfectly placed to check the French advance, while if it had been overwhelmed Wellington could have brought up the First and Seventh Divisions. The risk of the French breaking the allied centre was very slight indeed.

Nonetheless, Bonnet and Clausel were only driven back after much hard fighting, while Ferey's rearguard covered their retreat admirably and showed just how well French infantry could defend a strong position. Something seems to have gone awry in the conduct of the allied attack here, although it is not clear if the fault lies with Wellington, Clinton or Hulse. But this was a relatively small blemish on a most successful day's operations. It is interesting that, even in the centre, the French lost significantly more casualties than the allies: 4,182 compared to 3,541.[12] Defeated troops normally do suffer more than victorious ones, but the disparity here is rather surprising as there were no allied cavalry on this part of the field – unless we accept d'Hautpoul's explanation of Clausel's defeat – and little effective pursuit: evidently the men of Clinton's division inflicted even more damage than they suffered.

Both generals played their most important part in shaping the battle before Pakenham's men advanced up the slope of the Pico de Miranda and the serious fighting began. Indeed, it is probable that by this point Marmont was already *hors de combat*. Yet even if we acquit him of the old charge of having deliberately extended the French left, he still bears a very great share of the responsibility for the French defeat. His operations on 22 July, as on the previous days of the campaign, were daring and well conceived, but they needed to be executed faultlessly if they were not to involve great risks. He was manoeuvring in close proximity to an enemy army which was slightly stronger than his own; and there is little doubt that he greatly underestimated both Wellington's boldness and the capabilities of the allied army. This is not to say that he was ridiculously rash. The evidence suggests rather that he was simply careless and somewhat overconfident, his concentration wavering when, after a week's intense work, he saw his goal almost within his grasp and relaxed slightly. As a result, he failed to ensure that each step was methodically consolidated before the next was embarked upon. He allowed his leading divisions to be those commanded by his most impetuous subordinate (Maucune) and his two most junior divisional commanders (Thomières and Taupin – both brigadiers acting for absent senior officers). These mistakes were venial: against most opponents they would not have mattered, and the day, and the whole campaign, would have ended in a successful action against the allied rearguard and a triumphant return to Salamanca. But Marmont had placed his army in a position where even venial mistakes made it vulnerable, and he was facing no ordinary opponent.

Salamanca destroyed Marmont's always fragile reputation. For years he had had to live with the suggestion that his promotion and opportunities had been the result of Napoleon's favour rather than proven ability. He had performed well in his previous independent commands, but suppressing brigands in the Balkans earned little fame or glory. Until 22 July he had showed marked ability and had had considerable success in his command of the Army of Portugal, yet if Foy can be believed he had not gained the respect of his subordinates. The reputation of a Soult, a Ney or a Masséna might have survived the defeat, but Marmont's name was not closely associated with any great victories and could not withstand the blow. Months later Napoleon told Caulaincourt, 'Marmont shows a really high quality of judgement and logic in discussing war, but is not even moderately able in action.'[13] When he recovered from his wound, Marmont commanded a corps, competently but without particular distinction, in the difficult campaigns of 1813-14. He would no doubt have been remembered as one of the more obscure and less successful of Napoleon's marshals had it not been for his fateful decision to order his troops to surrender to the allies after the fall of Paris in 1814, thus attracting the opprobrium – whether fairly or not – for betraying Napoleon in his greatest need.

Clausel's reputation, on the other hand, was enhanced by the battle. He has been praised for his quickness in conceiving, and boldness in executing, the counterattack in the centre following the repulse of Cole and Pack, and for his coolness and skill in organizing the retreat.[14] Unfortunately, there is little contemporary evidence which either supports or casts doubt on this praise, or indeed which gives any information at all about his role in the battle, and much of what has been taken for granted appears to be based on little more than plausible supposition. The wisdom or folly of the counterattack, which saw the two strongest divisions in the army broken with nothing achieved and little prospect of success, could be debated at length, but it is by no means certain that there was any choice involved: the French troops may have been too far committed to make disengagement and withdrawal practical. On the other hand, Foy's warm praise for Clausel must be given considerable weight.

Wellington displayed great skill and judgment throughout the campaign and the battle, but even more remarkable than these was his subordination of his pride to his intellect. He had been outmanoeuvred on the Duero and had then submitted to the withdrawal to Salamanca because Marmont had given him no opportunity to attack with advantage, and because he reasoned that it was not in his interests to fight unless the odds were distinctly favourable. Few generals had such patience or determination; most would either have attacked Marmont sooner, or would have been so cowed in spirit by the afternoon of 22 July that they would have failed to recognize the opportunity when it finally came, and would have thought only of securing their retreat. But Wellington kept his ultimate object in view throughout the campaign. The aborted attack in the late morning of the 22nd probably reflected his frustration at the thought of abandoning Salamanca without a fight, but when Beresford showed that the French behind the Greater Arapile were stronger than Wellington had realized, and hence that the attack would involve more risk, he cancelled it rather than jeopardize the safety of the army.

Wellington's handling of his army during the morning and early afternoon was nearly perfect. He made excellent use of the cover provided by the undulating ground, and kept his divisions in good order – ready to move in one direction or another, to meet a sudden French attack or launch one of their own. And while it was obvious that Pakenham would be brought across the river at some point, the decision to send him to Aldea Tejada proved inspired, laying the foundations of victory. Possibly Wellington can be criticized for not occupying the Greater Arapile early in the day, although it may have proved almost as awkward to maintain in allied hands as it was in French hands. From Wellington's point of view, the hill was a considerable nuisance either way, and his task would have been much easier if the space it occupied had been a flat plain. The movements of the First Division are also a little odd; after he had brought it into the front line behind the village of Arapiles, on Cole's right, it is not clear why Wellington later drew it back into the second line behind the Lesser Arapile and subsequently brought the Fifth Division into the line next to Cole. With hindsight it certainly seems as if it would have been better had the First Division remained behind the village, extending part of the way towards the Lesser Arapile. Pack's brigade could then have been withdrawn into reserve, while Cole would have occupied a shorter, more compact line. The Sixth Division would still have supported this line, and Pack, the Light Division and Bock's heavy cavalry were surely enough to guard the left flank. However, we cannot reconstruct the manoeuvres of the morning and early afternoon with any precision, so it is both unfair and unwise to criticize movements which were probably undertaken for excellent reasons at the time.

When the moment came to launch the attack, the allied army was already in position, so that its plan of operations was relatively simple. Once Pakenham's division turned the French flank, the rolling attack along the line devoured almost half of the French army before finally losing its momentum. Wellington's orders to his subordinates were brief but sufficient, and the sequence of attacks was nicely staggered so as to gain the full advantage from Pakenham's advance. The fighting in the centre was less well handled, mostly because Cole's division was spread too thinly and expected to do too much, while it would have been better if Pack's brigade had held back and masked, not assaulted, the Greater Arapile. Still, it says much for Wellington's dispositions that the Sixth Division was perfectly placed to fill the gap and that he was present to order it forward at the critical moment. This was entirely characteristic: throughout the battle he was almost invariably at the vital point, personally giving his subordinates clear, concise orders which left no room for misunderstanding. Every Anglo-Portuguese division saw him in turn during the battle, and his presence and alertness strengthened the confidence of the troops.

Not everything went perfectly for the allies at Salamanca: the defeat of Cole and Pack in the centre and the ineffectiveness of the pursuit were both significant blemishes on the victory. Some might wonder whether, in the light of these flaws, Wellington's handling of the battle was really so masterly. The answer is simple: war is not chess, and operations seldom if ever go entirely according to plan, while the more ambitious the operation, the greater the number of accidents that will occur. None of Napoleon's victories was unblemished: at Marengo the day was almost lost when Dessaix's division arrived and turned the tide; at Jena, Napoleon fought only the lesser half of the Prussian army and, even so, Ney's corps got into difficulties; while at Austerlitz, Napoleon's greatest triumph, only part of his plan succeeded, for Lannes's corps, which was to lead the French attack, was held in check by Bagration's men. Some of Wellington's more limited actions came closer to perfection – Oporto, Busaco and the Crossing of the Bidassoa – but none achieved so much, or displayed such a marvellous combination of courage and skill. It was Wellington's finest victory. William Napier writes:

> I saw him late in the evening of that great day, when the advancing flashes of cannon and musketry stretching as far as the eye could command showed in the darkness how well the field was won; he was alone, the flush of victory was on his brow and his eyes were eager and watchful, but his voice was calm and even gentle. More than the rival of Marlborough, since he had defeated greater generals than Marlborough ever encountered, with a prescient pride he seemed only to accept this glory as an earnest of greater things.[15]

Chapter Twelve
The Aftermath

Three days after the battle Sergeant Richard Davey, of the Royal Artillery Drivers, wrote home to his wife and children:

> The engagement then begun to be very heavy. I expected my ammunition would be wanted, as they was firing so fast, so I marched up to them, and such a sight I never saw for the ground was strew'd with Heads, Arms, Legs, Horses. Wounded men lay bleeding and groaning, women screaming and crying for the loss of their husbands, guns roaring and the shot flying about our heads in such a manner, seemed to me a most dreadful spectical [sic], but God preserved me this once again.[1]

Davey's description is a salutary reminder that even a rapid, decisive victory such as Salamanca involved much hard fighting, and that this fighting was brutal, savage and horrible. The soldiers of the day understood this well, but they seldom emphasized it in their letters or memoirs, not wishing to distress their families or readers, or dwell on it over-much themselves. For, despite the horrors of the battlefield, most soldiers were proud of their trade and looked on battle, not as a necessary evil, but as the climax of the campaign and a moment of higher, more intense feeling than they might otherwise experience in all their lives. Naturally their feelings were a mixture of apprehension and fear, excitement and confident pride, and almost all agreed that the hardest part of the day was waiting passively, perhaps under distant artillery fire, for their part in the battle to begin. At the close of the day, the men would be both exhausted and highly stimulated: Captain Tomkinson heard that the men of the Sixth Division 'were so tired when ordered to halt for the night that they could not possibly have marched much further, yet they sat up through the night talking over the action, each recalling to his comrade events that had happened.'[2]

The life of a Napoleonic soldier did not encourage squeamishness or delicacy, and Private Wheeler has no hesitation in recording that on the night after the battle he and his comrades 'collected what dead bodies were near and made a kind of wall with them. We did this to break the wind which was very cutting has [sic] we were very damp with sweat. Under this shelter we slept very sound till morning.'³ Corporal Douglas of the Royal Scots found the bivouac almost as dangerous as the fighting:

> We halted for the night on the ground occupied by the enemy during the morning (or during the action) and sent out parties for water, having nearly 5 miles to travel before it was found, and then it was as green as the water you may have seen during the heat of summer in a stagnant pond. However, it went down with a fine relish. The only piece of plunder either I or my comrade had got happened to be a leg of mutton off a Frenchman's knapsack, which I put down in a kettle to boil, having made a fire of French firelocks. I was sitting on a stone watching the fire, musing over the day's work, when, rising up to look into the kettle, one of the pieces went off, the ball passing between my legs. This was the nearest visible escape I had, for if providence had not so ordered it that I rose at the instant, the contents would have been through my body. The breaking up of the ammunition wagons might be heard at a great distance as the men wanted firewood for cooking.⁴

The Third Division was also short of water and the men suffered much as a result, for it had been a long, hot day and their natural thirst was exacerbated by the gritty dryness caused by the gunpowder when they tore cartridges open with their teeth. Lieutenant Grattan of the 88th remembered that the parties sent out for water had still not returned at 2 am when the sleeping men were roused by the arrival of the mules carrying rum. Inevitably the parched men drank far more than their allowance, which only made their thirst much worse.⁵

Private Green of the 68th, in the Seventh Division, was more struck by another aspect of the aftermath of battle:

> we encamped on that part of the field where the carnage had been most dreadful, and actually piled our arms amongst the dead and dying. We immediately sent six men from each company to collect the wounded, and carry them to a small village, where doctors were in attendance to dress their wounds. It really was distressing to hear the cries and moans of the wounded and dying, whose sufferings were augmented by the Portuguese plunderers stripping several of them naked. We took a poor Frenchman, who had been stripped by an unfeeling Portuguese: the adjutant gave him a shirt, an old jacket and trousers, and sent him to the village hospital.⁶

Lieutenant Frederic Monro, who had only reached the army a few weeks before, was shocked by what he saw, and he too blamed the Portuguese: 'The field of battle presented a sad spectacle as I rode over it ... I found myself amongst the dead and dying, and, to the shame of human nature be it said, BOTH stripped, some half-naked, others quite so; and this done principally by those infernal devils in mortal shape, the cruel, cowardly Portuguese camp-followers, unfeeling ruffians.'[7]

But it was not only the Portuguese who plundered the fallen: T. H. Browne writes vehemently of the wives of British soldiers who, 'in spite of orders, threats & even deprivation of rations', had insisted on following the army:

> All ideas of conduct or decency had disappeared – plunder & profligacy seemed their sole object, & the very Soldiers their Husbands evidently estimated them in proportion to their proficiency in these vices. They covered in number the ground of the field of battle when the action was over, & were seen stripping & plundering friend and foe alike. It is not doubted that they gave the finishing blow to many an Officer who was struggling with a mortal wound; & Major Offley of the 23rd Regiment, who lay on the ground, unable to move, but not dead, is said to have fallen victim to this unheard of barbarity. The daring & enterprize of these creatures, so transformed beyond anything we have heard of in man, is not to be described.[8]

It was easy to blame camp-followers and the Portuguese for this macabre plundering, less easy to admit that British soldiers took part. However, there is abundant evidence, from this and other battles, that many regular soldiers of all nationalities scoured battlefields looking for loot. Private Wheeler admits that at Salamanca he 'examined a few dead Frenchmen for money etc'; while there is something plaintive about John Douglas's statement that the 'only piece of plunder' he or his mate secured was a leg of mutton from 'a Frenchman's knapsack', which suggests that he had hoped for richer pickings.[9] This is a subject on which it is easy to feel indignation or repugnance in the well-fed comfort of a modern library, but which quickly becomes more difficult on closer examination. Only the harshest judge would blame hungry, thirsty soldiers for taking water bottles or provisions from the dead, whether friend or foe, at the end of the day when their own supplies might take hours to arrive, if they arrived at all. And is it realistic to expect that they would leave money on a corpse if they found it when looking for food or water? Clearly there is a great difference between using the water bottle of a dead comrade and wandering the battlefield at night, stripping the dead and dying of their clothes, and killing wounded men who might otherwise have survived. But this difference is made up of many fine gradations as impropriety becomes turpitude.

After such horrors it is pleasant to record that early on the following day many inhabitants of Salamanca ventured onto the battlefield, bringing fresh fruit, water and other provisions which they gave freely to the victorious soldiers. Having exhausted their supplies, they then loaded their carts with wounded, either leaving them at hospitals or taking them into their own homes and nursing them there.[10]

Unfortunately, the number of wounded overwhelmed all these efforts. The figures are uncertain, but it seems likely that the battle saw about two thousand men killed and approximately twelve or thirteen thousand wounded. Five or six thousand French wounded managed to retreat with the army, leaving about eight thousand wounded of all nationalities to be cared for in Salamanca and surrounding villages.[11] Neither army stayed long in the vicinity after the battle – the French were in full flight and the allies were pursuing them. Consequently many of the wounded spent several days in the open before they were rescued or managed to make their way to the town. William Warre, a young officer who remained in Salamanca in attendance on Marshal Beresford, describes the result:

Owing to the Army having advanced and the few means of transport, many of the wounded, particularly of the French, have suffered horribly, for, three days after, I saw a great many still lying, who had received no assistance or were likely to till next day, and had lain scorching in the sun without a drop of water or the least shade. It was a most dreadful sight. These are the horrid miseries of war. No person who has not witnessed them can possibly form any idea of what they are. Humanity shudders at the very idea, and we turn with detestation and disgust to the sole author of such miseries. What punishment can be sufficient for him! Many of the poor wretches have crawled to this. Many made crutches of the barrels of the firelocks and their shoes. Cruel and villainous as they are themselves, and even were during the action to our people, one cannot help feeling for them and longing to be able to assist them. But our own people have suffered almost as much, and they are our first care.[12]

Quite a few of the soldiers whose accounts of the fighting have been quoted in earlier chapters were wounded, and often they give graphic descriptions of their experiences. There are too many to quote them all here, but three British accounts give a representative sample. First, Captain Harry Ross-Lewin of the 32nd Foot in Hinde's brigade of the Sixth Division, who suffered a serious wound in his left arm, just under the shoulder, in the attack on El Sierro:

I had nearly reached the French position when a musket ball struck me, and, from the loss of blood, I soon found it requisite to go to the rear for surgical assistance; but, as it was already dusk, I wandered about, ignorant whether I was or was not taking the right direction for a village. I had walked for some time in this state of perplexity, when I suddenly heard the trampling of horses, and, on calling out to know who went there, I found, to my great satisfaction, that the party belonged to my own regiment, and that my batman was one of their number. They conducted me to the village of Arapiles, where we found the men breaking open the houses for the admittance of wounded officers, seven of whom were of my regiment. All the habitations and outhouses, even to the very pigsties, were speedily filled with wounded men, whose cries to have the dead taken away from them were incessant throughout the whole night.[13]

This suggests some of the confusion which must have existed behind the fighting line as night was falling and wounded men sought aid and shelter.

The second account, by Charles Synge, Pack's aide-de-camp, gives an idea of the suffering of an immobilized soldier who remained near the front. He fell just below the summit of the Greater Arapile with a broken thigh, and the French soldiers stripped him:

> I could not perceive that any near me were alive. It was some time too before I could realise the particulars of my own situation. I was a prisoner. I was wounded. I was naked. An open artery was bleeding fast. I was dying. Could this be death? There could be no doubt about it, and in a few moments I should be dead. Having come to that conclusion I lay down to die, and, having said my prayers, waited with composure for the last struggle. After lying some little time expecting faintness and some of the usual symptoms of death, my attention was attracted by some cannon shot. The balls were literally ploughing the ground all about me. They were from our own Artillery, who were in reserve on the other hill of the Arapiles, and who had opened their guns on those with whom my body lay. I thought it probable that one of those balls must hit me, and I am afraid I must acknowledge that I sat up and stretched my head as high as I could in the hope of a friendly ball ending my misery. But it was not to be. God in His mercy willed it otherwise. I began to think that I should be a long time dying, for, though I had lost much blood, I still felt no faintness. Then, for the first time, it came into my head that somehow I might have 'a chance', and I have often since thought of that 'trying to put my head in the way of a friendly ball.'[14]

Finally, there is the anonymous private soldier in the 1/38th in Leith's division, who was wounded in the right foot in the attack on Maucune:

> I felt quite in a composed state of mind until after I received my wound. But I lay in the Field 4 or 5 hours after I was wounded before I was taken away, and while I lay my spirits failed me so that I was filled with doubts and fear and began to think I should be separated from my few pious comrades, and I should not have one pious friend to converse with.[15]

Fortunately, in hospital he found a religious man from the 5th Foot whom he had met previously in Ireland, and whose presence and conversation proved a comfort.

The medical services were not highly developed and after a battle were placed under enormous pressure by the sheer number of wounded. Surgeons operated in the most primitive conditions, sometimes in the open air on a table made from a door. They worked until their instruments were blunt and their arms powerless from fatigue; and they had no anaesthetics or antiseptics. The surgeon who operated on Marshal Beresford found him lying on his back dressed in a blue frock coat with a white waistcoat. Just below the left breast was a star of blood, bright and defined as a star of knighthood. It was about the size of that chivalrous decoration, and occupied the exact spot where it is usually fixed. There was a small rent in its centre, black and round. The eyes were half closed; the countenance in perfect repose, perhaps a little paler than when I had last seen it. In an instant the marshal's dress was torn open, and my forefinger, that best of probes, was deep in his side. Not a muscle moved, not a sound was uttered. I felt the rib, smooth and resisting below, while the track of the bullet led downward and backwards, round the cavity of his ample chest. I now spoke for the first time, and said, 'General, your wound is not mortal.' This observation of mine seemed to have been heard with perfect indifference; for without taking the slightest notice, he looked up and asked, 'How does the day go?' 'Well,' I replied, 'the enemy has begun to give way.' 'Hah!' rejoined the marshal, 'it has been a bloody day.' I proceeded to cut out the bullet. My knife was already buried deep in the flesh, its point grating against the lead, when the marshal, feeling I had ceased to cut, and calculating, perhaps, that my steadiness as an operator might be influenced by the rank of my patient, again turned round and with as much *sang-froid* as if he had been merely a spectator, said in an encouraging tone, 'Cut boldly, doctor; I never fainted in my life': almost at the same moment I placed the bullet in his hand.[16]

Crude as the surgery was, it was surprisingly effective. There are no figures for the recovery rates after Salamanca, but after Waterloo two-thirds of the British and King's German Legion wounded had rejoined their units within ten months, while only 11 per cent had died. Amputations were unexpectedly rare: only 3 per cent, although this would not include those who died before the return was prepared.[17] These figures are all the more remarkable as conditions in the improvised hospitals were usually far from ideal. Edward Costello's memoirs give a vivid impression, although as usual his touch is light:

There we were, French and English, laid up together; and there, I must say, I saw sufficient practice daily in the use of the surgeon's knife to become perfectly familiar with every form attendant upon amputation. While lying in hospital, at all times a wretched place, from the groans of the numerous sufferers, I was here placed under the immediate attendance of Sergeant Michael Connelly, in charge of our ward, who being sufficiently recovered from a slight wound, was appointed sergeant to the hospital. He was one of the most singular characters I ever met ... Mike was exceedingly attentive to the sick, and particularly anxious that the British soldier, when dying, should hold out a pattern of firmness to the Frenchmen, who lay intermixed with us in the same wards.

'Hould your tongue, ye blathering devil,' he would say, in a low tone, 'and don't be after disgracing your country in the teeth of these ere furriners, by dying hard. Ye'll have the company at your burial, won't you? Ye'll have the drums beating and the guns firing over ye, won't you? Marciful God! what more do you want? ye are not at Elvas, to be thrown into a hole like a dog – ye'll be buried in a shroud and coffin, won't you? For God's sake, die like a man before these ere Frenchers.'[18]

When Costello adds that Mike 'drank like a whale' and did not scruple to consume the wine rations of his dead and dying patients, we can form some idea of the quality of post-operative care he provided. Nor is there any reason to believe that this was below the usual standard of military hospitals in the Peninsula, so that the recovery of the majority of the patients must be attributed to their youth and strength.

Costello mentions that French and allied soldiers were mixed together in the wards, and the account of Alphonse d'Hautpoul of the 59th Ligne in Clausel's division confirms this, while adding other details of hospital life, some of which might have been experienced by any wounded soldier, while others were limited to men from the defeated army. D'Hautpoul had been wounded by a musketball in the hip and a bayonet wound in the right arm, and spent the night on the battlefield without receiving any help. The following morning he was stripped naked by some Spanish guerrillas and was fortunate that they did not further abuse him, especially as he kicked one of them – who was pulling his boots off – in the stomach. It was dreadfully hot, and the full July sun burnt him. He lay in a field where the wheat had recently been cut, and he pulled up some stubble and loose soil to cover his head and give him some protection against heat-stroke, but nonetheless developed a fever. Nearby a fellow officer raged against his fate until he died in the middle of the afternoon. A little later a Spanish youth, fifteen or sixteen years old, and armed with an ancient musket, cursed him for having no plunder and threatened him, but did not fire – from humanity, or perhaps the musket was unloaded.

About 7 o'clock that evening some English soldiers found him and piled him onto a waggon with other wounded men and carried him into Salamanca. They left him in a cattle yard where there were already a number of French officers – some wounded, some not – who managed to find a few clothes to cover him. He does not complain of his treatment: 'It was natural that the English surgeons dealt first with their own wounded in the hospitals and houses of Salamanca. My wounds were not dressed until 10 or 11 in the evening of the 23rd, twenty-nine hours after I had been wounded.' As this was only a few hours since he had been brought in from the battlefield, it does not seem that he had been much neglected.

The following day he was carried into a church which had been converted into a hospital and laid on a bed of chopped straw. He does not mention it, but the move must have been agonizing. An English surgeon changed the dressing on his wounds every day, but gangrene soon appeared in the hip. 'The surgeon with his scalpel cut away a lump of flesh with the musketball and filled the wound with quinine and powdered lemon juice. I suffered horribly, but the treatment saved my life. In the morning he pulled away the putrefying flesh with pincers and cut it with scissors, put in the same ingredients as on the day before and covered it with a wad of linen.' The wound in his arm was also painful, but remained free of gangrene and healed fairly quickly.

It was three weeks before he was clear of the fever and gangrene, and he attributes his survival in part to the treatment he received, but principally to his noble blood – which, he says, enabled him to endure his suffering and misery!

D'Hautpoul remained in the church for two and a half months, without proper clothing and existing on a diet of broth made from salt beef from England. As he began to recover and look to the future his spirits sank:

> I would be a prisoner for a long time for the war between France and England would never end. The Emperor would not agree to a partial exchange of prisoners . . . There I was, twenty-three years old, without hope of regaining my liberty and my career ruined. This unhappiness was made worse by the low spirits resulting from my wound. I have a good temper, but I was near dying from my despair, sickness and the ruin of my hopes.[19]

The unwounded and slightly wounded prisoners posed a problem on the night after the battle. It was too late to make arrangements to march them immediately to the rear, and there were enough of them to pose some danger. In the end most were collected in an angle of the river where the stream was deep and rapid. A few sentries were placed on the bank to prevent any trying to swim to freedom, while a Portuguese battalion supported by a few cavalry mounted guard. At first the prisoners were 'very silent & sulky', but gradually they relaxed and were soon 'as merry & gay as if they had been going to a dance'. No doubt they talked over the events of the day and who was to blame for their defeat with as much animation as the men of the allied army, camped nearby. They had no food except what was in their knapsacks, but nor did most of the allied soldiers, and at least they had plenty of good water.[20]

The one concern which the prisoners expressed to their captors was that they not be escorted to the rear by Spanish soldiers, 'from whom they had everything that was cruel & inhuman to apprehend'.[21] Nonetheless, three days after the battle, Colonel Waters, the acting Adjutant-General, issued orders that the prisoners be sent to the rear in relatively small parties, the officers separately, under Spanish escort. All Waters could do was to urge his representative to 'impress on the minds of the Spanish officers the necessity of treating the prisoners with mildness', but this was disregarded. A British officer who encountered some of the prisoners at Almeida at the end of July recorded that, 'The Spaniards have treated them, by all accounts, with a most revolting cruelty during the march from Salamanca, and the joy of the poor fellows was unbounded when they were delivered into the custody of the Portuguese. A French officer told me, and I had it confirmed in various ways, that if any of the prisoners through fatigue lagged behind in the route, they were immediately bayoneted.'[22] Moyle Sherer's *Recollections* includes a later glimpse of the prisoners at Abrantes, towards the end of their long march south, when the charms of their new escort had worn thin:

> They were in a very exhausted state, from the length of their march, the heat of the weather, and the want of shoes and other necessaries; and ... they had neither a word or a laugh to disguise their mortification. I never saw Frenchmen more thoroughly cut down; and, what appeared not a little to increase their vexation, they were escorted by four hundred awkward-looking, ill-appointed Portuguese militia-men; whose air of pride and importance, as they regulated the motions of these 'vainqueurs d'Austerlitz', was truly entertaining.[23]

One may wonder whether or not the prisoners would have been pleased to know that their captivity would be shorter than they expected. Within two years the war was over, Napoleon had abdicated, and they were free to go home.

The armies marched away from Salamanca in one direction, the prisoners in another, while the wounded in the hospitals slowly recovered or died. The dead remained where they had fallen on the battlefield. The local inhabitants did their best to solve the problem, but the results were not satisfactory. A British officer who visited the scene a few weeks later

> found a long line of vultures on the battle-ground; these ill-omened birds stand quite erect, and might be mistaken by a distant spectator for a regiment drawn up in a single rank. Here was a fine field for them; the bodies of men and horses, which an attempt had been made to burn, lay everywhere in heaps, only half consumed. After the action, wherever the carcase of a horse was found, such human bodies as had fallen near were collected and thrown over it, and these again were covered with branches of trees, which, being quite green, made too weak a fire to reduce them to ashes; consequently the air had become very offensive, and the whole scene was extremely revolting. A vast number of pigs, which had been driven hither by their owners, also roamed about the field, and shared the loathsome feast with the vultures.[24]

Chapter Thirteen
Consequences

On the morning after the battle the French army continued its hasty and disordered flight east, towards Peñaranda, which it reached that evening. Clausel had left Foy's division at Alba to act as a rearguard, but, although Foy's men had seen little fighting and suffered few casualties, their confidence had been shaken by the defeat. Wellington resumed the pursuit early on the 23rd. Bock's heavy dragoons crossed the Tormes at the fords of Huerta,[1] Anson's brigade at Alba, and they were closely followed by the Light and First Divisions, the rest of the army advancing more slowly in their wake.

The value of such pursuit was demonstrated when the leading allied troops caught up with the French rearguard at Garcia Hernandez, some seven miles beyond Alba. Foy had his whole division, a brigade of Curto's cavalry and some artillery, amounting in all to more than five thousand men, under his command. Wellington at first had little more than a thousand horsemen, for both allied brigades had made many detachments and Bock's brigade was only just beginning to arrive, while the leading British infantry were still some way off. But Foy's task was to cover the retreat, not to fight, so when the allied troops appeared he began sending his regiments to the rear. Wellington appears to have seen only the French cavalry, and ordered Anson to drive it off. There followed one of the most celebrated combats of the Peninsular War. The French chasseurs fled before Anson who was joined by Bock at the head of his leading squadron. In their charge the Germans suffered from the fire of the French infantry, formed in square, which they had either not noticed or ignored. Seeing this, Captain von der Decken, commanding the 3rd squadron, wheeled his men and charged the infantry directly. This square was formed by a battalion of the 76th Ligne, and as it was well formed and in good order it should have been invulnerable to unsupported cavalry as long as its men held their nerve. What happened in the next minute or so must have been very confusing and obscured by smoke and dust; nonetheless, it is generally agreed that the infantry fired twice and maintained their composure. Neither fire checked the cavalry's momentum, but the second, disastrously for the infantry, brought a mortally wounded horse crashing down onto the square itself. The resulting chaos naturally led to panic and the square was broken, almost the entire battalion being taken prisoner.

Inspired by this success, the remaining German squadrons pressed forward and a second French battalion, from 6th Léger, was also overwhelmed, although it is not clear whether this unit was in a properly formed square and the men panicked, or in a more irregular, improvised formation. Several further charges were made, and the dragoons suffered quite heavily. But while they incurred 127 casualties, the French lost about 1,100, including hundreds of unwounded prisoners.[2]

After this disaster, Foy succeeded in drawing off his remaining regiments, but the morale of the defeated army had suffered another heavy blow. With fear urging them on the French made good speed. 'I have seen a Person,' wrote a senior British officer two days later, 'who passed through them Yesterday, when they were still running as fast as weakness, fatigue, and hunger would allow them, not merely along the Road, but in Crowds on each side of it, and all in the greatest hurry and disorder, a very large proportion having thrown away their Arms.'[3] This picture is confirmed by Clausel, who admitted that he had only 22,000 men left with the colours (although thousands more followed the army) and told the Minister for War in Paris: 'It is usual to see armies discouraged after a reverse, but it is difficult to find one in which the discouragement is greater than in this; and I must not conceal from you that there reigns and has reigned for some time past a very bad spirit in this army; our steps in this retreat have been marked everywhere by the most revolting disorders and excesses.' No wonder Tomkinson noted in his diary that the French 'leave many stragglers dead in the corn by the side of the road, and any person leaving the column is killed by the peasants.'[4]

On the afternoon of the 23rd July Clausel was joined by Chauvel's brigade of cavalry from the Army of the North, which was able to cover Foy's retreat more effectively than Curto's chasseurs. Nonetheless, the French made no attempt to stand or even to delay the allied pursuit. On the following morning the allied advanced guard entered Peñaranda, only to find that the French had left it at dawn. Their rearguard was briefly sighted a few miles beyond the town, but escaped before any horse artillery, let alone infantry, could be brought up. The following day, at Flores de Avila, Wellington abandoned the chase. The French had always been able to outmarch the allies and now, by discarding most of their equipment and heavy vehicles, they had succeeded in making their escape. The allied troops were weary and outpacing their supplies. If another blow could be struck at the French it would be worth pressing on, but it was now clear that this was most unlikely, and there was little point in exhausting the army simply to harass Clausel's already broken units and gather in a few hundred more prisoners. Not everyone agreed with the decision, either at the time or since, but Wellington evidently feared that a sustained pursuit without proper supplies would undermine the health and discipline of his troops. He may also have been influenced by the lack of a trustworthy and enterprising cavalry commander to lead the chase, for, with Cotton wounded and Le Marchant dead, the command had devolved onto Bock, who was very gallant, but also short-sighted and inexperienced at this level.[5]

Wellington therefore gave the army a day's rest and then advanced more slowly, entering Valladolid on 30 July. He was received with loud acclamations from the populace, despite their reputation for sympathizing with the French. Here he captured Marmont's base hospital with nearly a thousand sick and wounded soldiers, a considerable magazine of reserve ammunition and seventeen cannon. But even before he entered the city, his attention was turning south, for he had received reports that King Joseph's army, rather than securing its retreat across the Guadarramas, was lingering at Segovia. It will be remembered that Joseph had scraped together an army of fourteen thousand men and marched to assist Marmont. He had left Madrid on 21 July and was within a march or two of Peñaranda when he learnt of the defeat on the morning of the 25th. If he had advanced sooner, or if French communications or luck had been better, he might have prevented Marmont's defeat; but equally, if his luck had been worse, he might have been caught up in the disaster, advancing into the midst of the allied army before he learnt what had happened. Instead, the news arrived in time for the small French army to fall back into the shadow of the mountains after only a slight clash between outposts. However, having secured his retreat, Joseph hesitated to use it and marched to Segovia, misled, it is said, by an over-optimistic letter from Marmont. Wellington attempted to cut off his retreat, but after waiting for three days at Segovia, Joseph's army escaped across the Guadarrama pass and back to Madrid.[6]

This was the first time, since Wellington's advance to Talavera three years before, that the capital of the Bonaparte Kingdom of Spain had been seriously threatened, and the war, which had seemed comparatively distant and irrelevant to daily life, suddenly assumed a pressing urgency. Joseph's army was far too weak to hope to oppose Wellington's main force, while Suchet and Soult were too far away to lend immediate assistance. There was no alternative but flight, despite the blow this would strike against the authority of the regime, and the destruction it would cause to the little domestic support it had been able to gather. Orders were hurriedly issued to collect what could be salvaged, and the government's supporters faced the unenviable choice of either following their French master into an uncertain exile, or remaining and facing the retribution of the patriotic authorities. Several thousand chose to escape with their families, dependants and, often, much of their worldly goods, creating a vast, cumbersome, ill-prepared civilian convoy. At first they headed south, reaching Aranjuez on 13 August, where they turned east, taking the road to Valencia. The march which followed was one of great suffering, for the convoy had insufficient supplies, including water, and the midsummer heat was intense. Guerrillas and other scavengers were attracted by the promise of rich pickings and, of course, the march was not conducted by hardened soldiers, but by civilians of all ages, including many women and children. The exhausted refugees finally reached Valencia on 31 August.[7]

Meanwhile Wellington had entered Madrid on 12 August to an extraordinary welcome. 'When Ld. Wellington approached with his staff, in the group of which I rode,' recalled one British officer,

> a deputation of the principal Authorities & inhabitants came out to meet him, amidst loud & continued acclamations from thousands who had joined this procession. They had already found time to decorate the gate thro' which he was to enter, as a triumphal arch. The streets were lined with well dressed persons of both sexes, waving handkerchiefs and vociferating, 'Vivan los Ingleses', & 'Viva Fernando settimo'. The windows & balconies were filled with people, principally females elegantly dressed, repeating the acclamations of their friends below in the streets. Garlands & tapestry were suspended from all parts of the houses; the stirrups of the Officers, as they rode along, were taken hold of, & they were gently stopped to be saluted with every possible expression of good will & joy. Many were taken into the ice and lemonade shops by the rejoicing citizens of this delivered capital, & made to partake abundantly of these delicacies, nor would any money be received in payment. The inhabitants contended with each other, who should take British Officers into their houses. . . . For three successive nights the city was brilliantly illuminated, & British Officers were seen in all directions with Spanish Ladies leaning on their arms, who were pointing out to them, the different habitations of their Grandees by the light of the lamps. Priests & Monks too joined in this festive scene. Portuguese & Spanish Officers also, mixed abundantly in it, & the whole presented one of the most curious & interesting spectacles I ever beheld. The whole city was in a sort of confusion of joy for several days.[8]

Jonathon Leach of the 95th records the regimental point of view more succinctly: 'Few of us were ever so caressed before, and most undoubtedly never will be again.'[9] Wellington's triumph appeared complete.

At the same time as the allied army was advancing from Salamanca to Madrid, the news of its victory was spreading. On the night of the battle there were spontaneous celebrations in the streets of Salamanca. While some inhabitants nursed the wounded or took supplies out to the weary troops, others formed joyful crowds. One British officer remembered: 'Guitars sounded in the streets, patriotic sequidillas were composed and sung, the lively noise of castanets proclaimed the progress of the fascinating bolero. The town exhibited an appearance of the gayest carnival.'[10] A few days later Wellington was to complain that many of his soldiers who had assisted wounded comrades into the town had remained there, eating, drinking and taking part in the rejoicings rather than returning to their units.[11]

Other parts of unoccupied Spain greeted the news with similar festivities. In

Ferrol, for example, there were processions in the streets, with illuminations and fireworks in the evening; the guns of the fortress were fired in salute, and a special high mass was performed. In Cadiz an enthusiastic crowd formed outside the house of the British ambassador, Sir Henry Wellesley, hailing Wellington as the saviour of Spain; while the Cortes, which had already made Wellington Duque de Ciudad Rodrigo, now conferred upon him Spain's highest honour, the Order of the Golden Fleece.[12]

Rumours and vague stories of a battle circulated widely in England from the beginning of August. On 3 August, *The Times* was able to report only that dispatches from Sir Home Popham announcing a victory were said to have reached Falmouth, but that the Admiralty telegraph (a form of semaphore) had been interrupted by fog before confirmation or any details could be received. It was not until 5 August that the paper could report the news more fully, and even then the accounts of the battle were unofficial, being based on brief letters from Wellington to Castaños and other officers. Lord Bathurst wrote to Wellington that, after they had been in a state of suspense for days, the arrival of Popham's dispatches had 'now thrown us into a tumult of joy', and *The Times* declared that it would 'be absurd' to indulge in any further scepticism on the subject of the victory. But this was no comfort to those with friends or relatives in the army, whose anxiety could only be relieved when the dreaded casualty lists arrived with Wellington's formal dispatch. On 8 August Granville Leveson Gower wrote to Lady Bessborough, Frederick Ponsonby's mother: 'The suspense in which we are kept as to the battle is really terrible, and I fear that some days more may elapse before we have any official dispatch.'[13]

This uncertainty continued for more than another week, with the papers reduced to printing daily variations of the simple fact that there was no fresh news. The sight of the Admiralty telegraph in operation, reports that a ship had arrived from Lisbon and other portents were eagerly grasped, only to prove erroneous or irrelevant. The days dragged by until Sunday 16 August, when Captain Lord Clinton, Wellington's aide-de-camp, arrived in London in a chaise and four at about 10 o'clock in the morning:

> the drivers and horses were decorated with laurel. The eagles and flags were displayed out of the windows of the chaise. One of the eagles is besmeared with blood, supposed to be in consequence of the Ensign's head who held it being shot away. His Lordship drove to Lord Bathurst's residence, in Mansfield street. The state of the chaise soon spread the report throughout the neighbourhood, and a great concourse of people were collected in a few minutes. The glad tidings spread to Lady Wellington's, who resides near the spot, in Harley street. Her Ladyship ran with all possible speed to Lord Bathurst's house, with a naturally anxious desire to enquire after the welfare of her husband. Lord Clinton of course paid every possible attention to her Ladyship's enquiries; and on her receiving a satisfactory account, she was so much overwhelmed with joy, that she nearly fainted. The eagles and flags were left in Lord Bathurst's house.[14]

Bathurst abandoned his breakfast and took Clinton to the War Department in Downing Street, where they arrived just before 11 o'clock. A large crowd soon assembled, Wellington's dispatches were read, and then Bathurst and Clinton set off across the park on foot, to take the news to the Prince Regent at Carlton House, followed by a mass of people cheering and huzzahing.

The next few days were filled with celebrations in London and throughout the country as the news spread. Houses were lit up: sometimes with lights forming patriotic mottos or illuminated transparencies painted with scenes of battle. Some of the festivities got out of hand: late on the Monday night, or rather in the early hours of Tuesday morning, a crowd of 'idle apprentice-boys and fellows of the lowest description' invaded the West End, letting off fire-works, blunderbusses and muskets, and demanding that the houses in Piccadilly and St James's Street, most of which had doused their lights about 1 o'clock, be re-illuminated. A number of windows were broken, including those of Sir Francis Burdett, the prominent radical and critic of the war, who only two years before had been the hero of the London mob.[15]

Somewhat earlier in the evening Lord Wellesley had ventured into the streets in a plain carriage to view the illuminations. He was recognized in Charing Cross and the crowd insisted upon unhorsing his carriage and drawing it along the Strand and Fleet Street to St Paul's, then on to the Mansion House, and then all the way back to Apsley House. This triumphal progress was fol-lowed by an enormous throng which halted frequently to cheer Wellington and his brother who made many brief impromptu speeches extolling Wellington and thanking the crowd. So good-humoured were the people that they even cheered the Prince Regent, and heartily followed Wellesley's lead in cheering the King, the Duke of York and the army. What Wellington thought of his wife and his brother thus separately making public spectacles of themselves does not survive, but his disdain for the favour of the mob is well known and would prove to be amply justified by the many fluctuations in his own popularity over the next forty years.[16]

Similar, if less exuberant, scenes were repeated in other parts of the country. The artist Joseph Farington left London for Norwich and Cromer on the morning of 16 August, and so carried the news with him, recording in his diary the delight it produced. At Wymondham even a Quaker ('a very respectable looking man') appeared to be filled with pleasure by the announcement, and in Norwich the church bells were rung to welcome the tidings. In Scotland, Sir Walter Scott assembled some forty or fifty locals and workmen around a bon-fire on the banks of the Tweed and plied them with 'an ocean of whiskypunch' to celebrate.[17] And Charles Knight, remembering the days of his youth in Windsor, recalls that, on the evening the news arrived, he had been struggling to compose some verses on the death-song of a Spanish guerrilla:

Suddenly, from the not distant barracks, rose the burst of 'God Save the King', and the cheers of a multitude. I rushed to the town. The 29th Regiment was marching out of Park Street along the Frogmore Road to the inspiriting tune which revolutionary Frenchmen call 'ça ira', but which loyal Englishmen translated into 'The Downfall of Paris'. The Extraordinary Gazette, containing Wellington's despatches relating to the great victory of Salamanca, had been published on that Sunday morning, and had arrived at Windsor, to demand from the enthusiasm of the moment this hasty night march. I followed the measured tramp of the soldiery, in common with the great mass of our population, unknowing what was to be done, and yet filled with the passionate desire of the hundreds around me to give expression to the belief that the tide had turned – that England might shout for a mighty victory by land, as she had shouted for the Nile and for Trafalgar.[18]

The government naturally encouraged this enthusiastic spirit. The Archbishop of Canterbury prepared a special prayer of thanks for the success in Spain which was read in every church in England and Ireland. Liverpool and Bathurst both wrote to Wellington lavishly praising the victory and his skill. The Prime Minister declared that, 'whilst it reflects the highest lustre upon every individual who was engaged in it, [it] redounds so peculiarly to the Commander by whose foresight, decision, and science those operations were conducted which have led to a result of such incalculable importance.' He added that he had never seen such popular excitement as the news had produced.[19] The cabinet and Prince Regent eagerly agreed on raising Wellington to the rank of marquess, with a grant of £100,000 to support the honour. ('An income of nine or ten thousand is after all a poor support for a marquess,' wrote Liverpool, who was himself only an earl.) However, the Horse Guards succeeded in blocking a suggestion, supported by Liverpool, Bathurst and the Wellesley family, that Wellington should be made a field marshal, arguing that it would only exacerbate the jealousy which a number of senior officers already felt towards him.[20]

The celebrations were brought to a formal climax on the last day of September when, with an elaborate ceremony, the captured Eagles and colours were deposited in Whitehall Chapel. The three regiments of Foot Guards, and the two regiments of Life Guards, with their bands, together with contingents from other regiments in the capital, took part, watched by the Queen and her daughters. At 10.30, mounted on a white charger, and attended by the Dukes of York and Kent and a suite of officers and courtiers, the Prince Regent arrived. After he had inspected the soldiers, the parade commenced with the trooping of the colours. The Eagles and French flags made obeisance before the Regent and the Royal Family, to the acclamations of the thousands of spectators; and the favoured few then proceeded into the chapel to hear divine service. Catching the mood of the moment, *The Times* reflected that 'It was impossible to view, without feelings of exultation, those trophies which bore witness to the prowess of British soldiers, and which were won from no despicable enemy, but from troops whose military reputation stands so high in Europe.'[21]

Liverpool took advantage of the patriotic mood, which coincided with a good harvest and the end of the Luddite disturbances, to go to the polls. Elections at this period did not decide governments, but rather allowed the ministers in power at the moment to consolidate their position through the use of official patronage. Liverpool's weak administration was strengthened by the election, while some of the most vociferous Whig critics lost their seats and temporarily found themselves out of Parliament. The ministry was not yet quite secure – it would have to endure a concerted onslaught by Canning and Lord Wellesley in December and January – but it was rapidly gaining assurance, and would go on to endure for no fewer than fifteen years. Thus Salamanca helped to confirm in office the ministers who would guide Britain to victory in the war against Napoleon; its effect was probably not decisive, but if Wellington had been defeated by Marmont, the ministry would surely have fallen, although no one can say for certain what would have taken its place.

On the other side of Europe the news of Salamanca was less welcome. Captain Fabvier set out with Marmont's dispatch on 5 August and rode for thirty-two days before he reached Napoleon's headquarters on the eve of Borodino. Napoleon was naturally preoccupied with the impending battle with the Russians and affected to dismiss the news as of no account: 'The English have their hands full there. They cannot leave Spain and go to make trouble for me in France and Germany. That is all that matters.'[22] But the regency council in Paris could not dismiss the matter so lightly. It worried that the French armies in Spain might be defeated in detail and driven across the Ebro, or even the Pyrenees, and that Wellington might threaten the sacred soil of France, while Napoleon was thousands of miles away, deep in Russia. In desperation it recalled Marshal Masséna from retirement and ordered him to take command of the Army of Portugal and halt the allied advance on the Duero. Masséna reached Bayonne before he fell ill – or had second thoughts – and resigned the command on 26 August.[23] The fears of the French regency, like the hopes of the British government, proved exaggerated, or at least premature. Nonetheless, General Savary (the Duc de Rovigo), the Minister of Police, records that the defeat had a considerable effect on French public opinion, shaking confidence and making even loyal supporters of Napoleon anxious and eager for some decisive news from Russia. Borodino and the occupation of Moscow brought only muted joy, and it was not long before fresh and greater doubts arose. Napoleon's domestic support was already beginning to be eroded, even before the retreat from Moscow began.[24]

The allies did not gain a final victory in the Peninsula in 1812. The Battle of Salamanca transformed the prospects facing Wellington, rendered Marmont's army incapable of serious operations for a time, and opened the road to Madrid; but it altered rather than completely overturned the balance of forces in Spain. There were still more than 200,000 French soldiers south of the Pyrenees, far more than Wellington could hope to oppose if they combined against him. The allied army was suffering from the demands of the campaign and the heat of the summer, with a staggering total of twenty thousand British rank and file (not counting the Portuguese) reported sick on 25 August.[25] By occupying Madrid, Wellington had gained the central position, but found himself faced with the difficult, perhaps insoluble, problem of how best to use it. He considered marching south and attacking Soult in Andalusia, but decided to postpone this until a cooler season. In the meantime he returned to the north, leaving part of his army, including his best troops, in Madrid. His intention was to drive Clausel beyond the Ebro and, if possible, discover some means of protecting this flank when he again moved south. This led him to undertake the siege of Burgos, despite lacking the necessary means. The siege proved a protracted, costly and demoralizing failure; but even if it had succeeded, it is unlikely that it would have achieved his objectives, for the French were collecting vast forces against him.

The allied capture of Madrid had posed a threat to all the French armies in Spain and forced the marshals to subordinate their local concerns to the requirements of the wider war. Soult reluctantly raised the siege of Cadiz, evacuated his rich viceroyalty and marched through Granada and Murcia to join Joseph and Suchet in Valencia. In the north, Souham took command of the Army of Portugal, which had regained its order and composure, if not its confidence, remarkably quickly; while Caffarelli, threatened by Wellington's advance on Burgos, lent him ample support. Although Wellington brought Hill up from Estremadura to Madrid and received a small reinforcement from the garrison of Cadiz, the allies were soon heavily outnumbered on both fronts. Wellington raised the siege of Burgos on 22 October and began to withdraw, and nine days later Hill's rearguard abandoned Madrid. On 8 November the allied army was reunited on the Tormes, but the retreat continued. A week later, at Salamanca, Wellington offered battle, but although the combined French army under Joseph and Soult was much stronger than the allies, it would not fight and instead sought to manoeuvre Wellington into retreat by threatening his lines of communication. This time there was no mistake, and the allied army, weary and dispirited, was forced back to the Portuguese frontier, where it sullenly went into winter quarters after eleven months of extremely demanding operations.

And so the year ended as it began, with the allied army cantoned along the frontier. At first glance nothing appeared to have been gained except the capture of Ciudad Rodrigo and Badajoz in the winter and spring. But such glances are apt to mislead; much more than this had been accomplished. The allied army had proved its ability to manoeuvre and attack in the open field, and had established a psychological superiority over the French which remained unchallenged for the rest of the war. The siege of Cadiz had been raised and Andalusia had been freed. Madrid had been liberated and, although lost again, the authority of Joseph Bonaparte's government had been dealt an irreparable blow. French garrisons had been weakened or withdrawn from almost every province in Spain, opening the way for the guerrillas who flourished in their absence. The lasting results of this were not yet apparent, but would become obvious as the insurrection in northern Spain gained strength in the winter and spring, paving the way in turn for Wellington's rapid advance to Vitoria in 1813. Beyond the Pyrenees all Europe had seen that the French war in Spain was not going well; that it was no mere matter of suppressing brigands; and that there was no end in sight for the conscription needed to sustain Napoleon's armies. Of course, if Napoleon had triumphed in Russia, the new year might have seen another great influx of reinforcements such as that which had followed the defeat of Austria in 1809. Wellington might have been driven back to the Lines of Torres Vedras, Andalusia might have been overrun again and Joseph's authority might have been supported by another 200,000 French soldiers. But all the gains of the past three years (except Valencia) had been lost, and the Spanish guerrillas were vastly more confident, experienced and well organized. The war was not being won, and the cost of continuing it – in men, in money and above all in domestic support in France – was rising steeply. The illusion was shattered, and the Emperor's Spanish policy stood revealed in all its nakedness.

Appendix I

Casualties Suffered on 18 July 1812

ALLIED CASUALTIES

From the return in PRO WO 1/255, pp. 91–2.

	officers		men			total
	killed	wounded	killed	wounded	missing	
Fourth Division (Cole)						
3/27th Foot	2	1	11	58	–	72
1/40th Foot	–	1	8	59	1	69
1/7th Foot	–	1	1	14	3	19
1/23rd Foot	–	–	–	2	2	4
1/48th Foot	–	–	–	5	1	6
Fifth Division (Leith)						
3/1st Foot	–	–	–	2	–	2
detachments of 5/60th	–	–	–	1	2	3
Portuguese (all arms)	1	6	33	90	27	157
G. Anson's brigade						
11th Light Dragoons	–	2	3	11	–	16
12th Light Dragoons	–	1	5	12	1	19
16th Light Dragoons	–	1	3	8	3	15
V. Alten's brigade						
1st Hussars KGL	–	4	7	45	4	60
14th Light Dragoons	–	3	14	49	9	75
Bock's brigade						
1st Dragoons KGL	–	–	–	1	–	1
2nd Dragoons KGL	–	–	5	1	1	7
Le Marchant's brigade						
3rd Dragoons	–	1	–	9	–	10
Horse artillery	–	1	2	2	–	5
German artillery	–	–	–	2	–	2
Total	3	22	92	371	54	542

FRENCH CASUALTIES

Officer casualties come from Martinien; those for the men are based on the overall losses given in Lamartinière's return (printed in Sarramon, *La Bataille des Arapiles*, pp. 423–5) for the whole campaign divided in the same proportions as overall officer losses. For example, if a unit loses ten officer and one hundred rank-and-file casualties in the campaign as a whole, and Martinien identifies three of these officer casualties as occurring on 18 July, it is assumed that thirty of the casualties among the men also occurred on the 18th. For further discussion see Appendix III.

2nd Division (Clausel)
25th Léger lost 1 officer killed and 5 wounded = 6 officer casualties, suggesting 102 men, a total loss of approx. 108, or 7.0%

6th Division (Taupin)
17th Léger lost 2 officers killed, and 6 wounded (1 mortally) = 8 officer casualties, suggesting 184 men, a total loss of approx. 192, or 17.1%
65th Ligne lost 2 officers killed, and 1 wounded = 3 officer casualties, suggesting 87 men, a total loss of approx. 90, or 5.7%
22nd Ligne lost 5 officers wounded (1 mortally) = 5 officer casualties, suggesting 188 men, a total loss of approx. 193, or 12.5%

Light Cavalry Division (Curto)
3rd Hussars lost 2 officers wounded, suggesting 22 men, a total loss of approx. 24, or 9.7%
14th Chasseurs lost 3 officers wounded, suggesting 29 men, a total loss of approx. 32, or 9.9%

Dragoon Division (Boyer)
Brigadier Carrié was wounded and captured
15th Dragoons lost 1 officer killed and 1 wounded = 2 officer casualties, suggesting 26 men, a total loss of approx. 28 or 8.2%
25th Dragoons lost 4 officers wounded, suggesting 24 men, a total loss of approx. 28, or 8.4%

Total Loss
Infantry 22 officers and approx. 561 men, total 583
Cavalry 12 officers and approx. 101 men, total 113
Total 34 officers and approx. 662 men, total 696

Increasing these figures to allow for unwounded prisoners and slightly wounded men who had returned to the ranks by 8 August (see Appendix III for more details) produces an estimate of total losses on 18 July of 40 officers and 794 men, or 834 casualties in all.

Appendix II

Allied Strength and Losses

The following table gives the strength of the allied army on 15 July, the date of the last return before the battle. The figures for the British are based on the original manuscript weekly state in the Public Record Office at Kew (WO 1/255), and are much the same as those given by Oman, with a few minor corrections.* The figures for the Portuguese come from a less detailed morning state dated 12 July, also in the PRO (WO 1/255). This agrees very closely with the figures printed by Oman from a return in the archives in Lisbon;† unfort-

---

* Oman, *History*, vol. 5, pp. 595–9. Oman correctly gives the 5th Dragoon Guards as having 22 officers and 313 men, but due to a misprint gives a total of 325 instead of 335. This misprint goes uncorrected in Fortescue, Young and Lawford, and Sarramon, who all copy their figures for the allied army from Oman, even though the correct total is used later in calculating the full strength of the allied army.

  The other minor errors in Oman's figures are:

2nd Line Battalion KGL	should be 606 men, not 601
1/7th Foot	should be 463 men not 471
2/4th Foot	should be 647 men not 627
Brunswick Company in Pringle's brigade of the 5th Division	should have 2 officers, not 3
1/36th Foot	should have 410 men, not 400
1/43rd Light Infantry	should have 708 men, not 718

  The net effect is a reduction of one in the number of officers and an addition of seventeen men to the strength of the army.

† The variations from the figures given in Oman are as follows:

  Oman says that Stubbs's brigade had 137 officers, but the return says 127
  Oman says that Collins's brigade had 132 officers, but the return says 122
  Oman says that Pack's brigade had 85 officers, but the return says 87

A net reduction of 18 in the number of Portuguese officers; the figures for men agree exactly.

I have also followed S. G. P. Ward in preference to Oman on the composition of Bradford's brigade (the 24th Line, not the 14th). Ward, 'The Portuguese Infantry Brigades, 1809–1814', *JSAHR*, vol. 53 (1975), pp. 110–11.

unately, neither gives the strength of individual regiments or battalions, only the total for each brigade.

It is worth explaining that the original weekly state in the PRO is far more detailed than the version published here. There are almost fifty columns for each regiment, giving the number of officers of each rank; while sergeants, drummers and rank and file are each subdivided into 'Present', 'Sick – Present', 'Sick – Absent', 'Command' (men not currently serving in their normal place in the regiment, although fit for duty) and 'Prisoners of War and Missing'. Then follow columns for horses and for 'Alterations since last Return', which is further broken down under headings such as 'Joined', 'Deserted', 'Transferred', 'Promoted' and so on. Comparison shows that Oman disregarded most of these columns when calculating the effective strength of the regiment, and his practice has been followed here. The number of officers given is simply the total number of officers in the regiment: presumably sick or absent officers were returned separately. The number of 'men' is a little more complicated. For the infantry, Oman just adds together the sergeants, drummers and rank and file listed as 'Present' (not including 'Sick – Present'). But when dealing with the cavalry he looks instead to the column showing the number of horses present, which he equates with the number of men the regiment could put into the field. This decision is justified, for it gives a total strength for each brigade equal to the final column in the return: 'Effective Rank and File for Each Brigade and Division'. The phrase 'rank and file' here may cause some concern, but as the figure is based on the number of horses returned as present with the regiment, and as NCOs were certainly both present and mounted in action, it seems that it must be used loosely. On the other hand, the same column for the infantry gives simply the total rank and file listed as present and does not include sergeants or drummers.

The artillery returns present a puzzle. The manuscript 'state' does not give figures for individual batteries and includes units which were with Hill's corps in Estremadura and possibly also in the rear, and so is a poor guide to the strength of Wellington's artillery in the battle. *The Dickson Manuscripts* clearly identifies which batteries were present and the number and type of guns, but not the number of men; while a return referred to in the Ordnance Papers in the PRO is no longer present.* However, Oman gives reasonably detailed, plausible figures, and for want of any useful original returns these have been adopted, even though they may be an underestimate (see chapter two, commentary, p. 45).

The quite substantial reinforcements which joined the allied army between 15 and 22 July (such as the 1/38th) are included in the return, but no attempt has been made to deduct the losses which were suffered in this week – men falling out from exhaustion and the heat, and casualties, principally those

---

* *Dickson Manuscripts*, vol. 4, pp. 685–7; WO 55/1195, pp. 355–8 contains a report on the battle which mentions the return, but it is not present.

suffered on 18 July. A rough estimate puts this at about 1,200 men, most of whom would, of course, soon rejoin the army.[*]

The figures for British casualties in the battle come from the official return in the PRO (WO 1/255) and differ only slightly from those given in Oman.[†] However, there are two sets of figures for the Portuguese losses. Wellington reported in his official dispatch that the Portuguese suffered 2,038 casualties: 304 killed, 1,552 wounded and 182 missing; but Oman has found a detailed return in the archives in Lisbon which gives a lower figure of 1,627 casualties: 506 killed, 1,035 wounded and 86 missing. Oman notes the difference, but believes that there is a *prima facie* case for preferring 'the later and more carefully detailed document'.[‡] However, there are two powerful arguments against this choice: first, the sheer improbability of any general overstating his losses – or the losses of a significant part of his army – by 25 per cent; second, the proportion of killed to wounded in the later return is highly unusual. In Napoleonic battles for which we have reliable statistics, the killed normally amount to between 10 and 20 per cent of the casualties. Of the British casualties at Salamanca, 12.4 per cent were killed: the first Portuguese return shows 14.9 per cent killed; the second, 31.1 per cent. It is hardly likely that Portuguese soldiers fighting side by side with their British comrades were two and a half times as likely to be killed rather than wounded. A much more plausible explanation is that the second return was prepared some time – probably a few weeks – after the battle. Many of the slightly wounded men who had returned to the ranks were not counted (hence the fall in the overall total), while the number killed was swollen, both by the discovery of the bodies of men originally listed as missing and by the death of some of the most seriously wounded.

Unfortunately, this first return gives only the total numbers of Portuguese casualties, not those suffered by individual units; but the later return, which Oman prints, does give the losses of each brigade. If the explanation of the difference between the two returns given above is correct, one would expect the understatement of losses in this second return to be spread fairly evenly across the army. Therefore a rough calculation of the true losses of each brigade can be made by multiplying Oman's figure by 1.253, which, with a little rounding, produces the desired total of 2,038. Naturally the resulting figures cannot pretend to be precise, but they are plausible and appear to be the best that we can

---

[*] See chapter 2, commentary, pp. 43–4 for discussion of this point.

[†] The 2/38th should not have any missing (Oman says one man), so their total loss should be 51 not 52.

The 1/11th should have 15 officers wounded, not 14, and so their total loss should be 341 not 340.

The 1/36th should have 4 officers wounded, not 5, and so their total loss should be 98 not 99.

And the 14th Light Dragoons should have 7 men wounded, not 2, and so their total loss should be 8 not 3.

This represents a net increase in the army's casualties of 4.

[‡] Oman, *History*, vol. 5, pp. 470–1.

do. In the table, detailed figures for each Portuguese brigade are taken from Oman's return, with an adjusted total in brackets after the column for total casualties.

The strength of the Spanish division is given by Oman as 160 officers, 3,200 men, total 3,360. The round figures and exact proportion of one officer to twenty men suggest that this may be no more than an approximation. Recent Spanish research, using the papers of Don Julián Sánchez, states that he had a surprisingly powerful brigade of cavalry in the field: two regiments of lancers and a company of artillery (two 4-pounders), amounting to 950 men. Although this brigade was nominally subordinated to Don Carlos de España, it is said to have received its orders direct from Wellington's headquarters.[*] The strength and composition of the remainder of the Spanish force are uncertain: the assumption made here is that Oman's overall figure is correct, which means that the infantry under España's command amounted to 2,410 all ranks. It is not known how the six recorded Spanish casualties (two killed, four wounded) were distributed between the two elements.

No figures, whether for the strength or the losses of any army in any battle, are absolutely accurate. They include men who left the ranks early in the day and who took no part in the fighting, and fail to include the officially sick or absent soldier who went out of his way to join his comrades for the great occasion. Many officers refused to report themselves wounded for fear that their name appearing in the papers at home would alarm and distress their families, while others made the most of every scratch in the search for glory, promotion and renown. Some officers might understate their unit's losses by only recording men with comparatively serious wounds, while others would inflate their unit's casualty roll. These problems should deter us from regarding these statistics as being incontrovertible or above reproach; but in most cases their impact was probably slight, and the figures remain one of the most useful tools for seeking to understand what happened in the battle.

[*] Becerra, *Hazañas de Unos Lanceros*, p. 107.

Allied Army

FIRST DIVISION (H. CAMPBELL)

				officers		men				
	officers	men	total	killed	wounded	killed	wounded	missing	Total loss	% loss
Fermor's Brigade										
1st/Coldstream Guards	26	928	954	–	1	7	22	8	38	4.0%
1st Third Guards	23	938	961	–	1	1	20	2	24	2.5%
one coy 5/60th	1	56	57	–	–	–	–	–	–	–
Wheatley's Brigade										
2/24th	23	398	421	–	–	–	5	–	5	1.2%
1/42nd	40	1,039	1,079	–	–	–	3	–	3	0.3%
2/58th	31	369	400	–	–	–	3	1	4	1.0%
1/79th	40	634	674	–	–	–	1	3	4	0.6%
one coy 5/60th	1	53	54	–	–	–	–	–	–	–
Löwe's Brigade										
1st Line KGL btn	26	615	641	–	–	1	8	–	9	1.4%
2nd Line KGL btn	26	606	632	–	2	1	40	4	47	7.4%
5th Line KGL btn	30	525	555	–	1	1	17	–	19	3.4%
Total First Division	267	6,161	6,428	–	5	11	119	18	153	2.4%

THIRD DIVISION (PAKENHAM)

				officers		men				
	officers	men	total	killed	wounded	killed	wounded	missing	Total loss	% loss
Wallace's Brigade										
1/45th	26	416	442	–	5	5	45	–	55	12.4%
74th Foot	23	420	443	–	2	3	40	4	49	11.1%
1/88th	21	642	663	2	4	11	110	8	135	20.4%
3 coys 5/60th	11	243	254	–	3	6	24	3	36	7.6%*

*These losses are for all seven companies of the 5/60th with Wellington's army as no breakdown for individual companies is available.

				officers		men			Total loss	% loss
	officers	men	total	killed	wounded	killed	wounded	missing		
J. Campbell's Brigade										
1/5th	32	870	902	–	6	10	110	–	126	14.0%
2/5th	19	289	308	–	2	1	21	–	24	7.8%
2/83rd	24	295	319	–	2	2	30	–	34	10.7%
94th	24	323	347	1	3	3	21	–	28	8.1%
Power's Portuguese Brigade (8th Brigade)										
9th and 21st Line, 12th Caçadores	90	2,107	2,197	1	9	29	23	14	76 (= 95)	3.5% (4.3%)
Total Third Division	270	5,605	5,875	4	36	70	424	29	563 (582)	9.6% (9.9%)

(Portuguese = 37.4% of division and suffered 13.5% (16.3%) of its losses)

FOURTH DIVISION (COLE)

				officers		men			Total loss	% loss
	officers	men	total	killed	wounded	killed	wounded	missing		
W. Anson's Brigade										
3/27th	19	614	633	–	1	–	7	–	8	1.3%
1/40th	24	558	582	–	5	12	115	–	132	22.7%
one coy 5/60th	2	44	46	–	–	–	–	–	–	–
Ellis's Brigade										
1/7th	24	463	487	1	10	19	165	–	195	40.0%
1/23rd	19	427	446	1	6	9	90	–	106	23.8%
1/48th	22	404	426	–	10	9	60	–	79	18.5%
one coy Brunswick Oels	1	53	54	–	–	–	–	–	–	–
Stubbs's Portuguese Brigade (9th Brigade)										
11th and 23rd Line, 7th Caçadores	127	2,417	2,544	3	18	177	267	11	476 (= 596)	18.7% (23.4%)
Total Fourth Division	238	4,980	5,218	5	50	226	704	11	996 (1,116)	19.1% (21.4%)

(Portuguese = 48.8% of division and suffered 47.8% (53.4%) of its losses)

FIFTH DIVISION (LEITH)

	officers	men	total	officers		men			Total loss	% loss
				killed	wounded	killed	wounded	missing		
Greville's Brigade										
3/1st	32	729	761	–	8	23	129	–	160	21.0%
1/9th	31	635	666	–	1	3	42	–	46	6.9%
1/38th	36	764	800	2	12	14	115	–	143	17.9%
2/38th	20	281	301	–	2	9	40	–	51	16.9%
one coy Brunswick Oels	2	76	78	–	–	–	–	–	–	–
Pringle's Brigade										
1/4th	36	421	457	–	1	–	17	–	18	3.9%
2/4th	27	647	674	–	–	2	23	6	31	4.6%
2/30th	20	329	349	–	1	3	22	1	27	7.7%
2/44th	20	231	251	2	–	4	23	–	29	11.6%
one coy Brunswick Oels	2	66	68	–	–	–	–	–	–	–
Spry's Portuguese Brigade (3rd Brigade)										
3rd and 15th Line, 8th Caçadores	156	2,149	2,305	3	4	45	64	7	123 (=154)	5.3% (6.7%)
Total Fifth Division	382	6,328	6,710	7	29	103	475	14	628 (659)	9.4% (9.8%)

(Portuguese = 34.4% of division and suffered 19.6% (23.4%) of its losses)

SIXTH DIVISION (CLINTON)

	officers	men	total	officers		men			Total loss	% loss
				killed	wounded	killed	wounded	missing		
Hulse's Brigade										
1/11th	31	485	516	1	15	44	281	–	341	66.1%
2/53rd	25	316	341	–	11	26	105	–	142	41.6%
1/61st	29	517	546	5	19	39	303	–	366	67.0%
one coy 5/60th	2	59	61	–	–	–	–	–	–	–
	87	1,377	1,464	6	45	109	689	–	849	58.0%

	officers	men	total	\[officers\] killed	wounded	\[men\] killed	wounded	missing	Total loss	% loss

Hinde's Brigade

	officers	men	total	killed	wounded	killed	wounded	missing	Total loss	% loss
2nd Foot	27	381	408	1	6	13	77	12	109	26.7%
1/32nd	33	576	609	2	9	15	111	–	137	22.5%
1/36th	29	410	439	4	4	16	74	–	98	22.3%
	89	1,367	1,456	7	19	44	262	12	344	23.6%

Rezende's Portuguese Brigade (7th Brigade)

	officers	men	total	killed	wounded	killed	wounded	missing	Total loss	% loss
8th and 12th Line, 9th Caçadores	134	2,497	2,631	8	10	113	336	20	487 (= 610)	18.5% (23.2%)

	officers	men	total	killed	wounded	killed	wounded	missing	Total loss	% loss
Total Sixth Division	310	5,241	5,551	21	74	266	1,287	32	1,680 (1,803)	30.3% (32.5%)

(Portuguese = 47.4% of the division; suffered 29.0% (33.8%) of its losses)

SEVENTH DIVISION (HOPE)

Halkett's Brigade

	officers	men	total	killed	wounded	killed	wounded	missing	Total loss	% loss
1st KGL Light btn	25	544	569	–	2	–	7	–	9	1.6%
2nd KGL Light btn	21	473	494	1	1	5	9	–	16	3.2%
Brunswick Oels 9 coys	23	573	596	–	2	4	42	1	49	6.2%*

* These losses are for all twelve companies of the Brunswick Oels with Wellington's army as no breakdown for individual companies is available.

De Bernewiz's Brigade

	officers	men	total	killed	wounded	killed	wounded	missing	Total loss	% loss
51st Foot	27	280	307	–	–	–	2	–	2	0.7%
68th Foot	21	317	338	1	2	3	14	–	20	5.9%
Chasseurs Britanniques	27	686	713	–	–	5	10	14	29	4.1%

Collins's Portuguese Brigade (6th Brigade)

	officers	men	total	killed	wounded	killed	wounded	missing	Total loss	% loss
7th and 19th Line, 2nd Caçadores	122	2,036	2,158	–	1	5	10	1	17 (=21)	0.8% (1.0%)

	officers	men	total	killed	wounded	killed	wounded	missing	Total loss	% loss
Total Seventh Division	266	4,909	5,175	2	8	22	94	16	142 (146)	2.7% (2.8%)

(Portuguese = 41.7% of division and suffered 12.0% (14.4%) of its losses)

LIGHT DIVISION (CHARLES ALTEN)

	officers	men	total	officers		men			Total loss	% loss
				killed	wounded	killed	wounded	missing		
Barnard's Brigade										
1/43rd	30	708	738	–	1	–	15	–	16	2.2%
parts of 2 and 3/95th	19	373	392	–	–	–	5	–	5	1.3%
1st Caçadores	see below									
Vandeleur's Brigade										
1/52nd	28	771	799	–	–	–	2	–	2	0.3%
8 coys 1/95th	27	515	542	–	–	–	2	2	4	0.7%
3rd Caçadores	see below									
1st and 3rd Caçadores combined	30	1,037	1,067	–	1	5	12	–	17 (=21)	1.6% (2.0%)
Total Light Division	134	3,404	3,538	–	1	5	36	2	44 (48)	1.2% (1.4%)

(Portuguese = 30.2% of the division; suffered 38.6% (43.7%) of its losses)

INDEPENDENT PORTUGUESE BRIGADES

	officers	men	total	killed	wounded	killed	wounded	missing	Total loss	% loss
Pack's Brigade (1st Brigade)										
1st and 16th Line, 4th Caçadores	87	2,520	2,607	5	15	97	242	17	376 (= 471)	14.4% (18.1%)
Bradford's Brigade (10th Brigade)										
13th and 24th Line, 5th Caçadores	112	1,782	1,894	–	–	8	3	6	17 (= 21)	0.9% (1.1%)
Spanish Division (Carlos de España) 2nd Princesa; Tiradores de Castilla; 2nd Jaen; 3rd/1 Seville; one battery of 6-pounders: approx.	110	2,300	2,410	–	–	2	4	–	6*	0.2%
Total Infantry	2,176	43,230	45,406	44	218	810	3,388	145	4,605 (5,005)	10.1% (11.0%)

*The breakdown of Spanish casualties between España's infantry and Sánchez's cavalry is not known.

THE CAVALRY

	officers	men	total	officers killed	officers wounded	men killed	men wounded	men missing	Total loss	% loss
Le Marchant's Brigade										
3rd Dragoons	17	322	339	1	–	6	11	2	20	5.9%
4th Dragoons	22	336	358	–	1	7	21	–	29	8.1%
5th Dragoon Guards	22	313	335	–	2	9	42	3	56	16.7%
Total Le Marchant's Brigade:	61	971	1,032	1	3	22	74	5	105	10.2%
G. Anson's Brigade										
11th Light Dragoons	30	361	391	–	–	–	–	–	–	–
12th Light Dragoons	19	321	340	1	–	2	2	–	5	1.5%
16th Light Dragoons	14	259	273	–	–	–	–	–	–	–
Total Anson's Brigade	63	941	1,004	1	–	2	2	–	5	0.5%
V. Alten's Brigade										
14th Light Dragoons	23	324	347	–	–	1	7	–	8	2.3%
1st Hussars KGL	23	376	399	–	5	2	16	–	23	5.8%
Total Alten's Brigade	46	700	746	–	5	3	23	–	31	4.2%
Bock's Brigade										
1st Dragoons KGL	25	339	364	–	–	–	–	–	–	–
2nd Dragoons KGL	23	384	407	–	–	–	–	–	–	–
Total Bock's Brigade	48	723	771	–	–	–	–	–	–	–
D'Urban's Portuguese Brigade										
1st and 11th Portuguese Dragoons	32	450	482	2	2	5	18	10	37 (= 46)	7.7% (9.5%)
Julián Sánchez's Brigade										
1st and 2nd Lanceros de Castilla and two 4-pounders	50	900	950	–	–	–	–	–	–	–
Total Cavalry	300	4,685	4,985	4	10	32	117	15	178 (=187)	3.6% (3.8%)

(Portuguese = 9.7% of the cavalry and suffered 20.8% (24.6%) of its losses)

ARTILLERY AND SUPPORT SERVICES

	officers	men	total	officers killed	officers wounded	men killed	men wounded	men missing	Total loss	% loss
Royal Horse Artillery (troops of Ross, Macdonald, Bull and drivers)	18	403	421	–	–	1	2	–	3	0.7%
Field Artillery (coys of Lawson, Gardiner, Greene, Douglas, May* and drivers)	35	650	685	–	–	1	4	–	5	0.7%
King's German Legion Artillery (Sympher's battery)	5	75	80	–	–	2	4	–	6	7.5%
Portuguese Artillery (Arriaga's battery)	4	110	114	–	–	–	1	–	1	0.9%
Total Artillery	62	1,238	1,300	–	–	4	11	–	15	1.2%

(Also the Spanish battery in España's division and the two 4-pounders with Sánchez's lancers)

	officers	men	total	
Engineers	12	9	21	no casualties recorded
Staff Corps	5	81	86	no casualties recorded
Waggon Train	24	115	139	no casualties recorded
General Staff	?	?	?	2 officers killed, 9 wounded = 11 officer casualties
Total Support Staff	41	205	246	11 casualties 4.5%

	officers	men	casualties		%	
Total Infantry	2,176	43,230	4,605	(5,005)	10.1%	(11.0%)
Total Cavalry	300	4,685	178	(187)	3.6%	(3.8%)
Total Artillery	62	1,238	15	(15)	1.2%	–
Total Support Staff	41	205	11	(11)	4.5%	–
(Allow for rounding of Portuguese casualties)				(2)		
Grand Total:	2,579	49,358	4,809	(5,220)	9.3%	(10.0%)

* May's company was in charge of the reserve ammunition and brought no guns into the field.

Using the Amended (Higher) Figures for the Portuguese Losses

Infantry comprised	87.4% of the army and suffered	95.9% of its losses
Cavalry comprised	9.6% of the army and suffered	3.6% of its losses
Artillery comprised	2.5% of the army and suffered	0.3% of its losses
Support staff comprised	0.5% of the army and suffered	0.2% of its losses

Anglo–Germans	= 30,578 men or 58.9% of army and lost 3,176 or 60.8% of casualties
Portuguese	= 17,999 men or 34.7% of army and lost 2,038 or 39.0% of casualties
Spanish	= 3,360 men or 6.5% of army and lost 6 or 0.1% of casualties

Total 51,937 men   5,220 casualties

(The sum of the amended Portuguese casualties in the order of battle (those given in brackets) is only 2,036, not 2,038, owing to the rounding-down of fractions under 0.5, which happen to outnumber those above 0.5.)

Summary of Allied Army

(Using amended – higher – figures for Portuguese casualties. No deduction has been made from the strength of the army for losses suffered on 18 July, or for men who fell out in the days before the battle.)

	strength	casualties	% casualties
First Division	6,428	153	2.4%
Third Division	5,875	582	9.9%
Fourth Division	5,218	1,116	21.4%
Fifth Division	6,710	659	9.8%
Sixth Division	5,551	1,803	32.5%
Seventh Division	5,175	146	2.8%
Light Division	3,538	48	1.4%
Pack's Brigade	2,607	471	18.1%
Bradford's Brigade	1,894	21	1.1%
Spanish Division	2,410	6	0.2%
Le Marchant's Brigade	1,032	105	10.2%
G. Anson's Brigade	1,004	5	0.5%
V. Alten's Brigade	746	31	4.2%
Bock's Brigade	771	–	–
D'Urban's Brigade	482	46	9.5%
Sánchez's Brigade	950	–	–
Artillery	1,300	15	1.2%
Miscellaneous	246	11	4.5%
Allow for rounding of Portuguese casualties		2	
Total	51,937	5,220	10.0%

Appendix III

French Strength and Losses

The figures given below for the strength of the French army are based on a return dated 15 July 1812 and printed by Oman. Fortescue also prints this return in rather more detail – he gives the strength of each individual battalion rather than each regiment; a few slight differences between the two versions are noted. Sarramon prints a return dated 1 July, and while there are naturally some changes, this confirms the general picture given by Oman and Fortescue. After allowing for casualties suffered on 18 July, and for men falling out from fatigue caused by Marmont's long marches, Oman estimates the strength of Marmont's army on 22 July at 48,500. However, the fighting strength of the army on the 22nd, when non-combatants and detached troops are deducted, would have been rather lower: about 46,700. This figure does not include the thousands of men employed in garrisons as far afield as Astorga, or left in depots at Valladolid, or sick – these last alone amounted to between eight and nine thousand men.[*]

The losses of the French army pose much greater difficulties and cannot be determined with any certainty, although a rough approximation can be attempted. There are two main sources of information, but neither is complete. First, there is Martinien's valuable list of French officers killed and wounded between 1805 and 1815: not only the original 824-page book published in 1899

---

[*] Oman, *History*, vo.l 5, pp. 600–3 estimates the garrisons at about 4,200; the depots had been 3,300 but were now 'much less'; and the sick probably 'a trifle more' than 8,300, suggesting a total of approximately 14,000 or 15,000 men under Marmont's command but unable to join the field army. Fortescue, *History of the British Army*, vol. 8, pp. 632–6: the totals given for each division are evidently those in the original return and are often inaccurate. The net difference between Oman's and Fortescue's figures is that Oman gives Marmont's army 10 more officers (mostly in one unit) and 43 fewer men. The one instance where I have followed Fortescue rather than Oman is in giving 3rd Hussars two squadrons not three: this is supported by Sarramon's return and is more consistent with the strength of the squadrons in the other regiments of light cavalry. Sarramon, *La Bataille des Arapiles*, pp. 409–12. See chapter 2, commentary, p. 43 for the calculations employed to produce the fighting strength.

and reprinted *c.* 1980, but the much rarer and less well-known 196-page *Supplement* of 1909, which adds a further twenty-six officer casualties for the campaign. Oman uses both works extensively, but characteristically fails to give a precise reference – causing great confusion for anyone working on his figures who does not know of the *Supplement*'s existence. Martinien's work is highly accurate, but it does not include officers who, although unwounded, were taken prisoner, while a few officers who were wounded or even killed appear to have escaped his researches.

The second source of information is the official return of French casualties between 18 July and 8 August prepared by General Lamartinière, chief of staff of Marmont's army. This acknowledges total losses of 12,435 officers and men, made up as follows:

killed or captured	162 officers	+	7,529 men	=	7,691
wounded	232 officers	+	3,867 men	=	4,099
missing	–		645 men	=	645
	394 officers	+	12,041 men	=	12,435

The original return is in the French military archives at Vincennes (C7–15). Oman knew of it, but regarded it as worthless and ignored it in his calculation of French casualties. Fortunately, Sarramon recognized its significance and printed it (albeit with a few trifling inaccuracies).[*] It certainly *is* incomplete, as a few examples will show:

[*] I must thank Général Bach and Chef de Bataillon Porchet of the Service Historique de l'Armée de Terre, Château de Vincennes, for sending me a photocopy of the original return. Sarramon's table (*La Bataille des Arapiles*, pp. 423–5) contains the following minor errors:

4th Division	2nd Léger should have 43 not 42 men killed or captured total 154
	4th Léger should have 52 not 53 men killed or captured total 87
8th Division	118th Ligne should have 12 not 13 officers wounded total casualties 407
Cavalry	28th Chasseurs should have 6 not 7 men wounded total casualties 12
	15th Dragoons should have 39 not 40 men killed or captured total 40

Artillery should have 5 officers and 51 men wounded not 4 and 52   total 160
Etat-Major should have 5 officers killed or taken, not 4; and 9 wounded, not 7   total 14.
The net effect is an increase of one officer killed or captured and two wounded and a decrease of one man killed or captured and two wounded; so that the total of casualties overall remains unchanged.

Oman and Fortescue both refer to this return and give a summary of its totals which is quite wrong in one important respect, for they confuse the number of wounded men with the number 'killed or captured'. They think that,

162 officers and 3,867 men were killed or taken, and
232 officers and 7,529 men were wounded

whereas the correct figures are:

162 officers and 7,529 men killed or taken, and
232 officers and 3,867 men wounded.

As it is most unlikely that both these fine historians misread the original return in the same way, it seems probable that one copied the other. Oman's volume was published three years before Fortescue's, but in his preface he thanks Fortescue for the loan of copies of

– Lamartinière lists 14 officer casualties from the staff: 5 killed or captured and 9 wounded; but Martinien names 23 staff officers casualties: one killed, three mortally wounded and 19 wounded (21 in the battle, 2 in other engagements in the campaign).

– In the 13th Chasseurs, Lamartinière shows the loss of 60 men killed or taken, 19 wounded and 4 missing, or 83 in all from 496 rank and file, but not one of its twenty officers; Martinien, however, lists 7 officer casualties, all wounded.

– The 69th Ligne in Foy's division is almost as bad. According to Lamartinière, it had 120 men killed or taken, 81 wounded and 4 missing, but only 3 officer casualties (all three being listed as killed or taken). Martinien names two officers who were mortally wounded and 8 other wounded officers.

Many other examples could be given, although these are among the most glaring; and there is every reason to suppose that this understatement of losses extended to the rank and file as well as to the officers, although there is no independent check for the former of the kind Martinien provides for the latter.

Nonetheless, Lamartinière's return was not a cynical whitewash designed to conceal the scale of the defeat. It acknowledged the loss of over 12,000 casualties in a short campaign, including more than 7,500 men listed as 'killed or captured', and so permanently lost to the army. Clearly it was not designed to support Marmont's claim to have suffered only 6,000 casualties in the battle. It seems likely that it minimized French losses in the same way as the Portuguese return discussed in Appendix II, by disregarding slightly wounded officers and men who had returned to the ranks (or never left them) by the time it was prepared, about 8 August. This might account for the fact that the difference between Lamartinière's return and Martinien's list is greatest for the cavalry (especially the light cavalry) and the staff: many minor wounds were inflicted in cavalry melees, and it is reasonable to suppose that cavalry and staff officers might be eager to have such wounds recorded on their service record even if they did not force them to leave their unit. (Lamartinière records ten officer casualties in Curto's division of light cavalry compared to the thirty listed by Martinien.) This explanation of slight wounds does not cover every case, and it may be that some fudging went on, either by Lamartinière or by the responsible officer in some regiments. Alternatively some figures may have been distorted when the army picked up small garrisons and men from its depots in its retreat: if these accessions were not conscientiously deducted they would take the place

---

documents from the French archives, and this return may have been among them. The mistake leads Fortescue to doubt Wellington's statement that he had captured 137 officers and between six and seven thousand men, while the correct figure fits neatly with these totals. Oman, *History*, vol. 5, pp. ix, 469n; Fortescue, *History of the British Army*, vol. 8, p. 504n; Sarramon, *La Bataille des Arapiles*, pp. 423–5; *Wellington's Dispatches*, vol. 5, p. 756.

in the figures of men who had been killed, wounded or captured in the campaign. But with all its problems, Lamartinière's return provides by far the most detailed and useful insight into the losses of Marmont's army in the campaign.[*]

Altogether Martinien lists 447 French officer casualties for the campaign, Lamartinière 394. However, comparing the figures for each unit shows that there are 94 officers listed by Martinien but not included by Lamartinière, most of whom were, presumably, slightly wounded; while a further 41 officers are listed by Lamartinière but not by Martinien, these largely being unwounded prisoners. This gives a total of 488 French officer casualties, but this is certainly still an underestimate, for there must have been many occasions when the true figure was greater than that given by either authority. For example, a unit which had seven wounded officers, plus three more slightly wounded, plus three unwounded prisoners: both Martinien and Lamartinière would show this unit as having lost ten officer casualties, although the true result is thirteen. There is no way of accurately calculating the scale of this problem, but if we make a moderate guess and add a further 32 casualties to allow for it, and for those occasions when Lamartinière's figures were subject to fudging or some other distortion, we are left with a total of 520 French officer casualties for the campaign as a whole. Obviously this figure is far from precise, but it seems quite plausible.

If we accept the figure of 520 officer casualties, at least as a working hypothesis, it means that Lamartinière's 394 understates the 'correct' figure by one-quarter. Applying this to Lamartinière's figure for rank-and-file losses would give a total of 520 officers and 16,055 men, or 16,575 casualties suffered in the campaign.[†] However, it seems probable that this figure is too high, and that Lamartinière's figures are somewhat more accurate for rank and file than for officers. Certainly officers appear underrepresented in his table of casualties: there is barely one officer for every 31 men, while in the army there was one officer for every 25 men. It was most unusual for officers to suffer casualties at a lower rate than their men, although this may be because of the thousands of

---

[*] There is one well-documented case where the 'slightly wounded' explanation will not work, which helps to explain Oman's distrust of Lamartinière's return. At Garcia Hernandez, one battalion of the 76th Ligne was caught by Bock's cavalry and suffered severely. Martinien records 8 officer casualties (one killed and seven wounded); Lamartinière records 16 (eleven killed or taken, five more wounded). But Oman's painstaking search through official British prisoner rolls produced the names of sixteen officers of the regiment who were captured on the occasion, only two of whom appear in Martinien's list. When the remaining six officers whom Martinien names are added, the total losses of the 76th rise to 22 officers. This example certainly warns us against trusting too much to the combination of our two authorities, but if it damages Lamartinière's credibility (17 officers were captured or killed, not the 11 he gives), it counts even more heavily against any attempt to calculate French losses purely by extrapolating from Martinien's record of officer casualties, for Martinien, of course, only counts the eight officers who were killed or wounded.

[†] To make up for the lost quarter, one needs to add one-third of the lower figure: one-third of three-quarters is one-quarter.

prisoners included in the figures (officers where normally underrepresented among prisoners). It is also easy to imagine that slightly wounded officers would be more likely to stay with their unit than similarly wounded men, especially in the aftermath of a defeat. It therefore seems reasonable to increase Lamartinière's figure for rank and file by a rather lower proportion than the figure for officers. Again there is no reliable guide, but an increase of 20 per cent (compared to 33 per cent for the officers) seems a reasonable compromise. This produces the following French losses for the campaign:

officers	520
men	14,449
total	14,969

From here it is relatively simple to calculate French losses in the actual battle, by simply deducting losses in the lesser actions between 18 July and 8 August (the period covered by Lamartinière's return). Two methods are used. Foy's division was little engaged in the battle, but lost very heavily on the following day at Garcia Hernandez, and unfortunately Martinien combines the losses for both actions. Therefore an arbitrary figure of 200 casualties is supposed to cover its losses on 22 July in the skirmishing around Nuestra Señora de la Peña in the morning and late in the day in the course of its retreat. The remainder of its losses are assumed to have occurred at Garcia Hernandez or at other points in the campaign. For other units, the casualties given by Lamartinière are divided in the same proportion as the officer casualties given by Martinien. Thus, if Martinien says that a unit lost three officer casualties on the 18th and seven on the 22nd, 30 per cent of its total losses are assumed to have occurred on the 18th and 70 per cent in the battle. Clearly the small number of officer casualties in individual units will produce distortions, but these are likely to cancel each other out. The result of these calculations (adjusted to allow for Lamartinière's understatement in the same way as the figures for the campaign as a whole) is that the lesser actions of the campaign cost the French army 91 officers and 2,403 men, or 2,494 in all.

Losses in the whole campaign	14,969
deduct losses in lesser actions	2,494
leaves losses in the battle	12,475

No one who has followed these calculations will believe that this figure is anything more than a rough approximation: it rests on too many untestable assumptions, although a figure of between twelve and thirteen thousand seems about right, given the very large number of prisoners taken in the battle. It is reassuring that Sir Charles Oman comes to a fairly similar figure by a quite different route. He bases his calculations on a combination of extrapolating from

French officer casualties as given by Martinien, and the figures given in some French regimental histories. He concludes that Marmont's army lost some 14,000 men in the campaign, which, when his estimates of losses on the Guarena, on the march and at Garcia Hernandez are deducted, leaves losses in the battle at 11,700.[*]

In the following table the first column identifies the unit, the next three give its strength on 15 July (officers, men, total). The next column gives the total number of officer casualties for the campaign as recorded by Martinien. Then follow figures from Lamartinière's return:

> – officers listed as killed or taken
> – officers listed as wounded
> – men listed as killed or taken
> – men listed as wounded
> – men listed as missing
> – total according to Lamartinière.

Finally, there are the losses according to Lamartinière as a percentage of the unit's total strength on 15 July.

---

[*] Oman does not always make it clear that the figure of 14,000 is for the campaign as a whole, not just the battle; indeed, on page 469 he implies the opposite, but the truth emerges unmistakably from a close study of his calculations which are based on officer casualties covering the whole campaign. Oman, *History*, vol. 5, pp. 600–6.

French Army

	Strength on 15 July from Oman, History, vol. 5, pp. 601–3			Martinien officer casualties	Lamartinière's return					Total loss	% Loss
	officers	men	total		officers killed or taken	wounded	men killed or taken	wounded	missing		
1st Division (Foy)											
6th Léger (2 btns)	46*	1,055	1,101*	11	7	7	390	87	2	493	44.8%
69th Ligne (2 btns)	50	1,408	1,458	10	3	–	120	81	4	208	14.3%
39th Ligne (2 btns)	49	918	967	2	–	2	57	30	–	89	9.2%
76th Ligne (2 btns)	56	1,351	1,407	8	11	5	314	176	–	506	36.0%
Artillery etc	7	207	214	no separate figures: see combined total at end							
Total	208	4,939	5,147	31	21	14	881	374	6	1,296	26.3%†
2nd Division (Clausel)											
25th Léger (3 btns)	54	1,485	1,539	20	5	11	116	206	17	355	23.1%
27th Ligne (2 btns)	40	1,637	1,677	7	5	6	150	165	26	352	21.0%
50th Ligne (3 btns)	52	1,490	1,542	27	10	16	280	203	–	509	33.0%
59th Ligne (2 btns)	47	1,531	1,578	19	9	6	217	202	68	502	31.8%
Artillery etc	7	219	226	no separate figures: see combined total at end							
Total	200	6,362	6,562	73	29	39	763	776	111	1,718	27.1%†
3rd Division (Ferey)											
31st Léger (2 btns)	46	1,359	1,405	9	2	5	66	203	–	276	19.6%
26th Ligne (2 btns)	44	1,145	1,189	6	1	5	286	53	–	345	29.0%
47th Ligne (3 btns)	67†	1,558‡	1,625†	17	4	10	97	106	57	274	16.9%
70th Ligne (2 btns)	49	1,114	1,163	5	3	1	36	43	23	106	9.1%
Artillery etc	5	302	307	no separate figures: see combined total at end							
Total	211	5,478	5,689	37	10	21	485	405	80	1,001	18.6%†

* Fortescue says 6th Léger had 36 officers and a total of 1,091 all ranks.

† This percentage is based on the strength and losses of the infantry regiments only, as the casualties for each battery are unavailable.

‡ Fortescue says 47th Ligne had 66 officers and 1,628 men, a total of 1,694 all ranks.

				Martinien officer casualties	Lamartinière's return						
	officers	men	total		officers killed or taken	officers wounded	men killed or taken	men wounded	missing	Total loss	% loss
4th Division (Sarrut)											
2nd Léger (3 btns)	66	1,772	1,838	3	3	2	43	54	55	154	8.4%
36th Ligne (3 btns)	69	1,570	1,639	3	—	2	63	47	31	143	8.7%
4th Léger (3 btns)	63	1,219	1,282	2	—	1	52	19	15	87	6.8%
Artillery etc	5	238	243	no separate figures: see combined total at end							
Total	203	4,799	5,002	8	—	5	158	120	101	384	8.1%†
5th Division (Maucune)											
15th Ligne (3 btns)	52	1,615	1,667	16	9	8	336	177	77	607	36.4%
66th Ligne (2 btns)	38	1,131	1,169	17	5	5	468	61	49	588	50.3%
82nd Ligne (2 btns)	41	966	1,007	8	1	9	185	60	17	272	27.0%
86th Ligne (2 btns)	30	1,155	1,185	3	3	2	196	69	—	270	22.8%
Artillery etc	4	212	216	no separate figures: see combined total at end							
Total	165	5,079	5,244	44	18	24	1,185	367	143	1,737	34.5%†
6th Division (Taupin)											
17th Léger (2 btns)	46*	1,074*	1,120*	11	4	5	130	104	19	262	23.4%
65th Ligne (3 btns)	59	1,527	1,586	12	3	7	204	106	39	359	22.6%
22nd Ligne (3 btns)	61	1,486	1,547	26	21	7	849	129	—	1,006	65.0%
Régiment de Prusse (remnant)	9	79	88	no casualty figures appear for this detachment							
Artillery etc	4	213	217	no separate figures: see combined total at end							
Total	179	4,379	4,558	49	28	19	1,183	339	58	1,627	38.3%†
7th Division (Thomières)											
1st Ligne (3 btns)	80	1,683	1,763	4	1	2	176	22	29	230	13.0%
62nd Ligne (2 btns)	47	1,076	1,123	15	12	8	637	203	8	868	77.3%
101st Ligne (3 btns)	61	1,388	1,449	25	19	12	920	225	10	1,186	81.8%
Artillery etc	5	203	208	no separate figures: see combined total at end							
Total	193	4,350	4,543	44	32	22	1,733	450	47	2,284	52.7%†

* Fortescue says 17th Léger had 46 officers, 1,047 men, a total of 1,091 all ranks.

† This percentage is based on the strength and losses of the infantry regiments only, as the casualties for each battery are unavailable.

	officers	men	total	Martinien officer casualties	Lamartinière's return officers killed or taken	officers wounded	men killed or taken	men wounded	missing	Total loss	% loss
8th Division (Bonnet)											
118th Ligne (3 btns)	53*	1,584	1,637*	20	2	12	231	162	–	407	24.9%
119th Ligne (3 btns)	64	1,265	1,329	26	5	15	145	169	–	334	25.1%
120th Ligne (3 btns)	63	1,745	1,808	8	–	5	158	132	17	312	17.3%
122nd Ligne (3 btns)	55	1,582	1,637	16	4	17	181	274	51	527	32.2%
Artillery etc	3	107	110	no separate figures: see combined total at end							
Total	238	6,283	6,521	70	11	49	715	737	68	1,580	24.6%
Light Cavalry Division (Curto)											
3rd Hussars (2 sqdns)	17	231	248	4	1	1	22	22	–	46	18.5%
22nd Chasseurs (2 sqdns)	17	236	253	6	–	1	8	23	–	32	12.6%
26th Chasseurs (2 sqdns)	16	278	294	4	–	–	19	38	–	57	19.4%
28th Chasseurs (1 sqdn)	7	87	94	2	–	1	5	6	–	12	12.8%
13th Chasseurs (5 sqdns)	20	496	516	7	–	–	60	19	4	83	16.1%
14th Chasseurs (4 squadrons)	14	308	322	8	4	2	38	19	21	84	26.1%
Escadron de marche	11	141	152	–	–	–	–	–	–	–	–
Total	102	1,777	1,879	31	5	5	152	127	25	314	16.7%
Dragoon Division (Boyer)											
6th Dragoons (2 sqdns)	19	376	395	9	–	6	45	37	–	88	22.3%
11th Dragoons (2 sqdns)	19	411	430	5	–	7	58	60	–	125	29.1%
15th Dragoons (2 sqdns)	15	328	343	3	1	–	39	–	–	40	11.7%
25th Dragoons (2 sqdns)	18	314	332	10	–	6	36	24	–	66	19.9%
Artillery Attached to Cavalry	3	193	196	no separate figures: see combined total at end							
Total	74	1,622	1,696	27	1	19	178	121	–	319	21.3%†
Total Cavalry	176	3,399	3,575	58	6	24	330	248	25	633	18.7%†‡

* Fortescue says 118th Ligne had 54 officers and a total of 1,638 all ranks.

† This percentage is based on the strength and losses of the dragoons alone, as the casualties for the attached artillery are not given separately, but combined with the rest of the artillery.

‡ This percentage is based on the strength and losses of the cavalry alone, as the casualties for the attached artillery are not given separately, but combined with the rest of the artillery.

| | | | | Martinien | Lamartinière's return | | | | | | |
	officers	men	total	officer casualties	officers killed or taken	officers wounded	men killed or taken	men wounded	men missing	Total loss	% loss
Artillery Reserve, Park etc	50	1,450	1,500	no breakdown of casualties available							
Artillery Attached to Divisions (as already given above)	43	1,894	1,937								
Total Artillery	93	3,344	3,437	7	2	5	96	51	6	160	4.7%
Engineers and Sappers	17	332	349	3	–	1	–	–	–	1	–
Gendarmerie	6	129	135	–	–	–	–	–	–	–	–
Équipages militaires	26	742	768	–	–	–	–	–	–	–	–
État-Major Général	54	–	54	23	5	9	–	–	–	14	–
Total Auxiliary Arms	103	1,203	1,306	26	5	10	–	–	–	15	1.1%
Totals											
Infantry Divisions*	1,557	39,968	41,525*	356	149	193	7,103	3,568	614	11,627	28.0%
Cavalry Divisions*	173	3,206	3,379*	58	6	24	330	248	25	633	18.7%
Total Artillery	93	3,344	3,437	7	2	5	96	51	6	160	4.7%
Auxiliary Arms	103	1,203	1,306	26	5	10	–	–	–	15	1.1%
				447	162	232	7,529	3,867	645	12,435	25.0%

Total strength on 15 July   1,926 officers; 47,721 men: 49,647 total

Total officer casualties listed by Martinien   447

Total casualties according to Lamartinière:

	officers	men	total
killed or captured	162	7,529	7,691
wounded	232	3,867	4,099
missing	–	645	645
Total	394	12,041	12,435	25.0%

Of these casualties:
61.8% are listed as killed or captured
33.0% are listed as wounded
5.2% are listed as missing

*Excludes divisional artillery.

Estimate of French Losses on the 22nd

The strength of each unit is based on the return of 15 July – no deduction is made for losses on the 18th or men who fell out on the campaign. Column A gives the total losses of each division according to Lamartinière's return, minus an estimate of their losses in the other actions of the campaign. Column B adjusts the figure in A to allow for slightly wounded men who had returned to the ranks by 8 August and other understatements in Lamartinière's return. The result is only a rough estimate – too inaccurate to apply to individual regiments. The percentages which follow are based on the strength of each division not counting the divisional artillery (whose losses are collected in the single-line entry for artillery). The gunners are included in the strength of each division and again under artillery, but this double counting has been removed from the total.

	strength	A	B	A as %	B as %
1st Division (Foy)	5,147	200	(241)	4.0%	(4.9%)
2nd Division (Clausel)	6,562	1,610	(1,941)	25.4%	(30.6%)
3rd Division (Ferey)	5,689	939	(1,131)	17.4%	(21.0%)
4th Division (Sarrut)	5,002	384	(462)	8.1%	(9.7%)
5th Division (Maucune)	5,244	1,737	(2,090)	34.5%	(41.6%)
6th Division (Taupin)	4,558	1,152	(1,386)	26.5%	(31.9%)
7th Division (Thomières)	4,543	2,284	(2,748)	52.7%	(63.4%)
8th Division (Bonnet)	6,521	1,457	(1,755)	22.7%	(27.4%)
Light Cavalry (Curto)	1,879	253	(304)	13.5%	(16.2%)
Dragoon Division (Boyer)	1,696	188	(237)	12.5%	(15.8%)
Artillery	3,437	137	(163)	4.0%	(4.7%)
Miscellaneous	1,306	13	(17)	1.0%	(1.3%)
Total	49,647*	10,354	(12,475)	20.9%	25.1%

* Gross total 51,584 minus 1,937 to allow for gunners counted both with the divisions to which they were attached and in the line for Artillery leaves a net total of 49,647.

Other French Losses in the Campaign

On 18 July (see Appendix I for details)	34 officers	+	662 men	=	696 (834)
At Garcia Hernandez (Foy's division only)	30 officers	+	1,066 men	=	1,096 (1,314)
Minor actions, mostly 24 July–8 August	14 officers	+	275 men	=	289 (346)
Total	78 officers	+	2,003 men	=	2,081 (2,494)

(The figures for officers are from Martinien; those for men are based on Lamartinière. The figure in brackets is adjusted to allow for the understatement in each source: Martinien is multiplied by approximately 1.163 (520 ÷ 447); Lamartinière by 1.2 – see text of this appendix for explanation.)

Losses in minor actions other than 18 July and Garcia Hernandez are based on officer casualties recorded by Martinien with a proportionate number of men added:

3rd Division (Ferey)	lost 2 officers	+	60 men	=	62 casualties
8th Division (Bonnet)	lost 5 officers	+	118 men	=	123 casualties
Light Cavalry (Curto)	lost 1 officer	+	4 men	=	5 casualties
Dragoons (Boyer)	lost 4 officers	+	71 men	=	75 casualties
Artillery	lost 1 officer	+	22 men	=	23 casualties
Miscellaneous	lost 1 officer	+	– men	=	1 casualty
Total	14 officers	+	275 men	=	289 casualties

Appendix IV

Letter Describing the Battle, Possibly Written by Major-General Henry Campbell

Among the Hope of Luffness Papers in the National Archives of Scotland in Edinburgh, there is a contemporary copy of a letter to Colonel Herbert Taylor from a senior officer in Wellington's army. Taylor had been private secretary to both the Duke of York (1799–1805) and King George III (1805–12) and remained an important, though discreet, figure at Court and at the Horse Guards. The copy of the letter is written in a clear clerk's hand and is signed only 'H. C.', but it is headed 'Copy of a Letter from M. General Henry Clinton, Commanding the 6th Division of Lord Wellington's Army, to Colonel Taylor'. However, there are several reasons for believing that this was a mistake – presumably made by the copyist – and that the letter was actually written by Major-General Henry Campbell, commander of the First Division. Here is the full text of the letter:

Cantaracillo, Saturday 25th July 1812

I cannot let the Mail go without a line to tell you that I am quite safe and well after the Action which has terminated a week of almost incessant Marching and Manoeuvring by the most complete defeat and total deroute of Marmont's Army. I have seen a Person who passed through them Yesterday, when they were still running as fast as weakness, fatigue, and hunger would allow them, not merely along the Road, but in Crowds on each side of it, and all in the greatest hurry and disorder, a very large proportion having thrown away their Arms. I cannot attempt now to give you an account of the Battle, but I will try a short sketch of the events of this highly interesting week.

On Sunday last our whole Army was collected near Canizal, and on the south side of the River Guarena (only a muddy ditch) in the Evening we moved out to a Position with our Left towards Canizal, and our rear to Vallesa.

On Monday morning both Armies were in sight opposite each other the French did not begin to move till long after Daylight, when they filed off to their left in high style, Bands playing etc etc. We formed in two Lines and offered them Battle, but they heeded us not, and walking quietly and steadily, yet rapidly round us made a great Circuit, and got on some very Commanding Hills on our right. We then wheeled our two Lines into Columns & moved along the Valley parallel to them, making a much smaller Circle within theirs, at one place where the Valley narrowed, they Cannonaded us, and several Shot fell over and near our Column but did no harm, soon after, we separated more, kept away to our Right and halted at the Village Cabeza Vellosa [Cabezabellosa], they bore away to their left down towards the Tormes.

The new Day at daybreak we also moved down to the Tormes, and halted on the right bank a very little above Salamanca; in the Evening we crossed the River at the Ford of St Martha and took up a Position with our Left on the River, our Right on high strong Ground, Salamanca being in our rear. We had a dreadful night of Thunder, Lightning, and Rain – The Horses of the Heavy Cavalry frightened at the Thunder, broke away and linked together as they were went directly over the Men who were asleep and maimed a great many – 50 Horses were missing in the Morning.

On Wednesday all was again quiet till long after daylight, but then a popping began in front, and kept increasing for some time. About 9 O'Clock we got an Order to quit the Ground we had occupied in the night, and the whole Army moved gaining Ground to the right, and to the front also; the French in the mean-while had got on a very Commanding Hill close in our front, from which they could see all that we did, and behind which they were playing the old Game again and stretching away to turn our right. Lord W. at one time determined to attack them, and sent for me, and told me to move forward in two Columns up a Hill in front of our Right, where this Division then was, and attack their left, while the 4th Division was to attack them in front, but I had hardly put the Columns in motion, before I recd. a Counter Order and moved back to the Ground I had quitted. We remained there some time and then got an order to Countermarch and move quite to the left to occupy some high Ground that other Divisions were quitting; but by the time we got there, the French shewed a large Force on the Hill we were to have attacked and opened a great many Guns there and kept advancing them from one point to another & Cannonading us in a very bullying way, treating us exactly like a beaten and retreating Army. This at last roused the Earl's indignation, and he determined to shew them, it was not come exactly to that, and attack them which was done as soon as thought, they were driven from all the strong Ground they had occupied on our Right in high style and their Left completely beat back, they then made a stand in their Centre, where the Portuguese giving way, made things look a little awkward for a time, but they were driven back from that by the 6th Division; their Right then formed on a Hill and made a last effort, where they were attacked just as the Moon was rising by the Light Division in two Lines supported by the 1st. They kept up a smart fire as we ascended the Hill, but on some Guns opening from a Hill on our Left they turned and ran for it, and must have made very good play for we followed them in the same order, the Light Division in two Lines, and the first in two Columns, one on each of its Flanks to support it till near 1 O'Clock in the Morning, going all the time at the rate of near 4 miles an hour, without over-taking more than a very few stragglers and wounded, but as a great deal of our way was thro' a very thick wood, we must have passed a great many that were picked up by others in our Rear. It is the first time I suppose, that ever Troops marched in Line for four hours across Country in the night, and they were in a very good Line when they halted, and our Columns also were in order to have wheeled into Line directly. We halted about one near the Village of Calvarrasa de Abajo.

At 5 we marched again and crossed the Tormes, a little below Alba de Tormes, and soon after near the Village of La Serra; the Cavalry that led our Columns came up with their Rear Guard, which they attacked in the most brilliant style, and made about 1,500 Prisoners at one haul [?]; as we got to one brow we could see them going up in the greatest disorder, but too far ahead to get up with them; the Peer tried to get them to stop, by showing only one Brigade, but they knew better & after following for nine Hours, we halted at Coca [Coca de Alba]; we moved from thence here yesterday, and today we halt to get up Stragglers that had been left with the wounded &c and Provisions; we are also nearly all barefooted, and want a day's rest or two.

The Guards have suffered but little. Two Officers Wounded, Captn Whyte, 3rd Regiment badly; Ens[ign] Hotham, Coldstreams, slightly and about 10 Men killed and 40 Wounded. Germans about the same. I believe Poor Le Marchant's death is most unfortunate, with so large a Family. All the <u>Guardsmen</u> safe and untouched, Clinton, Anson, Hulse, Wheatley, and all their Staff. God bless you, I have not time to say more – say every thing for me to all & Believe me
most truly Yours
H. C.
If Marmont had not rode the Winning Horse too hard & bullied us, we should have gone quietly back, over the Agueda; he has paid dearly for it.[*]

There are a number of reasons for believing that this letter was written by Campbell and not Clinton, some comparatively trivial, others more compelling. Both Clinton and Campbell were Guardsmen, and both would almost certainly have known Taylor, but Campbell's connection to Taylor and the Court was much stronger: Clinton had been aide-de-camp to the Duke of York, 1793–5, but Campbell had been aide-de-camp to the King in 1803 and a groom of the bedchamber from about 1809 to 1812, and went on to hold other Court appointments.[†]

The letter is dated from Cantaracillo, two or three miles east of Peñaranda. Wellington's headquarters on this day were at Flores de Avila a few miles further east, but John Mills and John Aitchison, both of the Guards brigade of the First Division, date letters of 25 July from Cantaracillo.[‡] Unfortunately, we do

[*] Hope of Luffness Papers, NAS GD 364/1/1224.

[†] Biographical details for both from Thorne, ed., *The History of Parliament, The Commons, 1790–1820*, vol. 3, pp. 372 and 451.

[‡] Aitchison, *Ensign in the Peninsular War*, p. 178 spells it Contaracilla; Mills, *For King and Country*, p. 183: his letter is dated 24 July but is continued: 'July 25th. The whole army halted this day ...' (p. 185).

not know where the Sixth Division was on this day: the only relevant source for the division is a letter from Lieutenant Robert Garrett, dated 'Camp near Penaranda, July 25th 1812',* so it is possible – although unlikely – that both the First and Sixth Divisions were in the same village on this day.

Turning to the text of the letter, there is nothing surprising in the account of the campaign, which is too general and impersonal to provide any evidence of the identity of the author. However, the description of the day of battle is more fruitful. The detailed account of Wellington's plans for an attack on the Greater Arapile, which was then cancelled, is particularly significant. Many other sources state that this operation was to be undertaken by the First and Fourth Divisions, while they give no hint that the Sixth Division was to take part.† As it is clear that this letter was written by the commander of the division which – with the Fourth Division – was to lead the attack, we must either attribute it to Campbell, or completely recast our understanding of the episode.

The letter continues by saying that the division 'move[d] quite to the left to occupy some high Ground that other Divisions were quitting'. This fits neatly with the strange movement of the First Division from behind the village of Arapiles to the left, where it replaced the Fifth Division behind the Lesser Arapile. It is not compatible with any known movement made by the Sixth Division.

Consider next the brief, bare description of the fighting in the centre: '[the French] then made a stand in their Centre, where the Portuguese giving way, made things look a little awkward for a time, but then were driven back from that by the 6th Division.' Is this really all that the commander of the Sixth Division would have to say of its advance to fill the yawning hole in the centre of the allied line, its deployment under heavy fire, its succouring of the broken units of the Fourth Division, and then of its checking and finally breaking Bonnet's counterattack? Such reticence surely goes beyond the limits of soldierly modesty.

What follows? An account of the Sixth Division's heroic – if costly – assault on Ferey's position? No, that is passed over in silence and instead we have a lengthy account of the advance of the First and Light Divisions in pursuit of the French. Furthermore, this account is full of the first person plural: '*we* ascended the hill ... *we* followed them in the same order, the Light Division in two Lines, and the first in two Columns ... a great deal of *our* way ... *we* must have passed. ... *We* halted about one ...' (emphasis added). No excessive modesty here: the account is detailed, confident and proud, although not unpleasantly boastful. Its final sentence leaves little room for argument: 'We halted about one near the Village of Calvarrasa de Abajo' – so did the First Division, while the Sixth remained near El Sierro, some six miles to the southwest.

---

* Garrett, 'A Subaltern in the Peninsular War', p. 10.
† See chapter three, pp. 56–8, 77.

The letter ends with comments on the losses of the Guards and German brigades (both in the First Division) and on the safety of various senior officers who had served in the Guards, which was a subject of particular interest at Court. This list includes 'Clinton' – odd if the letter was written by Henry Clinton, but perfectly natural if the author was Henry Campbell, commander of the First Division.

Appendix V

The Battlefield Today

The battlefield of Salamanca is generally well preserved; there have been relatively few changes since that bloody July afternoon almost two hundred years ago. It is easily accessible to visitors to Spain, being only a few miles south of the beautiful city of Salamanca, whose glorious cathedrals, ancient university and magnificent Plaza Mayor, all built in honey-coloured stone, attract thousands of tourists every summer – which in turn means that there are many excellent hotels and other facilities. The most convenient way to tour the battlefield is by car, but the most dedicated could do so on foot, by bicycle or even, conceivably, on horseback. Moving generally from west to east, one can follow the unfolding of the battle fairly well, although it means that the heights of Calvarrasa de Arriba, the scene of the skirmishing in the morning, come at the end rather than the beginning of the tour.

Start by leaving the city on the C512, which ultimately goes to Tamames. After only a few miles one reaches the village of Aldea Tejada, near which Pakenham's division, D'Urban's Portuguese dragoons and Arentschildt's light cavalry rested for an hour or two in the middle of the day. The substantial hills around the village provide ample cover, and Pakenham and his staff may have taken advantage of the extensive views from the top of the steep height immediately to the east – although this is speculation, for we do not even know exactly where the troops halted. A little unsealed country road leaves the village to the south-east: like most of the by-roads which cross the battlefield, it is quite rough but perfectly negotiable provided one is careful and remembers that there may be deep gutters on either side. This road will take one along the route probably followed by Pakenham's division in the first part of its advance. The low north–south ridge which screened the allies is clearly apparent, but the track which used to run along its foot to the south has disappeared. Instead, the by-road crosses the ridge and joins the main N 630 (E-803) road from Salamanca. Go south along the main road for less than a mile then turn right at a crossroads on to the sealed road to Miranda de Azan.

In approaching Miranda de Azan, the road runs between two steep hillsides with barely the width of the road separating them. The one on the left (south) is the Pico de Miranda, the western extremity of the Monte de Azan; the one on the right is the end of the north–south ridge – the batteries of Bull and Douglas were stationed a little way north along this rise. The village of Miranda de Azan lies a few hundred yards beyond this pass, and it is difficult to see how the five thousand infantry and thousand cavalry under Pakenham, D'Urban and Arentschildt could have deployed in such a confined space. The slopes of the Pico de Miranda are steep but not unmanageable. Climbing them with fifty pounds of equipment on one's back, under enemy fire, while maintaining one's place in close formation would be less easy, but all part of a day's work for Napoleonic infantry. The summit is flat but narrow: only fifty yards across, although it broadens considerably to the east.

Pedestrians can continue walking along the ridge, but those with cars or other means of transport need to return to them and leave Miranda de Azan the way they came, heading now north-east. Back at the main N 630 (E803) road one can turn south and follow the road up the north face of the Monte de Azan, but it is probably better to cross it and continue east towards the village of Los Arapiles. Just before the village there is a minor road turning off sharply to the south-west leading to a large, modern industrial farm. If one parks on the side of this road, one can climb across open fields to the top of the Monte de Azan due south of Las Torres. (But remember, there is no *right* of trespass, however innocent one's motives, and do nothing which could disturb stock or damage crops.) The land here accords perfectly with Leith Hay's description of his advance. It is very tempting to say to oneself at the top, 'Yes, this was the very spot on which he fell wounded.' More seriously, one can note that, while the forward slope is wide and open, there are ripples and irregularities in it, some caused by water running down it, which would have created difficulties for troops advancing in line. Equally, the summit, though broad and expansive, is not perfectly flat: there is a slight reverse slope, almost a lip, at the northern edge, then a wide expanse of open ground rising gently to another skyline perhaps half a mile away. Undulations in the ground on either side obscure the view to the east and west: one can easily see how Maucune and Clausel fought in separate compartments of the plateau, and also (although less easily) how Maucune may not have noticed the advance of Le Marchant's cavalry or Pakenham's infantry.

On returning to your car, drive into the village of Arapiles. Like all the villages on the battlefield, it has grown considerably and is not particularly picturesque or beautiful. An unsealed road heads south from the centre of the village, soon ascending the steep slope which is the north face of the Monte de Azan at this point. Beyond the slope the land is again wide, open and rolling, with another hillside perhaps a thousand yards to the south. This is probably the line of advance of Cole's Fusilier brigade – Stubbs's Portuguese were further east – and it is uncertain whether their clash with Clausel occurred at the first or second crest, although the latter seems more probable. Beyond this second crest (where this is a good view of the rear of the French position) the road becomes private so one must return to the village.

From Los Arapiles one heads east along the narrow strip of bitumen for about a mile until it reaches the railway line and divides into a number of unsealed roads. Here one is at the foot of the Lesser Arapile: those with a super-abundance of energy can climb it. An equally useful digression is to take the track north-west parallel to the railway line for a few hundred yards, then turn left (west) and drive or walk across the gap between the Lesser Arapile and the Teso de San Miguel, and then up the surprisingly steep eastern slope of the latter hill and look out across the shallow valley to the rolling country of the Monte de Azan to the south. Viewed from either the Greater or Lesser Arapile, the Teso de San Miguel appears insignificant, but closer inspection shows that, while it is far from being a mountain, it would have had considerable military importance.

However, there is no denying that the Greater and Lesser Arapiles dominate the battlefield, and that few visitors will be able to resist the temptation to climb the former, survey the view and examine the obelisk. The ground is rough and the slope steep, but it is not difficult to climb the northern face, although stout shoes and long trousers are clearly advisable. As one climbs one cannot help but think of Charles Synge's experiences, and sympathize with him and even with the Portuguese soldier he mentions who shammed death rather than face the French at the summit. The view from the top is superb: wide, bare and open. The hill itself was severely vandalized a century ago when the railway was built and it was used as a quarry. Fortunately, the north face, western end and over-all profile remain unaffected: the destruction was on the southern side, where it ate away two-thirds of the width of the hill. One can only hope that such dese-cration would not be allowed today, although the fate of the battlefield of Talavera does not give much grounds for confidence.

Again we return to the car and drive a little way back towards Los Arapiles, before turning south onto an unsealed road which passes close under the west-ern end of the Greater Arapile, and then on for almost a mile through smooth, bare country to the long, low rise of El Sierro, where Ferey made his stand. The ridge – although is scarcely deserves the name – marks a sharp boundary even today, for on the further side are low trees and scrub extending to the south-east, while on the near side the land has been swept clear for crops.

Return past the Greater Arapile to the dusty junction of minor roads by the railway line, and head east across open country which saw little or no fighting. After the road has turned north-east for a while, and when you are approach-ing Calvarrasa de Arriba (the local rubbish dump indicates its proximity), there is a side road to the left (north-west). This unpromising track leads to the foot of the heights of Calvarrasa de Arriba – a line of low cliffs which are the most striking natural feature on the generally undramatic battlefield. The Pelagarcia brook at their foot is trifling, although the reed-beds which enclose it might be thirty or even fifty yards wide in places. The heights themselves dwindle as they go north, but it is well worth the scramble to climb up to the chapel of Nuestra Señora de la Peña near their summit. Look west across the shallow valley to the gentle, low heights which were occupied by the allied army at the beginning of the day, while further to the south are the Lesser and Greater Arapiles.

For those with the time and energy, it is not a long drive (about six miles) from Calvarrasa de Arriba to Alba de Tormes (on the C510). Much of the country is broken and some of it wooded, and although none is really difficult, Marmont's battered army would not have had an easy march in the dark. One can see why Wellington's men, weary after a long, hot and immensely demand- ing day, did not press on for the five miles from El Sierro and push the French into the river. Alba de Tormes is not a particularly pretty town, but the situ- ation is most attractive. The river is unexpectedly wide, and the fairy-tale castle rises high above the town. Whether a small Spanish garrison could have held the tower against a determined French assault – and whether, if they had done so, they really could have sustained a fire which would have prevented the flee- ing French from using the bridge at night – seems somewhat doubtful; but in any case, too much has generally been made of this issue, for, as Soult's retreat from Oporto showed, a French army could almost always find some means of escape and, however much it suffered in the process, it would soon recover and be ready to take the field again.

Although the distances on the battlefield are short it would take a minimum of one very full day to visit and appreciate the points mentioned above. If poss- ible, at least two days should be allowed, and any time over can be spent most enjoyably exploring the city.

Notes

Chapter One: The Campaign

1. There were bridges across the Tagus at Arzobispo and Talavera, but the roads leading to them were so poor that Wellington regarded them as useless for substantial bodies of troops, Wellington to Liverpool, 26 and 28 May 1812; *The Dispatches of Field Marshal the Duke of Wellington...*, compiled by Colonel Gurwood, 8 vols (London, Parker, Furnivall and Parker, 1844–7, 'enlarged edition'), vol. 5, pp. 672–3, 681. (Henceforth cited as *Wellington's Dispatches.*)

2. Wellington to Liverpool, 26 May 1812, *Wellington's Dispatches*, vol. 5, pp. 672–3.

3. Wellington to Liverpool, 18 and 25 June 1812, *Wellington's Dispatches*, vol. 5, pp. 713–16, 721–3; Major-General Sir W. F. P. Napier, *History of the War in the Peninsula and in the South of France*, 6 vols (London, Boone, 1853, new edition, revised by the author), vol. 4, p. 240 (henceforth cited simply as Napier, *History*) comments on the rough ground at the foot of the position.

4. Lieutenant-Colonel William Tomkinson, *The Diary of a Cavalry Officer in the Peninsular War and Waterloo Campaign, 1809–1815* (London, Swan Sonnenschein, 1895, 2nd edition), p. 166 gives an example of this surprise. For more on this, see commentary p. 18 and for further discussion of Wellington's reasons, see chapter 2, p. 37–9.

5. Girod de l'Ain, *Vie Militaire du Général Foy* (Paris, Plon Nourrit, 1900), pp. 165–6, quoting Foy's journal; see also Sir Charles Oman, *A History of the Peninsular War*, 7 vols (Oxford, Clarendon Press, 1902–30), vol. 5, pp. 367–8 (henceforth cited as Oman, *History*), and Jean Sarramon, *La Bataille des Arapiles (22 Juillet 1812)* (Toulouse, University of Toulouse, 1978), p. 53; Marmont does not mention the council of war in the brief account he gives of this episode in Marshal A. F. L. V. de Marmont, Duc de Raguse, *Mémoires du Maréchal Marmont, Duc de Raguse*, 9 vols (Paris, Perrotin, 1857), vol. 4, p. 117.

6. Wellington's views are reflected in his letters: for his early hopes see his letters to Graham, 3 July 1812 and to Bathurst, 4 and 7 July, *Wellington's Dispatches*, vol. 5, pp. 731–2, 733, 735–6; for his growing concern see the two letters quoted: to Hill, 13 July, and to Sir Henry Wellesley, 14 July, *ibid.*, pp. 741–2, 745, and also other letters of this period. The changing plans are also recorded in the letters of Alexander Gordon, one of Wellington's most trusted ADCs, to his brother Lord Aberdeen, 7 and 14 July, and to Lord Bathurst, 14 July which criticizes Bentinck, Aberdeen Papers, BL Add. Ms 43,224, ff. 88–9, 90–1 and Bathurst Papers, BL Loan Ms 57, vol. 5, f. 487.

7. Napier, *History*, vol. 4, p. 249.

8. Charles Boutflower, *The Journal of an Army Surgeon during the Peninsular War* (Staplehurst, Spellmount, 1997, first published 1912), p. 145; Augustus Mockler-Ferryman, *The Life of a Regimental Officer during the Great War, 1793–1815 ... from the Correspondence of Col. Samuel Rice, 51st Light Infantry* (Edinburgh, Blackwood, 1913), pp. 210–11.

9. For an account of this see Mark Urban, *The Man Who Broke Napoleon's Codes* (London, Faber, forthcoming), esp. chapters 10–14.

10. The Hon. J. W. Fortescue, *A History of the British Army*, 13 vols in 20 (London, Macmillan, 1899–1930), vol. 8, p. 472.

11. Wellington to Clinton, 7 pm, 16 July 1812, *Wellington's Dispatches*, vol. 5, pp. 748–9.

12. Napier, *History*, vol. 4, p. 254.

13. Captain J. Kincaid, *Adventures in the Rifle Brigade and Random Shots from a Rifleman* (Glasgow, Richard Drew, 1981, first published 1830–5), p. 78; Tomkinson, *Diary of a Cavalry Officer*, pp. 180–2.

14. Charles Broke Vere, *Marches, Movements and Operations of the 4th Division* ... (Ipswich, privately printed, 1841), p. 28 describes the halt by the river as short; Burgoyne (also Fourth Division) says 'about an hour' in George Wrottesley, *The Life and Correspondence of Field Marshal Sir John Burgoyne*, 2 vols (London, Bentley, 1873), vol. 1, p. 197; Leith Hay (of the Fifth Division) implies that the halt was fairly brief, Sir Andrew Leith Hay, *A Narrative of the Peninsular War* (London, Captain John Hearne, 1839, 3rd edition), p. 244; T. H. Browne (staff) also implies a halt, Captain T. H. Browne, *The Napoleonic War Journal of Captain Thomas Henry Browne, 1807–1816*, ed. by Roger Norman Buckley (London, Bodley Head for the Army Records Society, 1987), p. 163; Fortescue, *History of the British Army*, vol. 8, p. 475n cites several Light Division sources, implying only a brief, and

perhaps undisciplined, scramble for water. Many other sources naturally do not mention the episode at all.

15. P. Castel, *Relation de la Bataille et Retraite des Arapiles* (Toulouse, J.-B. Cazaux, 1854), p. 11; Sarramon, *La Bataille des Arapiles*, pp. 173–4; Oman, *History*, vol. 5, p. 405.

16. Captain William Bragge, *Peninsular Portrait, 1811–1814. The Letters of Captain William Bragge, Third (King's Own) Dragoons*, ed. by S. A. C. Cassels (London, Oxford University Press, 1963), p. 73 – see commentary, pp. 20–1 for discussion.

17. Sarramon, *La Bataille des Arapiles*, p. 174.

18. See Appendix I for details of losses on 18 July, and commentary, pp. 21–2 for discussion.

19. So say Oman, *History*, vol. 5, p. 406, and Sarramon, *La Bataille des Arapiles*, p. 175, but it is not clear on what authority, other than the fact that all three regiments lost quite heavily.

20. Castel, *Relation de la Bataille et Retraite des Arapiles*, p. 11.

21. Vere, *Marches, Movements ...*, *4th Division* p. 29, confirmed by Browne, *Napoleonic War Journal*, p. 163.

22. Browne, *Napoleonic War Journal*, p. 163.

23. Boutflower, *Journal of an Army Surgeon*, p. 146; Browne, *Napoleonic War Journal*, p. 163 (Browne was a lieutenant at the battle and subsequently promoted); George Hennell, *A Gentleman Volunteer. The Letters of George Hennell from the Peninsular War, 1812–1813*, ed. by Michael Glover (London, Heinemann, 1979), p. 28.

24. Castel, *Relation de la Bataille et Retraite des Arapiles*, pp. 11–12.

25. Sarramon, *La Bataille des Arapiles*, p. 175, although first-hand British accounts are more inclined to mention the French artillery than any fresh force of infantry.

26. A. Martinien, *Tableaux par Corps et par Batailles des Officiers Tués et Blessés pendant les Guerres de l'Empire (1805–1815)* (Paris, Éditions Militaires Européennes, nd [1980s], – first

published 1899) and *Supplement* (Paris, Fournier, 1909) (henceforth the combined evidence from both is cited simply as Martinien). The British took some 240 prisoners, most of whom would have been wounded men who could not make their escape when their unit broke, Wellington to Bathurst, 21 July 1812, *Wellington's Dispatches*, vol. 5, p. 750. See commentary, pp. 21–2 and Appendices I and III for further discussion of casualty figures.

27. See Appendix I and commentary, p. 21 for casualty details and discussion.

28. Napier, *History*, vol. 4, pp. 258–9.

29. Cathcart to Sir Thomas Graham, 31 July 1812, Lynedoch Papers, NLS Ms 3610, ff. 187–96. Cathcart had been on Graham's staff and had remained with the army when Graham returned home, although his precise position in July 1812 is not clear.

30. Tomkinson, *Diary of a Cavalry Officer*, p. 188; however, neither Oman (*History*, vol. 5, p. 415) nor Fortescue (*History of the British Army*, vol. 8, p. 478) repeats this, and some of the details, such as the strength of the Spanish force, are incorrect.

31. John Green, *The Vicissitudes of a Soldier's Life ... 1806–1815* (Louth, privately printed, 1827), pp. 97–8.

32. Kincaid, *Adventures in the Rifle Brigade*, p. 81.

33. Pakenham to Murray, 24 August 1812, Murray Papers NLS, Adv. Ms 46.2.15, vol. 38, ff. 148–51.

34. Anon *The Personal Narrative of a Private Soldier, Who Served in the Forty-Second Highlanders, for Twelve Years, during the Late War* (Cambridge, Trotman, 1996, first published 1821), pp. 122–3. The author had been made a corporal at Salamanca (p. 121). The suggestion that Graham went home in disgust appears to be ill-founded – the problem with his eyes was both genuine and serious. Antony Brett-James, *General Graham, Lord Lynedoch* (London, Macmillan, 1959), p. 254.

35. Spencer Moggridge [Thomas Hamilton], 'Letters from the Peninsula. No IV: The Battle of Salamanca', *Blackwood's Edinburgh Magazine*, vol. 23, no. 138 (May 1828), p. 537 – see p. 81 for a discussion of this source.

36. Tomkinson, *Diary of a Cavalry Officer*, pp. 180–1.

37. Lord Granville Leveson Gower, *Lord Granville Leveson Gower (First Earl Granville), Private Correspondence, 1781–1821*, ed. by Castalia, Countess Granville, 2 vols (London, John Murray, 1916), vol. 2, p. 450; for casualties see Appendix I.

38. Lieutenant-Colonel C. Campbell to Torrens, 25 July 1812, Hope of Luffness Papers, NAS GD 364/1/1224; Hennell, *A Gentleman Volunteer*, p. 28; Browne, *Napoleonic War Journal*, p. 162.

39. Major George Simmons, *A British Rifleman. The Journals and Correspondence of Major George Simmons ...*, ed. by Lieutenant-Colonel W. Verner (London, A&C Black, 1899), p. 239; see also Lieutenant-Colonel J. Leach, *Rough Sketches of the Life of an Old Soldier* (Cambridge, Trotman, 1986, first published 1831), p. 266.

40. Burgoyne in Wrottesley, *Life and Correspondence of ... Burgoyne*, pp. 196–7; Boutflower, *Journal of an Army Surgeon*, p. 146.

41. Castel, *Relation de la Bataille et Retraite des Arapiles*, pp. 10–11.

42. N. L. Beamish, *History of the King's German Legion*, 2 vols (London, T&W Boone, 1832–7), vol. 2, pp. 64–5; Daniel S. Gray, 'The Services of the King's German Legion in the Army of the Duke of Wellington: 1809–1815' (unpublished PhD thesis presented to Florida State University in 1970), pp. 245–8.

43. Burgoyne in Wrottesley, *Life and Correspondence, of ... Burgoyne*, p. 198; Bragge, *Peninsular Portrait*, p. 73 – see also Lieutenant John Massey (3rd Dragoons) to his brother Dick, 4 August 1812. Letters of Lieutenant John Massey NAM Ms 7804–14; Browne, *Napoleonic War Journal*, p. 163.

44. Wellington to Bathurst, 21 July 1812, *Wellington's Dispatches*, vol. 5, p. 750; Burgoyne in Wrottesley, *Life and Correspondence of ... Burgoyne*, pp. 197–8; Browne, *Napoleonic War Journal*, p. 163.

45. Cathcart to Graham, 31 July 1812, Lynedoch Papers, NLS Ms 3610, ff. 187–96; Campbell to Torrens, 25 July 1812, Hope of Luffness Papers, NAS GD 364/1/1224; Pakenham to Murray, 24 August 1812, Murray Papers, NLS Adv. Ms 46.2.15, vol. 38, ff. 148–51; Hennell, *Gentleman Volunteer*, p. 28; Castel, *Relation de la Bataille et Retraite des Arapiles*, pp. 11–13.

46. PRO WO 1/255, pp. 91–2, 'Return of Killed, Wounded and Missing on 18th July 1812'. G. Anson's three regiments lost sixteen, nineteen and fifteen casualties – seventeen more than Oman gives, *History*, vol. 5, p. 607. *Wellington's Dispatches*, vol. 5, p. 752; Tomkinson, *Diary of a Cavalry Officer*, pp. 182–3.

47. Napier, *History*, vol. 4, pp. 253–7; Oman *History*, vol. 5, pp. 401–7; Fortescue, *History of the British Army*, vol. 8, pp. 473–6; Peter Young and J. P. Lawford, *Wellington's Masterpiece. The Battle and Campaign of Salamanca* (London, Allen & Unwin, 1973), pp. 186–91; Sarramon, *La Bataille des Arapiles*, pp. 173–6.

Chapter Two: Armies and Generals

1. For more on this issue see my *Tactics and the Experience of Battle in the Age of Napoleon* (New Haven and London, Yale University Press, 1998), pp. 201–7.

2. Figures: French from Fortescue, *History of the British Army*, vol. 8, p. 636; allies from Sir A. Dickson, *The Dickson Manuscripts*, ed. by J. H. Leslie, 5 vols (Cambridge, Trotman, 1990, first published 1908), vol. 4, pp. 685–6. These figures assume that the Spanish battery of 6-pounders included one howitzer.

3. One of the four 18-pounders that had

originally advanced with the army had been disabled and rendered unfit for further service during the siege of the forts, Major-General John T. Jones *Journal of the Sieges Carried On by the Army under the Duke of Wellington ...*, 3 vols (London, John Weale, 1846, 3rd edition), vol. 1, pp. 259, 262.

4. [William Grattan], 'Reminiscences of a Subaltern: Battle of Salamanca', *USJ*, June 1834, p. 175; John Aitchison, *An Ensign in the Peninsular War. The Letters of John Aitchison*, ed. by W. F. K. Thompson (London, Michael Joseph, 1981), p. 178.

5. Oman, *History*, vol. 3, p. 542, vol. 4, p. 361.

6. *Ibid.*, vol. 4, p. 225.

7. Although the 120th Ligne had served at Medina del Rio Seco in 1808 – see Martinien.

8. Most of the prior history of the regiments has been derived from Martinien supplemented by histories of particular campaigns: for example, on the 122nd Ligne at Coruña see Oman, *History*, vol. 1, p. 585n and vol. 5, p. 391n.

9. *Dickson Manuscripts*, vol. 4, p. 685; Emilio Becerra de Becerra, *Hazañas de Unos Lanceros – Diarios de Julián Sánchez 'El Charro'* (Diputación Provincial de Salamanca, 1999), p. 107. I am grateful to Bernabe Saiz Martínez de Pisón for bringing this source to my attention.

10. Counting detachments of 2nd and 3rd/95th Rifles as one battalion and the eight companies of 1st/95th as another.

11. Wellington to Bathurst, 14 July 1812, *Wellington's Dispatches*, vol. 5, p. 743 mentions that the 5th, 38th and 83rd Regiments are en route, and that he also expects two thousand drafts and convalescents to join in the following three weeks.

12. There is a good account of the origins and reputations of each division in Sir Charles Oman, *Wellington's Army, 1809–1814* (London, Greenhill, 1986, first published 1913), pp. 167–75, especially pp. 172–3.

13. Oman, *History*, vol. 4, p. 391.

14. The best sketch of Marmont's career is

in R. P. Dunn-Pattison, *Napoleon's Marshals* (London, Methuen, 1909), pp. 200–18; but see also John Pimlott's essay in David Chandler, ed., *Napoleon's Marshals* (London, Weidenfeld & Nicolson, 1987), pp. 254–69.

15. Napier, *History*, vol. 4, p. 229.

16. Girod de l'Ain, *Vie Militaire du Général Foy*, pp. 170–1, quoting Foy's diary for 16 July 1812.

17. *Ibid.*, p. 177n.

18. See chapter three, commentary, p. 80 for more on this.

19. M. A. Thiers *History of the Consulate and Empire ...*, 20 vols (London, Willis & Sotheran, 1857), vol. 15, p. 55 (Book XLVI); there are some useful notes on Clausel's career, and on Marmont's other subordinates, in Young and Lawford, *Wellington's Masterpiece*, pp. 288–301; see also David Chandler, *Dictionary of the Napoleonic Wars* (London, Arms & Armour, 1979).

20. Etienne-François Girard, *Les Cahiers du Colonel Girard, 1766–1846 ...*, ed. by Paul Desachy (Paris, Plon, 1951), pp. 194–6 et seq.; Marmont, *Mémoires*, vol. 4, p. 127.

21. Oman, *History*, vol. 5, p. 367n.

22. Lemonnier-Delafosse quoted in Oman, *History*, vol. 5, p. 392.

23. Tomkinson, *Diary of a Cavalry Officer*, p. 188; see also Anon, *Personal Narrative of a Private Soldier*, p. 123: 'But I suppose my Lord Wellington's orders were *not to engage unless we were attacked*' (original emphasis).

24. Wellington to Liverpool, 9 June 1812, *Supplementary Despatches and Memoranda of Field Marshal Arthur, Duke of Wellington*, ed. by the 2nd Duke of Wellington, 15 vols (London, John Murray, 1858–72), vol. 7, p. 343.

25. Wellington to Liverpool, 29 June 1812, Liverpool Papers, BL Loan Ms 72, vol. 21, ff. 187–8.

26. Wellington to Bathurst, 21 July 1812, *Wellington's Dispatches*, vol. 5, pp. 749–52; see also Wellington to Liverpool, 25 June 1812, *ibid.*, p. 722.

27. Oman *History*, vol. 2, pp. 538–42; see also my *Tactics and the Experience of Battle in the Age of Napoleon*, pp. 95–100.

28. Cathcart to Graham, 31 July 1812, Lynedoch Papers, NLS Ms 3610, ff. 187–96.

29. Burgoyne in Wrottesley, *Life and Correspondence of ... Burgoyne*, pp. 203–4.

30. Earl of Ellesmere, *Personal Reminiscences of the Duke of Wellington* (London, John Murray, 1904), p. 107n; see also chapter one, commentary, p. 18.

31. Wellington to Bathurst, 9 July 1812, Wellington Papers WP 1/347, printed with the name suppressed in *Wellington's Dispatches*, vol. 5, pp. 738–9.

32. Boutflower, *Journal of an Army Surgeon*, p. 145.

33. Campbell to Torrens, 25 July 1812, Hope of Luffness Papers, NAS GD 364/1/124.

34. Quotation from 'The Bingham Manuscripts', ed. by T.H. McGuffie, *JSAHR*, vol. 26, no. 107 (1948), p. 107; for his temper and much warm praise see George Napier, *Passages in the Early Military Life of Sir George T. Napier, K.C.B.*, ed. by W.C.E. Napier (London, John Murray, 1884), pp. 151–2.

35. Alexander Gordon to Lord Aberdeen, 8 August 1811, Aberdeen Papers, BL Add. Ms 43,224, ff. 11–15.

36. Michael Glover, *Wellington as a Military Commander* (London, Sphere, 1973), p. 195.

37. W. M. Gomm, *Letters and Journals of Field Marshal William Maynard Gomm ...*, ed. by Francis Culling Gomm (London, John Murray, 1881), p. 189.

38. George Napier, *Passages in the Early Military Life*, p. 238; Edward Costello, *The Peninsular and Waterloo Campaigns* (London, Longmans, 1967, first published 1852), p. 23n; Wellington to Torrens, 7 September 1812, *Wellington's Dispatches*, vol. 6, p. 55.

39. Torrens to Wellington, 'Private', 24 August 1811, Wellington Papers, WP 1/337.

40. For example, Wellington to Clinton, 7 am, 16 July 1812, *Wellington's Dispatches*, vol. 5, pp. 747–8.

41 Quoted in 'The Bingham Manuscripts', p. 108.

42. Clinton's inspection report on the 2nd in WO 27/106 (unfoliated).

43. Leach, *Rough Sketches*, p. 262; W. Verner, *History and Campaigns of the Rifle Brigade*, 2 vols (London, John Bale & Sons, 1919), vol. 2, p. 393.

44. Wellington to Torrens, 7 September 1812, *Wellington's Dispatches*, vol. 6, pp. 55–56; but cf Glover, *Wellington as a Military Commander*, p. 196, which suggests that this praise should not be taken at face value; however, the story that Glover links to Hope does not fit exactly.

45. Biographical information about Campbell is difficult to find, but see R. G. Thorne, ed., *The History of Parliament. The House of Commons 1790–1820*, 5 vols (London, Secker & Warburg for the History of Parliament Trust, 1986), vol. 3, p. 372 and also Appendix IV of the present work.

46. Bragge, *Peninsular Portrait*, pp. 18, 38.

47. 'An Essex Soldier's Letter of Long Ago', edited by Miss E. Vaughan, *The Essex Review*, July 1917, p. 143 (letter of Private Alexander Thompson, 2 January 1812).

48. Oman, *History*, vol. 5, p. 600.

49. Castel, *Relation de la Bataille et Retraite des Arapiles*, pp. 19–20; Sarramon, *La Bataille des Arapiles*, p. 223 and note; Oman, *History*, vol. 5, p. 598n.

50. Oman, *History*, vol. 5, p. 595; see Appendix I of the present work for losses on 18 July.

51. Napier, *History*, vol. 4, p. 296; Oman, *History*, vol. 5, p. 600.

52. Oman, *History*, vol. 5, p. 603; the return of 1 July printed by Sarramon, *La Bataille des Arapiles*, pp. 409–12, while organized differently, gives a similar strength for the French artillery.

53. PRO WO 1/255; Oman, *History*, vol. 5, p. 598.

54. My thanks to Steven H. Smith, Howie Muir and George Nafziger, whose contributions to the Napoleonic Discussion Forum helped to clarify, if not resolve, this problem.

55. Sarramon, *La Bataille des Arapiles*, p. 151 and note; return of 1 July in *ibid.*, pp. 409–12; return of 15 July in Fortescue, *History of the British Army*, vol. 8, pp. 632–6.

56. Girod de l'Ain, *Vie Militaire du Général Foy*, pp. 178–9.

Chapter Three: Preliminary Manoeuvres and Skirmishing: Morning and Early Afternoon

1. Corporal John Douglas, *Douglas's Tale of the Peninsula and Waterloo*, ed. by Stanley Monick (London, Leo Cooper, 1997), pp. 42–3; see also James Hale, *The Journal of James Hale, Late Serjeant in the Ninth Regiment of Foot* (Cirencester, Philip Watkins, 1826; reprinted by Peter Catley and IX Regiment, 1997), p. 85 (p. 79 of reprint); Anonymous memoirs of a private soldier in 1/38th, NAM Ms 7912–21, f. 20; and Kincaid, *Adventures in the Rifle Brigade*, p. 80.

2. Wellington to Bathurst, 24 July 1812, *Wellington's Dispatches*, vol. 5, p. 753.

3. Colonel Jackson to Graham, 24 July 1812, Lynedoch Papers, NLS Ms 3610, ff. 181–4.

4. Leith Hay, *Narrative of the Peninsular War*, pp. 250–1; Gomm, *Letters and Journals*, pp. 276–7; Campbell to Torrens, 25 July 1812, Hope of Luffness Papers, NAS GD 364/1/1224.

5. *Wellington's Dispatches*, vol. 5, pp. 753–4; Beamish, *History of the King's German Legion*, vol. 2, pp. 70–1; Cathcart to Graham, 31 July 1812, Lynedoch Papers, NLS Ms 3610, ff. 187–96.

6. Green, *Vicissitudes of a Soldier's Life*, pp. 98–9.

7. For casualty figures see Appendices II and III; see also commentary, pp. 72–4.

8. [Denis Le Marchant,] *Memoirs of the Late Maj-General Le Marchant* (London, Bentley, 1841), pp. 277. But compare this to William Legh Clowes to Denis Le Marchant, 4 June (*c.* 1841?), Le Marchant Papers, in the Royal Military Academy Library, Sandhurst,

Packet 29a, Item 4, who denies that such a detachment was made, at least from the 3rd Dragoons. It seems possible that this story is actually based on the part played by the 3rd Dragoons on 18 July, but without knowing the source of the story it is hard to dismiss it out of hand. I am grateful to Mark Urban for sending me a copy of this letter.

9. Beamish, *History of the King's German Legion*, vol. 2, p. 70 and note.

10. Girod de l'Ain, *Vie Militaire du Général Foy*, pp. 173–4; Marmont, *Mémoires*, vol. 4, p. 133.

11. Marmont, *Mémoires*, vol. 4, pp. 133–4; see also Sarramon, *La Bataille des Arapiles*, pp. 198–9, and Girod de l'Ain, *Vie Militaire du Général Foy*, pp. 174–5.

12. Vere, *Marches, Movements ... 4th Division*, p. 31; Napier, *History*, vol. 4, p. 263.

13. Cathcart to Graham, 31 July 1812, Lynedoch Papers, NLS Ms 3610, ff. 187–96: a note on the manuscript in another hand says 'omit this sentence' in reference to the first sentence quoted here. Presumably the letter was to be copied for private circulation among family and friends, as was common at the time, rather than being published.

14. Lillie in H. A. Bruce, *The Life of General Sir William Napier, KCB*, 2 vols (London, John Murray, 1864), vol. 1, pp. 277–8; Charles Synge, 'Captain Synge's Experiences at Salamanca', ed. by F. St L. Tottenham, *Nineteenth Century and After*, July 1912, p. 55; *Wellington's Dispatches*, vol. 5, p. 753.

15. Vere, *Marches, Movements ... 4th Division*, p. 32.

16. *Wellington's Dispatches*, vol. 5, p. 754; see also commentary, pp. 75–6.

17. Fortescue, *History of the British Army*, vol. 8, p. 483n.

18. Sir F. Maurice, *The History of the Scots Guards ...*, 2 vols (London, Chatto & Windus, 1934), vol. 1, p. 363 quoting a diary; John Mills, *For King and Country. The Letters and Diaries of John Mills, Coldstream Guards, 1811–1814*, ed. by Ian Fletcher (Staplehurst,

Spellmount, 1995), p. 181; Aitchison, *An Ensign in the Peninsular War*, pp. 175–6.

19. 'H.C.' to Colonel Taylor, 25 July 1812, Hope of Luffness Papers, NAS GD 364/1/1224; see commentary, p. 77 and Appendix IV for further discussion of this letter.

20. Aitchison, *An Ensign in the Peninsular War*, p. 180.

21. See commentary, pp. 77–8 for discussion of sources for all these points.

22. Thomas Dyneley, *Letters Written by Lieut.-General Thomas Dyneley C.B., R.A., While on Active Service between the Years 1806 and 1815*, ed. by Colonel F. A. Whinyates (Cambridge, Trotman, 1984), p. 32; on Sympher see Vere, *Marches, Movements ... 4th Division*, p. 32.

23. Castel, *Relation de la Bataille et Retraite des Arapiles*, p. 16 says he was sent with these orders at 8 am; it was only seven or eight miles as the crow flies, so the 27th should have rejoined their division soon after midday, but they may have been delayed.

24. Marmont, *Mémoires*, vol. 4, pp. 136–7.

25. Aitchison, *An Ensign in the Peninsular War*, p. 176; General Friedrich Ludwig von Wachholtz, 'Auf der Peninsula 1810 bis 1813', ed. by H. L. von Wachholtz, *Beihefte zum Militär-Wochenblatt*, 1907, p. 293; Beamish, *History of the King's German Legion*, vol. 2, p. 72; see also Mills, *For King and Country*, p. 181.

26. Wachholtz, 'Auf der Peninsula', pp. 292, 294; see Appendix II for allied casualties; Maurice, *History of the Scots Guards*, pp. 363–4; D. Mackinnon, *Origins and Services of the Coldstream Guards ...*, 2 vols (London, Bentley, 1833), vol. 2, p. 176; see also a much later letter from Captain George Browne of the 23rd Fusiliers in A.D.L. Cary and S. McCance, *Regimental Records of the Royal Welch Fusiliers*, 4 vols (London, RUSI, 1921–9), vol. 1, pp. 253–4.

27. Marmont, *Mémoires*, vol. 4, p. 138.

28. Cathcart to Graham, 31 July 1812, Lynedoch Papers, NLS Ms 3610, ff. 187–96; see also *Wellington's Dispatches*,

vol. 5, p. 754, and Alexander Gordon to Lord Aberdeen, 25 July 1812, Aberdeen Papers, BL Add. Ms 43,224, ff. 95–101. See Vere, *Marches, Movements … 4th Division*, p. 33 and Leith Hay, *Narrative of the Peninsular War*, p. 256 for estimates of the French having twenty guns; and for the Fifth Division's lack of cover, *ibid.*, p. 256 and Gomm, *Letters and Journals*, p. 277.

29. Douglas, *Douglas's Tale*, p. 43.

30. Robert Eadie, *Recollections of Robert Eadie: Private of the 79th Regiment of Infantry* (London, Maggs, 1987, first published, 1829), pp. 122–4.

31. Green, *Vicissitudes of a Soldier's Life*, pp. 99–100; see also W. Wheeler, *The Letters of Private Wheeler, 1809–1828*, ed. by Captain B. H. Liddell Hart (London, Michael Joseph, 1951), p. 87 – Wheeler was in the same division, though not the same regiment, and his account provides general confirmation of Green's description.

32. Marmont, *Mémoires*, vol. 4, pp. 137–9.

33. Sarramon, *La Bataille des Arapiles*, pp. 212–13 – see commentary, p. 80 for more on this point.

34. Marmont, *Mémoires*, vol. 4, pp. 138, 430–48; Fortescue, *History of the British Army*, vol. 8, p. 486.

35. Oman, *History*, vol. 5, pp. 428–33, 438–9; Sarramon, *La Bataille des Arapiles*, pp. 204–6, 211–13; Fortescue, *History of the British Army*, vol. 8, p. 486, 502–3; Young and Lawford, *Wellington's Masterpiece*, pp. 217–21; see commentary, pp. 78–80.

36. Girard, *Les Cahiers du Colonel Girard*, pp. 199–200, cf Napier, *History*, vol. 4, pp. 296–7.

37. Girod de l'Ain, *Vie Militaire du Général Foy*, pp. 175–6.

38. *Ibid.*, p. 175; Marmont, *Mémoires*, vol. 4, pp. 139, 444; Oman, *History*, vol. 5, p. 437 accepts Foy's 'between three and four o'clock in the afternoon', adding only the rider 'certainly nearer the latter than the former hour'.

39. C. C. F. Greville, *The Greville Memoirs. A Journal of the Reigns of King George IV, King William IV and Queen*

Victoria, ed. by Henry Reeve, 8 vols (London, Longmans, Green, 1888), vol. 4, p. 40, 2 January 1838. Oman's citation 'Greville's *Memoirs* ii p. 39' is confusing but not inaccurate: in the 1885 edition it is in the 'second part' of the *Journal of the Reign of Queen Victoria*, vol. 1, p. 39.

40. Greville, *Greville Memoirs*, vol. 4, p. 141, 18 November 1838.

41. For example, Muriel Wellesley, *The Man Wellington* (London, Constable, 1937); p. 239; Edward Fraser, *The Soldiers Whom Wellington Led* (London, Methuen, 1913), p. 239; James Lunt, *Scarlet Lancer* (London, Hart-Davis, 1964), p. 57.

42. Oman, *History* vol. 5, p. 419 and note; Sarramon, *La Bataille des Arapiles*, p. 190; Fortescue, *History of the British Army*, vol. 8, p. 480; Napier, *History*, vol. 4, p. 263 gives Chauvel two thousand horsemen and twenty guns.

43. Leith Hay Papers, NAS GD 225, Box 40, manuscript narrative of the campaign of 1812.

44. Boutflower, *Journal of an Army Surgeon*, pp. 147–8.

45. Cartografía Militar de España, Mapa General Serie L, Salamanca 13–19 (478) E. 1:50,000 (1993).

46. I must particularly thank Howie Muir for first pointing out to me the discrepancies between Fortescue and the ordnance map, and for an extended and most useful correspondence on this whole subject.

47. Leith Hay, *Narrative of the Peninsular War*, p. 254.

48. Leith Hay Papers, NAS GD 225, Box 40, manuscript narrative of the campaign of 1812.

49. Mills, *For King and Country*, p. 187.

50. Oman, *History*, vol. 5, pp. 421–2; Muir, *Tactics and the Experience of Battle in the Age of Napoleon*, pp. 58–9; Sarramon, *La Bataille des Arapiles*, p. 196n; *Wellington's Dispatches*, vol. 5, pp. 753–4.

51. Synge, 'Captain Synge's Experiences at Salamanca', p. 58.

52. *Wellington's Dispatches*, vol. 5, pp. 753–4; Green, *Vicissitudes of a Soldier's*

Life, pp. 98–9; Marmont, *Mémoires*, vol. 4, pp. 133–4; Girod de l'Ain, *Vie Militaire du Général Foy*, pp. 173–4; Sarramon, *La Bataille des Arapiles*, pp. 196–7.

53. McGrigor to [Wellington ?], 25 July 1812, Bathurst Papers, BL Loan Ms 57, vol. 5, f. 509.

54. Wellington to Croker, 8 August 1815, Wellington Papers, WP 1/478, printed with Croker's name suppressed in *Wellington's Dispatches*, vol. 8, pp. 231–2.

55. Mills, *For King and Country*, p. 179; Aitchison, *An Ensign in the Peninsular War*, p. 175.

56. Sarramon, *La Bataille des Arapiles*, p. 199; M. Lemonnier-Delafosse, *Campagnes de 1810 à 1815. Souvenirs Militaires ... Tome Second* (Havre, Imprimerie du Commerce Alph. Lemale, 1850), p. 157.

57. Sarramon, *La Bataille des Arapiles*, p. 199; Oman, *History*, vol. 5, p. 426.

58. Marmont, *Mémoires* vol. 4, p. 134; Mills, *For King and Country*, p. 181; Aitchison, *An Ensign in the Peninsular War*, p. 175; Tomkinson, *Diary of a Cavalry Officer*, p. 188; Oman, *History*, vol. 5, pp. 426–7; Ellesmere, *Personal Reminiscences of the Duke of Wellington*, p. 107n.

59. Wrottesley, *Life and Correspondence of ... Burgoyne*, p. 200; *Wellington's Dispatches*, vol. 5, p. 754; Marmont, *Mémoires*, vol. 4, p. 136.

60. Leith Hay, *Narrative of the Peninsular War*, p. 256; Mills, *For King and Country*, p. 181.

61. Sarramon, *La Bataille des Arapiles* p. 209; Napier, *History*, vol. 4, p. 266; Andrew Leith Hay to his father, 24 July 1812, Leith Hay Papers NAS GD 225; Box 34/26; Andrew Leith Hay, manuscript narrative of the campaign of 1812, *loc. cit.*, GD 225, Box 40; Mills, *For King and Country*, p. 181.

62. Campbell in H. C. Wylly, *History of the 1st and 2nd Battalions, The Sherwood Foresters ...*, 2 vols (Frome, for the regiment, 1929), vol. 1, p. 223; Edward Pakenham, *Pakenham Letters, 1800 to 1815* (Privately printed, 1914) p. 173,

but cf *ibid.*, p. 170; Sarramon, *La Bataille des Arapiles*, p. 210; Moggridge [Thomas Hamilton], 'Letters from the Peninsula', p. 546; Oman, *History*, vol. 5, p. 436; Major-General Benjamin D'Urban, *The Peninsular Journal of Maj-Gen. Sir Benjamin D'Urban*, ed. by I. J. Rousseau (London, Greenhill, 1988, first published 1930), p. 274.

63. Fortescue, *History of the British Army*, vol. 8, p. 485 and note; Oman, *History*, vol. 5, pp. 425–6; Young and Lawford, *Wellington's Masterpiece*, pp. 210, 215–16; D'Urban, *Peninsular Journal*, p. 274; Campbell in Young and Lawford, *Wellington's Masterpiece*, p. 215.

64. Beamish, *History of the King's German Legion*, vol. 2, pp. 71, 415–17 (Arentschildt's report); *Wellington's Dispatches*, vol. 5, p. 754.

65. Sarramon, *La Bataille des Arapiles*, p. 199; Marmont, *Mémoires*, vol. 4, p. 134.

66. Dyneley, *Letters*, pp. 33, 36; Macdonald in Captain Francis Duncan, *History of the Royal Regiment of Artillery*, 2 vols (London, John Murray, 1872–3), vol. 2, p. 327; Wachholtz, 'Auf der Peninsula', p. 292; Synge, 'Captain Synge's Experiences at Salamanca', pp. 59–60.

67. Aitchison, *An Ensign in the Peninsular War*, p. 175; Mills, *For King and Country*, p. 181; Tomkinson, *Diary of a Cavalry Officer*, p. 185; Maurice, *History of the Scots Guards*, p. 363.

68. Marmont, *Mémoires*, vol. 4, p. 135; Cathcart to Graham, 31 July 1812, Lynedoch Papers, NLS Ms 3610, ff. 187–96; Alexander Gordon to? nd [July or August 1812], fragment, Tomes Mss; Browne, *Napoleonic War Journal*, p. 169; Tomkinson, *Diary of a Cavalry Officer*, p. 188; see also H. Arbuthnot, *The Journal of Mrs Arbuthnot, 1820–1832*, ed. by Francis Bamford and the Duke of Wellington, 2 vols (London, Macmillan, 1950) vol. 1, p. 212, 7 February 1823.

69. Browne, *Napoleonic War Journal*, pp. 168–70; Scovell Papers, PRO WO 37/7, p. 10; *Wellington's Dispatches*, vol. 5, p. 754.

70. Oman, *History*, vol. 5, p. 427; Vere,

Marches, Movements ... 4th Division p. 31–2; Cathcart to Graham, 31 July 1812, Lynedoch Papers NLS Ms 3610, ff. 187–96. Cathcart states that the commissariat and baggage were ordered to retreat 'in the afternoon'; but Daniel, who is not as reliable a source but who was directly affected, says that this order was received at 10 o'clock in the morning. [J. E. Daniel], *Journal of an Officer in the Commissariat Department of the Army* ... (Cambridge, Trotman, 1997, first published 1997), p. 133.

71. Dyneley, *Letters*, pp. 32, 35; Vere, *Marches, Movements ... 4th Division*, p. 32; Young and Lawford, *Wellington's Masterpiece*, p. 207; Beamish, *History of the King's German Legion*, vol. 2, p. 71.

72. *Wellington's Dispatches*, vol. 5, pp. 754, 759.

73. Dyneley, *Letters*, p. 36; Wachholtz, 'Auf der Peninsula', p. 294; Leith Hay also praises Sympher's battery, which 'kept up a constant and well directed fire against the moving masses of the enemy' (*Narrative of the Peninsular War*, p. 256).

74. Leith Hay, *Narrative of the Peninsular War*, pp. 253–4; see chapter five, p. 105 and commentary, pp. 116–17 for more on this incident.

75. Oman, *History*, vol. 5, p. 433.

76. Castel, *Relation de la Bataille et Retraite des Arapiles*, pp. 16–17.

77. Napier, *History*, vol. 4, p. 267; Fortescue, *History of the British Army*, vol. 8, p. 490; Oman, *History*, vol. 5, p. 439 and note, which gives an excellent discussion of the conflicting sources; Sarramon, *La Bataille des Arapiles*, p. 212.

78. Napier, *History*, vol. 4, p. 297; Castel, *Relation de la Bataille et Retraite des Arapiles*, pp. 16–17; Charles Parquin, *Napoleon's Army*, trans. and ed. by B. T. Jones (London, Longmans, 1969), pp. 147, 149: Parquin says that the luncheon was aborted some time before Marmont was wounded.

79. Marmont, *Mémoires*, vol. 4, p. 139; Marmont to King Joseph, 25 July 1812, *Mémoires et Correspondance Politique et Militaire du Roi Joseph*, ed. by A. du Casse, 10 vols (Paris, Perrotin, 1854–5), vol. 9, p. 57; Oman, *History*, vol. 5, p. 440; Young and Lawford, *Wellington's Masterpiece*, pp. 293–4 and note; Sarramon, *La Bataille des Arapiles*, pp. 212–13.

80. Mills, *For King and Country*, p. 181; *The Times*, 19 August 1812.

81. Moggridge [Thomas Hamilton], 'Letters from the Peninsula', p. 545; Hamilton is identified as the author of the article in the *Wellesley Index to Victorian Periodicals*, ed. by Walter E. Houghton, *et al.*, 5 vols (University of Toronto Press, 1966–89), vol. 1, p. 26; biographical information about him from the *Dictionary of National Biography* and the obituary in *Blackwood's Edinburgh Magazine*, February 1843, p. 280.

82. J. W. Croker, *The Croker Papers. The Correspondence and Diaries of ... John Wilson Croker*, ed. by Louis J. Jennings, 3 vols (London, John Murray, 1884), vol. 2, p. 120, 24 May 1831; James Thornton, *Your Most Obedient Servant. James Thornton, Cook to the Duke of Wellington* (Exeter, Webb & Bower, 1985), p. 65.

83. Napier, *History*, vol. 4, p. 266; Sir Herbert Maxwell, *The Life of Wellington. The Restoration of the Martial Power of Great Britain*, 2 vols (London, Sampson Low, Marston, 1900), vol. 1, pp. 281–2; Elizabeth Longford, *Wellington. The Years of the Sword* (London, Weidenfeld & Nicolson, 1969), p. 285; Young and Lawford, *Wellington's Masterpiece*, p. 221n.

84. Fortescue, *History of the British Army*, vol. 8, pp. 486–7; Young and Lawford *Wellington's Masterpiece*, pp. 221–2; *Wellington's Dispatches*, vol. 5, p. 754; Oman, *History*, vol. 5, pp. 437–9.

Chapter Four: Pakenham and Thomières

1. D'Urban, *Peninsular Journal*, p. 274.

2. William [Grattan,] 'Reminiscences of a

Subaltern: Battle of Salamanca,' p. 181; Greville, *Greville Memoirs*, vol. 4, p. 141, 18 November 1838, Pakenham, *Pakenham Letters*, p. 173.

3. The other regiment, the 12th Dragoons, had been detached to escort the baggage train.

4. Wallace quoted in [Richard Cannon,] *Historical Records of the 88th* (London, Clowes, 1838), p. 46; other details from Colonel James Campbell, *The British Army As It Was – Is – and Ought to Be* (London, T&W Boone, 1840), p. 224.

5. Campbell, *The British Army*, p. 224.

6. James Wyld, (publisher), *Maps and Plans Showing the Principal Movements, Battles, and Sieges in Which the British Army Was Engaged . . .* (London, James Wyld, 1841) shows two tracks following this route south; one, at the foot of the ridge, has since disappeared. Not that troops needed a road to cross such open country.

7. Young and Lawford, *Wellington's Materpiece*, p. 237n.

8. D'Urban quoted in Oman, *History*, vol. 5, p. 441; see commentary, pp. 101–2 for a discussion of this episode.

9. [Grattan,] 'Reminiscences of a Sub-altern', p. 182; Moggridge [Thomas Hamilton], 'Letters from the Peninsula', p. 546 (for Pakenham's speech); [Stephen Morley,] *Memoirs of a Serjeant of the 5th Regiment of Foot . . .* (Ashford, Elliott, 1842), pp. 112–13.

10. William Grattan, *Adventures with the Connaught Rangers 1808–1814*, ed. by Charles Oman (London, Arnold, 1902), p. 258.

11. Pakenham, *Pakenham Letters*, p. 173.

12. Campbell, *The British Army*, p. 225.

13. [Grattan,] 'Reminiscences of a Subaltern', pp. 182–3: I have changed 'Packenham' to Pakenham, and substituted Thomières for Foy throughout the quotation.

14. See Appendix II. These figures exclude the three companies of the 5/60th attached to the brigade, as Grattan is clearly referring to the main line, not its screen of skirmishers. However, including them would make very little difference: the whole 5/60th lost only

thirty-six casualties from 472 officers and men, or 7.6 per cent in the battle.

15. Campbell, *The British Army*, p. 225.

16. Grattan, *Adventures with the Connaught Rangers*, p. 258. According to Cannon's *Historical Records of the 88th*, p. 47 at the same moment Murphy was hit, 'a ball struck the pole of the King's colour, cutting it neatly in two, and taking the epaulette off the shoulder of Lieutenant D'Arcy who carried it.'

17. Moggridge [Thomas Hamilton], 'Letters from the Peninsula', p. 546 (for the Germans); Colonel P.H. Dalbiac, *History of the 45th: 1st Nottinghamshire Regiment* (London, Swan Sonnenschein, 1902), p. 106 (for Pakenham).

18. Quoted in Wylly, *History of . . . the Sherwood Foresters*, vol. 1, p. 225 – see commentary, p. 103 for a discussion of the problems posed by this quotation.

19. [Morley,] *Memoirs of a Serjeant*, p. 113.

20. Arentschildt's report in Beamish, *History of the King's German Legion*, vol. 2, pp. 415–17; Gray, 'The Services of the King's German Legion', pp. 251–3; Sarramon, *La Bataille des Arapiles*, pp. 217–18; Curto's losses have been adjusted to take into account casualties suffered on 18 July.

21. Campbell, *The British Army*, p. 226; [Grattan,] 'Reminiscences of a Subaltern', p. 184.

22. Campbell, *The British Army*, p. 224; Lightfoot quoted in Wylly, *History of . . . the Sherwood Foresters*, vol. 1, p. 224.

23. Charles William Vane, Marquess of Londonderry [and G. R. Gleig], *Story of the Peninsular War* (London, Colburn, 1848), p. 328. Londonderry was, of course, the same Charles Stewart who had been Wellington's Adjutant-General until April 1812; he changed his surname to Vane on his second marriage.

24. *Wellington's Dispatches*, vol. 5, p. 754; Pakenham, *Pakenham Letters*, p. 173; D'Urban, *Peninsular War Journal*, p. 274; Campbell, *The British Army*, p. 225; [Grattan,] 'Reminiscences of a Subaltern', p. 182; Young and Lawford, *Wellington's Masterpiece*, p. 229; Oman,

History, vol. 5, p. 440; Fortescue, *History of the British Army*, vol. 8, p. 487. Dalbiac's account, which Oman follows, is clearly based on Campbell: Dalbiac, *History of the 45th*, p. 103. For another example of an officer using 'the right brigade' to mean the first or leading brigade of the division, see [Daniel,] *Journal of an Officer in the Commissariat Department*, pp. 186–7, 2 December 1812.

25. [Grattan,] 'Reminiscences of a Subaltern', p. 182: as well as replacing Foy with Thomières, I have again changed 'Packenham' to Pakenham. This passage may be found in vol. 2, pp. 55–6 of the first edition of Grattan's *Adventures of the Connaught Rangers from 1808 to 1814*, 2 vols (London, Colburn, 1847), and on pp. 242–4 of the abridged edition edited by Oman.

26. Campbell, *The British Army*, pp. 224–5.

27. Moggridge [Thomas Hamilton], 'Letters from the Peninsula', p. 546.

28. Wellington to Bathurst, 24 July 1812, *Wellington's Dispatches*, vol. 5, p. 754; Pakenham to Hercules Pakenham, 25 July 1812, *Pakenham Letters*, p. 173.

29. D'Urban, *Peninsular War Journal*, p. 273n; Oman, *History*, vol. 5, pp. 441–2; Napier, *History*, vol. 4, p. 464.

30. Oman, *History*, vol. 5, p. 433. The implication (perhaps unintended) that it was nearly three miles from Maucune's left flank to the Pico de Miranda is misleading – it was about half that – but Oman may have meant that Thomières had marched nearly three miles since advancing onto the Monte de Azan.

31. Oman, *History*, vol. 5, p. 442n; Sarramon, *La Bataille des Arapiles*, pp. 207, 214.

32. Fortescue, *History of the British Army*, vol. 8, p. 490; Young and Lawford, *Wellington's Masterpiece*, p. 244; Oman, *History*, vol. 5, p. 469; Sarramon, *La Bataille des Arapiles*, p. 218.

33. Oman, *History*, vol. 5, p. 444; [Sergeant Joseph Donaldson,] *The Eventful Life of a Soldier* (Edinburgh, Tait, 1827), p. 264; Brown quoted in Wylly, *History of the . . . Sherwood Foresters*, vol. 1,

p. 225; [Morley], *Memoirs of a Serjeant*, p. 113; Campbell, *The British Army*, pp. 225–6; Moggridge [Thomas Hamilton], 'Letters from the Peninsula', p. 546.

34. Beamish, *History of the King's German Legion*, vol. 2, pp. 415–17; *Wellington's Dispatches*, vol. 5, p. 754; Sarramon, *La Bataille des Arapiles*, p. 217.

Chapter Five: Leith and Maucune

1. Leith Hay, *Narrative of the Peninsular War*, pp. 253–5; Douglas, *Douglas's Tale*, p. 43; see commentary, pp. 116–17 for more on this incident.

2. Gomm, *Letters and Journals*, p. 277; Douglas, *Douglas's Tale*, p. 45.

3. Leith Hay, *Narrative of the Peninsular War*, p. 257.

4. *Ibid.*

5. Anonymous memoirs of a private soldier in 1/38th, NAM Ms 7912–21, f. 20: the quotation has been slightly edited – an unedited transcript is given in the commentary, p. 117; Ensign Freer quoted in J. P. Jones, *History of the South Staffordshire Regiment (1705–1923)* (Wolverhampton, Whitehead Brothers, 1923), p. 37; Douglas, *Douglas's Tale*, p. 45; 'bragadocian' means 'arrogant and boastful'.

6. Sir Philip Bainbrigge, 'The Staff at Salamanca', *USJ*, January 1878, pp. 72–3.

7. Douglas, *Douglas's Tale*, p. 44 and p. 117 quoting Luke 18:3.

8. Anonymous memoirs of a private soldier in 1/38th, NAM Ms 7912–21, f. 21: for an unedited transcript of this quotation see commentary, p. 117.

9. Leith Hay Papers NAS GD 225, Box 40, Andrew Leith Hay's manuscript narrative of the campaign of 1812 and his *Narrative of the Peninsular War*, pp. 258–9.

10. [Sir Andrew Leith Hay,] *Memoir of the Late Lieutenant-General Sir James Leith . . .* (Barbados, privately printed, 1817), pp. 96–7.

11. Douglas, *Douglas's Tale* p 45; Leith Hay Papers NAS GD 225, Box 40,

Andrew Leith Hay's manuscript narrative of the campaign of 1812, cf his *Narrative of the Peninsular War*, p. 259.

12. Andrew Leith Hay to his father, 24 July 1812, Leith Hay Papers, NAS GD 225, Box 34/26; Gomm, *Letters and Journals*, p. 278; Douglas, *Douglas's Tale*, p. 46.

13. Douglas, *Douglas's Tale*, p. 46.

14. In the first edition of his book Leith Hay wrote 'contiguous squares', changing this to 'columns' by the third edition – that quoted here.

15. Leith Hay, *Narrative of the Peninsular War*, pp. 259–60.

16. Gomm, *Letters and Journals*, p. 278.

17. Anonymous memoirs of a private soldier in 1/38th, NAM Ms 7912–21, f. 21; for an unedited transcript of this quotation see commentary, p. 118.

18. Hale, *Journal of James Hale*, p. 86 (p. 79 of reprint).

19. Douglas, *Douglas's Tale*, p. 46.

20. *Ibid.*

21. See Appendix II.

22. Quotation from Leith Hay Papers, NAS GD 225, Box 40, Andrew Leith Hay's manuscript narrative of the campaign of 1812; on Dowson see Leith Hay's *Narrative of the Peninsular War*, p. 261, and John A. Hall, *A History of the Peninsular War. Vol viii. The Biographical Dictionary of British Officers Killed and Wounded, 1808–1814* (London, Greenhill, 1998), p. 174.

23. Oman, *History*, vol. 5, pp. 431–2; Leith Hay, *Narrative of the Peninsular War*, pp. 253–4; [Leith Hay,] *Memoir of Sir James Leith*, p. 94; Tomkinson, *Diary of a Cavalry Officer*, pp. 185–9; Lawson in *The Dickson Manuscripts*, vol. 4, p. 705; Douglas, *Douglas's Tale*, p. 43.

24. Leith Hay, *Narrative of the Peninsular War*, p. 257.

25. *Ibid.*; Colonel L. I. Cowper, *The King's Own. The Story of a Royal Regiment*, 2 vols (Oxford, for the regiment, 1939), vol. 1, p. 396; Hall, *Biographical Dictionary*, p. 199 names him as Edmund Faunce.

26. Leith Hay Papers, NAS GD 225, Box 40, Andrew Leith Hay's manuscript narrative of the campaign of 1812;

Anonymous memoirs of a private soldier in 1/38th, NAM Ms 7912–21, f. 19; Oman, *History*, vol. 5, p. 446n states that it joined the division 'only twelve hours back', but it is not clear whether this means the previous evening or the small hours of the morning, while on p. 597 Oman says that it joined 'on the battle-morning'.

27. Fortescue, *History of the British Army*, vol. 8, p. 491, cf p. 627n; Oman, *History*, vol. 5, p. 596n; Oman, *Wellington's Army*, p. 360.

28. Anonymous memoirs of a private soldier in 1/38th, NAM Ms 7912–21, ff. 20–1.

29. [Leith Hay,] *Memoir of the Late Lieutenant-General Sir James Leith*, pp. 96–7; Richard Cannon, *Historical Record of the Ninth, or the East Norfolk, Regiment of Foot* (London, Parker, Furnivall & Parker, 1848), p. 61; Anonymous memoirs of a private soldier in 1/38th, NAM Ms 7912–21, f. 20.

30. Thomas Carter, *Historical Record of the Forty-Fourth or the East Sussex Regiment* (Chatham, Gale & Polden, 1887), p. 65; Lieutenant-Colonel Neil Bannatyne, *History of the Thirtieth Regiment ...* (Liverpool, Littlebury, 1923), p. 281.

31. Leith Hay, *Narrative of the Peninsular War*, p. 259 – see above, n. 14 for the change from squares to columns.

32. Andrew Leith Hay to his father, 24 July 1812, Leith Hay Papers, NAS GD 225, Box 34/26; Leith Hay, *Narrative of the Peninsular War*, p. 258; Anonymous memoirs of a private soldier in 1/38th, NAM Ms 7912–21, f. 21.

33. Other examples include the quotation on p. 451 from [Le Marchant,] *Memoirs of Le Marchant*, where the reference is also wrong (it should be to p. 296, not p. 285).

Chapter Six: Le Marchant and the Destruction of the French Left

1. [Le Marchant,] *Memoirs of Le Marchant*, pp. 288–9.
2. Tomkinson, *Diary of a Cavalry Officer*, p. 185; [Le Marchant,] *Memoirs of Le Marchant*, p. 288; Bragge, *Peninsular Portrait*, p. 66.
3. [Le Marchant,] *Memoirs of Le Marchant*, pp. 290–1; Bruce, *Life of Napier*, vol. 1, p. 275, quoting letter from Dalbiac.
4. [Grattan,] 'Reminiscences of a Subaltern', p. 184.
5. Dalbiac in Bruce, *Life of Napier*, vol. 1, p. 274.
6. Mary Viscountess Combermere and Captain W. Knollys, *Memoirs and Correspondence of Field Marshal Viscount Combermere*, 2 vols (London, Hurst & Blackett, 1866), vol. 1, p. 274: see commentary, pp. 136–7 for more on this subject.
7. [Grattan,] 'Reminiscences of a Subaltern', p. 185.
8. 'A.Z.', 'The Heavy Cavalry at Salamanca', *USJ*, November 1833, p. 353 – quoted in commentary, pp. 140–1; Leith Hay Papers, NAS GD 225, Box 40, Andrew Leith Hay's manuscript narrative of the campaign of 1812; Douglas, *Douglas's Tale*, p. 46; P. Arvers, *Historique de 82e Régiment d'Infanterie de Ligne* ... (Paris, Typographie Lahue, 1876), p. 127.
9. [Le Marchant,] *Memoirs of Le Marchant*, pp. 296–9 (quotation on p. 299); 'A.Z.', 'The Heavy Cavalry at Salamanca', p. 353; see also Young and Lawford, *Wellington's Masterpiece*, p. 251.
10. [Le Marchant,] *Memoirs of Le Marchant*, pp. 297–301.
11. 'A.Z.', 'The Heavy Cavalry at Salamanca', p. 353.
12. Bragge, *Peninsular Portrait*, pp. 63–4.
13. D. Scott Daniell, *4th Hussar: The Story of the 4th Queen's Own Hussars, 1685–1958* (Aldershot, Gale & Polden, 1959), p. 121.
14. Lieutenant John Massey to Richard Massey, 4 August 1812, letters of Lieutenant John Massey, NAM Ms 7804–14; Lunt, *Scarlet Lancer*, p. 57; Grattan, *Adventures with the Connaught Rangers*, p. 259.
15. Parquin, *Napoleon's Army*, p. 148. The 20th Chasseurs were not present in Marmont's army, but Parquin may have been thinking of the 22nd, the 26th or the 28th, all of which were.
16. Quoted in full in Major-General J. C. Dalton, 'A Family Regiment in the Peninsular War', *Cavalry Journal*, vol. 18 (April 1928), pp. 285–7.
17. [Grattan,] 'Reminiscences of a Subaltern', p. 185.
18. Calculated on its strength after the losses of the 18th have been deducted, which is why the figures appear odd.
19. Castel, *Relation de la Bataille et Retraite des Arapiles*, pp. 19–20; Sarramon, *La Bataille des Arapiles*, p. 223 and note.
20. Edward Fraser, *The War Drama of the Eagles* (London, John Murray, 1912) pp. 253–4. I have changed the spelling of the names from 'Pierce' to 'Pearce' – the form given in Carter's *Historical Record of the Forty-Fourth*, pp. 65–6 – and 'Cruickshank' to 'Crookshank' – the form used by Captain L. S. Challis in 'British Officers Serving in the Portuguese Army, 1809–1814', *JSAHR*, vol. 27, no.110 (1949), p. 54.
21. Bannatyne, *History of the Thirtieth Regiment*, pp. 279–81 deals authoritatively with Pratt and Maguire. Pakenham, *Pakenham Letters*, p. 173 confirms the capture of the Eagle of the 22nd.
22. Douglas, *Douglas's Tale*, p. 47.
23. [Le Marchant], *Memoirs of Le Marchant*, pp. 288–9; Combermere and Knollys, *Memoirs and Correspondence*, vol. 1, p. 274; Tomkinson, *Diary of a Cavalry Officer*, p. 187.
24. Clowes to Scovell, 17 March 1859, letter stuck into the front of the second volume of Scovell's diary and signed 'Legh', Scovell Papers, PRO WO 37/7B.
25. Napier, *History*, vol. 4, p. 270; [Le Marchant,] *Memoirs of Le Marchant*, pp. 301–2; Combermere and Knollys,

Memoirs and Correspondence, vol. 1, p. 275.

26. For Denis Le Marchant see the *Dictionary of National Biography*; for Carey Le Marchant see R. H. Thoumine, *Scientific Soldier. The Life of General Le Marchant, 1766–1812* (London, Oxford University Press, 1968), p. 198 and, for the date of death, Hall's *Biographical Dictionary*, p. 341. Light's diary entry is quoted in Geoffrey Dutton and David Elder, *Colonel William Light – Founder of a City* (Melbourne University Press, 1991), p. 60. For Money and Dalbiac see Bruce, *Life of Napier*, vol. 1, pp. 269–76: Bruce prints 'Money' as 'Moore' but this seems to be a misreading of the name; Napier himself cites 'Col. Money' (*History*, vol. 4, p. 463), and while the Army List shows a Colonel Archibald Money in the 11th Light Dragoons, see also Charles Dalton, *The Waterloo Roll Call* (London, Arms & Armour, 1978, reprint of 1904 edition), pp. 71–2 for more on Colonel Money.

27. Napier, *History*, vol. 4, pp. 463–4: the full version of the two letters from Dalbiac is printed in Bruce, *Life of Napier*, vol. 1, pp. 270–6; Tomkinson, *Diary of a Cavalry Officer*, pp. 186–9; *Intelligence Officer in the Peninsula. Letters and Diaries of Major the Hon. Edward Charles Cocks, 1786–1812* , ed. by Julia Page (Tunbridge Wells, Spellmount, 1986), pp. 187–90; Ms journal of Captain William Smith, 11th Light Dragoons, NAM 6807–52; Anonymous pen-and-ink sketch map, Ashworth Papers, NAM 7510–27.

28. Anonymous pen-and-ink sketch map, Ashworth Papers, NAM 7510–27.

29. Printed in Beamish, *History of the King's German Legion*, vol. 2, pp. 415–17.

30. Becerra, *Hazañas de Unos Lanceros – Diarios de Julián Sánchez*, pp. 108–11.

31. Oman, *History*, vol. 5, p. 450; Anonymous pen-and-ink sketch map, Ashworth Papers, NAM 7510–27; Bainbrigge, 'The Staff at Salamanca', p. 73.

32. Carter, *Historical Record of the Forty-Fourth*, p. 65; Douglas, *Douglas's Tale*, pp. 45 and 116n28; Roger Evans, *The Story of the Fifth Royal Inniskilling Dragoon Guards* (Aldershot, Gale & Polden, 1951), pp. 54–5; Anonymous 'Memoirs of a Dragoon' NAM 6807–213, p. 11.

33. Dalbiac in Bruce, *Life of Napier*, vol. 1, pp. 272, 274; Clark-Kennedy in H. T. Siborne, ed., *Waterloo Letters* (London, Trotman, 1983, first published 1891), pp. 77–8.

34. 'A.Z.', 'The Heavy Cavalry at Salamanca', p. 353.

35. Oman, *History*, vol. 5, pp. 450–2.

36. [Grattan,] 'Reminiscences of a Subaltern', p. 184.

37. *Ibid.*, p. 183.

38. Sarramon, *La Bataille des Arapiles*, pp. 219, 221–4.

39. Girard, *Les Cahiers du Colonel Girard*, p. 201.

40. Castel, *Relation de la Bataille et Retraite des Arapiles*, pp. 16–20.

41. See chapter eleven, p. 211.

42. Lamartinière; 'A.Z.', 'Heavy Cavalry at Salamanca', p. 353; Arentschildt in Beamish, *History of the King's German Legion*, vol. 2, pp. 415–17.

43. Oman, *History*, vol. 5, p. 470; Fortescue, *History of the British Army*, vol. 8, p. 505n; Sarramon, *La Bataille des Arapiles*, p. 246; P. Charrié, *Drapeaux et Etendards de la Révolution et de l'Empire* (Paris, Copernic, 1982), pp. 206, 209–10, 212 – I am indebted to John Cook for bringing this source to my attention.

44. John R. Elting, *Swords around a Throne. Napoleon's Grande Armée* (London, Weidenfeld & Nicolson, 1988), pp. 347–8; Oman, *History*, vol. 5, p. 470n.

45. Hall, *Biographical Dictionary*, supplemented with appendices from S. G. P. Ward, *Wellington's Headquarters* (London, Oxford University Press, 1957).

46. Tomkinson, *Diary of a Cavalry Officer*, p. 185.

Chapter Seven: Collapse and Recovery in the Centre

1. Oman, *History*, vol. 4, pp. 631–2 for allied losses at Albuera.
2. M. L. Cole and S. Gwynn, *Memoirs of Sir Lowry Cole* (London, Macmillan, 1934), p. 80, letter of 5 June 1812.
3. Vere, *Marches, Movements ... 4th Division*, pp. 34–5.
4. Captain Barralier, 'Adventure at the Battle of Salamanca', *USJ*, October 1951, p. 274; Wachholtz, 'Auf der Peninsula', p. 294.
5. Wachholtz, 'Auf der Peninsula', p. 295; Vere, *Marches, Movements ... 4th Division*, p. 35; Sarramon, *La Bataille des Arapiles*, pp. 226–7.
6. Bainbrigge, 'The Staff at Salamanca', p. 73; Sarramon, *La Bataille des Arapiles*, p. 227.
7. Cole and Gwynn, *Memoirs of Sir Lowry Cole*, p. 85, quoting a letter from Colonel Wade of Cole's staff, 24 July 1812.
8. Anonymous letter from an officer of the Fusilier brigade, Fourth Division, 27 July 1812, NAM 6807–333.
9. Burgoyne to his sister, 25 July 1812, in Wrottesley, *Life and Correspondence of Burgoyne*, vol. 1, p. 204.
10. Bainbrigge, 'The Staff at Salamanca', pp. 73–4.
11. *Ibid.*, p. 74.
12. Quoted in Anon., *History of the King's Shropshire Light Infantry*, 4 vols (1970), vol. 1, p. 156.
13. Quoted in 'Bingham Manuscripts', p. 108.
14. So says Charles Vere, *Marches, Movements ... 4th Division*, p. 36.
15. Quoted in Bruce, *Life of Napier*, vol. 1, pp. 278–9.
16. Vere, *Marches, Movements ... 4th Division*, p. 36.
17. Marmont, *Mémoires*, vol. 4, p. 448; Captain T. Marcel, *Campagnes du Capitaine Marcel du 69e de Ligne ...*, ed. by Commandant Var (Paris, Plon-Nourrit, 1913), p. 165; Castel, *Relation de la Bataille et Retraite des Arapiles*, p. 21.
18. Oman, *History*, vol. 5, p. 460n; private information from Steven H. Smith of California, citing Ernesto Augusto Pereira Sales, *Bandeiras e Estandartes Regimentais do Exercito e da Armada e Outras Bandeiras ...* (Lisbon, [Centro Tipografico Colonial,] 1930).
19. Quoted in Bruce, *Life of Napier*, vol .1, p. 279.
20. 61st Regiment Digest, pp. 188–9. I am grateful to Lieutenant-Colonel R. E. R. Robinson who kindly sent me a copy of his notes from this source, held by the regimental museum in Gloucester, some parts of which are published in his excellent *The Bloody Eleventh: History of the Devonshire Regiment* (Exeter, Devonshire & Dorsetshire Regiment, 1988), vol. 1, pp. 425–8.
21. Printed in Bruce, *Life of Napier*, vol. 1, p. 280. See commentary, p. 161 for reasons for believing that this letter was written by Major Newman.
22. Aitchison, *An Ensign in the Peninsular War*, p. 180; Henry Brackenbury, 'A Letter from Salamanca', *Blackwood's Magazine*, vol. 165 (February 1899), p. 381, original emphasis.
23. Hall, *Biographical Dictionary*, p. 71.
24. Browne, *Napoleonic War Journal*, pp. 170–1.
25. Brackenbury. 'Letter from Salamanca', p. 382.
26. Sir William Warre, *Letters from the Peninsula, 1808–1812* (London, John Murray, 1909, reprinted Spellmount, 1999), p. 288 (p. 183 of the reprint).
27. General Marquis Alphonse D'Hautpoul, *Mémoires du Général Marquis d'Hautpoul ...* (Paris, Perrin, 1906), pp. 68–70.
28. Oman, *History*, vol. 4, p. 631 for Albuera strength and losses. Lieutenant Robert Knowles, *The War in the Peninsula. Some Letters of Lieutenant Robert Knowles ...*, ed. by Sir Lees Knowles (Bolton, Tillotson, 1913), pp. 21–22 for the detachment sent out to the 1/7th in July 1811.
29. Vere, *Marches, Movements ... 4th Division*, p. 37; letter of Colonel Wade of 24 July 1812, in Cole and Gwynn, *Memoirs of Sir Lowry Cole*, p. 85.

30. Browne, *Napoleonic War Journal*, p. 170.
31. Quoted in William Wheater, *Historical Record of the Seventh or Royal Regiment of Fusiliers* (Privately printed, 1875), p. 120.
32. Burgoyne to his sister, 25 July 1812, in Wrottesley, *Life and Correspondence of Burgoyne*, vol. 1, p. 204.
33. Wachholtz, 'Auf der Peninsula', p. 296.
34. Bruce, *Life of Napier*, vol. 1, pp. 279–82; Robinson, *The Bloody Eleventh*, vol. 1, p. 668n70 and private correspondence with Lieutenant-Colonel Robinson, who identified Newman as the probable author of the letter.
35. Oman, *History*, vol. 5, pp. 459–60; Fortescue, *History of the British Army*, vol. 8, p. 496.
36. Young and Lawford, *Wellington's Masterpiece*, p. 264.
37. 61st Regiment Digest, pp. 188–9 – see above n. 20, and Major Newman's account printed in Bruce, *Life of Napier*, vol. 1, p. 280.
38. 61st Regiment Digest, pp. 188–9.
39. Captain De Gyves, *Historique du 122me Régiment d'Infanterie* (Montpellier, Imprimerie Centrale du Midi, 1890), pp. 119–20; Marcel, *Campagnes du Capitaine Marcel*, p. 165 (Marcel was in the 69th Ligne in Foy's division, and so was not a witness).
40. Bainbrigge, 'The Staff at Salamanca', p. 74.
41. H. Ross-Lewin, *With the 'Thirty-Second' in the Peninsula* (Dublin, Hodges, 1904), pp. 182–3.
42. Quoted in Richard Cannon, *Historical Record of the Eleventh, or, the North Devon Regiment of Foot ...* (London, Parker, Furnivall & Parker, 1845), p. 68.

Chapter Eight: Pack's Attack on the Greater Arapile

1. John Colville, *The Portrait of a General* (Salisbury, Michael Russell, 1980), p. 55 (May 1811); Dalton, *Waterloo Roll Call*, p. 21.

2. *Wellington's Dispatches*, vol. 5, p. 754; Pack quoted in Peter Carew 'A Gallant "Pack"', *Blackwood's Magazine*, vol. 260 (1946), p. 394, citing a family memoir; Synge, 'Captain Synge's Experiences at Salamanca', pp. 57–8.
3. *Wellington's Dispatches*, vol. 5, p. 755; Vere, *Marches, Movements ... of the 4th Division*, pp. 35–6; Synge, 'Captain Synge's Experiences at Salamanca', p. 58.
4. Synge, 'Captain Synge's Experiences at Salamanca', pp. 58–61.
5. Dyneley, *Letters*, p. 33.
6. *Ibid.*, p 36.
7. Lamartinière states that the 120th suffered 312 casualties in the campaign, which suggests total losses of about 375 casualties when the lightly wounded are taken into account. However Martinien's figures for killed and wounded officers suggest that a significant proportion of these casualties occurred in a separate combat later in the campaign. Extrapolating from this reduces the losses of the 120th in the battle to approximately 225 casualties. Yet according to Oman, the regimental history of the 120th acknowledged the loss of 458 casualties, but it seems unlikely that this is well-founded. Lamartinière – see Appendix III; Martinien; Oman, *History*, vol. 5, p. 605.
8. Napier, *History*, vol. 4, p. 271.
9. Synge, 'Captain Synge's Experiences at Salamanca', pp. 57–8.
10. *Wellington's Dispatches*, vol. 5, p. 755; Vere, *Marches, Movements ... 4th Division*, pp. 35–6.
11. Dyneley, *Letters*, p. 56.
12. Quoted in Carew, 'A Gallant "Pack"', p. 394.
13. Ingilby in *The Dickson Manuscripts*, vol. 4, p. 695; Colonel Jackson to Graham, 24 July 1812, Lynedoch Papers, NLS Ms 3610, ff. 181–4; Anon, *Personal Narrative of a Private Soldier*, pp. 132–3 (quoted here pp. 202–3); Wheatley's brigade lost sixteen casualties (all wounded or missing men) from 2,574 all ranks (excluding Brunswick Oels) – see Appendix II.

14. Lillie quoted in Bruce, *Life of Napier*, vol. 1, p. 278.
15. Marmont, *Mémoires*, vol. 4, p. 140.

Chapter Nine: Ferey and the French Last Stand

1. Dalton 'Family Regiment in the Peninsular War', p. 286; Martinien and supplement; cf Oman, *History*, vol. 5, pp. 454 and 461, Sarramon, *La Bataille des Arapiles*, pp. 232–3.
2. Sarramon, *La Bataille des Arapiles*, pp. 233, 236n.
3. *Ibid.*, pp. 231–2.
4. *Ibid.*, pp. 233–4.
5. Napier, *History*, vol. 4, p. 274.
6. Moggridge [Thomas Hamilton], 'Letters from the Peninsular', p. 548.
7. De Lancey to Murray, 4 August 1812, Murray Papers, NLS Adv. 46.2.15, vol. 38, ff. 113–16.
8. Sarramon, *La Bataille des Arapiles*, pp. 232–6.
9. Newman quoted as 'Major Nott' in Bruce, *Life of Napier*, vol. 1, pp. 280–1: see chapter seven, p. 161.
10. Ross-Lewin, *With the 'Thirty-Second' in the Peninsula*, pp. 184–5.
11. Douglas, *Douglas's Tale*, pp. 46–7. The 11th and 61st were in Hulse's brigade, the 2nd Queen's in Hinde's.
12. Vere, *Marches, Movements ... 4th Division*, p. 37.
13. Wachholtz, 'Auf der Peninsula', p. 296–7.
14. Lemonnier-Delafosse, *Campagnes de 1810 à 1815*, pp. 159–60.
15. *Ibid.*, p. 161.
16. De Lancey to Murray, 4 August 1812, Murray Papers, NLS Adv. 46.2.15, vol. 38, ff. 113–16; Newman quoted in Bruce, *Life of Napier*, vol. 1, p. 282; Bingham's letter of 24 July 1812, 'Bingham Manuscripts', p. 108.
17. Browne, *Napoleonic War Journal*, p. 171; Andrew Leith Hay to his father, 2 August 1812, Leith Hay Papers, NAS GD 225, Box 34/26; *Royal Military Panorama*, vol. 1, no. 3 (December 1812), pp. 257–8; Boutflower, *Journal of an Army Surgeon*, p. 149.

18. Sarramon, *La Bataille des Arapiles*, pp. 232–6.
19. Oman, *History*, vol. 5, p. ix.
20. *Wellington's Dispatches*, vol. 5, p. 755.
21. Campbell quoted in Wylly, *History of ... the Sherwood Foresters*, vol. 1, p. 228.
22. 61st Regiment Digest, p. 190, courtesy of R. E. R. Robinson – see n. 20 in chapter seven; Napier, *History*, vol. 4, p. 274; Moggridge [Thomas Hamilton], 'Letter from the Peninsula', p. 547; Ross-Lewin, *With the 'Thirty-Second' in the Peninsula*, pp. 183–4.
23. 61st Regiment Digest, p. 190, courtesy of R. E. R. Robinson.
24. Napier, *History*, vol. 4, p. 274.
25. Lieutenant F. Monro, 'Centenary of the Battle of Salamanca', ed. by Sir Charles Oman, *Fortnightly Review*, vol. 98 (July 1912), p. 74.
26. Ross-Lewin, *With the 'Thirty-Second' in the Peninsula*, p. 185n.
27. Lemonnier-Delafosse, *Campagnes 1810 à 1815*, pp. 161–70.
28. Wachholtz, 'Auf der Peninsula', p. 297.
29. Brent Nosworthy, *Battle Tactics of Napoleon and his Enemies* (London, Constable, 1995), pp. 196–201, 208; Sir Harry Smith, *Autobiography of Sir Harry Smith, 1787–1819* , ed. by G. C. Moore Smith (London, John Murray, 1910), p. 134.
30. Leith Hay, manuscript narrative, Leith Hay Papers, NAS GD 225, Box 40.

Chapter Ten: Foy and the French Retreat

1. Donaldson, *Eventful Life of a Soldier*, pp. 266–7.
2. Ashworth Papers, NAM 7510–27. I have transposed 'heavy' and 'steady': the original reads 'were very heavy under a steady cannonade', which, while possible, seems likely to have been a slip of the pen. It is also possible that Julián Sánchez's lancers played a more active part than is suggested by these casualty figures – see chapter six, p. 138.

3. Costello, *The Peninsular and Waterloo Campaigns*, pp. 107–8.
4. Girod de l'Ain, *Vie Militaire du Général Foy*, pp. 176–7.
5. V.-M. Duplan, *Mémoires et Campagnes. Vie Militaire du Lieutenant-Colonel Victor-Marie Duplan* (Moutiers-Tarentaise, Ducloz, 1901), p. 161. According to Martinien, Desgraviers was mortally wounded, not killed outright, and died on 26 July.
6. Tomkinson, *Diary of a Cavalry Officer*, p. 187.
7. Sir Richard Levinge, *Historical Records of the Forty-Third Regiment . . .* (London, Clowes, 1868), p. 167.
8. Anon, 'Sketch of the Battle of Salamanca', *USJ*, vol. 1, no. 1 (1829), p. 294; reprinted with very slight textual differences in W. H. Maxwell, *Peninsular Sketches by Actors on the Scene*, 2 vols (London, Colburn, 1845), vol 1 pp. 345–7.
9. Quoted in Bruce, *Life of Napier*, vol. 1, pp. 101–2.
10. Hennell, *A Gentleman Volunteer*, pp. 29–30.
11. Leveson Gower, *Lord Granville Leveson Gower. Private Correspondence*, vol. 2, p. 450.
12. See Hall, *Biographical Dictionary*, pp. 166–7.
13. Sarramon, *La Bataille des Arapiles*, p. 237; Fortescue, *History of the British Army*, vol. 8, p. 509.
14. 'H. C.' to Colonel Taylor, 25 July 1812, Hope of Luffness Papers, NAS GD 364/1/1224: see Appendix IV for the full text of this letter, and the reasons for believing that it was written by Henry Campbell.
15. Colonel Jackson to Graham, 24 July 1812, Lynedoch Papers, NLS Ms 3610, ff. 181–4.
16. Mills, *For King and Country*, pp. 187–8.
17. Eadie, *Recollections of Robert Eadie*, pp. 125–6.
18. Combermere and Knollys, *Memoirs and Correspondence*, vol. 1, pp. 277–8, 317; Napier, *History*, vol. 4, p. 275 on Cotton's movements.
19. Lemonnier-Delafosse, *Campagnes 1810 à 1815*, pp. 163–4.

20. Sarramon, *La Bataille des Arapiles*, p. 236.
21. For Cotton's order see Tomkinson, *Diary of a Cavalry Officer*, pp. 186–7.
22. *Wellington's Dispatches*, vol. 5, p. 758.
23. Tomkinson, *Diary of a Cavalry Officer*, p. 187.
24. J. Robert Hume to Graham, Madrid, 29 August 1812, Lynedoch Papers, NLS Ms 3610, ff. 216–17; Napier, *History*, pp. 272–3.
25. Anon., *Personal Narrative of a Private Soldier*, pp. 132–4.
26. Napier to his wife, 25 July 1812, printed in Bruce, *Life of Napier*, vol. 1, pp. 106–7; other details from Anon., 'Sketch of the Battle of Salamanca', p. 291.
27. Hennell, *A Gentleman Volunteer*, pp. 30–1.
28. Napier, *History*, vol. 4, pp. 273–4; see also Sarramon, *La Bataille des Arapiles*, p. 238.
29. Girod de l'Ain, *Vie Militaire, du Général Foy*, p. 176.
30. Lady Bessborough to Granville Leveson Gower, 21 August 1812, printed in Leveson Gower, *Lord Granville Leveson Gower*, vol. 2, p. 452.
31. Alexander Gordon to Lord Aberdeen, 25 July 1812, Aberdeen Papers, BL Add. Ms 43,224, ff. 95–101.
32. Browne, *Napoleonic War Journal*, pp. 171–2.
33. [Cocks], *Intelligence Officer in the Peninsula*, p. 188.
34. Sarramon, *La Bataille des Arapiles*, p. 238; Jack A. Meyer, 'Wellington's Generalship: A Study of his Generalship' (Unpublished PhD thesis presented to the University of South Carolina in 1984), pp. 218–19; Young and Lawford, *Wellington's Masterpiece*, pp. 270–1.
35. Napier, *History*, vol. 4, p. 275.
36. Girard, *Les Cahiers du Colonel Girard*, pp. 201–2.

Chapter Eleven: The Victory

1. J. Robert Hume to Graham, 29 August 1812, Lynedoch Papers, NLS Ms 3610,

ff. 216–17; Cathcart to Graham, 31 July 1812, *loc. cit.* ff. 187–96; Colonel Jackson to Graham, 24 July 1812, *loc. cit.*, ff. 181–4; Foy in Girod de l'Ain, *Vie Militaire du Général Foy*, pp. 177–8.

2. Calculation of Taupin's losses excludes any estimate of casualties suffered on 18 July on the Guarena, both from its initial strength and from its losses, which adds another element of uncertainty into these figures.

3. Calculation of the losses of Clausel, Boyer and Curto excludes estimated casualties suffered on 18 July.

4. This is based on the official return in PRO WO 1/255; the figures given by Oman and reproduced in Appendix II total 896 killed, 3,753 wounded and 160 missing. See Appendix II for a discussion of these returns.

5. Wellington says 137 officers and between six and seven thousand ordinary soldiers were taken prisoner, but this certainly includes those taken at Garcia Hernandez (nearly one thousand) and may also include those taken on 18 July. *Wellington's Dispatches*, vol. 5, p. 756.

6. Lamartinière.

7. *Wellington's Dispatches*, vol. 5, p. 756n; 'Return of Ordnance etc Taken at the Battle of Salamanca, 22nd July 1812', WO 1/255, p. 123.

8. Sergeant William Lawrence, *The Autobiography of Sergeant William Lawrence* (London, Sampson Low, 1886), pp. 124–5.

9. See chapter seven, pp. 152–4.

10. Or 15,693 French against 14,830 allies if losses on 18 July are deducted.

11. That is 14,104 French against 13,086 allies if losses on 18 July are deducted (assuming that 140 of the 157 Portuguese casualties suffered on that day came from Cole's division).

12. French losses do not include those of 15th Dragoons which are estimated at twelve casualties on 22 July.

13. A. de Caulaincourt, *With Napoleon in Russia* (New York, Morrow, 1935), p. 304.

14. Oman, *History*, vol. 5, p. 458; General Sarrazin, *History of the War in Spain*

and Portugal, from 1807 to 1814 (London, Henry Coburn, 1815), pp. 279–80 even argues that Marmont's wound was a blessing for the French cause, because it brought Clausel to the command.

15. Napier, *History*, vol. 4, p. 299.

Chapter Twelve: The Aftermath

1. Sergeant Richard Davey, 'A Sussex Soldier of Wellington's. The Letters of an Old Campaigner: 1811–1816' ed. by W. A. Woodward, *Sussex County Magazine*, February–April 1928, p. 90.

2. Tomkinson, *Diary of a Cavalry Officer*, p. 187.

3. Wheeler, *Letters of Private Wheeler*, p. 88.

4. Douglas, *Douglas's Tale*, pp. 47–8.

5. Grattan, *Adventures with the Connaught Rangers*, p. 257.

6. Green, *Vicissitudes of a Soldier's Life*, p. 102.

7. Monro, 'Centenary of the Battle of Salamanca', p. 75.

8. Browne, *Napoleonic War Journal*, p. 174.

9. Wheeler, *Letters of Private Wheeler*, p. 88; Douglas, *Douglas's Tale*, p. 47.

10. On food, [Daniel,] *Journal of an Officer of the Commissariat Department*, p. 140 and [Grattan,] 'Adventures of a Subaltern', p. 257; on the wounded, Aitchison, *An Ensign in the Peninsular War*, pp. 177–8; see also Leith Hay, *Narrative of the Peninsular War*, p. 265.

11. These figures include an estimate of lightly wounded Frenchmen, not counted in Lamartinière's return: see Appendix III.

12. Warre, *Letters from the Peninsula*, pp. 293–4 (p. 186 of new edition).

13. Ross-Lewin, *With the 'Thirty-Second' in the Peninsula*, p. 187.

14. Synge, 'Captain Synge's Experiences at Salamanca', pp. 61–2.

15. Anononymous memoirs of a private soldier in the 1/38th, NAM 7912–21, f. 21.

16. Quoted in Michael Glover, *Wellington's Army in the Peninsula, 1808–1814*,

(Newton Abbot, David & Charles, 1977), pp. 127–8.

17. Return printed in Wellington, *Supplementary Despatches and Memoranda*, vol. 14, p. 633.

18. Costello, *The Peninsular and Waterloo Campaigns*, p. 109. Costello went to hospital a day or two after Salamanca, suffering from exhaustion and the after-effects of a wound suffered at Badajoz.

19. D'Hautpoul, *Mémoires*, pp. 69–73.

20. Browne, *Napoleonic War Journal*, p. 173.

21. *Ibid.*, p. 173.

22. The Adjutant-General to Captain Hare, D. A. A. G., Salamanca, 25 July 1812, printed in *Wellington's Despatches*, vol. 5, p. 761; [E. W. Buckham,] *Personal Narrative of Adventures in the Peninsula during the War in 1812–1813. By an Officer Late in the Staff Corps Regiment of Cavalry* (Cambridge, Trotman, 1995, first published 1827), p. 60, letter dated 30 July 1812.

23. Moyle Sherer, *Recollections of the Peninsula* (Staplehurst, Spellmount, 1996, first published 1824), p. 184.

24. Ross-Lewin, *With the 'Thirty-Second'*, p. 191.

Chapter Thirteen: Consequences

1. Oman (*History*, vol. 5, p. 475) says the ford of Encinas, but Fortescue (*History of the British Army*, vol. 8, p. 499) says Huerta, and Beamish (*History of the King's German Legion*, vol. 2, p. 80) says 'the ford near Babila-fuente', which is Huerta.

2. Oman, *History*, vol. 5, pp. 476–81; Fortescue, *History of the British Army*, vol. 8, pp. 499–502; Beamish, *History of the King's German Legion*, vol. 2, pp. 81–8; Gray, 'Services of the King's German Legion', pp. 257–61.

3. 'H. C.' to Colonel Taylor, 25 July 1812, Hope of Luffness Papers, NAS GD 364/1/1224; see Appendix IV for the full text of this letter.

4. Clausel quoted in Fortescue, *History of the British Army*, p. 551, see also

Clausel to King Joseph, 25 July 1812, in *Mémoires et Correspondance Politique et Militaire du Roi Joseph*, vol. 9, pp. 54–5, and Oman, *History*, vol. 5, p. 483; Tomkinson, *Diary of a Cavalry Officer*, p. 192.

5. Fortescue, *History of the British Army*, vol. 8, pp. 551–2, but cf Leach, *Rough Sketches*, p. 278 on the benefits of the halt.

6. Oman, *History*, vol. 5, pp. 488–92.

7. *Ibid.*, pp. 506–7; Gabriel H. Lovett, *Napoleon and the Birth of Modern Spain*, 2 vols (New York University Press, 1965), vol. 2, pp. 540–1.

8. Browne, *Napoleonic War Journal*, p. 177.

9. Leach, *Rough Sketches*, p. 282.

10. Leith Hay, *Narrative of the Peninsular War*, p. 265.

11. Wellington to Sir Thomas Graham, 25 July 1812, *Wellington's Despatches*, vol. 5, pp. 759–60.

12. On Ferrol, *The Times*, 11 August 1812; on Cadiz, Charles J. Esdaile, *The Duke of Wellington and the Command of the Spanish Army, 1812–1814* (Basingstoke, Macmillan, 1990), p. 47.

13. *The Times*, 3 and 5 August 1812; Bathurst to Wellington, 6 August 1812, Wellington, *Supplementary Despatches and Memoranda*, vol. 7, pp. 374–5; Leveson Gower, *Lord Granville Leveson Gower. Private Correspondence*, vol. 2, p. 444.

14. *The Times*, 17 August 1812.

15. *The Times*, 19 August 1812.

16. *Ibid.*

17. Joseph Farington, *The Farington Diary*, 8 vols (London, Hutchinson, 1922–8), vol. 7, pp. 98, 102; Sir Walter Scott, *The Letters of Sir Walter Scott, 1787–1832*, ed. by H. J. C. Grierson, 12 vols (London, Constable, 1932–7), vol. 3, p. 156.

18. Charles Knight, *Passages of a Working Life*, 3 vols (London, Bradbury & Evans, 1864), vol. 1, p. 139.

19. Sidmouth to the Prince Regent, 21 August 1812, *Letters of King George IV*, ed. by A. Aspinall, 3 vols (Cambridge University Press, 1938), vol. 1, p. 134; Liverpool to Wellington, 19 August

1812, and Bathurst to Wellington, 16 and 20 August 1812, Wellington, *Supplementary Despatches and Memoranda*, vol. 7, pp. 401–2, 383–4 and 404–5.

20. Liverpool to Bathurst, 17 August 1812, Historical Manuscripts Commission, *Report of the Manuscripts of Earl Bathurst Preseved at Cirencester Park* (London, HMSO, 1923), pp. 196–7; Torrens to the Duke of York, 'Private', Horse Guards, 22 August 1812, PRO WO 3/603, pp. 9–10.

21. *The Times*, 1 October 1812.

22. Napoleon quoted in Caulaincourt, *With Napoleon in Russia*, p. 96; for Fabvier see A. G. Macdonell, *Napoleon and his Marshals* (London, Macmillan, 1934), p. 257.

23. James Marshall-Cornwall, *Marshal Massena* (London, Oxford University Press, 1965), p. 251; Oman, *History*, vol. 6, p. 33.

24. A. J. M. R. Savary, Duc de Rovigo, *Memoirs of the Duke of Rovigo (M. Savary)*, 3 vols (London, Colburn, 1828), vol. 3, pt 1, pp. 201–3, 212–15.

25. PRO WO 17/2470, Monthly Returns, July–December 1812.

Bibliography

Primary sources are normally listed under the name of the participant, not the editor, even when published as an article by the editor. The exceptions occur when there are only a few quotations from the primary source, or when several different primary sources are quoted in one article.

UNPUBLISHED SOURCES
Archives Historiques de la Guerre (AHG) du Service Historique de l'Etat-Major de l'Armée de Terre (Château de Vincennes)
C7–15 Général Lamartinière. Etat Numérique des Pertes Eprouvées par l'Armée du Portugal depuis le 18 Juillet jusqu'au 8 Août 1812 (Official French casualty return, 18 July to 8 August)

British Library
Add. Ms 43,224 Aberdeen Papers. Letters of Lieutenant-Colonel Sir Alexander Gordon to his brother Lord Aberdeen, with some replies, 1811–15
Loan Ms 57 Bathurst Papers, vol. 5, 1812
Loan Ms 72 Liverpool Papers, vol. 21. Correspondence with Wellington, 1811–14

National Army Museum, London
NAM 6807–52 Manuscript journal of Captain William Smith, 11th Light Dragoons (Anson's brigade)
NAM 6807–214 Journal of Sergeant William Stephenson, 3rd King's Own Dragoons (Le Marchant's brigade)
NAM 6807–213 Anonymous 'Memoirs of a Dragoon' (A ranker in the 5th Dragoon Guards: typescript copy of ms memoirs)
NAM 6807–333 Anonymous letter from an officer of the Fusilier brigade, Fourth Division, 27 July 1812
NAM 7510–27 Papers of Major-General Charles Ashworth, including an anonymous pen-and-ink sketch map of the battle with extensive annotations
NAM 7804–14 Letters of Lieutenant John Massey, 3rd Dragoons, 1811–12
NAM 7912–21 Anonymous memoirs of a private soldier in 1/38th (Fifth Division)
NAM 8408–37 Manuscript 'Journal of the Campaigns in the Peninsula by Charles Whitman of the Royal Horse Artillery, 1811–14'

National Library of Scotland, Edinburgh
NLS MS 3610. Lynedoch Papers. Correspondence, 1812

NLS Ms 15,371. Typescript copies of the letters on active service from the sons of William Marshall, factor to the Duke of Gordon, 1790–1815
Murray Papers
    NLS Adv. Ms 46.2.15, vol. 38, 1812
    NLS Adv. Ms 46.4.19, Distribution Book, 13 July 1812–8 February 1813

National Archives of Scotland, Edinburgh
NAS GD 364/1/1224. Hope of Luffness Papers. Miscellaneous re Peninsular War, 1811–12
NAS GD 225. Leith Hay Papers. Box 34/26 Letters, 1809–12
Box 40 Includes manuscript narrative of the campaign and battle, with significant variations from his published *Narrative*
RHP 44684 Sketch plan of the battle of Salamanca

Public Record Office, Kew
WO 1/255 In letters from Wellington, July to December 1812 (Includes many returns etc.)
WO 3/603 Out letters of CinC (Private), August–December 1812
WO 17/2469–70 Monthly returns, 1812
WO 27/106–7 Inspection reports, 1812
WO 37/7A&B Scovell Papers: Diary of Sir George Scovell (Staff)
WO 55/1195 Ordnance Department. Letters from Officers on Foreign Service, 1810–13

University of Southampton
Ms 296 Pack and Reynell Papers:
    Ms 296/1 Correspondence of Sir Denis Pack, 1809–23
    Ms 296/7 Letters from Sir Denis Pack to Sir T. Reynell, 1810–23
Wellington Papers:
    WP 1/337 From Wellington, August 1811
    WP 1/345 To Wellington, January–July 1812
    WP 1/347 From Wellington, May–August 1812
    WP 1/348 To Wellington, 1–16 August 1812
    WP 1/349 To Wellington, 17–31 August 1812
    WP 1/359 Miscellaneous, 1812
    WP 1/478 From Wellington, August 1815

Mrs J. N. Tomes:
Some family papers of Alexander Gordon

PRIVATE INFORMATION
Lieutenant-Colonel R. E. R. Robinson kindly provided me with copies of his notes of the manuscript Digest of the Services of the 61st Regiment held by the Regimental Museum in Gloucester
Steven H. Smith supplied me with information from Ernesto Augusto Pereira Sales, *Bandeiras e Estardartes Regimentais do Exercito e do Armada e Outras Bandeiras* ... (Lisbon, Centro Tipografico Colonial, 1930)
Bernabe Saiz Martínez de Pisón sent me a copy of the maps relating to the battle of Salamanca in Arteche's *Guerra de la Independencia – Historia Militar de España de 1808 a 1814*
Mark Urban sent me copies of several letters describing the battle from the Le Marchant Papers and another private collection

PUBLISHED SOURCES
Aitchison, John, *An Ensign in the Peninsular War. The Letters of John Aitchison*, ed. by W. F. K. Thompson (London, Michael Joseph, 1981) (Third Guards, First Division)

Anon., *Historique du 65e Régiment d'Infanterie* (Paris and Limoges, Charles-Lavauzelle, 1886) (Taupin's division)

Anon., *The Personal Narrative of a Private Soldier, Who Served in the Forty-Second Highlanders, for Twelve Years, during the Late War* (Cambridge, Trotman, 1996, first published 1821) (First Division)

Anon., 'Sketch of the Battle of Salamanca'; *USJ*, vol. 1, no. 1 (1829), pp. 283–95 (Light Division) (Reproduced almost exactly in Maxwell's *Peninsular Sketches*)

Anon., *History of the King's Shropshire Light Infantry*, 4 vols (1970). Vol. 1: *The 53rd (Shropshire) Regiment, 1775–1881* (Includes reprint of Rogerson's *Historical Records of the 53rd*) (Sixth Division)

Arbuthnot, H., *The Journal of Mrs Arbuthnot, 1820–1832* , ed. by Francis Bamford and the Duke of Wellington, 2 vols (London, Macmillan, 1950)

Arvers, P., *Historique de 82ᵉ Régiment d'Infanterie de Ligne ...* (Paris, Typographie Lahue, 1876) (Maucune's division)

Atkinson, C. T., *The South Wales Borderers, 24th Foot, 1689–1937* (Cambridge, for the Regiment, 1937) (First Division)

Aubrey-Fletcher, H. L., *A History of the Foot Guards to 1856* (London, Constable, 1927) (First Division)

'A. Z.', 'The Heavy Cavalry at Salamanca', *USJ*, November 1833, pp. 351–4 (Le Marchant's brigade)

Bainbrigge, Sir Philip, 'The Staff at Salamanca', *USJ*, January 1878, pp. 72–5

———, 'Sketch of the River Tormes, near Salamanca, Made in the Presence of the Enemy ... 24th June 1812', *Minutes of the Proceedings of the Royal Artillery Institution*, vol. 12 (1884), pp. 513–16

Bannatyne, Lieutenant-Colonel Neil, *History of the Thirtieth Regiment ...* (Liverpool, Littlebury, 1923) (Fifth Division)

Barralier, Captain, 'Adventure at the battle of Salamanca', *USJ*, October 1851, pp. 274–7 (Stubbs's brigade, Fourth Division)

Bathurst, Earl: see Historical Manuscripts Commission

Beamish, N. L., *History of the King's German Legion*, 2 vols (London, T&W Boone, 1832–7)

Becerra, Emilio Becerra de, *Hazañas de Unos Lanceros – Diarios de Julián Sánchez 'El Charro'* (Diputación Provincial de Salamanca, 1999)

Bigarré, A., *Mémoires du Gal. Bigarré Aide de camp du Roi Joseph, 1775–1813* (Paris, Kolb, nd [1893]) (Not at battle)

Bingham, Sir G.R., 'The Bingham Manuscripts', ed. by T. H. McGuffie, *JSAHR*, vol. 26, no. 107 (1948), pp. 106–11 (2/53rd, Sixth Division)

——— 'The Bingham Papers and the Peninsular War, Part II' ed. by T. H. McGuffie, *Army Quarterly*, July 1949, pp. 254–6 (ditto)

Boutflower, Charles, *The Journal of an Army Surgeon during the Peninsular War* (Staplehurst, Spellmount, 1997, first published 1912) (40th, Fourth Division)

Brackenbury, Henry, 'A Letter from Salamanca', *Blackwood's Magazine*, vol. 165 (February 1899), pp. 376–84 (Lieutenant Edward Brackenbury, Spry's brigade, Fifth Division and his brother Lieutenant William Brackenbury, 61st, Sixth Division)

Bragge, Captain William, *Peninsular Portrait, 1811–1814. The Letters of Captain William Bragge Third (King's Own) Dragoons*, ed. by S. A. C. Cassels (London, Oxford University Press, 1963) (Le Marchant's brigade)

Bray, E. W., *Memoirs and Services of the Eighty-Third Regiment ...* (London, Smith, Elder & Co, 1863) (Third Division)

Brett-James, Antony, *General Graham, Lord Lynedoch* (London, Macmillan, 1959)

Brialmont, A., *History of the Life of Arthur Duke of Wellington*, with emendations and additions by Rev. G. R. Gleig, 4 vols (London, Longman, Green, Longman & Roberts, 1860)

Broke: *see* Vere

Brotherton, T., *A Hawk at War. The Peninsular War Reminiscences of General Sir Thomas Brotherton*, ed. by Bryan Perrett (Chippenham, Picton, 1986)

Browne, Captain T. H., *The Napoleonic War Journal of Captain Thomas Henry Browne, 1807–1816*, ed. by Roger Norman Buckley (London, Bodley Head for the Army Records Society, 1987) (Staff)

Bruce, H. A., *The Life of General Sir William Napier, K.C.B.*, 2 vols (London, John Murray, 1864)

[Buckham, E. W.,] *Personal Narrative of Adventures in the Peninsula during the War in 1812–1813. By an Officer Late in the Staff Corps Regiment of Cavalry* (Cambridge, Trotman, 1995, first published 1827)

Burgoyne, Sir John, *The Life and Correspondence of Field Marshal Sir John Burgoyne*, by George Wrottesley, 2 vols (London, Bentley, 1873) (Fourth Division)

Butler, Lieutenant-Colonel Lewis, *The Annals of the King's Royal Rifle Corps. Vol. 2: The Green Jacket* (London, John Murray, 1923) (5/60th, First, Third, Fourth and Sixth Divisions)

Campbell, Colonel James, *The British Army As It Was – Is – and Ought to Be* (London, T&W Boone,1840) (Third Division staff)

Cannon, Richard, *Historical Records of . . .* (London, 1835–53). Series of volumes: consulted for the following regiments: 3rd Dragoons, 5th Dragoon Guards, 12th and 14th Light Dragoons, 1st, 2nd, 4th, 5th, 7th, 9th, 11th, 23rd, 36th, 53rd, 61st, 74th and 88th Foot

Carew, Peter, 'A Gallant "Pack" ', *Blackwood's Magazine*, vol. 260 (1946), pp. 391–401 (Pack's brigade)

Carter, Thomas, *Historical Record of the Forty-Fourth or the East Sussex Regiment* (Chatham, Gale & Polden, 1887) (Fifth Division)

Cary, A. D. L. and S. McCance, *Regimental Records of the Royal Welch Fusiliers*, 4 vols (London, RUSI, 1921–9) (23rd, Fourth Division)

Cassels: *see* Bragge

Castel, P., *Relation de la Bataille et Retraite des Arapiles* (Toulouse, J.-B. Cazaux, 1854) (staff)

Caulaincourt, A. de, *With Napoleon in Russia* (New York, Morrow, 1935)

Challis, Captain L. S., 'British Officers Serving in the Portuguese Army, 1809–1814', *JSAHR, vol.* 27, no. 110 (1949), pp. 50–60

Chandler, David, *Dictionary of the Napoleonic Wars* (London, Arms & Armour, 1979)

———, ed., *Napoleon's Marshals* (London, Weidenfeld & Nicolson, 1987)

Charrié, P., *Drapeaux et Etendards de la Révolution et de l'Empire* (Paris, Copernic, 1982)

Christophe, Robert, *Les Amours et les Guerres du Maréchal Marmont, Duc de Raguse* (Paris, Hachette, 1955)

Cocks, E. C., *Intelligence Officer in the Peninsula. Letters and Diaries of Major the Hon. Edward Charles Cocks, 1786–1812*, ed. by Julia Page (Tunbridge Wells, Spellmount, 1986) (16th Light Dragoons, Anson's brigade)

Cole, John W., *Memoirs of British Generals Distinguished during the Peninsular War*, 2 vols (London, Richard Bentley, 1856)

Cole, M. L. and S. Gwynn, *Memoirs of Sir Lowry Cole* (London, Macmillan, 1934) (A life with letters etc, not memoirs by Cole)

Colville, John, *The Portrait of a General* (Salisbury, Michael Russell, 1980) (Not at battle, but quoted)

Combermere, Sir Stapleton, Viscount, *Memoirs and Correspondence of Field Marshal Viscount Combermere* by Mary Viscountess Combermere and Captain W. Knollys, 2 vols (London, Hurst & Blackett, 1866) (A life of Stapleton Cotton, not his recollections)

Cooper, J. S., *Rough Notes of Seven Campaigns in Portugal, Spain, France and America during the Years 1809–1815* (Staplehurst, Spellmount, 1996, first published 1869) (7th Fusiliers, Fourth Division, but Cooper not at battle)

Cope, Sir William, *The History of the Rifle Brigade . . .* (London, Chatto & Windus, 1877)

Costello, Edward, *The Peninsular and Waterloo Campaigns* (London, Longmans, 1967, first published 1852) (95th, Light Division)

Cowper, Colonel L. I., *The King's Own. The Story of a Royal Regiment*, 2 vols (Oxford, for the Regiment, 1939) (4th, Fifth Division).

Croker, J. W., *The Croker Papers. The Correspondence and Diaries of . . . John Wilson Croker*, ed. by Louis J. Jennings, 3 vols (London, John Murray, 1884)

Dalbiac, Colonel P. H., *History of the 45th: 1st Nottinghamshire Regiment* (London, Swan Sonnenschein, 1902) (Third Division)

Dalton, Charles, *The Waterloo Roll Call* (London, Arms and Armour, 1978 – reprint of 1904 edition)

Dalton, Major-General J. C., 'A Family Regiment in the Peninsular War', *Cavalry Journal*, vol. 18 (April 1928), pp. 282–9 (4th Dragoons, reprints Norcliffe's letter – see under Norcliffe – with additional material) (Le Marchant's brigade)

[Daniel, J. E.,] *Journal of an Officer in the Commissariat Department of the Army . . .* (Cambridge, Trotman, 1997, first published 1820)

Daniell, D. Scott, *4th Hussar: The Story of the 4th Queen's Own Hussars, 1685–1958* (Aldershot, Gale & Polden, 1959) (4th Dragoons, Le Marchant's brigade)

———— *Cap of Honour. The Story of the Gloucestershire Regiment* (London, Harrap, 1951) (28th and 61st – latter in Sixth Division)

Davey, Sergeant Richard, 'A Sussex Soldier of Wellington's. The Letters of an Old Campaigner: 1811–1816', ed. by W. A. Woodward, *Sussex County Magazine* February–April 1928, pp. 48–55, 88–92, 134–40 (Royal Artillery Drivers)

Davis, Lieutenant- Colonel John, *The History of the Second, Queen's Royal Regiment . . .*, vol. 4 (London, Eyre & Spottiswoode, 1902) (Sixth Division)

Davson, Captain H. M., 'Napoleon's Marshals: 6. Marmont', *Journal of the Royal Artillery*, vol. 35 (1908–9) pp. 377–89

De Gyves, Captain, *Historique du 122me Régiment d'Infanterie* (Montpellier, Imprimerie Centrale du Midi, 1890) (Bonnet's division)

Delbauve, Captain E., *Historique du 26e Régiment d'Infanterie* (Paris and Nancy, Berger-Levrault, 1889) (Ferey's division)

D'Hautpoul, General Marquis Alphonse, *Mémoires du Général Marquis Alphonse d'Hautpoul . . .* (Paris, Perrin, 1906) (59th Ligne, Clausel's division)

Dickson, Sir A., *The Dickson Manuscripts*, ed. by J. H. Leslie, 5 vols (Cambridge, Trotman, 1990, first published 1908) (Artillery, staff)

Dictionary of National Biography, ed. by Sir Leslie Stephen and Sir Sidney Lee, 22 vols (Oxford University Press, 1921–2)

[Donaldson, Sergeant Joseph,] *The Eventful Life of a Soldier* (Edinburgh, Tait, 1827) (94th, Third Division)

Douglas, Corporal John, *Douglas's Tale of the Peninsula and Waterloo*, ed. by Stanley Monick (London, Leo Cooper, 1997) (3/1st, Fifth Division)

Du Fresnel, Commandant, *Un Régiment à travers l'Histoire, Le 76ᵉ ex 1er Léger* (Paris, Flammarion, 1894) (Thomières's division)

Duncan, Captain Francis, *History of the Royal Regiment of Artillery*, 2 vols (London, John Murray, 1872–3)

Dunn-Pattison, R. P., *Napoleon's Marshals* (London, Methuen, 1909)

Duplan, V.-M., *Mémoires et Campagnes. Vie Militaire du Lieutenant-Colonel Victor-Marie Duplan* (Moutiers-Tarentaise, Ducloz, 1901) (Foy's division)

D'Urban, Major-General Benjamin, *The Peninsular Journal of Maj-Gen. Sir Benjamin D'Urban*, ed. by I. J. Rousseau (London, Greenhill, 1988, first published 1930)

Dutton, Geoffrey, and David Elder, *Colonel William Light – Founder of a City* (Melbourne University Press, 1991) (Staff, Le Marchant's brigade)

Dyneley, Thomas, *Letters Written by Lieut.-General Thomas Dyneley C.B., R.A., While on*

Active Service between the Years 1806 and 1815 ed. by Colonel F. A. Whinyates (Cambridge, Trotman, 1984)

Eadie, Robert, *Recollections of Robert Eadie: Private of the 79th Regiment of Infantry* (London, Maggs, 1987, first published 1829) (First Division)

Ellesmere, Earl of, *Personal Reminiscences of the Duke of Wellington* (London, John Murray, 1904)

Elting, John R., *Swords around a Throne. Napoleon's Grande Armée* (London, Weidenfeld & Nicolson, 1988)

Esdaile, Charles J., *The Duke of Wellington and the Command of the Spanish Army, 1812–1814* (Basingstoke, Macmillan, 1990)

Evans, Roger, *The Story of the Fifth Royal Inniskilling Dragoon Guards* (Aldershot, Gale & Polden, 1951) (Le Marchant's brigade)

Farington, Joseph, *The Farington Diary*, 8 vols (London, Hutchinson, 1922–8) (On reaction in Britain)

Fletcher, Ian, *Salamanca, 1812. Wellington Crushes Marmont* (London, Osprey, 1997: Campaign Series no. 48)

Fortescue, the Hon. J. W., *A History of the British Army*, 13 vols of 20 (London, Macmillan, 1899–1930) (The maps of Salamanca are in a separate, accompanying volume, *Maps and Plans Illustrating Fortescue's History of the British Army, Vol. viii*, 1917)

Foster, William C., *Sir Thomas Livingston Mitchell and his World, 1792–1855* (Sydney, Institute of Surveyors of NSW, 1985)

Foy, M., *Vie Militaire du Général Foy* by Girod de l'Ain (Paris, Plon Nourrit, 1900) (Prints extensive extracts from Foy's diary)

Fraser, Edward, *The War Drama of the Eagles* (London, John Murray, 1912)

———, *The Soldiers Whom Wellington Led* (London, Methuen, 1913)

Garrett, Lieutenant Robert, 'A Subaltern in the Peninsular War. Letters of Lieutenant Robert Garrett, 1811–1813', ed. by A. S. White, *JSAHR* vol. 13 (1934), pp. 3–22 (2nd, Sixth Division)

Gates, David, *The Spanish Ulcer. A History of the Peninsular War* (London, Allen & Unwin, 1986)

———, *The British Light Infantry Arm, c. 1790–1815* (London, Batsford, 1987)

George IV, *The Letters of King George IV*, ed. by A. Aspinall, 3 vols (Cambridge University Press, 1938)

Girard, Etienne-François, *Les Cahiers du Colonel Girard, 1766–1846 . . .*, ed. by Paul Desachy (Paris, Plon, 1951) (Maucune's chief of staff)

Girod de l'Ain, M.: *see* Foy

Glover, Michael, *Wellington's Peninsular Victories* (London, Batsford, 1963)

———, *Wellington as a Military Commander* (London, Sphere, 1973)

———, *Wellington's Army in the Peninsula, 1808–1814* (Newton Abbot, David & Charles, 1977)

———: *see* Hennell

Gomm, W. M., *Letters and Journals of Field Marshal Sir William Maynard Gomm . . .*, ed. by Francis Culling Gomm (London, John Murray, 1881) (Fifth Division staff)

Gower: *see* Leveson Gower

[Grattan, William,] 'Reminiscences of a Subaltern: Battle of Salamanca'; *USJ*, June 1834, pp. 175–87 (88th, Third Division)

———, *Adventures of the Connaught Rangers from 1808 to 1814*, First Series, 2 vols, Second Series, 2 vols (London, Colburn, 1847, 1853) (88th, Third Division)

———, *Adventures with the Connaught Rangers 1808–1814* , ed. by Charles Oman (London, Arnold, 1902)

Gray, Daniel S., 'The Services of the King's German Legion in the Army of the Duke of Wellington: 1809–1815' (Unpublished PhD thesis presented to Florida State University in 1970)

Green, John, *The Vicissitudes of a Soldier's Life ... 1806–1815* (Louth, privately printed, 1827) (68th, Seventh Division)

Greville, C. C. F., *The Greville Memoirs. A Journal of the Reigns of King George IV, King William IV, and Queen Victoria*, ed. by Henry Reeve, 8 vols (London, Longmans, Green, 1888)

Gurney, Lieutenant-Colonel R., *History of the Northamptonshire Regiment, 1742–1934* (Aldershot, Gale & Polden, 1935) (48th, Fourth Division and 58th, First Division)

Hale, James, *The Journal of James Hale, late Serjeant in the Ninth Regiment of Foot* (Cirencester, Philip Watkins, 1826; reprinted by Peter Catley and IX Regiment, 1997) (Fifth Division)

Haley: *see* Pearson

Hall, John A., *A History of the Peninsular War. Vol. viii. The Biographical Dictionary of British Officers Killed and Wounded, 1808–1814* (London, Greenhill, 1998)

Hamilton, F. W., *The Origin and History of the First or Grenadier Guards* , vol. 2 (London, John Murray, 1874) (First Division)

Hamilton, H. B., *Historical Record of the 14th, (King's) Hussars ... 1715–1900* (London, Longmans, 1901)

[Hamilton, Thomas,] 'Letters from the Peninsula. No IV: The Battle of Salamanca', purportedly by 'Captain Spencer Moggridge', *Blackwood's Edinburgh Magazine*, vol. 23, no. 138 (May 1828), pp. 535–49 (Third Division)

———, *Annals of the Peninsular War ...*, 3 vols (Edinburgh, Blackwood, 1829)

———, obituary in *Blackwood's Edinburgh Magazine*, vol. 53 (February 1843), p. 280

Hay: *see* Leith Hay

Haythornthwaite, Philip, *The Armies of Wellington* (London, Arms & Armour, 1994)

Hennell, George, *A Gentleman Volunteer. The Letters of George Hennell from the Peninsular War, 1812–1813*, ed. by Michael Glover (London, Heinemann, 1979) (43rd, Light Division)

Historical Manuscripts Commission, *Report of the Manuscripts of Earl Bathurst Preserved at Cirencester Park* (London, HMSO, 1923)

Hodenberg, Captain Carl von, 'A Dragoon of the Legion' (Hodenberg's letters edited by Charles Oman), *Blackwood's Magazine*, vol. 193 (March 1913), pp. 293–307 (Bock's brigade)

Hough, Lieutenant H., 'The Diary of 2nd Lieutenant Henry Hough, Royal Artillery', ed. by Major J. H. Leslie, *Journal of the Royal United Service Institution*, vol. 61 (November 1916), pp. 839–80

Houghton, Walter E., *et al.* (eds), *The Wellesley Index to Victorian Periodicals, 1824–1900*, 5 vols (University of Toronto Press, 1966–89)

Ingilby, Lieutenant, 'Diary of Lt. Ingilby R.A. in the Peninsular War and Waterloo Campaign', *Minutes of the Proceedings of the Royal Artillery Institution*, vol. 20 (1893), pp. 250–62

Jones, J. P., *History of the South Staffordshire Regiment (1705–1923)* (Wolverhampton, Whitehead Brothers, 1923) (38th Foot, Fifth Division)

Jones, Major-General John T., *Journal of the Sieges Carried On by the Army under the Duke of Wellington ...*, 3 vols (London, John Weale, 1846 3rd edition)

Joseph, King of Spain, *Mémoires et Correspondance Politique et Militaire du Roi Joseph*, ed. by A. du Casse, 10 vols (Paris, Perrotin, 1854–5)

Jourdain, Lieutenant-Colonel H. F. N., and Edward Fraser, *The Connaught Rangers*, vol. 1 (London, 1924) (88th, Third Division)

Kincaid, Captain J., *Adventures in the Rifle Brigade and Random Shots from a Rifleman* (Glasgow, Richard Drew, 1981, first published 1830–5) (95th, Light Division)

Knight, Charles, *Passages of a Working Life*, 3 vols (London, Bradbury & Evans, 1864) (On reaction in Britain)

Knowles, Lieutenant Robert, *The War in the Peninsula. Some Letters of Lieutenant Robert Knowles ...* ed. by Sir Lees Knowles (Bolton, Tillotson, 1913) (7th, Fourth Division)

Laurie, Lieutenant-Colonel G. B., *History of the Royal Irish Rifles* (London, Gale & Polden,

1914) (83rd, Third Division) (The chapter on the Peninsula is written by Oman, and the account of Salamanca adds nothing new)

Lawford, J. P., and Peter Young *see* Young, Peter and J. P. Lawford.

Lawrence, Sergeant William, *The Autobiography of Sergeant William Lawrence* (London, Sampson Low, 1886) (40th, Fourth Division, but Lawrence not at battle)

Leach, Lieutenant Colonel J., *Rough Sketches of the Life of an Old Soldier* (Cambridge, Trotman, 1986, first published 1831) (95th, Light Division)

Leask, J. C., and H. M. McCance, *The Regimental Records of the Royal Scots* (Dublin, Thom, 1915) (1st Foot, Fifth Division)

Leith Hay, Sir Andrew, *A Narrative of the Peninsular War* (1st edition, 2 vols, Edinburgh, Daniel Lizars, 1831; 3rd edition – that cited except when specified – 1 vol., London, John Hearne, 1839) (Fifth Division, staff)

[————,] *Memoir of the Late Lieutenant-General Sir James Leith* ... (Barbados, privately printed, 1817)

[Le Marchant, Denis,] *Memoirs of the Late Maj-General Le Marchant* (A life by his son Denis) (London, Bentley, 1841)

Lemonnier-Delafosse, M., *Campagnes de 1810–1815. Souvenirs Militaires* ... *Tome Second* (Havre, Imprimerie du Commerce Alph. Lemale, 1850) (Ferey's division)

Leveson Gower, Lord Granville, *Lord Granville Leveson Gower (First Earl Granville), Private Correspondence, 1781–1821*, ed. by Castalia, Countess Granville, 2 vols (London, John Murray, 1916) (Includes letter from Colonel Frederick Ponsonby, 12th Light Dragoons, Anson's Brigade)

Levinge, Sir Richard, *Historical Records of the Forty-Third Regiment* ... (London, Clowes, 1868) (Light Division)

Longford, Elizabeth, *Wellington. The Years of the Sword* (London, Weidenfeld & Nicolson, 1969)

Lovett, Gabriel H., *Napoleon and the Birth of Modern Spain*, 2 vols (New York University Press, 1965)

Lunt, James, *Scarlet Lancer* (London, Hart-Davis, 1964) (Includes extracts from the letters of John Luard, 4th Dragoons, Le Marchant's brigade)

Macdonell, A. G., *Napoleon and his Marshals* (London, Macmillan, 1934)

McGrigor, Sir James, *Autobiography and Services of Sir James McGrigor* (London, Longman, 1861) (Medical staff)

McGuffie: *see* Bingham

Mackenzie, Captain T. A., *et al.*, *Historical Records of the 79th Queen's Own Cameron Highlanders* ... (London, Hamilton, Adams & Co, 1887) (First Division)

Mackinnon, D., *Origins and Services of the Coldstream Guards* ..., 2 vols (London, Bentley, 1833) (First Division)

Marcel, Captain T., *Campagnes du Capitaine Marcel du 69e de Ligne* ..., ed. by Commandant Var (Paris, Plon-Nourrit, 1913) (Foy's division)

Marindin, A. H., *The Salamanca Campaign* (London, Hugh Rees, 1906)

Marmont, Marshal A. F. L. V., Duc de Raguse, *Mémoires du Maréchal Marmont, Duc de Raguse* ..., 9 vols (Paris, Perrotin, 1857)

————, *The Spirit of Military Institutions* (Westport, Greenwood, 1974)

Marshall-Cornwall, James, *Marshal Massena* (London, Oxford University Press, 1965)

Martinien, A., *Tableaux par Corps et par Batailles des Officiers Tués et Blessés Pendant les Guerres de l'Empire (1805–1815)* (Paris, Editions Militaires Européennes, nd [1980s], first published 1899)

————, *Tableaux par corps et par Batailles des Officiers Tués et Blessés pendant les Guerres de l'Empire (1805–1815) (Supplément)* (Paris, Fournier, 1909)

Maurice, Sir F., *The History of the Scots Guards* ..., 2 vols (London, Chatto & Windus, 1934) (First Division)

Maxwell, Sir Herbert, *The Life of Wellington. The Restoration of the Martial Power of Great Britain*, 2 vols (London, Sampson Low, Marston, 1900)

Maxwell, W. H., ed., *Peninsular Sketches by Actors on the Scene*, 2 vols (London, Henry Colburn, 1845) (Light Division: see above under Anon.)

Meyer, Jack A., 'Wellington's Generalship: A Study of his Peninsular Campaigns' (Unpublished PhD thesis presented to the University of South Carolina in 1984)

Mills, John, *For King and Country. The Letters and Diaries of John Mills, Coldstream Guards, 1811–1814*, ed. by Ian Fletcher (Staplehurst, Spellmount, 1995) (First Division)

Mockler-Ferryman, Augustus: *see* Rice, Col. Samuel

Moggridge: see [Hamilton, Thomas]

Monro, Lieutenant F., 'Centenary of the Battle of Salamanca' (two letters by Lieutenant Frederic Monro, R.A.), ed. by Charles Oman, *Fortnightly Review*, vol. 98 (July 1912), pp. 68–75

Moorsom, W.S., *Historical Record of the Fifty-Second Regiment ...* (London, Bentley, 1860) (Light Division)

[Morley, Stephen,] *Memoirs of a Serjeant of the 5th Regiment of Foot ...* (Ashford, Elliott, 1842) (Third Division)

Muir, Rory, *Britain and the Defeat of Napoleon, 1807–1815* (New Haven and London, Yale University Press, 1996)

———, *Tactics and the Experience of Battle in the Age of Napoleon* (New Haven and London, Yale University Press, 1998)

———, 'The British Government and the Peninsular War', in Paddy Griffith, ed., *A History of the Peninsular War. Vol IX. Modern Studies of the War* (London, Greenhill, 1999) (A detailed assessment of Oman's *History* with particular reference to the role of the British government in the war)

Mullaly, Colonel B. R., *The South Lancashire Regiment* (Bristol, White Swan Press, nd) (40th, Fourth Division)

Napier, George, *Passages in the Early Military Life of Sir George T. Napier, KCB*, ed. by W. C. E. Napier (London, John Murray, 1884) (Not present at battle, but quoted)

Napier, Major-General Sir W. F. P., *History of the War in the Peninsula and in the South of France*, 6 vols (London, Boone, 1853, 'new edition, revised by the author')

———: *see* also H. A. Bruce

Napoleon, *The Confidential Correspondence of Napoleon Bonaparte with his Brother Joseph ...*, 2 vols (New York, Appleton, 1856)

Nettleship, Andrew, *That Astonishing Infantry! A History of the 7th Foot (Royal Fusiliers) in the Peninsular War, 1809–1814* (Privately printed, 1989) (Fourth Division)

Norcliffe, Lieutenant N., 'A Dragoon's Experiences at Salamanca', ed. by C. Dalton, *Cavalry Journal*, October 1912, pp. 458–60 (4th Dragoons, Le Marchant's brigade)

———: *see* also Dalton

Nosworthy, Brent, *Battle Tactics of Napoleon and his Enemies* (London, Constable, 1995)

Oatts, L. B., *Proud Heritage: The Story of the Highland Light Infantry*, vol. 2 (London, Nelson, 1959) (74th, Third Division)

Oman, Sir Charles, *A History of the Peninsular War*, 7 vols (Oxford, Clarendon Press, 1902–30)

———, *Wellington's Army, 1809–1814* (London, Greenhill, 1986, first published 1913)

Page: *see* Cocks

Pakenham, Edward, *Pakenham Letters, 1800 to 1815* (Privately printed, 1914)

Parquin, Charles, *Napoleon's Army*, trans. and ed. by B. T. Jones (London, Longmans, 1969)

Paton, Colonel George, *et al.*, *Historical Records of the 24th Regiment ...* (London, Simpkin, Marshall, 1892) (First Division)

Pearson, Andrew, *The Private Who Walked Away. Autobiography of Andrew Pearson, A Peninsular War Veteran*, ed. by Arthur H. Haley (Liverpool, Bullfinch, nd) (61st Regiment, Sixth Division)

Petre, F. L., *The History of the Norfolk Regiment, 1685–1918* (Norwich, Jarrold, 1924) (9th, Fifth Division)

Ponsonby: *see* Leveson Gower

Redway, Major G. W., 'The Centenary of Salamanca', *USJ* vol. 156 (1912), pp. 390–402

Rice, Col. Samuel, *The Life of a Regimental Officer during the Great War, 1793–1815 . . . from the Correspondence of Col. Samuel Rice, 51st Light Infantry* (Edinburgh, Blackwood, 1913) (Seventh Division)

Rigaud, Gibbes, *Celer et Audax. A Sketch of the Services of the 5th Battalion, 60th Regiment* (Oxford, Hall & Stacy, 1879) (Companies scattered through the army)

Robertson, Ian C., *Wellington at War in the Peninsula 1808–1814. An Overview and Guide* (Barnsley, Leo Cooper Pen & Sword Books, 2000)

Robinson, R. E. R., *The Bloody Eleventh: History of the Devonshire Regiment*. Vol. 1: 1685–1815 (Exeter, Devonshire & Dorsetshire Regiment, 1988) (Sixth Division)

Rogerson: *see* Anon.

Ross, H. D., *Memoir of Field Marshal Sir Hew Dalrymple Ross R. H. A.* (Woolwich, Royal Artillery Institution, 1871)

Ross-Lewin, H., *With the 'Thirty-Second' in the Peninsula* (Dublin, Hodges, 1904) (Sixth Division)

Rovigo: *see* Savary

Royal Military Panorama. Vol. 1: 1812–13

Sarramon, Jean, *La Bataille des Arapiles (22 Juillet 1812)* (Toulouse, University of Toulouse, 1978)

Sarrazin, General, *History of the War in Spain and Portugal, from 1807 to 1814* (London, Henry Colburn, 1815)

Savary, A. J. M. R., Duc de Rovigo, *Memoirs of the Duke of Rovigo (M. Savary) . . .* 3 vols (London, Colburn, 1828) (On reaction in France)

Scott, Sir Walter, *The Letters of Sir Walter Scott, 1787–1832*, ed. by H. J. C. Grierson, 12 vols (London, Constable, 1932–7) (On reaction in Britain)

Sherer, Moyle, *Recollections of the Peninsula* (Staplehurst, Spellmount, 1996, first published 1824) (Not at battle)

Siborne, H. T., ed., *Waterloo Letters* (London, Trotman, 1983; first published 1891)

Simmons, Major George, *A British Rifleman. The Journals and Correspondence of Major George Simmons . . .*, ed. by Lieutenant-Colonel W. Verner (London, A&C Black, 1899) (95th, Light Division)

Smith, Sir Harry, *The Autobiography of Sir Harry Smith, 1787–1819*, ed. by G. C. Moore Smith (London, John Murray, 1910) (95th, Light Division)

Smythies, R. H. R., *Historical Records of the 40th (2nd Somerset) Regiment* (Devonport, Swiss, 1894) (Fourth Division)

Southey, Robert, *History of the Peninsular War*, 6 vols (London, John Murray, 1837)

Stanhope, Philip Henry, Earl of, *Notes of Conversations with the Duke of Wellington, 1831–51* (London, John Murray, 1888)

Sutcliffe, Victor, *The Sandler Collection. An Annotated Bibliography of Books Relating to the Military History of the French Revolution and Empire in the Library of John Sandler* (Cambridge, Trotman, 1996)

Swiney, G. C., *Historical Records of the 32nd (Cornwall) Light Infantry* (London, Simpkin, Marshall, Kent, 1893) (Sixth Division)

Synge, Charles, 'Captain Synge's Experiences at Salamanca,' ed. by F. St L. Tottenham, *Nineteenth Century and After* July 1912, pp. 54–68

Tarragon, Lieutenant de, *Historique du 15e Régiment d'Infanterie* (Paris and Limoges, Charles-Lavauzelle, 1895) (Maucune's division)

Thiers, M. A., *History of the Consulate and the Empire . . .*, 20 vols (London, Willis & Sotheran, 1857)

Thompson, Private Alexander, 'An Essex Soldier's Letter of Long Ago', ed. by Miss E.

Vaughan, *The Essex Review*, July 1917, pp. 141–7 (5th Dragoon Guards, letter of 2 January 1812 describing Le Marchant)

Thorn, Captain G. W. P., 'The Salamanca Campaign, 1812. An Illustration of Modern Ideas', *Army Quarterly*, October 1934, pp. 117–24

Thorne, R. G., ed., *The History of Parliament. The House of Commons, 1790–1820*, 5 vols (London, Secker & Warburg for the History of Parliament Trust, 1986)

Thornton, James, *Your Most Obedient Servant. James Thornton, Cook to the Duke of Wellington* (Exeter, Webb & Bower, 1985)

Thoumine, R. H., *Scientific Soldier. The Life of General Le Marchant, 1766–1812* (London, Oxford University Press, 1968)

Times, The

Timewell, John, 'The Diary of a Private Soldier in the Peninsular War', ed. by W. Verner, *Macmillan's Magazine*, 77 (November 1897) pp. 1–10 (Light Division)

Tomkinson, Lieutenant-Colonel William, *The Diary of a Cavalry Officer in the Peninsular War and Waterloo Campaign, 1809–1815* (London, Swan Sonnenschein, 1895, 2nd edition) (16th Light Dragoons, Anson's brigade)

Tulard, Jean, *Nouvelle Bibliographie Critique des Mémoires sur l'Époque Napoléonienne Écrits ou Traduits en Francais* (Droz, 1991, 'Nouvelle édition revue et enrichie')

Urban, Mark, *The Man Who Broke Napoleon's Codes* (London, Faber and Faber, forthcoming)

Vane, Charles William, Marquess of Londonderry, [and G. R. Gleig], *Story of the Peninsular War* (London, Colburn, 1848)

Vaughan: *see* Thompson

Vere, Charles Broke, *Marches, Movements and Operations of the 4th Division . . .* (Ipswich, privately printed, 1841)

Verner, W., *History and Campaigns of the Rifle Brigade*, 2 vols (London, John Bale & Sons, 1919)

Vichness, Samuel E., 'Marshal of Portugal: The Military Career of William Carr Beresford, 1785–1814' (Unpublished PhD thesis presented to Florida State University in 1976)

Wachholtz, General Friedrich Ludwig von, 'Auf der Peninsula 1810 bis 1813,' ed. by H. L. von Wachholtz, *Beihefte zum Militär-Wochenblatt*, 1907, pp. 261–326

Walker, H. M., *A History of the Northumberland Fusiliers, 1674–1902* (London, John Murray, 1919) (5th Foot, Third Division)

Ward, S. G. P. *Wellington's Headquarters* (London, Oxford University Press, 1957)

———, *Faithful: The Story of the Durham Light Infantry* (Edinburgh, Nelson for the Durham Light Infantry, nd [1963]) (68th, Seventh Division)

———, 'The Portuguese Infantry Brigades, 1809–1814', *JSAHR, vol.* 53 (1975), pp. 103–12

Warre, Sir William, *Letters from the Peninsula, 1808–1812* (London, John Murray, 1909, reprinted Spellmount, 1999) (On Beresford's staff)

Weller, Jac, *Wellington in the Peninsula, 1808–1814* (London, Nicholas Vane, 1962)

Wellesley, Muriel, *The Man Wellington* (London, Constable, 1937)

Wellington, Duke of, *The Dispatches of Field Marshal the Duke of Wellington . . .* compiled by Colonel Gurwood, 8 vols (London, Parker, Furnivall & Parker, 1844–7, in the 'enlarged edition')

———, *Supplementary Despatches and Memoranda of Field Marshal Arthur, Duke of Wellington*, ed. by the 2nd Duke of Wellington, 15 vols (London, John Murray, 1858–72)

———, 'Unpublished Letters of Wellington, July–August 1812', ed. by I. J. Rousseau, *Cambridge Historical Journal*, vol. 3, no. 1 (1929), pp. 96–101

Wetherall, J., *An Historical Account of His Majesty's First or the Royal Regiment of Foot . . .* (London, Clowes, 1832) (Fifth Division)

Wheater, William, *Historical Record of the Seventh or Royal Regiment of Fusiliers* (Privately printed, 1875) (Fourth Division)

————, *A Record of the Services of the Fifty-First* ... (London, Longmans, Green and Co, 1870) (Seventh Division)

Wheatley, Major-General William, 'Letters from the Front, 1812', ed. by G. E. Hubbard, *USJ*, March 1919, pp. 432–52 (Commanded a brigade in First Division)

Wheeler, W., *The Letters of Private Wheeler, 1809–1828*, ed. Captain B. H. Liddell Hart (London, Michael Joseph, 1951) (51st, Seventh Division)

Wrottesley, G.: *see* Burgoyne

Wyld, James (publisher), *Maps and Plans Showing the Principal Movements, Battles, and Sieges in Which the British Army Was Engaged* ... (London, James Wyld, 1841) (Maps surveyed by Sir Thomas Mitchell)

Wylly, H.C., *History of the 1st and 2nd Battalions, the Sherwood Foresters* ..., 2 vols (Frome, for the Regiment, 1929) (45th, Third Division)

————, *The History of the King's Own Yorkshire Light Infantry* (London, Lund Humphries, n.d. [1926]) (51st, Seventh Division)

Young, Peter and J. P. Lawford, *Wellington's Masterpiece. The Battle and Campaign of Salamanca* (London, Allen & Unwin, 1973)

Index

26th Ligne (Ferey's Division) 184

27th Ligne (Clausel's Division) 27, 43, 48, 60, 148, 280n23

36th Ligne (Sarrut's Division) 26, 177

39th Ligne (Foy's Division) 27

47th Ligne (Ferey's Division) 184, 188

50th Ligne (Clausel's Division) 27, 148

59th Ligne (Clausel's Division) 27, 148, 157

62nd Ligne (Thomières's Division) 27, 88, 95, 102, 126, 128, 133–5, 141, 142, 143, 145, 209

65th Ligne (Taupin's Division) 129, 132, 134, 176–8

66th Ligne (Maucune's Division) 111, 115, 118, 128, 133–4, 139, 140–2, 143, 145, 209

69th Ligne (Foy's Division) 27, 255

70th Ligne (Ferey's Division) 184, 188

76th Ligne (Foy's Division) 27, 228–9, 256n

82nd Ligne (Maucune's Division) 111, 115, 118, 128, 134, 143, 145

86th Ligne (Maucune's Division) 111, 115, 118, 128, 134, 143

101st Ligne (Thomières's Division) 27, 88, 95, 102, 126, 128, 133, 142–5, 209

118th Ligne (Bonnet's Division) 27, 151, 152, 154, 254n

119th Ligne (Bonnet's Division) 27, 151, 152, 178

120th Ligne (Bonnet's Division) 27, 55, 76, 151, 168, 171–2, 178, 277n7, 290n7

122nd Ligne (Bonnet's Division) 27, 60, 147–8, 151–2

Arriaga, Capt. S. J. de (Portuguese artillery) 193

Arteche y Moro (historian) 71–2

Ashworth, Brig. Charles, map in the papers of 138, 139, 192, 291n2

Astorga, siege of 5, 9, 10

Austerlitz, Battle of (2 December 1805) 26–7, 217

'A.Z.' (pseudonym) 140–1

Badajoz 2, 3, 4, 30, 31, 37, 107, 146

Bainbrigge, Capt. P. (staff) 108, 139, 151, 161, 163

Ballesteros, Gen. F. 5

Barralier, Capt. Joseph (23rd Portuguese) 147

Bathurst, Georgina, Countess 205

Bathurst, Henry, 3rd Earl (statesman) 78, 201, 232–3, 234

Beamish, N.L. (historian) 20, 60, 76, 78, 103

Beatty, Col. (7th Fusiliers) 160

Belshes, Capt. (ADC to Gen. Leith) 110, 123

Bentinck, Lt-Gen. Lord William 5, 9

Beresford, Sir William C., Marshal 3, 12, 20, 28, 40

influence on Wellington 18, 39, 58, 59, 77

attacks Clausel's flank 156–7, 161

wounded 157–210, 223–4

Bessborough, Lady 197, 205, 232

Bessières, Marshal J-B. 26

Big Ben 74

Bingham, Col G. R. (2/53rd) 152, 186

Blackwood's Edinburgh Magazine 81

Bobers, Lt. (1st KGL Hussars) 60

Bock, Maj-Gen. E. von 228–9, 230

Boinod, opinion of Marmont, quoted by Foy 33

Bonaparte see Joseph, King of Spain
see also Napoleon I, Emperor

Bonnet, Gen. J. P. F. 6, 7, 9, 10, 34

biographical sketch 34–5

junior to Clausel 34, 80

occupies Greater Arapile 55–6, 76

wounded 65–6, 210

Borodino, Battle of (7 Sept 1812) 235

Boutflower, Charles (surgeon) (40th) 10, 20, 70, 153, 187

Bouthmy, Col (120 Ligne) 178

Boyer, Gen. P. F. J. see under army, French

Brackenbury, Capt. E. (15th Portuguese Line) 155–7

Brackenbury, Lt. W. (1/61st) 155–6

Bradford, Lt-Col. H. H. (A.A.G. Sixth Division) 181

Bradford, Brig. T.: see under army, allied

Bragge, Capt. W. (3rd Dragoons) 21, 42, 129–30, 137, 139

Brennier, Gen. A. F. 13, 36, 165

British army see army, allied

Brown, Private William (1/5th) 94, 103

Browne, Lt T. H. (staff) 15, 19, 20, 21, 77

on Spry's attack 156–7

on Cole's attack 160

on attack on El Sierro 186

on the pursuit 205

on plunder of the wounded 221

Bruce, H. A. (historian) 161

Brunswick Oels see under army, allied

Bull, Capt. Robert (R.H.A.): see Army, Allied

Burdett, Sir Francis (M.P.) 233

Burgh, Lt-Col U. (ADC to Wellington) 39

Burgos, siege of (Sept–Oct. 1812) 236

Burgoyne, Maj. J. (R.E.)

on 18 July 20–1

victory proves army well disciplined 37

time of French advance on Monte de Azan 75

Cole's attack 149, 160

784 DATE DUE DAYS

DEC 1 6 2002		
JAN 1 6 2003		
JAN 2 7 2003		
FEB 2 4 2003		
MAR 0 8 2003		
APR 0 9 2003		
	WITHDRAWN	
GAYLORD		PRINTED IN U.S.A.